Church and Society
in Reformation Europe

Professor Robert M. Kingdon

Robert M. Kingdon

Church and Society
in Reformation Europe

VARIORUM REPRINTS
London 1985

British Library CIP data   Kingdon, Robert M.
    Church and society in Reformation Europe. —
    (Collected studies series; CS210)
    1. Reformation
    I. Title
    274'.06   BR305.2

    ISBN 0-86078-158-5

Copyright © 1985 by   Variorum Reprints

Published in Great Britain by   Variorum Reprints
    20 Pembridge Mews London W11 3EQ

Printed in Great Britain by   Butler & Tanner Ltd
    Frome, Somerset

    VARIORUM REPRINT CS210

CONTENTS

THE CHURCH IN CALVIN'S GENEVA

THE CHURCH AND THEORIES OF
POLITICAL RESISTANCE AND DEMOCRACY

viii

THE CHURCH AND THE PRINTING PRESS

This volume contains a total of 350 pages.

PUBLISHER'S NOTE

The articles in this volume, as in all others in the Collected Studies Series, have not been given a new, continuous pagination. In order to avoid confusion, and to facilitate their use where these same studies have been referred to elsewhere, the original pagination has been maintained wherever possible.

Each article has been given a Roman number in order of appearance, as listed in the Contents. This number is repeated on each page and quoted in the index entries.

PREFACE

For more than thirty years the focus of my historical research has been directed toward problems in the ecclesiastical history of western Europe during the early modern period. I have been interested above all in the development late in the sixteenth century of some particularly militant forms of Christian witness, primarily among Calvinists and Catholics. Three connected activities of these militant Christian communities have attracted most of my attention. I have tried to find out more about how Calvinists tried to gain a continuing place in European society by creating new institutions. I have tried to find out more about how Calvinists and Catholics resisted the persecution of hostile governments by developing and implementing new political ideas. I have tried to find out more about how Calvinists and Catholics spread their ideas through the communications media then available, above all the relatively new medium of print. All these sixteenth-century ecclesiastical activities and more I have tried to illuminate in both general essays and narrowly focused case studies. This volume contains a selected mixture of the two.

The twenty-one articles that make up this volume are divided into four topical categories. A first category contains four attempts to define the true church, primarily as that problem was viewed in the early modern period, ranging from an initial overview to consideration of three facets of the problem. A second category contains five studies of the impact of religious change on the city of Geneva during the period of Calvin's ministry there, beginning with a general essay arguing that this change was indeed revolutionary, continuing with four specialized analyses of specific ecclesiastical institutions that emerged in Geneva at that time. A third category contains seven articles on developments in political thought during the late sixteenth century, with special attention to reflections on the relative value of different types of government and to arguments by persecuted minorities for armed resistance against their governments. These articles explore primarily political ideas advanced by Theodore Beza, William Allen, and Peter Martyr Vermigli. I selected Beza, Calvin's successor as leader of that branch of the international Reformed movement that looked to Geneva for ideological direction, because of his intimate involvement in the French Protestant struggle for survival and recognition. I selected Allen, leader of the Catholic refugees from Elizabethan England on the continent, because of his similar involvement in the English Catholic struggle for survival and recognition. I selected Vermigli, more a closet thinker than an activist but one whose Biblical commentaries constituted an influential complement to Calvin's writings in the shaping of Reformed theology, because his political ideas were typical and influential. A fourth category contains five articles on the use of printing by these communities, beginning with a general essay on the role of printing and piety in the publishing industry, continuing with three more focused studies of specific printers in Calvinist Geneva and Catholic Antwerp, and concluding with another general essay on the present state of research in a part of this field.

Originally these articles appeared in a widely scattered variety of places, including five periodicals and twelve *Festschriften* or other types of symposium volumes, published in seven different countries over a period of nearly thirty years. That wide dispersion constitutes both the strength and the weakness of this volume. It brings together for the first time in one place studies that few readers, even the most devoted specialists, will have had a chance to consult in their entirety. I am particularly grateful to the editors of *Variorum* for making this possible. But since these studies were originally written for very different audiences and yet dwelt upon somewhat similar themes, there is a certain amount of overlap and repetition among them that will soon become evident to anyone patient enough to read through the entire book. If this had been a volume of reprints, some of that repetition could have been edited out. Since it is a volume of reproductions, I can only hope the systematic reader will be indulgent.

Several of these articles were written in connection with critical editions of sixteenth-century sources, editions that had either just appeared or were soon to appear. The serious reader will want to consult these editions for further documentation of the arguments contained in my articles. Of these editions let me mention particularly my own edition of Theodore Beza's *Du droit des magistrats* (Geneva: Droz, 1971) and its appendices, of special importance for the arguments contained in articles X, XI, and XIV; my edition of William Allen's *A True, Sincere, and Modest Defense of English Catholics* (Ithaca: Cornell University Press, 1965), the most important source of article XIII, the selected texts in my *The Political Thought of Peter Martyr Vermigli* (Geneva: Droz, 1980), supporting articles XV and XVI; the edition by Pierre Hurtubise of the *Correspondance du nonce en France Antonio Maria Salviati*, vol. 12 (for 1572-1574) in the series *Acta Nuntiaturae Gallicae* (Rome: Editions de l'Université Grégorienne, 1975), important for my article XIV. Other recent editions of some importance for a number of these articles are that of the *Registres de la Compagnie des Pasteurs de Genève* (Geneva: Droz, 1962--), which Jean-François Bergier and I launched and which continues with other editors, and that of the *Correspondance de Théodore de Bèze* (Geneva: Droz, 1960--), by Henri Meylan, Alain Dufour, and others.

Much of the material in these articles can also be freshened, corrected or placed in a wider context by more recent secondary works. Those wishing to place the articles on political thought in a broader context should consult Quentin Skinner, *The Foundations of Modern Political Thought* (Cambridge University Press, 1978), and the works there cited, particularly in volume two, *The Age of the Reformation*. Those wishing to place the articles on printing in a broader context should consult Elizabeth L. Eisenstein, *The Printing Press as an Agent of Change* (Cambridge University Press, 1979). For more on the printer Plantin, subject of articles XIX and XX, one should consult above all Leon Voet, *The Golden Compasses*, 2 vols. (Amsterdam: Vangendt, 1969, 1972), and for more on the printers of Geneva, subject of article XVIII, one should consult, in addition to the monographs mentioned in article XXI, the important new book by Jean-François Gilmont on *Jean Crespin* (Geneva: Droz, 1981). The material on Vermigli in articles IV, XV, and XVI, can be complemented by a number of excellent recent studies, of which one has particularly influenced me: John P. Donnelly, *Calvinism and Scholasticism in Vermigli's Doctrine of Man and Grace* (Leiden: Brill, 1976). The material on the administration of charity in Calvin's Geneva in articles VI and VII is complemented in important ways by two recent dissertations: Elsie McKee, *John Calvin on the Diaconate and Liturgical Almsgiving* (Geneva: Droz, 1984); Jeannine Evelyn Olson, *The Bourse française: deacons and social welfare in Calvin's Geneva* (Stanford University Ph.D. dissertation in history, 1980, scheduled for publication by Brill in Leiden). The material on the control of morals in Calvin's Geneva in article VIII is complemented and corrected in important ways by E. William Monter, "The Consistory of Geneva, 1559-1569," *Bibliothèque d'Humanisme et Renaissance* XXXVIII (1976), 467-484. Other complementary studies are cited in Articles I and XXI. And there are, of course, many others. But this list should supply readers with at least a preliminary guide. I hope at least a few will share my continuing fascination with these subjects.

My special thanks go to Amy Nelson Burnett for shrewd and generous help in preparing the index to this volume.

ROBERT M. KINGDON

Institute for Research in the Humanities
University of Wisconsin — Madison
July 1984

I

The Church: Ideology or Institution

I am greatly honored but a bit puzzled to find myself president of the
American Society of Church History. Most of my predecessors in this
position have been professors within theological faculties or departments of
religion. Even those who have been, like me, members of secular departments
of history, have generally received some formal instruction in religious
studies. But this year you have chosen a president who is entirely secular in
both education and career, whose graduate training was in diplomatic
history of the Reformation period and whose teaching has been largely
limited to secular state universities. I descend, to be sure, from a line of
Protestant missionaries, ministers and religious educators, and over the years
I have learned a good deal of historical theology from some very gifted
students. But neither asset, I fear, places me very securely within the line of
succession in which I now find myself.

Furthermore I am afraid I joined the Society with serious misconceptions
of its character. Some thirty years ago, when John T. McNeill offered to
nominate me for membership, I accepted because I was then planning a
doctoral dissertation on the diplomacy of an ecclesiastical institution—the
Company of Pastors created in the city of Geneva by John Calvin—and I
thought I would meet scholars within this society with similar interests in
ecclesiastical institutions.[1] I soon discovered that many if not most members
of this society had radically different interests. They were working on what
seemed to me to be the history of religious ideas. It is this discrepancy,
between the focus on institutional history which I expected in this Society
and the focus on intellectual history which I discovered within it, which
furnishes the subject for my presidential address. In making this choice of
subject, obviously, I am departing from the model set by most of my
predecessors, who made of their presidential addresses solid and useful
reports of their own research. I am rather joining the arrogant few who made
of their addresses general reflections on the nature of the discipline of church
history.[2] I can only hope the results will provoke some useful thought.

1. My dissertation was later published as Robert M. Kingdon, *Geneva and the Coming of the
Wars of Religion in France, 1555–1563* (Geneva, 1956).
2. For example, Lewis W. Spitz, "History: Sacred and Secular," *Church History* 47 (1978):
5–22. I am particularly indebted to Spitz for his survey of other presidential addresses to
this society, pp. 5–9.

*This presidential address was delivered at the annual meeting of the
American Society of Church History, 28 December 1980. Mr. Kingdon is
director of the Institute for Research in the Humanities and professor of
history in the University of Wisconsin-Madison.*

Now the anomaly of a society of church history limiting itself to religious thought might first be demonstrated by suggesting some analogies to other types of historical societies. No society for the history of government would devote itself primarily to the history of political theory from Plato to the present without considerable complementary attention to the institutions of city-states, empires, kingdoms and republics. No society for the history of the economy would limit itself to the history of economic theory from Adam Smith to Friedman without considerable additional attention to the history of industrial and financial institutions. No society for the history of warfare would limit itself to military theory from Machiavelli to Clausewitz without considerable further attention to armies and navies. Is the church so radically different from these other social groups that its history can be better understood from the ideas by which it defined itself rather than from the institutional shapes it exhibited?

To begin answering that question, we can look at some other societies of scholars who call themselves church historians. When we do, we discover a good number which devote a considerable amount of their research to institutions. Members of the Ecclesiastical History Society in Britain, for example, tend to focus primarily on the history of Christian institutions and their place in society, publishing their findings in a periodical titled the *Journal of Ecclesiastical History,* supplemented by an annual series of volumes titled *Studies in Church History.* They leave to another group of scholars in Britain the focus on the history of Christian ideas which finds its outlet in an entirely different British periodical titled the *Journal of Theological Studies.* And the Ecclesiastical History Society of Britain is but one of a series of national societies for the study of the history of ecclesiastical institutions whose work is coordinated by the International Commission for the Comparative Study of Ecclesiastical History. I have long been puzzled and distressed, incidentally, that there has not been more American participation in this international scholarly organization. I am, therefore, particularly pleased to report that one of the officers of this Society, Robert F. Trisco, was recently elected a member of the executive committee of the International Commission, thus guaranteeing a formal American participation in the general planning of its program on a sustained basis hitherto impossible.

But why, to return to my central problem, should so many members of this Society approach our discipline as a form of intellectual history rather than as a form of institutional history? One important part of the answer surely lies in our American experience; another important part of the answer, I suspect, lies in our predominantly Protestant character. Since early in our postcolonial or national history, Americans have ben accustomed to regard churches as free and voluntary associations rather than the legal establishments to which our European colleagues are accustomed. And Americans have come to accept as churches such a variety of institutions that they defy easy categorization, much less systematic and synthetic study. It is therefore far easier for the European to identify the church with a visible institution that is part of his experience and far more difficult for the American who cannot equate the church with any one institution unless, of course, he belongs to one of those fortunate denominations which is convinced that it is the only true church of Christ and that outside its membership there is no salvation.[3]

My second explanation for this focus on intellectual history may seem more problematic. No one will deny that the American Society of Church History is essentially American. But some will doubt that it is necessarily predominantly Protestant. So let me elaborate this part of my argument in more detail. Historians of our Society make it clear that its erudite and energetic founder, Philip Schaff, was motivated in good part by a desire to create an organization that would transcend denominational barriers, that would assist ecumenical activity throughout the United States. But the ecumenical outreach he achieved, it seems to me, was primarily among Protestant groups. This in spite of Schaff's fervent hope that what he called "Evangelical Catholicism" would be the form Christianity should develop in this country.[4] Schaff himself, observe, was of a Swiss and German Reformed background, thus ultimately Calvinist; and many of the more prominent early members of the Society were Presbyterian or Congregational, thus also of a background ultimately Calvinist. To be sure, there has been a very considerable broadening in the leadership of our Society in the twentieth century. But the most obvious element in that broadening, it seems to me, has been Lutheran. Think of the contributions to our Society of two of the three editors of our journal, Brauer and Marty. Think of the contributions of such sterling scholars and charismatic teachers as Ahlstrom and Pelikan, Grimm and Spitz, Forrell and Hillerbrand, Lotz and Schwiebert. Think even of the contributions made by a number of Lutheran fellow travelers, of scholars not formally Lutheran but clearly fascinated by Luther's thought, like Bainton, Pauck, Gerrish and Steinmetz. The political sociologists who complain that Lutherans in America are apolitical and never involve themselves in community activity clearly did not investigate the American Society of Church History!

Now I should like to suggest that Protestants, perhaps particularly of German background, and maybe above all Lutherans, tend to define the church more as an ideology than as an institution. And from this definition of the church, inevitably, flows a definition of church history as a discipline

---

3. This point is made more amply by L. J. Trinterud, "The Task of the American Church Historian," *Church History* 25 (1956): 3–15, especially p. 15.
4. Henry Warner Bowden, *Church History in the Age of Science: Historiographical Patterns in the United States, 1876–1918* (Chapel Hill, N.C., 1971), especially p. 60.

devoted primarily to the history of an ideology. I reach this conclusion not so much from my impressions of the points of view of our current members as from my reading of a part of the historic record. I reach it, to be specific, from my reading of certain debates during the period of the Reformation on the identity of the true church. These debates, in a period of ferocious, even fratricidal competition among institutions each claiming to be the only true church, tried to identify the *notae* or marks by which the true church can be recognized. Debate over marks of the true church, to be sure, was not an innovation of the Reformation period. It had also characterized debates between the orthodox and such groups as the Gnostics in the early church. But since I know the Reformation period better than others, I shall draw my examples from it.

For the classic Protestant definition of the church, the obvious first place to look is the Augsburg Confession. In its article VII, we do indeed find the church defined as the "congregation of the saints, in which the Gospel is purely taught and the sacraments rightly administered."[5] This article clearly specifies two marks by which the real church can be recognized: true teaching and correct administration of the sacraments. No additional marks are specified. Thus any institution, whether local, national or universal, whether governed democratically, aristocratically or monarchically, whether independent or a branch of some political entity, whether the product of a long history or newly created, can fairly claim to be the church if it satisfies these two criteria.

Many early Protestants found this definition intellectually satisfactory and polemically useful. John Calvin, the most prominent representative of a Protestant movement which parted company with the Evangelical Lutherans on many issues, found no reason to quarrel with this definition of the church. In edition after edition of his classic *Institutes of the Christian Religion,* he defined the church by saying, "wherever we see the word of God to be purely preached and heard, [and] the sacraments to be administered according to the institution of Christ, there we cannot doubt that a church exists."[6]

Some early Protestants, to be sure, did not find this definition complete. Most of them belonged to the Reformed rather than the Evangelical branch of Protestantism. They seem to have been disturbed by an antinomian tendency in much of the early theology of the movement, an emphasis on justification by faith alone so extreme that it left too little room for the encouragement of ethical behavior which is another traditionally important

5. "Est autem ecclesia congregatio sanctorum, in qua evangelium pure docetur et recte administrantur sacramenta." See *Die Bekenntnisschriften der evangelisch-lutherischen Kirche,* 5th ed. (Göttingen, 1963), p. 61 for both Latin and German texts, and pp. 233–246 for a more extended explanation of this article.

6. "Car par tout où nous voyons la parolle de Dieu estre purement preschée et escoutée, les Sacremens estre administrez selon l'institution de Christ, là il ne faut douter nullement qu'il n'y ait Eglise." 4.1.9. In the critical edition of Jean-Daniel Benoît (Paris, 1957–1963), 4.20.

part of Christian teaching. And they seem to have felt a need for more practical guidance on the institutional shape the true church should assume. In any event they added to their definition of the church a third mark, the mark of discipline. One particularly clear statement of this expanded definition can be found in the writings of Peter Martyr Vermigli, the Italian Reformed associate of Martin Bucer in Strasbourg and England, and of Henry Bullinger in Zurich, whose works constituted important references for several generations of Reformed clergymen in the late sixteenth and early seventeenth centuries. Vermigli emphatically and repeatedly includes three marks in his definition of the church. Thus at one point he defines the church as "a company of believers and regenerate persons whom God gathereth together in Christ by the word and the holy Ghost, and by his ministers governeth the same with pureness of doctrine, with lawful use of the sacraments and with discipline." He then elaborates on the utility of this definition by saying, "if thou wilt conclude hereby that the church shall be unknown, we will deny it . . . because there be proper marks assigned by which the same may be very well known. . . . For wheresoever the pureness of doctrine flourisheth, the sacraments are purely ministered and discipline exercised, thou hast a congregation whereunto which thou mayest safely join thyself." And elsewhere he refers again to the "three marks of the church which are wont to be shewed by men of our side: namely doctrine, the right administration of the sacraments and the care of discipline."[7] This three-mark definition of the church receives official endorsement in a number of Reformed confessions of faith, including the Belgic Confession, the Hungarian Confession and the Scots Confession.[8] Its adoption by the Scots, of course, makes it a part of the tradition from which modern Presbyterianism descends.

In the later Reformation, these definitions of the church in terms of marks are considerably elaborated and adapted for polemical purposes. One which happens to intrigue me was drafted by Theodore Beza, Calvin's successor as the theological and ecclesiastical director of that branch of Reformed Protestantism which continued to look to Geneva for leadership. In 1579, Beza published a Latin treatise on the marks of the true church, then reissued it in French in 1592 in a considerably revised form. An English translation of the Latin version was first published in 1582. Now Beza in this treatise on occasion mentions three marks of the church, but they are no

7. From Vermigli's loci De ecclesia and De schismate, as excerpted and translated in the posthumous Common Places collected from his writings, in the 1583 English ed. (STC 24669), 4.1.1 and 4.6.16, with spelling, capitalization and punctuation modernized. Also quoted and discussed at more length in Robert M. Kingdon, "Peter Martyr Vermigli and the Marks of the True Church," in F. Forrester Church and Timothy George, eds., Continuity and Discontinuity in Church History: Essays Presented to George Huntston Williams (Leiden, 1979), especially p. 205.

8. Pointed out and documented by Tadataka Maruyama, The Ecclesiology of Theodore Beza (Geneva, 1978), p. 211.

longer the marks of true doctrine, correct sacraments and discipline, as in Vermigli and several of the Reformed confessions. They are rather true doctrine, proper succession of ministers and proper ordination of ministers. And the three marks are not of equal importance. The second and third flow from the first, and are very much subordinate to it. Thus succession is not defined by persons but by doctrines. The true successors of the apostles are those who teach apostolic doctrine, not those who can claim lineal descent from Christ's closest associates. And ordination requires adherence to true doctrine to be effective, rather than fulfillment of some canonically prescribed rite. Thus there is really only one mark of the true church for Beza, and that is orthodox doctrine. As he summarizes his own argument, "Christ is the true, perpetual, necessary, and, to be short, the only mark of the church . . . as he from the beginning has most perfectly . . . revealed himself, both in the writings of the prophets and of the apostles. . . . Therefore wheresoever the word is heard, as it ought to be, there indeed Christ reigns, and where Christ reigns, there indeed we judge the catholic, visible church to be, neither tied to any certain place, nor unto the multitude."[9] In this statement, of course, Beza is retorting to claims by the Roman Catholic Church that the location of its headquarters in Rome and the widespread acceptance of its authority are evidence that it is the only true church. In this statement he is also following the traditional Protestant expedient of basing doctrine on scripture alone. He explicitly allows, however, for the use of other early written authorities as guides to understanding scripture. Thus he accepts the creeds and legislation of the earliest ecumenical councils and the writings of the early church Fathers wherever they do not contradict scripture. But he refuses to accept any tradition not written down at an early period as truly orthodox. For Beza the church has come to be primarily a vehicle for education in this amplified scriptural message. At one point he even defines the church as "the congregation of them, that must be taught of God," and again as "a school, in which the word of the Lord is not only barely to be read, as out of the letter written, but also to be taught, that it may be rightly understood."[10] The church has now come to be defined entirely by its beliefs. It is an ideology, not an institution.

Thinking of Beza's sort, it seems to me, underlies much of the approach to church history which I have labeled ideological. From my secular point of view, however, it poses problems. It tends to overlook the fact that any ideology to have influence and to endure must be institutionalized, or must

9. Theodore Beza, *A Discourse of the True and Visible Markes of the Catholique Churche,* 1582 (STC 2014), sigs. Dv-[D]2 (hereafter cited as Beza, *Marks;* spelling, capitalization and punctuation again modernized). See Maruyama, *The Ecclesiology of Theodore Beza,* pp. 164–173, for an extended analysis of this treatise.
10. Beza, *Marks,* sigs. [C6], [C7]v.

become incarnate, if you will permit me a theological metaphor. Luther's ideas, for example, would never have survived, much less had significant influence, if they had not been taught in schools, preached from pulpits, applied to practical problems by laws enforced in courts. To understand his influence fully, we need to know more of the teachers, preachers and lawyers who mediated his ideas to the general public. And in studying that process of mediation we may well need to accept the possibility that parts of the original ideological impulse were significantly modified, weakened, distorted or even lost.

In addition, this ideological approach has a source rooted in vitriolic polemic of the Reformation period, and that poses additional problems. For there was another side to the sixteenth-century debate, and that, of course, was the Roman Catholic side. So let me now examine that briefly.

For a Catholic definition of the church dating from the sixteenth century, I turn to the *Controversies* of Saint Robert Bellarmine. The legislation promulgated by the Council of Trent obviously would provide a more authoritative source. But the Tridentine Fathers, for a variety of reasons, sidestepped formal pronouncements on the nature of the church, forcing modern scholars to deduce their views from canons and decrees devoted primarily to other matters. Bellarmine, on the other hand, tackles squarely the problems of defining the true church and of discerning the marks by which it can be distinguished from it rivals. And the *Controversies* in which these and the whole range of other issues then separating Protestants from Catholics were examined was a manual of enormous influence on generations of Roman polemicists.

The key difficulty with Protestant definitions of the church, Bellarmine argues, is that they "make the true church invisible," that they fail to recognize that the church is as much a "visible and palpable assembly of people as the assembly of the people of Rome, the kingdom of France or the republic of Venice."[11] To Bellarmine, therefore, the church must have concrete institutional shape, which its members can recognize and support. And to help define this shape, he proposes a list of fifteen marks of the true church, having first rejected the classic Lutheran and Calvinist lists of marks as incomplete and insufficient. Some of Bellarmine's marks remain

---

11. "propterea Ecclesiam veram invisibilem faciunt. . . . Ecclesia enim est coetus hominum ita visibilis, et palpabilis, ut est coetus populi Romani, vel Regnum Galliae, aut Respublica Venetorum." Robert Bellarmine, *Controversiarum de conciliis*, lib. 3, cap. 2; in the J. Fèvre ed. of his *Opera Omnia*, 12 vols. (Paris, 1870; reprinted Frankfurt, 1965), 2:318. This passage was called to my attention by Robert W. Richgels of Viterbo College, the author of an unpublished University of Wisconsin-Madison Ph.D. dissertation of 1973 on "Bellarmine's Use of Calvin in the *Controversies*." The passage is also cited by Quentin Skinner, *The Foundations of Modern Political Thought*, 2 vols. (Cambridge, England, 1978), 2:147, as a part of an analysis of the sixteenth-century Thomist theory of the church, pp. 144–148, to which I am indebted.

ideological, for he says the true church must teach doctrine which is sacred and doctrine which is efficacious. And some of them are supernatural, including the glory of miracles, prophetic light, the invariably unhappy fate of those who oppose the church and the happy state of those who defend it. But others describe institutional characteristics. For Bellarmine the true church must also be ancient, must be able to trace an uninterrupted history from the beginning, must have gained a broad measure of support and must be ruled by a succession of bishops within the Roman communion dating from the apostles down to our own times.[12]

Thinking of Bellarmine's sort, it seems to me, underlies much of the approach to church history which I have labeled institutional. But from my secular point of view it again poses problems. It is even more obviously rooted in polemic of the Reformation period than the Protestant arguments I examined earlier. And it is thus susceptible to the battery of arguments advanced by all who challenge the claims of the Roman papacy to sole leadership of the Christian community; just one example is the argument that the theoretical possibility of the choice of a heretic as pope makes it unthinkable that the pope can invariably be accepted as Christ's only vicar on earth. And Bellarmine's definitions are less than useful for the secular historian faced with one very important and very obvious empirical fact: a great many people who claim to be Christians are not members of the Roman Catholic Church. If one wants to study the institutional shape of the community of those who call themselves Christian, one must examine several institutions, not just one.

Now of these two views of the church, one which sees the church primarily as an ideology and which I argue appeals particularly to Protestants, and the other which sees the church primarily as an institution and which I argue appeals particularly to Catholics, it seems to me clear that the former prevails within our Society. I find it, in highly sophisticated forms to be sure, in the theoretical writings of some of our most thoughtful members. Let me cite as examples two I particularly admire, Sidney Mead and Wilhelm Pauck. In a seminal essay published in 1963, Mead offered to explain church history. He began by analyzing in a general way the discipline of history, stating that it includes "First . . . assertions about the activities of people done in the past. . . . Second are assertions about "ideology"—where the word "ideology" merely points to the content and way of thinking that character-izes an individual, or a group, or an era. . . . Third are assertions about unquestioned presuppositions."[13] What I miss from this pattern of analysis, with its emphasis on activities, ideologies and presuppositions, is any attention to structures—entities that in the last few decades an ex-tremely imaginative and influential group of French historians

12. Robert Bellarmine, *Controversiarum de conciliis,* lib. 4, cap. 1–18; in the Fèvre ed., 2:361–407.
13. Sidney E. Mead, "Church History Explained," *Church History* 32 (1963): 19–20.

have demonstrated to us merit close attention. Since Mead has no room for structures in general history, he obviously need provide no room for them in church history. He thus calls on church historians to work "within the context of the whole theological tradition of Christendom," to accept "the overwhelming consensus of Christians" that the church "is one body" and thus to develop "a more excellent conception of what and where the true church was, and is, and ought to be."[14] The denominational institutions which claim to be churches, thus, do not for Mead deserve intensive study. What is really important is a core of ideas animating and uniting a number of these institutions in ways to which their members may not even be sensitive.

In another seminal essay published in 1952, Pauck came closer to a definition of the church I find satisfactory. He granted that some notion of church is essential for all Christianity: "the Christian mind is marked by a special kind of self-consciousness induced by the awareness that the Christian faith is not fully actualized unless it is expressed in the special social context suggested by the term 'church.' "[15] And he admonished us never to forget that the apostle Paul, by inaugurating the "era of Christian institutionalism, *thereby* secured the permanence of the Christian movement."[16] But Pauck then proceeded to develop this theme in a swift and masterly essay on the *idea* of the church from Jesus to the World Council of Churches rather than dealing with any messy institutional embodiments of the idea.

Now I do not want to denigrate research on the history of Christian thought. Some of the most exciting contributions to knowledge to issue forth from this society within the last generation have been the work of historians of theology like Wilhelm Pauck and Heiko Oberman and their many students. Their approaches are certainly not exhausted and deserve development and elaboration. But I do wish to press for more consideration of the institutional matrixes which shape some of these bodies of thought and which make them relatively permanent. Let me develop this point by offering a brief list of projects which have recently impressed me and which I would like to see imitated.

(1) A first type of study I would like to see developed further is of the smallest units into which Christian communities are divided ecclesiastically, local parishes or congregations. In 1973, William Clebsch made of his presidential address to this society a plea for changing church history from investigation of Christian doctrine to a study of "life-styles of pragmatic piety" as they were provoked by succeeding "cultural crises."[17] He then developed this plea further in a provocative short book titled *Christianity in*

14. Ibid., pp. 25-27.
15. Wilhelm Pauck, "The Idea of the Church in Christian History," *Church History* 21 (1952): 191.
16. Ibid., p. 210.
17. William A. Clebsch, "Toward a History of Christianity," *Church History* 43 (1974): 5-16, especially p. 11.

European History (New York, 1979). Now I have considerable sympathy for Clebsch's plea, but I found his development of it disappointing. This is partly because that development was inevitably highly schematic, compressing the history of two millennia into a slight book of only about three hundred pages. But it was also because Clebsch's approach was macrocosmic, in a field where I suspect a microcosmic approach promises better results, for the present at least. The obvious microcosm of the Christian community, of course, is the local parish or congregation.

The possibilities of intensive study of local parishes were probably first appreciated by the great French religious sociologist Gabriel Le Bras. We owe to him and his students a number of fine monographs on the parishes within restricted parts of France over periods of a century or so, for example the study by André Schaer of parish clergy in upper Alsace from 1648 to 1789.[18] And the influence of Le Bras has spread to other countries. One which came to my attention in recent years is Poland, where I participated in a conference on ecclesiastical history in 1978. At the Catholic University of Lublin in that country, a suite of rooms has been set aside for intensive study of the geohistory of Polish religious institutions. Under a photograph of Le Bras mounted on one wall a team of historians and geographers works to develop maps of the exact dimensions of parishes from the rather late introduction of Christianity into Poland down to the present. Their main discovery to date has been of remarkable continuity. Many of the parishes established in Poland soon after the initial introduction of Christianity to that country still possess the same size, the same center and the same basic functions that were assigned to them at the beginning. It can be argued that the parish is the most durable of all institutions in Poland, far more durable than any of the rather ephemeral political institutions developed in that country, far more durable than any of the exploitative economic institutions saddled on the population, even more durable than the institutions of ecclesiastical superstructure such as dioceses.

But it is possible to bring even greater focus to the study of parishes. It is possible to apply to them the methods of "thick description" pioneered by anthropologists like Clifford Geertz. This has already been done with exciting results by a number of social historians specializing on Italian and French cities of the fifteenth and sixteenth centuries. One particularly striking example by an active member of this Society is Natalie Zemon Davis's analysis of the parish of Sainte Croix in Lyon from 1545 to 1575.[19] This fascinating study reveals a great deal about the class culture, the sexual systems and the religious forms of a rather patrician neighborhood dominated by clerical bureaucrats and lawyers. It shows us how the administra-

18. André Schaer, *Le clergé paroissial catholique en haute Alsace sous l'ancien régime, 1648–1789* (Paris, 1966).
19. Natalie Zemon Davis, "Religion in the Neighborhood: The Stones of Sainte-Croix Parish," read to an American Historical Association meeting in New York, 28 December 1979. I am grateful to Professor Davis for giving me a copy of this unpublished version.

tion of the religious rites of baptism, marriage and burial gave a significant measure of meaning to the daily life of this small community. It points out how the penetration of Calvinist Protestantism in these decades threatened to reorient and reorganize this community and how the new faith was ejected. It thus gives us a fresh appreciation of what the Reformation really meant to ordinary people in one neighborhood, how it seemed appealing to some but threatening to others, because of the ways in which it affected the texture of their daily lives.

Elsewhere I have pointed out that while most parish studies to date have been of Catholic parishes, there is much to be done on Protestant parishes.[20] For the parish system survived the Reformation in all those parts of Europe which turned to Lutheran Evangelical, Calvinist Reformed or Anglican versions of Christianity. And variants of parishes survive in religiously pluralistic societies like our own American society. I believe these microcosms of Christian life deserve the closest study, featuring the imaginative use of methods drawn from modern sociology and anthropology. If properly executed, they could be enormously revealing of "life-styles of pragmatic piety."

(2) A second type of study I would like to see developed further is of the ecclesiastical courts and other institutions of discipline created by Christian churches. I suspect they deserve considerable credit for the characteristic styles of life developed by Christians in different historical periods, for example the much maligned style of life labeled Puritan in early modern England. These institutions concerned themselves particularly with the protection of the family, the most basic of all social units, by regulating marriage, by protecting marriage from the threats posed to it by sexual irregularity and violence and by seeking to prevent the dissolution of marriage. They thus should be of particular interest to modern scholars trying to understand the history of marriage, of the family, of the roles conditioned by position within the family of children, women and men. Now the most elaborate body of legislation backed by institutions of enforcement developed within Christian history is obviously to be found within the Roman Catholic Church, beginning in the Middle Ages and reaching its peak for those areas remaining Catholic in the decades following the Tridentine reforms. And some of this machinery of control still survives within Catholic communities, particularly in Catholic countries. But the church court system, like the parish system, also survived the Reformation, and indeed seems to have become even more vigorous in certain Reformed communities than in any others. The Protestant ecclesiastical courts of the Reformation period happen to interest me particularly, so I would like to make a special appeal for the study of them.

These courts carried several different names. In Geneva and in many of

20. Robert M. Kingdon, "Protestant Parishes in the Old World and the New: The Cases of Geneva and Boston," *Church History* 48 (1979): 290–304.

the French Calvinist communities following her lead, they were called "consistories" in rather obvious imitation of the consistorial courts controlled by Catholic bishops before the Reformation in those same communities. In German-speaking communities, for example, Zurich and Basel, they were often called *Ehegerichten* or marriage courts. In England they were called by the general public "bawdy courts." These institutions saw to it that a new morality was not only preached but also practiced. They helped to internalize that approach to life which came to be labeled Puritan. Their records are beginning to attract attention but deserve far more. There has been a great flowering among social historians in recent years of research on the family. But many of the most influential reports on this research have depended very heavily on rather impressionistic use of literary and artistic evidence. This is certainly true of Philippe Ariès's pioneering essay on the history of the family.[21] But it is also true to a degree of Lawrence Stone's massive study of the English family between 1500 and 1800, and of Jean-Louis Flandrin's provocative study of families in early modern France.[22] All of these studies downgrade, it seems to me, the degree to which the Christian church remained the custodian of the family and the ways in which it exercised this custody through church courts. Valuable complements and correctives to these studies could well be provided with material drawn from the records of church courts, and records of this sort survive in enough places to make research of that sort quite feasible. The records of the Genevan Consistory, for example, into which I have dipped a number of times, happen to be unusually complete and well-preserved, if in an especially dreadful handwriting.

The Genevan Consistory, in fact, provides a particularly striking example of how pervasive and intensive the social control exercised by a church court could be. E. William Monter, in an important article on this Consistory, estimates that in 1569, five years after Calvin died, when the court was at its peak of activity, every year one in fifteen adults out of the entire population of the city was summoned for questioning, and one in twenty-five was punished by excommunication.[23] It is a mistake to conclude, however, as I once did myself, that this court initiated a "moral reign of terror."[24] For Monter's quantitative tallies indicate that the most common treatment of a complaint was simply discussion. A couple or neighbors or parents and children accused of quarreling, of physical abuse to each other or of other types of disruptive behavior would be called in, questioned closely and helped

---

21. Philippe Ariès, *Centuries of Childhood: A Social History of Family Life* (New York, 1962).
22. Lawrence Stone, *The Family, Sex and Marriage in England, 1500–1800* (New York, 1977); Jean-Louis Flandrin, *Families in Former Times: Kinship, Household and Sexuality in Early Modern France* (Cambridge, England, 1979).
23. E. William Monter, "The Consistory of Geneva, 1559–1569," *Bibliothèque d'Humanisme et Renaissance* 38 (1976): 467–484, especially p 484.
24. Robert M. Kingdon, "The Control of Morals in Calvin's Geneva," in *The Social History of the Reformation,* ed. Lawrence P. Buck and Jonathan W. Zophy (Columbus, 1972), p. 12.

to settle their differences. In most cases, in fact, the Consistory acted more like a counseling service than a court. If the accused was not sufficiently penitent or the charge was really serious, the Consistory, to be sure, could levy the penalty of excommunication. And if the accused had committed a crime, he could be handed over to a secular court for formal trial and punishment, including, with disconcerting frequency, mutilation and execution. This combination of restraints—counseling for the great majority of cases, excommunication for certain more serious cases, secular punishments including execution for the most serious cases—turned out to be extremely effective. Monter discovered that remarkably few excommunicates were ever called before the Consistory a second time. Over a sample span of three and a half years, the rate of repeaters amounted to only ten percent.[25] This is a far better rate of success than any modern penal system of which I have knowledge.

All over Europe in the seventeenth century, in both Catholic and Protestant countries, the position of the family was reinforced and strengthened. In many areas rates of illegitimacy dropped to record lows; in many communities prostitution was effectively abolished. This change was no doubt due in some part to the ethical teachings of Protestant and Catholic Reformers. But it was surely also due in good part to the activities of courts like the Consistory created by Calvin, even if few municipalities were able to sustain social pressure quite as intense and intrusive as that displayed in late sixteenth-century Geneva. And when this trend was reversed in much of Europe during the eighteenth century with widespread relaxations of restraints on extramarital sex coupled with frequent loosenings of family ties, we would do well to go beyond the evident decline in the authority of Christian teachings and teachers to see if there was not also a pronounced weakening in the activities and powers of ecclesiastical courts. At least these are hypotheses, I would contend, which merit examination.

(3) A third type of study I would like to see developed further is of the hospitals and other institutions of charity created by Christian communities. Since the creation of the church by the apostles, Christians have agreed that the church has a special obligation to relieve the sufferings of society's unfortunate. The institutions created to discharge this obligation deserve intensive study. Of these institutions, the ones about which I am best informed are again those created in sixteenth-century Geneva as a part of the Calvinist Reformation. Examples drawn from Geneva, to be sure, may be atypical, since the Reformation led to more abrupt and more extreme changes there than elsewhere. But there is some virtue in considering the extreme example, since it provides a limit against which more ambiguous and restrained types of change can be measured.

Before the Reformation, social welfare was handled in Geneva, as it was in most European cities, by a group of hospitals supplemented by a

25. Monter, "The Consistory of Geneva," pp. 477–478.

municipal fund. These hospitals were not limited to care of the sick, as in modern times, but were rather all-purpose institutions designed to provide assistance to orphans, the aged and others unable to care for themselves. There were seven of them in pre-Reformation Geneva, most of them founded by private bequests and perhaps housed in the deceased donor's residence, most of them staffed by a priest who would say masses for the donor and his family and help with the poor, assisted by a lay administrator. Each might house and support a dozen or so poor people. Their work was supplemented and coordinated by a municipal fund, designed to aid the poor who could remain in their own residences.

All these institutions were abolished by the Reformation. They were initially replaced by a single General Hospital, which housed several dozen poor people and also provided external relief, mostly in the form of food rations. This General Hospital was directed by a lay administrator with several assistants, supervised by a committee of prominent citizens chosen as a part of the city government. This institution was created before the establishment of the Reformation, before the arrival of Calvin in the city, by the same pious lay people who ejected the Roman Catholic clergy and hired Protestant ministers to take their place. The only contribution Calvin and the other ministers made to this institution was to consecrate it. Calvin informed the citizens of Geneva that the administrators of this Hospital were in fact deacons, of the sort described in the New Testament. He encouraged prominent lay people to accept the responsibilities of these positions and encouraged the rest of the population to support these deacons financially and in other ways. The whole early history of this institution provides a classic example of the common transfer by Protestants of religious duties from ordained clergymen to pious lay people.[26]

At a slightly later stage in the Genevan Reformation, a second charitable institution was created, the *Bourse française*. This was a fund raised by contributions from wealthy French refugees, administered by a group of these refugees who again were given the title of deacons, to meet the economic problems faced by the poor among the several thousand religious refugees who fled from France to Geneva. This *Bourse française* is the object of an excellent Stanford dissertation, just completed, by Jeannine Olson.[27] Calvin and the other ministers took a much more active role in the creation and administration of this institution than in that of the General Hospital. Some of them contributed to it financially. One of them was always formally represented in its board of deacons. The ministers also offered the *Bourse* plenty of advice on expenditures. This institution provides another example of the common transfer by Protestants of religious duties to pious lay people.

26. For elaboration and documentation, see Robert M. Kingdon, "Social Welfare in Calvin's Geneva," *American Historical Review* 76 (1971): 50–69.
27. Jeannine Evelyn Olson, "The Bourse Française: Deacons and Social Welfare in Calvin's Geneva," (Ph.D. diss., Stanford University, 1980).

The history of these two institutions taken together provides us with a detailed and graphic picture of how the earliest Calvinists actually grappled with social problems. And that picture is far more meaningful, it seems to me, than the attempts to extrapolate a Reformed social position from ethics or theology, particularly when it becomes as attenuated and strained as it does in the works of Max Weber and some of his disciples.

There are dozens of similar charitable institutions still waiting for similar investigation. I think particularly of medieval hospitals and Catholic confraternities of the Counter Reformation, but there are plenty of analogues from other periods and places and traditions. The close study of these institutions is surely one of the best ways to measure and evaluate the response of the Christian community to the endemic social problems of the societies within which it has been located. It might even provide some guidance to what Christian responses should be at the present day.

(4) A fourth type of study I would like to see developed further is of ecclesiastical diplomatic institutions. This was my original research interest. I must confess that the results of my earliest research disappointed me in some ways. For I discovered that while ecclesiastical leaders like Melanchthon, Calvin and Beza were occasionally involved in formal diplomatic negotiations, Protestant diplomacy tended to be dominated by the secular agents of great princes, with clergymen serving only as consultants or as manipulators of public reactions to princely policies. But I still believe ecclesiastical diplomacy has much to teach us of the Christian contributions to decisions on war and peace, often the most fateful decisions western societies have made. In recent years, I have become especially intrigued by the diplomatic institutions developed during the Renaissance and Reformation by the central administration of the Roman Catholic Church, and particularly by the significant growth and adaptation of those institutions to meet the Protestant threat by such militant popes of the late sixteenth century as Gregory XIII. For these Catholic institutions operated on a larger, better financed and more independent basis than Protestant diplomatic agencies, and thus give us a clearer picture of how the church could intervene upon the diplomatic scene. A group of scholars working out of Helsinki in Finland, led by Henri Biaudet, published several monographs on late sixteenth-century papal diplomacy several decades ago, centered on the pontificate of Gregory XIII.[28] But some of the raw material upon which they were building is only now being made generally available, and much of it still remains housed in archival collections of manuscripts. The most important of these collections, of course, is the Secret Archives of the Vatican;

28. Henri Biaudet, *Les nonciatures apostoliques permanentes jusqu'en 1648*, in *Annales Academiae Scientiarum Fennicae*, ser. B 2, vol. 1 (Helsinki, 1910); Liisi Karttunen, *Grégoire XIII comme politicien et souverain*, in ibid., ser. B 2, vol. 2 (Helsinki, 1911); P. O. von Törne, *Ptolémée Gallio, cardinal de Côme: étude sur la cour de Rome, sur la secrétairerie pontificale, et sur la politique des papes au XVIᵉ siècle* (Helsinki and Paris, 1907).

and of particular interest within it are the sets of instructions sent out by the papal Domestic Secretary, who acted as a secretary of state, and the reports back to him from the nuncios, resident ambassadors accredited by the Vatican to leading Catholic states. Some of these nuncios' correspondence was published or at least calendared some time ago, particularly correspondence with the nuncios dispatched to Germany at the time of the Reformation.[29] But other sets of correspondence are only now becoming available, for example the exchanges with the nuncios to France, publication of which is now being prepared by an international team of scholars coordinated by Pierre Blet, and apparently originally inspired, to some degree at least, by a church historian and former nuncio to France who became Pope John XXIII.[30] And there are voluminous reports of this character still remaining in the Vatican for scholarly inspection, in particular correspondence with the nuncios in Spain and the Italian states, in addition to accounts and other records providing information on how these diplomats were paid and assisted. These materials are making it more possible than ever before for scholars to understand how the Roman curia continued to exercise formidable political powers, both within national churches and within secular states, throughout the entire early modern period. And the exercise of those powers helps to explain much of the alternations of peace and war which dominated international politics during the sixteenth and seventeenth centuries and which ultimately frustrated the Protestant attempt to reshape the entire Christian church, leaving the Christian community in all those parts of the world dominated by western European culture permanently split into Catholic and Protestant segments.

These four types of ecclesiastical institutions—parishes, courts, hospitals and embassies—are the ones which have attracted my personal interest over the last thirty years. But there are many others which also merit intensive study. One obvious additional type is the educational institution. In almost all periods, the Christian church has taken seriously its responsibility to pass the fundamentals of the faith on to upcoming generations. At times it has even monopolized most of the formal education in western society. There is still much to be done on institutions created for this purpose, including elementary schools designed to shape the general population and universities designed to prepare religious elites.[31]

29. *Nuntiaturberichte aus Deutschland nebst ergänzenden Actenstücken,* ed. by the K. preussische historische Institut in Rom, especially section 3 (1572–1585), and by the Görres-Gesellschaft, especially section 1 (1585–1590, 1892–).

30. *Acta Nuntiaturae Gallicae* (Rome, 1961–), especially vols. 12, 13, *Correspondance du nonce en France Antonio Maria Salviati (1572–1578),* ed. Pierre Hurtubise and Robert Toupin, 1975.

31. Two particularly suggestive studies of educational institutions sponsored by religious bodies which have come to my recent attention are Gerald Strauss, *Luther's House of Learning: Indoctrination of the Young in the German Reformation* (Baltimore, 1978) and William J. Courtenay, "The Effect of the Black Death on English Higher Education," *Speculum* 55 (1980): 696–714.

This summary list of research projects on the history of Christian ecclesiastical institutions must now be terminated. Many of you could add to it. Some of you could challenge or modify some of the items on my list. But I hope it helps make my general point. I have deliberately sidestepped the question of whether the study of church history is or should be useful to the contemporary Christian church. Many Protestant church historians have already demonstrated that ideological church history can be used to strengthen Christianity, and many Catholic church historians have demonstrated that institutional history can be used in the same way. Both categories of church historians have also all too often permitted their devout intentions to color and even distort their reports of the historical record. Historians without Christian commitments of any kind, furthermore, have used both of these approaches to the study of church history, sometimes with remarkable imaginative empathy, sometimes with a stunning inability to comprehend the religious mentality. This problem I leave to those more involved in religious education than I. The main point I have tried to make is that a full understanding of the history of the Christian church requires study of both its ideas and its institutions, since both are necessary components of a living Christianity. While it is certainly true that an institution without ideology is sterile, it is also equally true that an ideology without institution is futile.

Reprinted by permission from Church History *50 (1981), 81-97.*

II

SOME FRENCH REACTIONS TO THE COUNCIL OF TRENT*

In this age of growing ecumenicism, many scholars are turning to the history of the sixteenth century for a fresh examination of the origins of those ideas and institutions which continue to divide the Christian community. During these years of the widely publicized meetings of an ecumenical council sponsored by the Roman Catholic Church, many are turning specifically to the canons and decrees drafted by the Council of Trent for a fresh study of the extent to which they do or must divide Christians. But fully to understand these Tridentine decisions from an ecumenical perspective requires not only a knowledge of their texts and of the debates from which they emerged. It requires also a knowledge of the hostile reactions which they aroused among the many Christians who would not accept these decisions or the authority of those who promulgated them. An interesting spectrum of such reactions can be found among French criticisms of Trent published during the sixteenth century. Of these publications, three seem to me to demonstrate this proposition neatly: one by a distinguished French theologian, John Calvin; a second by a distinguished French jurisconsult, Charles Dumoulin; a third by a prominent French lawyer and historian, Innocent Gentillet. These works have not been ignored by such experts on the historiography of Trent as Professor Jedin.[1] But I feel they merit a more detailed and more considered examination than they have as yet received. This paper sketches some of the lines upon which such an examination might proceed.

John Calvin's most extended comment on the Council of Trent was his *Acta Synodi Tridentinae cum antidoto*. It was published in 1547, after the first seven sessions of the Council, held under the sponsorship of Pope Paul III, had been completed. It was soon reissued in a French translation, which was somewhat longer and earthier than the Latin original.[2] And it quickly provoked a spirited retort by the German Catholic polemicist Cochlaeus. The main purpose of Calvin's pamphlet was to demonstrate that the canons and decrees of the Council of Trent do not conform to the basic truths of Christian doctrine revealed in Holy Scripture. It took the form of a full reprint of texts of the decisions by these early sessions of the Council, with Calvin's opinions of each appended. From a purely polemical point of view, this method would seem to have certain obvious disadvantages. It makes accessible to one's readers not only one's own views but also those of one's opponents. But it was a method that Calvin was to use many times. Another example is provided by his refutation of Servetus, when there was even more reason, from Calvin's point of view, to suppress statement of the rare but dangerous doctrinal position he was then combating. Such was Calvin's confidence in the irresistible logic of his own arguments, however, that it never seems to have occurred to him that his readers might find superior merit in those of his opponents.

Of the seven sessions upon which Calvin comments in this book, the one which absorbed by far the greatest amount of his attention was the sixth—at which the decree on justification and thirty-three related canons were adopted. Analysis of them occupies more than a third of the entire book. Since corollary to the doctrine of justification are elements of the doctrine of predestination, so commonly identified in the popular mind with Calvin, this should, perhaps, not seem surprising. Not, that is, unless one takes seriously the view of those interpreters of Calvin who hold that a rigid view of predestination was less of a preoccupation with him than with his followers.[3] Certainly in this particular pamphlet, however, it absorbed more of his attention than any other doctrine.

More incontrovertibly characteristic of Calvin are the sources he uses in this work. He depends above all upon Scripture, insists generally upon plain or literal readings of Scripture, and occasionally even hinges interpretations of its meaning on such fine points as the grammatical constructions of specific Scriptural passages. In his refutation of canon fourteen attached to the decree on justification, for example, Calvin's argument depends in part on the tense of a verb translated as "live" in a passage from "the prophet," apparently Habakkuk 2:4.[4] As a guide to authoritative interpretation of Scripture, Calvin is frequently willing to rely on such early Church Fathers as St. Augustine. In this work he makes particularly great use of Augustine's anti-Pelagian tracts, above all of the *Contra duas epistolas pelagianorum* and the *De praedestinatione sanctorum*.[5] Occasionally Calvin refers to a medieval figure like St. Bernard or a contemporary scholar like Erasmus. But he never depends very heavily upon their authority.

At first glance this work may seem to be a very unlikely one to study for any contribution to an ecumenical hope. This, indeed, seems to be the opinion even of those modern historians who enthusiastically claim Calvin to be one of the great ecumenical figures of the Reformation period. On close examination, their claim generally seems to be that he was irenic in his dealings with most other orthodox Protestants, but that he did not really consider seriously the possibility of reunion with Rome.[6] This latter view is certainly supported by a reading of the language he uses in this tract, particularly in the French version. While some may find a certain raw humor in his comparison of the Council of Trent to a diseased whore, his constant references to the Tridentine Fathers as "horned beasts" with "stinking muzzles," his labeling of sacramental chrism as "stinking grease"—such wordings are hardly likely to soothe Roman Catholics or contribute in any very helpful way to contemporary ecumenical dialogue.

Yet Calvin was too careful in his thought and too concerned for theology to base his argument entirely on cheap name-calling. And a more considered examination of his reactions to the Tridentine decisions reveals a degree of agreement which, to me at least, is surprising. To some of the many Tridentine texts he republishes, his only comment is a simple "Amen." This is the accolade he accords, for example, to a number of the canons anathematizing Pelagian views and some anathematizing Antinomian views. To other Tridentine texts he registers a partial assent. Occasionally he objects to details of wording. Occasionally he objects to philosophical assumptions or logical distinctions which he claims a given text implies and to which he takes exception. In doing this, incidentally, he reveals himself to be no fool in matters of scholastic theology. In one place, he takes malicious delight in exposing Erasmus' ignorance on a point of theology.[7] Calvin even makes some concessions which have far-reaching implications. In discussing the fundamentally divisive Tridentine decree on the Scriptures, adopted at the fourth session of the Council, Calvin grants some authority to an unwritten apostolic tradition,[8] although not as much, of course, as would most Roman Catholics. It is these areas of consensus between Tridentine Catholicism and orthodox Protestantism, recognized by Calvin himself, which seem to me to merit particular attention from those interested in the history of ecumenicism. And his entire argument can be profitably studied by all who seek to understand the deep Protestant concern that all Christian doctrine be securely based on Scripture.

Reactions to the Tridentine tradition are not all of them religious, however. And neither were contemporary reactions to Trent itself. This is demonstrated by the other pamphlets I have selected for analysis. The more secular reaction to Trent finds its first great statement in a jurisconsult's brief by Charles Dumoulin, published in 1564, shortly after the definitive adjournment of Trent. It was prepared, perhaps at the request of the Protestant Admiral Coligny, as a guide to the French courts which would soon be asked to consider formal reception of the Tridentine decrees and their integration into the body of French law. Dumoulin was a man whose religious position is not easy to define. During his mature life he was certainly not a Roman Catholic, except, perhaps, for a short time before he died. But neither was he any orthodox sort of Protestant—although he flirted with Calvinism, Lutheranism, and Zwinglianism. And neither was he a mere amateur in matters of religion. His published collation or harmony of the gospels, whose printing the Calvinists tried to prevent and whose appearance was harshly condemned by a national synod of the Reformed churches of France, has nevertheless been judged by such an expert and relatively impartial an authority as Richard Simon to be a good piece of work—superior even to Calvin's own harmony of the gospels. Dumoulin was a man, however, whose position in the history of French law is beyond dispute. In an age of great French jurisconsults, Dumoulin was among the greatest. His monumental studies of the legal customs of the Paris area influenced generations of French lawyers and servants of the crown.[9] Religion and law combined to make Dumoulin deeply suspicious of the temporal claims of the Roman Catholic Church, and this suspicion erupted in a predictably hostile way in his brief on the reception in France of Trent. It was issued in French, under the title *Conseil sur le fait du Concile de Trente,* and also issued almost simultaneously in Latin, in a slightly longer version. Like Calvin's critique, it became the target of a Catholic polemical retort drafted by a rising young jurisconsult named Pierre Grégoire, and released after a delay of some twenty years.[10] And it got Dumoulin into serious trouble with the French government, from which he was extricated only with the help of extremely powerful friends.

The announced intention of Dumoulin's brief was to persuade French courts that the Tridentine decrees were profoundly subversive of both church traditions and regal rights, and should consequently not be received in the kingdom. Its argument is denser and its style less popular than those of Calvin's treatise. And in form it is somewhat more analytical. Dumoulin considers in turn the convocation of the Council, attendance at the Council, the Council's dogmatic decrees, its reform decrees, and, finally, its provisions for promulgation of the decrees. In each of these aspects of conciliar activity, Dumoulin finds legal flaws. The convocation of the Council violated procedure dictated by natural law, since the defendant, the Pope, called it and appointed its presiding officers, and since the plaintiffs, the German Protestant princes, were neither summoned nor allowed to attend.[11] It also violated precedent, since all early ecumenical councils were convened by emperors and secular rulers.[12] Attendance at the Council similarly violated natural law since the delegates all were sworn enemies of the plaintiffs,[13] and it again violated precedent, since there were no official representatives from such important Christian countries as France at certain sessions.[14] As for the dogmatic decrees, Dumoulin argues that a number of them corrupt truth and promulgate heresy, as a study of Scripture and certain specified Church Fathers reveals.[15] This part of his argument is comparatively perfunctory. With more persuasiveness, he argues that many of the reform decrees cannot be accepted in France because they violate laws of centuries' standing, both in Christendom generally and in France particularly. In developing the latter part of this argument, Dumoulin is at his best, since he could draw on his own magnificent knowledge of French legal precedents.[16] But even this part of his argument is not documented in great detail. At several points, he contents himself with citing more substantial works of reference, including such works of his own as the monumental Commentaries on the customary laws of Paris.[17] The brief ends with Dumoulin's legal objections to the Council's submission of its decrees to the Pope for final promulgation.[18]

Underlying Dumoulin's entire argument is the assumption that in all matters affecting the temporal organization of human society, the state must take precedence over the church. Consequently in all matters pertaining to the organization and discipline of the French clergy, French law must take precedence over canon law or papal dictate. Equally basic to Dumoulin's entire argument is a general if not altogether consistent prejudice in favor of tradition and against innovation. He normally shares that conviction so widespread among lawyers of the common law tradition, that customary ways of doing things are legal and right. And this conviction goes far to explain his determination to resist acceptance of the Tridentine reforms, even at some real personal risk.

Here again the scholar concerned with history as a background to ecumenicism might not expect to find much of value. Dumoulin's language, if not as salty as Calvin's, is nonetheless strong and insulting. Yet Dumoulin's reaction epitomizes a persisting concern among non-Catholics, that the Roman Church is tampering with the structure of society in ways which are hardly necessary to its essential purpose. And the forms which this concern has taken then and since merit, I feel, extended attention.

Reactions to the Tridentine decisions were not all as doctrinaire as Calvin's and Dumoulin's. One of greater suppleness came from Innocent Gentillet. Again this reaction was in character. Gentillet was a lawyer, active in southeastern France late in the century, in the 1570's and 1580's. He became involved in practical politics, as a Protestant member of the *Chambre mi-partie* of the Dauphiné, a position requiring not only legal skill but also a tact rare in that day of raging religious passions. This activity led him to an interest in the theory of politics, which was expressed in a number of writings.[19] Perhaps the best known of them is his *Anti-Machiavel*, an extended refutation of the Florentine political analyst's cynical *Prince*. But his political interests also led him to an examination of Trent, and explain much of the form in which it is cast. This examination is titled *Le bureau du Concile de Trente*. It was published in 1586, in French and in Latin, was soon translated into German, and was later republished in at least two further Latin editions.[20] It was dedicated to Henry, King of Navarre. Its formal purpose was twofold: first to support the king's announced willingness to submit himself in matters of religion to a truly "free" general council; then to refute an argument this announcement had provoked from Catholic polemicists, that such a council had already been held, at Trent.

At the beginning of his book, Gentillet admitted that he was no theologian and therefore could not present authoritative arguments against the theological validity of the Tridentine formulations. But he did claim to be an expert both in law and in history.[21] And he argued that the Tridentine decrees, before being accepted as French law, not only had to pass the test of theological truth, but also had to meet certain standards of legal and historical acceptability. For Gentillet these standards were established, not, as for Dumoulin, primarily by French tradition, but above all by the internal history of the Christian church. In a way he was trying to meet Catholic polemicists on their own grounds, by arguing from church tradition. His evidence comes consequently less from Scripture and the early Church Fathers than in Calvin, and less from French legal history than in Dumoulin. It comes more from canon law. He uses Gratian extensively. And he also uses certain other collections of the canons and decrees of early councils, and even of early popes. Many of these councils were not, in the opinion of most canonists of our day, true ecumenical councils, representing the entire Christian church and possessing a peculiarly impelling authority. They were rather regional, national, or even provincial synods of the clergy, such as the synods of Carthage in Africa of the second to fifth centuries, the synods of Arles in France of the fourth century, the synods of Toledo in Spain held throughout the medieval period. If this be a technical flaw in Gentillet's method of argument, he was not aware of it, for his book is filled with references to decisions by councils of this character.

In form, Gentillet's book resembles Calvin's. He proceeds from session to session of the Council of Trent, recording and sometimes quoting decisions, and then registering his reactions. Unlike Calvin, he does not try to discuss all the decrees issued in the period he surveys. He rather discusses only those to which he takes exception, in company with most orthodox Protestants and many Gallicans. Unlike Calvin and Dumoulin, moreover, Gentillet goes well beyond the actual texts of the decrees and canons adopted. He discusses in more detail the ecclesiastical and secular intrigues enveloping certain of the Council sessions. He summarizes many of the orations delivered to the Council, appending his own acid comments on some of them. He discusses some of the Council's modes of operation. In this he reveals a greater sensitivity than his predecessors to the historical context in which the Tridentine decisions were reached. And he thus points out ways which were later to be followed by many of the really important historians of Trent.

Gentillet also reveals a considerable sensitivity to French political developments of the period in which he was writing. When he discusses the Tridentine decrees on the episcopal powers of excommunication, for example, he adds a lengthy aside, arguing that the recent excommunication of the King of Navarre by Pope Sixtus V is illegal and invalid.[22] And he tacks on to the end of his historical analysis of Trent proper, an extended refutation of two recent petitions which had been presented by the French clergy to King Henry III, requesting that the Tridentine decrees all be received as a part of French law.[23] In this, of course, he was carrying on Dumoulin's campaign, but in a more specific context.

In Gentillet, we also finally find a sixteenth-century French critic of Trent who is at last somewhat irenic in tone—who realizes, for example, that Catholics do not like to be called "papists,"[24] and that language of this sort does not encourage dialogue. But Gentillet remains deeply troubled by the impact of Trent upon the country in which he lived. And he is particularly disturbed by the ways in which issues raised by Trent upset the course of political events in his country, especially around the courts of Navarre and of the Valois king. This fear of intervention in the course of political events is, of course, as we Americans recently had cause to observe, yet another concern among non-Catholics which makes difficult the advance of religious reconciliation.

In summary, these sixteenth-century critics of the Council of Trent feared that its decisions would limit the religious authority of Scripture, would alter the structure of secular society, and would trouble the course of human events. In this, they articulated fears which are still with us, fears which must be faced with honesty by men of good will.

* This is a slightly revised version of a paper read at the joint session of the American Society of Church History and the American Catholic Historical Association in Philadelphia, December 29, 1963.

1. Hubert Jedin, Das Konzil von Trient: ein Überblick über die Erforschung seiner Geschichte (Rome, 1948), pp. 44, 67-69, 71-73. Cf. Generoso Calenzio, Esame Critico-Letterario delle Opere riguard-anti la Storia del Concilio di Trento (Rome & Turin, 1869), pp. 2-3, 5-6.

2. A convenient copy of the Latin edition can be found in Baum, Cunitz, and Reuss (ed.), Ioannis Calvini Opera, VII, pp. 365-506. The French edition, titled Les Actes du Concile de Trente, avec le remede contre la poison (1548), is somewhat less accessible. I have used the copy in the Folger Shakespeare Library, and all my references are

to this edition, hereafter cited as Calvin, *Actes*.

3. I would not, however, argue that Calvin's precise definition of his doctrine of predestination was quite as rigid at this stage in his career as it was among his most devoted followers. In fact a comparison between his largely favorable reaction to Trent's condemnation in canon 23 attached to the decree of justification, of an extreme doctrine of the perseverance of the saints (Calvin, *Actes*, pp. 278-280), and the affirmation of such a view of perseverance by the Synod of Dort, head 5, article 6, leads me to suspect that Calvin himself might not have been able to subscribe completely to this most quintessentially Calvinist definition of predestination.

4. Calvin, *Actes*, pp. 233-234: "Le Prophete ne dit pas seulement que le juste *vit* de foy, mais qu'il *vivra*." Cf. Habakkuk 2:4 "... but the just *shall* live by his faith." (Italics mine.)

5. Luchesius Smits, *Saint Augustin dans l'oeuvre de Jean Calvin* (Assen, Louvain, Paris, 1957-58), II, pp. 88-91, identifies and tabulates these references.

6. See particularly W. Nijenhuis, *Calvinus Oecumenicus* (the Hague, 1959), p. 247 and *passim*. Cf., however, John T. McNeill, "Calvin as an Ecumenical Churchman," *Church History*, XXXII, 4 (Dec. 1963), especially pp. 390-91.

7. Calvin, *Actes*, p. 333.

8. *Ibid.*, pp. 109 ff.

9. The fullest biography of Dumoulin is Julien Brodeau, *La vie de Maistre Charles du Molin*, in Charles Dumoulin, *Omnia quae extant opera* (Paris, 1681, 5 vols.), I, pp. 1-60. For text of synodical condemnations of his *Collatio et unio q u a t u o r Evangelistarum*, see John Quick, *Synodicon in Gallia Reformata* (London, 1692, 2 vols.), I, p. 67. For analysis of this work, see Richard Simon, *Histoire critique des principaux commentateurs du Nouveau Testament* (Rotterdam, 1693), pp. 772-74; cf. p. 745 for comparison to Calvin's harmony.

10. Charles Dumoulin, *Conseil sur le fait du Concile de Trente; Consilium super*

actis Conciliis Tridentini; Pierre Grégoire, *Response au Conseil donné par Charles du Molin sur la dissuasion de la publication du Concile de Trente en France,* republished in Dumoulin, *Opera* (1681 ed.), V, pp. 347-64, 365-93, 395-444. Dumoulin's brief is hereafter cited as Dumoulin, *Conseil*. Harold Bauman of the University of Oregon first called this work to my attention. For authoritative comment on it, see Victor Martin, *Le Gallicanisme et la réforme catholique* (Paris, 1919), pp. 70-73.

11. Dumoulin, *Conseil*, articles 5 and 6, re the Pope's role; 7 and 8, re the role of the German Protestant princes. In arguing that the plaintiffs had not been summoned (article 7), Dumoulin may well have meant that he felt they were not properly summoned. Or perhaps he was simply misinformed.

12. *Ibid.*, article 6.

13. *Ibid.*, article 9.

14. *Ibid.*, article 18.

15. *Ibid.*, articles 26 and ff.

16. *Ibid.*, articles 38 and ff.

17. *Ibid.*, article 64. Cf. articles 58, 59, 92 (French version), references to others of Dumoulin's works.

18. *Ibid.*, article 99.

19. For biographical sketches, see articles in *Nouvelle biographie générale*, XIX, pp. 948-50; Eug. and Em. Haag, *La France protestante*, V, pp. 247-48.

20. *Ibid.* I have used the Folger Shakespeare Library copy of the 1586 French edition; hereafter cited as Gentillet, *Bureau*. For another recent analysis of this work, which concentrates attention on Gentillet's remarks about French participation in Trent, see Philippe de Félice, "A propos d'un Concile: le Bureau du Concile de Trente par Innocent Gentillet," *Bulletin de la Société de l'histoire du protestantisme français*, CVIII (1962), pp. 185-191.

21. Gentillet, *Bureau*, sig. iii verso.

22. *Ibid.*, pp. 279 ff.

23. *Ibid.*, pp. 329 ff. For a discussion of the drafting of these petitions, see V. Martin, *op. cit.*, pp. 219-29.

24. *Ibid.*, p. 10. Gentillet's relative irenicism is also noted by de Félice, *op. cit.*, p. 191.

Reprinted by permission from Church History *33 (1964), 149-156.*

III

Problems of Religious Choice for Sixteenth Century Frenchmen[*]

THE PROBLEM of ideological conflict so intense as to force choice is one of the more agonizing men can face. It is, of course, a perennial problem. In our own day it has torn men's minds and bodies with forced choices between political parties, between economic systems, between national cultures. In the later stages of the European Reformation it was also an acute problem. Only then the ideologies in conflict were religious, the choices forced were between churches. A study of men grappling with these problems of choice might well help us to understand better that troubled era. It might also help us to deal more effectively with the forced choices of our own era.

One set of particularly sharp and well-documented examples of this problem recently came to my attention, in the course of some research in Switzerland on French religious politics during the decade following Calvin's death in 1564. It is upon them that I want to focus attention in this report. These examples are drawn from the career of a prominent sixteenth century French clergyman named Hugues Sureau, dit du Rosier.[1] They centre in two spectacular public conversions by Sureau which occurred within a single year. The first of these conversions took place late in 1572 and was from Calvinist Protestantism to Roman Catholicism. The second of these conversions took place in mid-1573 and was from Roman Catholicism back to Protestantism.

Religious conversion, of course, was not a rare phenomenon in the sixteenth century. Conversions of distinguished religious leaders, of kings and statesmen, of entire populations, created upheavals all over Europe, and made possible the emergence of the Reformed churches which are still such an evident part of the Christian ecclesiastical scene. If Sureau's conversions were different, that difference lies in the extraordinary publicity given to them, and the fact that much of it emanated from Sureau himself. Sureau was not the sort of man who wanted or

* This paper was prepared for reading at the Central Renaissance Conference, University of Missouri, Columbia, Missouri, April 18-20, 1963. Some of the material upon which it is based was collected while I was in Europe as a Fellow of the American Council of Learned Societies.
1. The most complete biographical sketch of Sureau is Beuzart, P., 'H. Sureau du Rosier (1530?-1575?)', *Bulletin, Société de l'histoire du protestantisme français,* LXXXVIII, 1939, pp. 249-68. For further biographical details, a more complete list of his books and references to other more recent work, see Kingdon, Robert M., 'Genève et les réformés français: le cas d'Hugues Sureau, dit du Rosier', *Bulletin. Société d'histoire et d'archéologie de Genève,* XII, 2, 1961, pp. 77-87.

could keep his religious problems to himself or within the private circle of his family or friends. And he had attained such prominence on the French ecclesiastical scene, that he was under considerable pressure to explain in print his changes of heart. Just such pressure, exerted by officials of the royal court and of the church establishment, led him to prepare a 'Confession' of the reasons for his return to Roman Catholicism at the time of the first of these public conversions. It was published, several months later, by a printer to the University of Paris.[2] Less open pressures, some of them stemming from his own conscience, led Sureau to prepare a 'Confession' of the reasons for his return to Protestantism shortly after the second of these conversions. It was published almost immediately, by a printer operating within the French refugee community in Heidelberg.[3] These two little books, consequently, provide us with an unusual look directly into the mind of a man grappling with the problem of ideological choice as it posed itself in the sixteenth century. In seeking to understand Sureau's conversions, we need not be forced to depend, as we must with Luther, on unreliable records of his conversation noted down decades after the spiritual torment which led to his historic break with Rome. Nor need we fall back, as we must with Calvin, upon the even vaguer memories of his associates as they tried, shortly after his death, to recall second-hand stories of the momentous early years in his career. Nor need we depend, as we must with Henry VIII of England, on the somewhat tendentious reports of courtiers, involved in the desperate intrigues enveloping his momentous religious choice. Rather with Sureau we have direct reports, prepared at the actual times of decision, by a man articulate enough to explain in fairly sophisticated fashion the motives which impelled him to these abrupt changes of heart. And we have two of them.

The fact that there are two, however, does not complicate an understanding of Sureau quite as much as one might think. For a reading of them reveals one startling fact: they are surprisingly similar. Though Sureau changed his formal religious affiliations twice within one year, he did not change radically his fundamental religious beliefs. And yet, according to Sureau himself, problems of belief helped drive him to each of these conversions. To explain this paradox, we must take a closer look at the confessions themselves.

The doctrine which provides the key to understanding the first of Sureau's dramatic conversions, the one to Roman Catholicism, is the doctrine of apostolic succession. Sureau had reluctantly come to be

2. *Confession de foy faicte par H. S. du Rosier avec abjuration & detestation de la profession Huguenotique: faicte tant par devant Prelats de l'Eglise Catholique & Romaine, que Princes du sang Royal de France & autres, ensemble la refutation de plusieu[r]s poincts, mis en avant par Calvin & Beze, contre la Foy & Eglise Apostolique* . . . . Paris, Sebastien Nivelle, 1573. The date at the end of this confession, however, is 16 September, 1572. I consulted the copy in the Geneva Bibliothèque publique et universitaire, Bc 3299. Hereafter cited as Sureau, *Catholic.*

3. *Confession et recognoissance de Hugues Sureau dit du Rosier touchant sa cheute en la Papauté, & les horribles scandales par lui commis, servant d'exemple a tout le monde, de la fragilité, & perversité de l'homme abandonné a soi, & de l'infinie misericorde, & ferme verité de Dieu envers ses esleuz,* Heidelberg, Ian Mayer, 1573. I consulted the copy in the Geneva Bibliothèque publique et universitaire, Ba 4363. Hereafter cited as Sureau, *Protestant.*

persuaded of its weight in the course of a full decade as an increasingly prominent Calvinist pastor. His growing prominence within the Calvinist Reformed Church was due partly to an evident polemical skill. Several times he had been chosen to represent the Protestant position in public debate with skilful Catholic theologians, either in print or in direct confrontation, under the auspices of powerful aristocrats anxious to gain expert guidance in their own religious choice. And in this public debate, Sureau apparently had had to grapple, perhaps for the first time in Protestant history, with a powerful new form of argument. This was a form of argument drawn from classical Scepticism, particularly from the thought of Sextus Empiricus. Its discovery and use by Catholic polemicists is but another of the battery of discoveries from the classics which are very nearly the essence of the Renaissance. One of these polemicists, a man named Gentian Hervet, was among the first to discover Sextus, and to recognize the utility of his arguments in fighting any system of thought as highly rational as Calvinist theology.[4] Hervet even translated the corpus of Sextus' writings into Latin, thus making his thought generally available to educated men. And Hervet was Sureau's main opponent in some of the public debate between confessions to which I have referred.[5] At this period, the Catholic polemicists in France had not as yet perfected their use of Scepticism as a tool to undermine Protestant rationalism. Indeed, it was only toward the end of this decade, in 1569, that Hervet published his translation of Sextus Empiricus. But these polemicists had developed arguments powerful enough to disturb Sureau. And one in particular struck home. Sureau began to have increasing doubts about the authority with which Calvinist ministers laid claim to be the true leaders of the entire Christian community. He was well aware that Farel, founder of the Reformed Church in Geneva, then serving as a model and mother to the entire developing Calvinist movement, had simply seized ecclesiastical power in that city, without any pretence of being invested with it by his predecessor, the Bishop of Geneva.[6] And he could not find in Calvinist theory, any more than in Calvinist history, a claim of authority as strong as that resting on the 'power of the keys' which the Roman Church claims to inherit by a direct line of personal succession from the Apostle Peter down to the reigning Roman pontiff. This point of Protestant weakness and Catholic strength had been vigorously forced upon Sureau's attention by his opponents in this public debate. And it had finally won him over. Doubts of his own authority and of that of his fellow clergymen in the Reformed churches, had led him to consider abandoning his clerical

4. Popkin, Richard H., *The History of Scepticism from Erasmus to Descartes*, Assen, 1960, pp. 35-6, and *passim*.

5. Kingdon, op. cit., p. 80 and n. 2, re Sureau's printed response to Hervet. Hervet's attacks on Sureau are listed in such standard references as the *Catalogue général des livres imprimés de la Bibliothèque Nationale*. N.B. his *L'Anti-Hugues . . .*, Reims, 1567.

6. Sureau, *Catholic*, fol. 29, '. . . Farel, quand il occupa la chaire de Geneve, il n'eut point de predecesseur. Car celuy qui estoit l'Evesque ordinaire fut dechassé'.

vocation and moving from the kingdom,[7] perhaps to some such relatively neutral area as the city of Basel. His actual decision to convert, however, as he himself makes clear, was triggered by a single bloody event—the St. Bartholomew's Massacres. These appalling atrocities not only made Sureau fear, with reason, for his own life. They also made him doubt the favour of Providence. The fact that the Almighty could permit such gory slaughter of so many devout and relatively innocent Protestants made Sureau and others wonder if God was not perhaps a Catholic after all.[8] And so he announced his decision to become a Catholic. He went even further: he accepted a request to join in a governmentally-sponsored campaign to convert other prominent Calvinists back to the Roman faith.

Even when his commitment to Catholicism was strongest, however, Sureau was not a complete Catholic. He could accept the authority of the Roman Church including the Pope. He could abandon the critical yet controversial Calvinist view of predestination. He felt no need for a distinctively Protestant version of justification. But there was one essential element of Catholic theology which he could not accept: the theology of the Mass. The doctrine of transubstantiation as an explanation of the way in which Christ is present in the Mass, the notion that Christ's sacrifice for us is repeated in the Mass, the very details of the way in which the Mass is administered, all upset Sureau.[9] They seemed to him to be in plain conflict with God's evident intent as revealed in His Word, the Holy Scriptures. In his published Catholic confession, Sureau accordingly fell back, after having mentioned some of his reservations about eucharistic theology, to a simple fideistic statement that in such matters one must simply rely upon the Church.[10] This statement is quite out of keeping with the general tone of this confession, which presents highly rational arguments for the Catholic position. It can be matched, in fact, only by a similarly fideistic statement on acceptance of vows, of fasting, and of certain doctrines about the Trinity.[11]

Sureau's reservations on eucharistic theology, furthermore, continued to prey on his mind. Even more important, they influenced his activity. In his Protestant confession, a year later, he reported that he had advised those whom he converted back to Catholicism to attend Mass, but not to believe the priest's explanation of the sacrament. As a replacement, he supplied them with an explanation of the nature of Christ's presence in the Lord's Supper which is unmistakably derived

7. Sureau, *Protestant*, sig. Biii$_v$, 'Et combien que j'eusse mieux aimé eschaper hors du Royaume (comme de fait je m'y preparoy) que d'y arrester plus longuement, . . .'; Sureau, *Catholic*, fol. 26v., 'Ce qui m'a tellement degousté de continuer au ministere auquel j'ay esté employé, que je desiroy trouver couleur d'en desister, & me retirer'.
8. Sureau, *Protestant*, sig. Biii$_v$, 'Mais voyant l'affliction exceder la mesure que j'eusse voulu donner a Dieu, je me prins a douter non de la doctrine en soy, mais de l'Eglise, pour le regard de la succession personnelle'.
9. Sureau, *Catholic*, fols. 26v.-27; Sureau, *Protestant*, sig. Av$_v$, 'comme principalement de la Messe, oblation & presence du cors de Christ'.
10. Sureau, *Catholic*, fols. 36-36v., 'Quant à la conversion de la substance des choses materielles au corps & sang de Jesus Christ, quittons nos subtilitez, demandes, repliques & objections: submettons nous au sens qui est enseigné en la saincte Eglise'.
11. Ibid., fol. 36v.

from orthodox Calvinism.[12] Even this evasion could not satisfy Sureau's own conscience, however. As his discontent increased, he began to lay plans to escape from France, during a tour by a conversion team to which he had been assigned, a tour which was to pass through the eastern French provinces bordering on Germany. The star of this particular conversion team was a renowned Spanish Jesuit orator and scholar, Juan Maldonado. And Maldonado supplied the incident which finally hardened Sureau's decision to abandon Catholicism. He preached a sermon on the Mass, developing an argument which seemed to Sureau so wildly at variance with Scripture[13] that he could not remain a good Catholic. And so he fled to Protestant Germany. He was never again to become a clergyman, however. He lived out the rest of a rather short and precarious life as an obscure assistant to several printers of religious and classical texts.[14]

Doubts about apostolic succession and eucharistic theology were thus the reasons which Sureau announced to the public as causing his dramatic conversions. There were, of course, others. Some of them he even acknowledged. His conversion to Catholicism had been induced partly by a well-founded fear for his life. He had, indeed, actually been in prison at the time of this decision. Another possible reason, which he does not acknowledge, can probably be found in an earlier quarrel within the Calvinist Church.[15] This quarrel was over the problem of whether Reformed church government should include powerful synods to maintain regional unity and powerful consistories to maintain local discipline. Sureau had become a leader of the anti-synodical party. His party had been crushed with vigour by Theodore Beza and others who dominated the Reformed movement in the years following Calvin's death. And this harsh treatment may well have left Sureau bitter. Yet more complex explanations of Sureau's behaviour are also possible. Students who try to apply psychoanalysis to the history of religious experience could no doubt supply several.

But it nonetheless remains instructive to consider the announced public reasons for Sureau's conversions. They reveal much of his mind and of the public to which he was appealing. They also reveal much of the context within which both operated. Among other things, they make it clear that it was impossible for any thinking man in sixteenth century France to profess belief in two doctrines which do not seem to an out-

---

12. Sureau, *Protestant*, sigs. [Avii-Avii$_v$], 'puis que c'est là [la Messe] un tel quel reste & trace du vray Sacrement de ce precieux cors: & qu'en regardant le sacrement, (encor qu'il soit grandement different & esloigné de l'institution de Jesus Christ, & de l'administration de l'Eglise ancienne) il suffit que nous levions le cueur au ciel, auquel lieu est seulement ce vray cors vivant, auquel nostre Seigneur regne & se sied a la dextre de Dieu son Pere'.

13. Ibid., sig. B$_v$, 'd'autant que j'apperceu clairement de quelle violence & audace ils falsifient l'Escriture sainte'.

14. See Kingdon, op. cit., p. 79, about material for study of this phase of his career.

15. Ibid., pp. 84-5, for a sketch of this aspect of Sureau's career. I am preparing an extended study of this ecclesiastical quarrel. For a note on one aspect of it, see Kingdon, Robert M., 'Calvinism and Democracy: some political implications of debates on French Reformed Church government, 1562-1572', *American Historical Review*, LXIX, 1964, pp. 393-401.

sider to be necessarily contradictory in themselves: the doctrine of apostolic succession as a rule of authority for the Church, and the doctrine of Christ's real but spiritual communion with the believer during the celebration of the Lord's Supper. There were, of course, nations of Europe in which this particular combination of doctrines could be embraced. England was one. In England, however, there were other combinations of Christian doctrines which were simply not permitted. And so the problem which Sureau faced was well-nigh universal in his day. In sixteenth century Europe, a man had to make religious choices. By the mid-sixteenth century, furthermore, his choice had to be between relatively hard bodies of dogma. He could not formulate a personal set of beliefs which seemed to him plausible or useful. He had no choice but to follow the dictates of one dogmatic church or another. This was the situation which created the agonies which wrecked Sureau's career, and which tormented thousands if not millions of others in a great diversity of ways.

Only a few, of course, reacted to these ideological tensions with the explosiveness of Sureau. But reactions of one sort or another were exceedingly common. A great many people were not able to accept dogmatic dictation of belief with the docility which was expected of them and which many superficial students of the period assume they displayed. Two further reactions are suggested by certain peripheral aspects of Sureau's career. Both became widespread and important in France, particularly in the decades following his spectacular conversions. Something should be said about them to round out our analysis.

These two reactions were those of Nicodemitism and Scepticism. My labels for them, incidentally, were used extensively within the period itself. And both, of course, are classical allusions.

The Nicodemite label derives from the New Testament Pharisee Nicodemus, who accepted Jesus' claim to speak for God but who would meet with Jesus only in secret, at night.[16] It became a label widely used within the sixteenth century for those who accepted one form of Christianity privately, while practising publicly, for a variety of expediential reasons, whatever other form was established in their communities. This dodge, certainly understandable in times of savage persecution, roused the indignation of the more resolute religious leaders of every persuasion. Calvin flayed its appearance among Protestants in France. Jesuits blasted its appearance among Catholics in England. And one could point to many other examples of attacks upon it. Sureau himself used the 'Nicodemite' label, in his 1573 Protestant confession, for those who had followed his advice to return to Roman Catholicism, but with reservations.[17] The Nicodemite expedient, involving, as it must, an element of hypocrisy, was one which Sureau himself could not long stomach. But there were clearly many who did, whether upon his advice, upon the advice of others, or upon their own initiative. Among the more prominent within France during the period immediately fol-

16. John iii. 1-2.
17. Sureau, *Protestant*, sig. [Avii], '. . . faux Nicodemites, & temporizeurs, . . .'

lowing Sureau's career, may well have been the great jurisconsult and political theorist, Jean Bodin. His manuscript comparison of various religious beliefs, circulated widely shortly after his death, makes it quite clear that by the end of his life he was neither the devout Catholic he had so often claimed to be, nor the Protestant he had at times appeared to be. His personal beliefs were apparently rather a curious amalgam of exotic Oriental ideas and purely rational constructs, which would have horrified most pious Christians if they had been made public during his lifetime.[18]

Not all Nicodemites were quite as secretive and as individual in their beliefs as Bodin, however. In fact, organized groups of them can be identified. One which has recently attracted my attention flourished within France's northern neighbour, the Netherlands. It called itself the 'House of Love'. It was not the original mystical sect of that name, however, founded by Hendrik Niclaes, which had certain rather interesting influences upon Elizabethan England. It was rather an offshoot of that group, directed by a man named Barrefelt.[19] This 'House of Love' included many ostensible Catholics. Among them were the great printer Christopher Plantin and many of his friends, perhaps even Benedictus Arias Montanus, the scholarly sometime chaplain to His Most Catholic Majesty, Philip II of Spain.[20] Among them were also certain ostensible Calvinists, resident in the parts of the Netherlands controlled by the troops of William of Orange. And among them also were certain ex-Jews, whose public conversions to Christianity had long been suspect to the Spanish, apparently with good reason. That such a group could persist in the very part of Europe where Catholic military might was strongest and most intolerant, is interesting testimony to the basic appeal of the Nicodemite attitude.

The Sceptic label, to turn now to the other form of reaction secondarily suggested by Sureau's career, was applied to those who used the corrosive arguments which had received that name in antiquity, in refutation of any body of thought which was essentially rational. We have already observed that such arguments were utilized by some of Sureau's early polemical opponents. But Scepticism is a many-edged weapon. It can be used not only against Calvinist theology, but also against any body of formal thought. And as my former colleague

---

18. See Baudrillart, Henri, *J. Bodin et son temps*, Paris, 1853, Part 2, ch. V, for an extended analysis of this problem. Modern Bodin specialists such as Pierre Mesnard have also commented on it.

19. For a useful survey of recent work on these groups, including some important new information, see Kirsop, Wallace, 'The Family of Love in France', *The Journal of Religious History*, III, 1964, pp. 103-18. He suggests, pp. 113-4, the possibility that Bodin was associated with them. For a sketch of Barrefelt, also called Hiel, see de la Fontaine Verwey, H., 'Trois hérésiarques dans les Pays-bas du XVIe siècle', *Bibliothèque d'Humanisme et Renaissance*, XVI, 1954, pp. 312-30.

20. On Plantin, see Voet, L., 'The Personality of Plantin', *Gedenkboek der Plantin-Dagen, 1555-1955*, Antwerp, 1956, especially pp. 200-5. On Montanus, see Maurits Sabbe, 'Hoe stond Benedictus Arias Montanus tegenover de Leeringen von Hendrik Jansen Barrefelt (Hiël)?', *De Moretussen en hun kring*, Antwerp, 1928, pp. 27-51; also Kirsop, article cited in n. 19, p. 106, and works there cited. Cf. Kingdon, Robert M., 'Christopher Plantin and his Backers, 1575-1590: a study in the problems of financing business during war', *Mélanges d'histoire économique et sociale en hommage au professeur Antony Babel*, Geneva, 1963, I, pp. 303-16.

Richard Popkin has demonstrated, although it was in fact first used by Catholic polemicists against Calvinist rationalism, it was also exploited by Calvinist polemicists to undermine the more rational brands of Catholic theology.[21] A few adventurous souls even discovered that it could be used against all theology. Pre-eminent among these may well have been the greatest of all sixteenth century Sceptics, Michel de Montaigne. This is a proposition not easy to demonstrate, however. Montaigne's personal religious convictions are very difficult to pin down with certainty, as a number of able scholars who have tried can testify.[22] But surely Montaigne was sceptical of most religious commitments. His comments about the rather simple and uncomprehending acceptance of religious dogmas which he saw in most of his compatriots are by turns ironic and pitying, but they are practically never sympathetic.

Not many Frenchmen were Sceptics in as technical a sense as Montaigne. But the sceptical attitude was clearly pervasive in France by the end of the sixteenth century. Indeed one could argue that it was dominant among the political leaders of French society, among the men who paved the way for the accession of King Henri IV, and who made up much of his entourage once his rule was secure.

These, then, were the intellectual consequences of intense ideological conflict during the sixteenth century in France: forced conversions, Nicodemitism, Scepticism. All of them have a sordid side. Two of them force conscience. All of them undermine the common core of belief to which religious leaders of every persuasion were then committed. From the point of view of these religious leaders, so passionately certain of their basic theological insight and so determined to win its general acceptance in society, these new alternatives were more disastrous than the dogmatic ones against which they directed their fire. But this is what happens when ideology becomes fanatic. One simply cannot impose a rigid body of dogma upon all the complex elements of most civilized societies. There are times when human thought cannot be dragooned. The attempt to do so can not only plunge a society into bloody confusion. It can also provoke reactions which few expect or want.

21. Popkin, op. cit., passim; Popkin, Richard H., 'Pierre Bayle's Place in 17th Century Scepticism', in Dibon, Paul (Ed.), Pierre Bayle, le philosophe de Rotterdam, Amsterdam, et al., 1959, pp. 1-19. See also Rex, Walter, Essays on Pierre Bayle and Religious Controversy, The Hague, 1965.
22. Inter alia, Raymond, Marcel, 'L'attitude religieuse de Montaigne', Génies de France, Les Cahiers du Rhône, no. 4, May, 1942, pp. 50-67; Popkin, The History of Scepticism, pp. 55-6, and others there cited; Peyre, Henri, in 'Religion and Literary Scholarship in France', Publications, Modern Language Association of America, LXXVII, 1962, pp. 349-50; Frame, Donald M., Montaigne, a Biography, New York, 1965, pp. 175-80, and passim.

IV

PETER MARTYR VERMIGLI AND THE MARKS OF THE TRUE CHURCH

One of George Huntston Williams' most important contributions to scholarship has surely been in the history of ecclesiology. The distinction, which he first drew more than twenty years ago in his monumental studies of the Radical Reformation, between a "Magisterial Reformation" of Lutherans, Zwinglians, Calvinists, and Anglicans on one hand, and a "Radical Reformation" of Anabaptists, Spiritualists, and Evangelical Rationalists on the other, has influenced an entire generation of specialists on the period. [1] It has made us all more aware of the importance of doctrines of church government in distinguishing among various groups of Christians. In Williams' own work, of course, ecclesiology has been used primarily to distinguish from each other the "Magisterials" with their attempts to co-operate closely with secular governments in the reform of the Church and the "Radicals" with their attempts to purify the Church by avoiding all collaboration with secular institutions. It has also been used, secondarily, to assist in the delicate job of distinguishing from each other the many often ephemeral and protean groups of "Radicals." Ecclesiology can also be used, however, to distinguish with greater precision among various groups of "Magisterials." That is the enterprise to which this article hopes to contribute. It will focus on one ecclesiological doctrine, that of the marks of the true Church of Christ.

When the Reformation of the sixteenth century began, Luther and his associates hoped to reform the entire Church, beginning with those parts of it in western Europe controlled by the Roman Catholic hierarchy. They obviously failed in that objective. Rome did not wish to be reformed along the lines suggested by Luther and resisted both

---

[1] George Huntston Williams, Introduction to Part I of *Spiritual and Anabaptist Writers: Documents Illustrative of the Radical Reformation ...*, vol. XXV in *The Library of Christian Classics* (Philadelphia, 1957), 19-38; "Studies in the Radical Reformation: a bibliographical survey," *Church History* 27 (1958), 46 ff.; Introduction to *The Radical Reformation* (Philadelphia, 1962), xxiii-xxxi.

strenuously and successfully all attempts to make it do so. What the early Reformers did do in the end was to stimulate the creation of a number of separate alternative churches in parts of western and northern Europe, each claiming to be the true Church of Christ. These, of course, were the ancestors of many of our modern Protestant denominations. The creation of these new churches led to vigorous competition between them and the Roman Catholic Church and sometimes among themselves as well. On the intellectual level the competition took the form of rival theologies, one important ingredient of which was generally an ecclesiology. And within these ecclesiologies one component was often a doctrine of the notes, or signs, or marks by which the true Church could be distinguished from its false competitors. Polemical exchanges on the marks of the true Church became particularly common and heated late in the sixteenth century and they continued well into the early seventeenth century. They remain useful in helping us understand how ecclesiastical spokesmen of the period wished to distinguish themselves from each other.

Roman Catholic apologists could assemble a considerable variety of marks of the true Church to justify their position. They could point to the numerical superiority of their constituency and the material wealth of their corporations as signs that God in His Providence had selected their institution as His own. More often they pointed to the unbroken history of their Church, stretching back to the time of Christ and His Apostles, sealed by the apostolic succession of its leaders and elaborated by the canonical ordination of its clergy.

"Magisterial" Protestants retorted by insisting that there were two and only two marks of the true Church: (1) the teaching of pure doctrine; (2) the correct administration of the sacraments. This was the general position of most Lutherans. It found particularly authoritative expression in article seven of the Augsburg Confession of 1530, which defines the Church as the congregation of the faithful in which the Gospel is purely preached and the sacraments rightly administered. [2] This position, furthermore, was endorsed by John Calvin. In every edition of his monumental *Institutes of the Christian Religion* from 1541 on, he defined the visible Church as a body in which the Word of God is purely preached and heard and in which the sacraments are

---

[2] For a fine critical edition of both German and Latin texts, which differ somewhat, see *Die Bekenntnisschriften der evangelisch-lutherischen Kirche,* 5th ed. (Göttingen, 1963), 61.

administered according to Christ's instructions. [3] This doctrine of the marks of the true Church is of obvious utility in developing a reply to the Roman Catholic position. It denies the importance of numbers, wealth, and tradition and substitutes the claims of ideology and its symbols. Since the doctrine is supported by such influential authorities within both the Evangelical Lutheran and Reformed Calvinist camps, one might suppose that it was one on which all Protestants could agree.

In fact, however, this two-mark doctrine did not fully satisfy many Protestants, including not only a good many Radicals, but also an increasing number of spokesmen for the Reformed Churches, which are commonly believed to have been founded by Zwingli and Calvin. These Protestants may have been disturbed by an antinomian tendency in much of the early theology of their movement, an emphasis on the doctrine of justification by faith alone so extreme that it left little room for the encouragement of ethical behavior which is commonly another important part of Christian teaching. Or they may have been disturbed by a lack of practicality associated with this doctrine, by its failure to provide any guidance for the institutional shape the true Church should take. The task of building new ecclesiastical institutions became increasingly important to later Reformers, as it became more and more obvious that nothing would come of early hopes for reform of the entire Church and that their movement would either have to create durable institutions to preserve itself or face the likelihood of collapse.

For whatever reason, a number of early "Magisterial" theologians developed an alternative doctrine of the marks of the true Church. They argued that there were in fact three fundamental marks. To the two classical marks suggested by the Lutheran confessions and Calvin they added the third mark of discipline. One of the earliest statements of this three-mark doctrine can be found in the writings of Martin Bucer, that seminal thinker who had such a pervasive influence on every branch of the Reformation. In his *Scripta duo adversaria D. Bartholomaei Latomi* . . ., a polemic directed against a Catholic theologian of Cologne and published in 1544, Bucer lists the Word, sacraments, and discipline of Christ as marks of the true Church. [4] The

---

[3] IV:1:9. See particularly in the critical variorum edition of Jean-Daniel Benoit (Paris, 1957-1963), IV, 20.

[4] Quoted in Tadataka Maruyama, "The Reform of the True Church: the Ecclesiology of Theodore Beza," Unpublished Th.D. dissertation, Princeton Theological Seminary, 1973, p. 38, n. 15. This splendid contribution to our knowledge of Reformed ecclesiology is to be published in 1978 by the Librairie Droz of Geneva. Hereafter cited as Maruyama.

same triad recurs in other works of his. This three-mark doctrine was later endorsed by such other Reformed theologians as John Knox, Pierre Viret, and Theodore Beza, although not always with consistency. It was also given more formal suport by inclusion in several Reformed confessions of faith, including the Scots Confession, and Belgic Confession, and the Hungarian Confession. [5] One expression of this point of view which was particularly sharp, clear, and influential was that of Peter Martyr Vermigli. It is upon his version of this doctrine that this paper concentrates.

There is a growing recognition among scholars of the value of the writings of Vermigli for a full understanding of early Reformed theology. These writings are comprehensive, covering almost all the topics . at issue during the period. They are organized and expressed with admirable clarity, avoiding much of the tendency to rhetorical flourish and tangential argument which characterizes the writing of other Reformers. And they are documented with impressive erudition. These qualities can be explained in part by the unusual strength of Vermigli's training and the unusual variety of positions he filled as a teacher and consultant. A quick sketch of his career should thus help us to understand his thought.

As a boy, Vermigli had entered the Lateran congregation of the Canons Regular of St. Augustine in his native Italy and had been sent to the order's study house at the University of Padua for training in theology and philosophy. He had become particularly interested in the neo-Aristotelian thought for which Padua was then distinguished and had mastered it to a degree rare among early Protestants. Unlike other Reformers, he saw this body of thought as of continuing value after his conversion to Protestantism and used it frequently, explicitly, and expertly in the elaboration of his own theological position. Unlike some Aristotelians of the period, moreover, Vermigli also shared the humanists' interest in the languages of antiquity. He learned Greek while in Padua and Hebrew while in Bologna where he was sent after completion of his formal education. Vermigli first became acquainted with Protestant thought in Naples where he settled next. There he became involved in a group of local Evangelicals and read certain of the books of Bucer and Zwingli. His final assignment from the order took him to Lucca, where through public teaching he stimu-

---

[5] *Ibid.,* 369. Beza's own shifting view is, of course, discussed at some length and summarized on pp. 365-70.

lated a serious attempt at reformation of the city. When this came to the attention of authorities in Rome, it helped provoke the repressive measures which signaled the beginning of the Counter Reformation in Italy. Vermigli fled to the Protestant north in 1542 and spent the rest of his life in exile. Bucer helped him obtain his first position in the north, as a teacher in the Strasbourg Academy. He stayed there until 1547. Thomas Cranmer then persuaded both Bucer and Vermigli to come to England, where Vermigli was assigned to teach at Oxford until 1553, when the accession of Mary forced him to resign and leave the country. He returned to Strasbourg, where he taught until 1556. The growth of orthodox Lutheranism in that city made him increasingly uncomfortable, however, so he moved to Zurich where he again served as a teacher until his death in 1562. [6]

Vermigli's early reading in Protestant theology and the acquaintances he made during his career as a Protestant teacher inclined him to align himself primarily with the theological positions of Bucer and Zwingli. After he settled in the north, he became increasingly interested in the theology of Calvin, entered into a cordial correspondence with him, and found himself in substantial agreement with the Reformer of Geneva on many doctrines in controversy. He also became well acquainted personally with the younger generation of leading theologians in this camp, notably Beza and Henry Bullinger.

Vermigli's teaching at Protestant schools consisted of lectures on books of the Bible. At Strasbourg and Zurich he lectured on books of the Old Testament, at Oxford he lectured on the New Testament.

---

[6] The primary source for biographical information on Vermigli is a funeral oration by Josiah Simler, prepared in consultation with Vermigli's student and secretary, Giulio Santerenziano, and published in a number of editions of Vermigli's Genesis commentary and his *Common Places*. See Philip McNair, *Peter Martyr in Italy: an anatomy of apostasy* (Oxford, 1967), xiv-xv. I have used the version in the 1583 English translation of the *Common Places*. For further and more recent accounts of Vermigli's career, see McNair, which is particularly reliable and detailed but covers only the period to 1542; Joseph C. McLelland, *The Visible Words of God: an exposition of the sacramental theology of Peter Martyr Vermigli, A.D. 1500-1562* (Grand Rapids, 1957), 1-68; Marvin Walter Anderson, *Peter Martyr, a Reformer in Exile (1542-1562): a chronology of biblical writings in England & Europe* (Nieuwkoop, 1975), I, 35-266. See also three expert recent studies of aspects of Vermigli's thought: Klaus Sturm, *Die Theologie Peter Martyr Vermiglis während seines ersten Aufenthalts in Strassburg, 1542-1547* (Neukirchen-Vluyn, 1971); John Patrick Donnelly, *Calvinism and Scholasticism in Vermigli's Doctrine of Man and Grace* (Leiden, 1976); Salvatore Corda, *Veritas Sacramenti: a study in Vermigli's doctrine of the Lord's Supper* (Zurich, 1975). Hereafter cited by author's last name.

He would pick one book for a term, and lecture on it in the usual Protestant way, going from verse to verse in *lectio continuo*. Over the years these lectures were published as Biblical commentaries. In their published form they include many set treatises of a rather formal sort on various topics not always closely related to the Biblical verses they are supposed to explain. These short treatises scattered throughout the commentaries are known as the *loci* or *common places* of Vermigli. Each *locus* can be identified by the Biblical verse or pericope to which it is attached.

During his own lifetime, Vermigli arranged for the publication of several of these Biblical commentaries and some polemical works. Many of his writings remained in manuscript at the time of his death, however, and it was left to his friends and students to arrange for their publication. Many of the printed works of Vermigli, as a consequence, are as much a product of the general Reformed community of scholars as of Vermigli himself. This is particularly true of the most influential of them, the *Loci Communes* or *Common Places*. Shortly after Vermigli's death, Beza asked Bullinger's opinion of a project to abstract the *loci* from Vermigli's Biblical commentaries, arrange them in a systematic form, and publish the collection. [7] It took some time for this project to materialize, but the collected *Loci Communes* of Peter Martyr were finally printed in 1576, in London. In the next eighty years this collection went through some thirteen further editions, some of them considerably expanded with the addition of polemical treatises, correspondence, and biographical material. They appeared in such important Reformed publishing centers as Basel, Zurich, Geneva, and Heidelberg, in addition to London. [8] These *Common Places* were arranged in the same general order as the topics in Calvin's *Institutes of the Christian Religion*. They were consciously designed to complement, expand, and document that theological classic. This collection became a standard textbook for the education of Reformed clergy-

---

[7] Beza to Bullinger, 1 July [1563], in Henri Meylan, Alain Dufour, and Arnaud Tripet, eds., *Correspondance de Théodore de Bèze,* IV (Geneva, 1965), 161-65.

[8] Professor Donnelly and I are gathering material for a full descriptive bibliography of Vermigli's writings. One or the other of us has examined copies of the following editions of his *Loci Communes*. All but one are in Latin. (1) London, 1576; (2) Zurich, 1580; (3) Basel, 1580-1582; (4) London, 1583; (5) London, 1583—in English; (6) Zurich, 1587; (7) Heidelberg, 1603; (8) Heidelberg, 1613; (9) Heidelberg, 1622; (10) Geneva, 1623; (11) Geneva, 1624; (12) Geneva, 1626; (13) Geneva, 1627; (14) Amsterdam and Frankfurt, 1656.

IV

men in the late sixteenth and early seventeenth centuries. It had a pervasive influence on several generations of the leaders of the Reformed movement.

Both the *Common Places* and the *Institutes* devote a fourth and last book to the two human institutions through which God leads men to Christ and His service—the Church and the state. The proportions of the books are somewhat different. Only one chapter in twenty of the fourth book in the *Institutes* is devoted to analysis of the state while nearly half of the fourth book in the *Common Places* deals with politics. Both books begin with discussions of ecclesiology, however, and develop them in significantly parallel ways. Vermigli's *loci* on ecclesiology fill the first twelve chapters of the *Common Places*. The most important of them are drawn from his commentary on First Corinthians, based on a series of lectures at Oxford, 1548-1549. The text of this epistle lends itself to reflection on ecclesiology, dealing as it does with the organizational problems of one of the earliest Christian churches. Vermigli's position in England also encouraged him to reflect on problems of church organization. Archbishop Cranmer frequently consulted his two distinguished guests from the continent, Bucer and Vermigli, for advice on how to go about the extensive reforms in the Church of England to which he was committed after the accession of Edward VI. Cranmer seems to have turned to Vermigli particularly for advice on institutional reform. Vermigli became a member of a committee charged with drafting an entire Reformed code of ecclesiastical laws for England. A surviving manuscript copy of this code contains corrections and annotations in the hands of both Cranmer and Vermigli, suggesting their contributions to the final draft were considerable. The code was never promulgated, to be sure. It was a victim of the abrupt end of the Edwardian reform program caused by the untimely death of the king. Attempts to revive it during the Elizabethan period failed. Even though it never became law, however, it provides striking proof of Vermigli's interest in institutional reform. [9]

Loci drawn from other commentaries are used to fill in the presentation of Vermigli's doctrine of ecclesiology in the *Common Places*. Most of them come from lectures he delivered later in life. They tend, however, simply to confirm and refine the views expressed in the commentary on First Corinthians. The most interesting of them is the

---

[9] James C. Spalding, "The *Reformatio Legum Ecclesiasticarum* of 1552 and the Furthering of Discipline in England," *Church History* 39 (1970), 162-71, especially p. 167 on the surviving manuscript. Hereafter cited as Spalding.

locus De Schismate on I Kings 12, from a lecture delivered in Zurich. His teaching there was interrupted during 1561 for an extended trip to France, where Vermigli joined Beza in the delegation of Protestants summoned by the royal court to a debate with Catholic bishops and theologians at the colloquy of Poissy. Vermigli was used in this debate primarily to argue the Protestant eucharistic position, a doctrine upon which he had become a respected authority as a result of debates in England. But ecclesiology was another important issue at Poissy and led to sharp exchanges between Beza and the moderate Catholic spokesman Claude d'Espence. [10] Perhaps the Poissy debate can be linked to Vermigli's commentaries on I Kings.

Vermigli's doctrine of the marks of the true Church is expressed most concisely in two of these *loci*. One is the *locus De Ecclesia* on I Corinthians 1, with which chapter 1 of book four of the *Common Places* begins. The other is the *locus De Schismate* on I Kings 12, which occupies all of chapter 6 of this book. In the first of these *loci*, Vermigli begins with a definition of the Church which contains the marks: "it [the Church] is a company of believers, and regenerate persons, whom God gathereth together in Christ, by the word and the holy Ghost, and by his Ministers governeth the same with pureness of doctrine, with lawful use of the sacraments, and with discipline." He then goes on to explain with more precision the value and nature of these marks: "But and if thou wilt conclude hereby that the Church shall be unknown, we will deny it to be a firm conclusion; because there be proper marks assigned, by which the same may be very well known, and be discerned from profane conventicles. For wheresoever the pureness of doctrine flourisheth, the sacraments are purely ministered, and discipline exercised, thou hast a congregation whereunto thou mayest safely join thyself." [11] At the end of this *locus* in the English translation, there is a cross-reference to other passages dealing with the marks of the true Church. The most developed of them is in *De Schismate* and reads: "the three marks of the Church which are wont to be shewed by men of our side: namely doctrine, the right administration of the sacraments, and the care of discipline (which these men

---

[10] Maruyama, chapter 3, pp. 63-97.
[11] My quotations are taken out of the 1583 English translation of the *Common Places*, hereafter cited as *C.P.*, compared with the 1583 Latin edition of the *Loci Communes*, hereafter cited as *L.C.*, both published in London, STC nos. 24669 and 24668. I have modernized spelling, capitalization, and punctuation, but have made no other changes. For these particular quotations, see *C.P.*, IV:1:1.

[Catholic opponents] cry out to be feigned by us and cannot be confirmed by the word of God) are very manifestly found in the Epistle to the Ephesians [5:25—which he then glosses]." He continues, in explicit retort to Cardinal Hosius who rejected Protestant arguments on the marks of the true Church, "he seeth that among us the pure word of God is exercised, the sacraments according to the institution of Christ administered, and discipline not altogether neglected," and for that reason Hosius must develop a more complex doctrine of marks to defend the Catholic position. [12]

The entire section on ecclesiology in Vermigli's *Common Places* can be analyzed as being built around the three marks he specifies at the beginning. This principle of organization is not explicit, and the obvious model remains Calvin's *Institutes*. But the three marks provide a useful pattern for analysis of the way in which this block of twelve chapters is assembled. The remainder of chapter 1 consists of a variety of *loci* on the preaching ministry and may be regarded as elaborating on the first mark. So may the next three chapters which are also on the ministry and are rather short, including *loci* on the use of property for the support of ministers, on the authority of ministers in relation to the spiritual leadership of the Church, and on the laws governing ministers. Chapter 5 includes a consideration of discipline and church polity and chapter 6 discusses schism. They may be regarded as elaborating on the third mark. Chapter 7 begins a consideration of the sacraments with discussion of Old Testament circumcision which Vermigli, in company with most "Magisterial" Protestants, sees as a forerunner of baptism, followed by chapters on baptism and communion, the two rites he accepts as sacraments. These chapters may be regarded as elaborating on the second mark.

Of these three subjects, Vermigli's doctrine of the sacraments has attracted the most attention from scholars. His eucharistic theology, in particular, has been subjected to considerable scrutiny and is the subject of two important recent books. [13] This is certainly understandable. Vermigli's treatises on the eucharist are particularly subtle and lengthy, lending themselves to careful analysis. And they were also of considerable influence, for Vermigli was regarded by contemporaries among the Reformed as a leading authority on the subject. He upheld the Reformed position on the eucharist in spirited formal debates with

---

[12] *C.P.*, IV :6 :16, 17.
[13] McLelland; Corda.

Catholic theologians at both Oxford and Poissy. And he elaborated and defended this position against certain Lutherans in polemics published after he settled in Zurich. In this study, however, I would rather concentrate on Vermigli's *loci* on discipline. This is the part of his argument which is most novel, it seems to me, flowing as it does from his emphasis on discipline as a third mark of the true Church. It sets him apart in a significant way from Luther and Calvin and makes of him a considerable influence in his own right, given the wide acceptance of this position among the Reformed by the seventeenth century.

The most important statement of Vermigli's position on discipline is to be found in his *loci* on I Corinthians 10:9 and on I Corinthians 5, published as the first eighteen sections of chapter 5 in book four of the *Common Places*. The title of this chapter, *De disciplina & politia Ecclesiae,* is in itself significant, since it makes clear the fact that for Vermigli discipline requires a consideration of church polity. The link is made explicit in his text. The chapter begins with a general discussion of ecclesiastical discipline, moves on to an extended consideration of excommunication as a particularly valuable tool of discipline, then turns to church polity, since "that we may rightly understand who ought to be excommunicate, it is needful to discuss in what sort the society of the Church is." [14] This linkage is important. In much of the Reformed writing on the subject during this period the terms "discipline" and "polity" are used almost interchangeably. This can be confusing to readers accustomed to modern usage. It is important to emphasize the fact that for most of the Reformed the attempt to establish standards of appropriate ethical behavior within the Christian community required the creation of a structure including institutions charged with enforcing those standards.

This chapter begins, as do most of Vermigli's really important *loci,* with a general definition: "Ecclesiastical discipline is nothing else but a power granted to the Church by God, by which the wills and actions of the faithful, are made conformable to the law of God: which is done by doctrine, admonitions, correction, and finally by punishments, and also by excommunication if need require." It then employs, and this again is characteristic, Aristotle's four-fold schema of causes as a method for elaborating the definition. It seeks to discern, in other words, the material, efficient, formal, and final causes of ecclesiastical

---

[14] *C.P.,* IV:5:9.

discipline. In Vermigli's own words: "the efficient cause is charity, for that it is no just correction, if it proceed of hatred, wrath, or injury. But the matter wherein it is occupied, be sins, and those grievous sins, seeing lighter faults pertain not to this kind of correction. The form is the manner prescribed by God. The end is, that evil may be taken away from among the faithful." [15]

Of the possible methods of discipline, excommunication clearly concerned Vermigli most. More than half of the chapter on discipline, sections 2-18, is devoted to his *locus De Excommunicatione* on I Corinthians 5. This *locus* begins again with a definition, this time starting with etymologies of the term excommunication, weighing the meaning of both Greek and Hebrew equivalents. It then announces an outline for the rest of the *locus,* promising to consider in turn how necessary excommunication is, what lesser steps should be taken before proceeding to this extreme measure, who should be excommunicated, and how this disciplinary tool should be used. [16] Vermigli sees excommunication primarily as a tool for enforcing standards of behavior and urges that it be used to punish not only "great crimes" like adultery or drunkenness which are matters of public notoriety, but also lesser sins which come to public knowledge. He would not limit its use solely to preventing misbehavior, however, but would also apply it to misbelief, against "they that be infected with ill doctrine." [17] The actual excommunication itself he sees as technically the work of the sinner, a deliberate alienation on his part from God. But this inner and private excommunication should be brought to the attention of the entire community in a public ecclesiastical rite "which is a token of this inward apostasy (indeed not a certain and necessary token, yet a great one and greatly to be feared)," a rite which should be "inflicted by the Church of Christ." [18]

When Vermigli turns to an explanation of how the Church should administer excommunication, he faces the problem of analyzing the polity of the Church, in order to locate within it appropriate responsibility for this type of discipline. Here he again uses Aristotle to structure his analysis, turning this time to the *Politics.* That Vermigli knew the *Politics* well is made abundantly clear in his political *loci,* most of which come from his commentaries on Judges, and many of which

---

[15] *C.P.,* IV :5 :1.
[16] *C.P.,* IV :5 :2.
[17] *C.P.,* IV :5 :5.
[18] *C.P.,* IV :5 :8.

are assembled in the second half of book four in the *Common Places*.
He found particularly useful Aristotle's analysis of the types of
government into six categories, according to the *locus* of sovereignty
in each: three good types—monarchy, aristocracy, and polity—matched
by three bad types into which they tend to degenerate—tyranny, oligarchy, and democracy. Near the beginning of his most comprehensive
locus on politics, *De Magistratu*, which constitutes chapter 13 of the
Common Places, he makes a statement which is close to a quotation
from Aristotle: "the form of magistrates is not of one sort but manifold: as monarchy (the government of one), aristocracy (the rule of
many good men), and polity (politic government). Or else tyranny
(where one rules for his own commodity), oligarchy (where a few
be in authority), and democracy (when the people bear the sway)."
While he does not refer specifically to the passage in Aristotle's
Politics (III.v.i-iv) which contains this analysis, he does give an
explicit credit to ancient thinkers by following his own analysis with
this comment: "the descriptions and natures of which forms Plato,
Aristotle, and other philosophers have elegantly described." [19] This
six-part analysis of the forms of government recurs again and again in
Vermigli's political *loci*. He did not insist that any single form was the
ideal type of secular government. Any one of the three good forms
would do. There was sound precedent in the Old Testament for each.
He did insist that any one of these good forms was preferable to
any of the three bad forms. And this moral distinction is connected later
to his interesting and influential arguments for political resistance to
established governments.

In analyzing the polity of the Church, Vermigli uses these same
Aristotelian political categories. He does not find in Aristotle a model
for an appropriate form of church government, however, but rather
finds that in another ancient source, the Roman Republic. He argues
that the Church, like the Roman Republic, should be a mixed government, adopting the best features of each of the three good forms
described by the ancient Greeks, in a careful balance. He may have
been following a commentator like Polybius in developing this theory
of mixed government but there are a number of other possible sources. Whatever his source, he finds in the Roman Republic a monarchic
principle in the institution of the dictator, an aristocratic principle

---

[19] *C.P.*, IV:13:2. I am currently preparing an edition of this and certain other
political *loci* of Vermigli.

in the institution of the Senate, and a democratic principle in the practice of referral of laws and decrees to the people for confirmation. [20] His use in this passage of the term "democratic," incidentally, is unusual and interesting. Normally he follows Aristotelian Greek practice in reserving the term "democratic" for the bad form of popular government, rule by the mob, and uses the term "politic" for the good form of popular government. In this *locus* he changes his usage and employs the word "democratic" in a more modern approving sense.

This Roman mixed government, Vermigli feels, is a better model for the government of the Church than any of the simpler forms described by the ancient Greeks. Here is his own full analysis of church polity: "It is not simple, but it is compounded of monarchy, aristocracy, and democracy. From it must be removed pernicious types of government, I mean tyranny, oligarchy, and corrupt domination of the people. If you respect Christ, it is called a monarchy, for He is our king who acquired the Church for himself with his own blood. He is now in heaven, yet rules this kingdom of his, not with a visible presence, but by the spirit and word of holy scriptures. And there are in the Church to execute this office for Him, Bishops, Presbyters, Doctors, and others who rule, in respect of whom it may justly be called an aristocracy. For they who are preferred to the government of churches, because of excellent gifts of God in doctrine and purity of life, must be promoted to these positions . . . . But because in the Church there are matters of very great weight and importance referred to the people (as appears in the Acts of the Apostles), it has an element of polity [here substituted for 'democracy']. But of the most weight are accounted excommunication, absolution, choice of ministers and the like, so it must be concluded that no man can be excommunicated without the consent of the Church." [21]

Observe that Vermigli reserves the right of excommunication to the people as a whole, rather than to more select institutions which represent them. He does not seem to be advocating either excommuni-

---

[20] *L.C.*, IV :5 :9. *C.P.* here supplies explanations of the Latin terms for "aristocratic" and "democratic," rather than using the terms themselves.

[21] *L.C.*, IV :5 :9. I have prepared a fresh translation, because in this instance *C.P.* does not use the significant political terms of *L.C.* For a recent edition of texts of both versions, see Robert M. Kingdon, *Geneva and the Consolidation of the French Protestant Movement, 1564-1572* (Geneva and Madison, 1967), in appendix III, pp. 217-218, hereafter cited as Kingdon.

cation of the Erastian type, limited to secular courts, or of the Calvinist type, limited to ecclesiastical courts on the model of the Genevan Consistory. He rather seems to be advocating congregational excommunication of the sort supported by Jean Morély and other dissidents within the French Reformed Church to the considerable distress of Calvin, Beza, and the other clerical leaders of that Church. [22] There is even some resonance of the Anabaptist approach to excommunication here. And there is more in a later passage in which he discusses appropriate treatment of the excommunicate, urging they be completely shunned, with all good Christians avoiding salutations, conversation, and even eating with them. Unlike the Anabaptists, however, he would make an exception to this general rule of shunning for the children, wives, and legal subjects of an excommunicate, since duty requires them to deal with such a sinner. [23] And elsewhere, to be sure, Vermigli explicitly repudiates many Anabaptist teachings.

This leads us to consideration of the influence of Vermigli's doctrine of the marks of the true Church. That it was considerable is suggested by the publication history of his works. Not only did his *Common Places* go through fourteen editions. Many of the commentaries upon which it is based went through a number of editions. The Commentary on First Corinthians, for example, went through four editions, and the Commentary on Kings through five. Most of these publications were in Latin, the only language that Vermigli normally used himself. They were clearly intended for the educated, not for the general public. A number of his works, however, including the *Common Places,* were translated into English and published in London. English is the only vernacular into which much of his work was translated. This suggests a particularly strong influence in Britain. Most of the Latin editions of his works were printed in such important Reformed publishing centers on the continent as Zurich, Geneva, and Heidelberg. Some of them also appeared in Basel, that great center for all kinds of printings, including a good many works produced by religious refugees from Italy, above all Pietro Perna. It was Perna, in fact, who produced the most complete single edition of Vermigli's *Loci Communes,* 1580-1582. [24]

---

[22] Kingdon, pp. 43-137, deals with the Morély affair. For a summary of Morély's argument on congregational discipline, see pp. 50 ff., specifically p. 52 on limitation of excommunication to the entire congregation.

[23] *C.P.,* IV :5 :18.

Clearly Vermigli had a considerable influence within the Reformed community. It will take a good deal of further work, however, to delineate the precise nature of that influence. In particular it is by no means clear which of the competing factions which developed within that movement were most faithful to the ecclesiological teachings of Peter Martyr. Indeed some influence can be traced in several directions. Several of Vermigli's most devoted students became leading Anglicans. Pre-eminent among them was John Jewel, bishop of Salisbury under Elizabeth I and a leading early apologist for the Church of England as established by Elizabeth. Jewel had become acquainted with Vermigli at Oxford, followed him into exile on the continent, joining him first in Strasbourg and then in Zurich, and maintained a warm correspondence with him after returning to England. [25] Edmund Grindal, Elizabeth I's first bishop of London and her second primate, probably also came to know Vermigli as one of the group of religious refugees in Strasbourg. In fact it seems probable that practically all of the important Elizabethan church leaders who had been members of the colonies of Marian exiles in Strasbourg and Zurich knew Vermigli personally. So did some of those leaders who remained in England during the Marian persecution. This network of personal contacts with the English elite helps to explain the high regard in which Vermigli was held by Elizabethans generally and the number of editions and translations of his work published in London. Since most of these men supported the episcopalian establishment of Elizabeth I, they obviously did not find a great incompatibility between the teachings of Vermigli and the practices of the Church of England.

Others among Vermigli's students and some of his best friends, on the other hand, became leading Presbyterians. Pre-eminent among them was Theodore Beza, Calvin's successor as Moderator of the Company of Pastors in Geneva. Beza was in frequent correspondence with Vermigli during his life and worked with him particularly closely in the

---

[24] See above, n. 8, on editions of the *Loci Communes*. Professor Donnelly or I have also examined copies of the following editions, all in Latin—of the Commentary on First Corinthians: (1) Zurich, 1551; (2) Zurich, 1567; (3) Zurich, 1572; (4) Zurich, 1579, and of the Commentary on Kings: (1) Zurich, 1566; (2) Zurich, 1571; (3) Zurich, 1581; (4) Zurich, again 1581; (5) Heidelberg, 1599.

[25] W. M. Southgate, *John Jewel and the Problem of Doctrinal Authority* (Cambridge, MA, 1962), especially the first two chapters, pp. 3-48. See also John E. Booty, *John Jewel as Apologist of the Church of England* (London, 1963), *passim*.

Protestant delegation at the Colloquy of Poissy. After Vermigli's death, it was Beza who first suggested the compilation of the *Loci Communes*. Beza also obtained possession of most of Vermigli's private library, making it the nucleus of the library of the comparatively new Geneva Academy. [26] Yet Beza became an ardent Presbyterian. On Calvin's death in 1564, he refused to accept the position of Moderator in Geneva on terms that would make it resemble the office of a bishop, insisting on annual election of the Moderator by the entire Company of Pastors. And after he had been routinely elected to the office for a number of years, he finally flatly refused to continue serving in 1580. Beza also worked hard to encourage Presbyterians in Scotland like Andrew Melville and Thomas Cartwright in their strenuous opposition to the rule of bishops in a Reformed Church. [27]

I have not as yet uncovered any direct personal connections between Vermigli and early Congregationalists. Most of them in his own lifetime were tainted with Anabaptism and that would have caused him to spurn their friendship on other theological grounds. But there is a good chance of influence in that direction, too, judging from the content of some of his writing. His opinion that the power to excommunicate should be reserved to the entire congregation, for example, must surely have appealed to later Congregationalists. It comes as no surprise, therefore, that we find copies of Vermigli's works in a place of honor within the libraries constructed in colonial New England to assist in the creation of a Congregational commonwealth. [28]

It might even be argued that, if the specific form of discipline suggested in the legal code Vermigli helped draft for England back in 1552 had prevailed, the later division among the English Reformed into Episcopalians, Presbyterians, and Congregationalists could have been avoided. This code ingeniously combines the guiding principles of these three factions, for example, in the procedure for excommuni-

---

[26] Alexandre Ganoczy, *La Bibliothèque de l'Académie de Calvin* (Geneva, 1969), supplies an inventory of the entire library. Donnelly, appendix, pp. 208-17, abstracts from it all of those items known to have belonged to Vermigli.

[27] On Beza's attitude toward the position of Moderator, see Olivier Labarthe, "Le changement du mode de présidence de la Compagnie des Pasteurs de Genève, 1578-1580," *Zeitschrift für Schweizerische Kirchengeschichte* 67 (1972), 160-86. On Beza's assistance to Presbyterianism in Scotland and England, see Maruyama, chapter 9, pp. 303-41.

[28] Giorgio Spini, "Riforma Italiana e Mediazioni Ginevrine nella Nuova Inghilterra Puritana," in Delio Cantimori, et al., *Ginevra e l'Italia* (Florence, 1959), 451-89, especially pp. 458 ff.

cation, suggesting that it be vested in the local congregation, on re-commendation of a group of elders, with the permission of a bishop. [29]

Even though Vermigli cannot be identified securely with any single one of these three factions seeking different types of church polity, however, he can be connected to the general concern they all shared for Christian discipline and polity. And this brings us back to the marks of the true Church. For it became characteristic of the entire Reformed movement that it was more concerned with questions of order than its main rival within the "Magisterial" camp, the Evangelical Lutheran movement. Vermigli's insistence that discipline must be the third mark of the true Church was surely both a symptom of this Reformed emphasis and a contribution to its growth and persistence.

---

[29] Spalding, p. 170. While Vermigli's ideas on excommunication may lend them-selves to compromise of this sort, there are other strands in his thought which would create problems for such a compromise. In particular there is an Erastian strand, pointed out by Erastus himself. See Donnelly, pp. 188-189. I am indebted to Professor Donnelly and Thomas M. Safley for close readings of earlier drafts of this essay.

V

WAS THE PROTESTANT REFORMATION A REVOLUTION? THE CASE OF GENEVA*

THE problem which I wish to consider is the problem of deciding whether the protestant reformation was a revolution. The problem should be of interest to a number of different scholars. There is no obvious reason, however, why it should interest those who define themselves primarily as ecclesiastical historians. I believe, however, that there is an ecclesiastical dimension to this problem and that earlier work upon it is flawed by a failure to recognize that fact. I see these flaws even in the work which has most stimulated my own recent thinking on the problem. This is the work of a number of modern english historians and above all a book published by that great english contribution to the american community of historians, Lawrence Stone, titled *The Causes of the English Revolution, 1529–1642*.[1] I found particularly useful Stone's lengthy analysis of the phenomenon of revolution, borrowing extensively from the recent work of political scientists, sociologists, and other behavioral scientists. And I found persuasive his application of that analysis to the puritan revolution. I found his ultimate conclusion, however, 'that the crisis in England in the seventeenth century is the *first* "Great Revolution" in the history of the world,'[2] to be nonsense. It is nonsense partly because he has ignored the illumination which can be shed on this topic by a consideration of ecclesiastical history. I shall argue that the protestant reformation of the early sixteenth century was also a revolution, anticipating Stone's by more than a hundred years. And I shall seek to demonstrate this argument with evidence drawn from ecclesiastical history.

Very few men at the time of the protestant reformation would have

---

* This essay is a revised version of one originally published in Robert M. Kingdon (ed) *Transition and Revolution: Problems and Issues of European Renaissance and Reformation History* (Minneapolis, Minnesota: Burgess Publishing Company, 1974). This version is published with the permission of the Burgess Company.

[1] New York 1972. Originally published in London 1972.

[2] p 147, italics mine.

called it a revolution.[3] In those days the term did not normally possess a political or social meaning. It was basically a scientific term, used primarily by astronomers. Its best known usage was in the title of the famous treatise in which Nicolaus Copernicus advanced his radical new heliocentric theory, *On the Revolution of the Heavenly Bodies*, first published in 1543. In this context the term 'revolution' referred to the motions of heavenly bodies in orbits around either the earth or sun.

There are obvious ways in which this astronomers' term can be applied, by analogy, to certain political and social changes. One can find a few scattered examples of such applications during the sixteenth and seventeenth centuries, but they are rare and ambiguous.[4] Only in the eighteenth century did the term 'revolution' come to be used in a way we would recognize. It was applied then to the two great upheavals we know as the american and french revolutions. At first these revolutions were conceived of as primarily dramatic political changes. Soon, however, they were interpreted as fundamentally social upheavals. The social interpretation, as developed by Marx and his disciples, has tended to prevail in the twentieth century. And the recent marxist revolutions, in Russia and China, tend to supply the type to which most modern usage of the term refers.

Modern behavioral scientists have tried to refine definitions of revolution still further. There are surely some who have tried to reduce them to mathematical formulae. I shall not try to follow them. I shall rather stop with a common-sense definition developed by Sigmund Neumann, an eminent and sensible and somewhat old-fashioned political scientist, imported to the United States from Germany. In this I follow Stone who, in spite of his enthusiasm for the most modern social sciences, also really stops at this point. Neumann defined revolution as 'a sweeping, fundamental change in political organization, social structure, economic property control, and the predominant myth of a social order, thus indicating a major break in the continuity

---

[3] On the history of the word revolution, see Hannah Arendt, *On Revolution* (New York 1965) cap I esp pp 34–40; Jacques Ellul, *Autopsie de la révolution* (Paris 1969) pp 51–2.

[4] For example Philippe du Plessis-Mornay, *Remonstrance aux Estats pour la paix* of 1576, repr *Mémoires et Correspondance de Duplessis-Mornay*, 2 (Paris 1824) p 75, in speaking of the evils brought to France by the catholic league, says: 'Les villes, qui de neutralité seront venues à liberté, de ceste liberté viendront à une licence populaire, de la licence retomberont à la tyrannie de quelqu'ung, et toutes les semaines par sedition auront nouvelles revolutions.' An even earlier example, drawn from a 1525 description of the revolt of the Comuneros in Spain is cited by [J. H.] Elliott, ['Revolution and Continuity in Early Modern Europe,'], *PP* no 42 (1969) p 40.

Reformation and revolution: the case of Geneva

of development.'[5] This formula seems to me to sum up modern opinion reasonably enough so that we can use it. Armed with this definition, we can now return to the original problem: was the protestant reformation a revolution?

At this point some scholars would object that to use the term 'revolution' in speaking of the reformation era, is to adopt an anachronism, the greatest sin any historian can commit. It seems to me that this objection is specious. In order to understand a period one need not restrict oneself to the language of that period. Indeed it is often possible to understand some aspects of a period in history even better than the men who lived through it, by use of concepts developed and refined since they died. Modern economic historians, for example, understand far more about the development of the european economy during the fifteenth and sixteenth centuries than did businessmen who participated in that development. Their superior understanding is based in part on the use of concepts derived from modern economics and mathematics, unknown to the sixteenth century. These scholars, for example, can construct price indices which show exactly what and where and how prices increased or decreased during the reformation. Men of that period often complained bitterly of rising prices but not even the best educated of them would have been able to construct a price index. That does not prevent modern scholars from creating price indices and then using them to explain many facets of the economic and social development of the period only imperfectly understood by contemporaries. These indices, for example, help us to explain more fully than ever before many of the food riots of the sixteenth century. I would argue that the concept of revolution is like the concept of a price index. If it is used with care, by someone who knows both what it means and what happened in the earlier period, it can be enormously illuminating.

A far more weighty objection to the suggestion that the protestant reformation was a revolution comes from specialists in the period itself. Many of them would argue that the reformation did not involve changes in political organisation, social structure, economic property control, and social myths which were fundamental enough to be fairly labeled revolutionary. It was not a revolution in Neumann's sense. One thoughtful expression of this point of view can be found in the writing of J. H. Elliott. He sums up his argument in these words:

---

[5] Sigmund Neumann, 'The International Civil War,' *World Politics*, I (1948–9) p 333, n 1, quoted and used by Stone p 48.

V

The sixteenth and seventeenth centuries did indeed see significant changes in the texture of European life, but these changes occurred inside the resilient framework of the aristocratic-monarchical state. Violent attempts were made at times to disrupt this framework from below, but without any lasting degree of success. The only effective challenge to state power and to the manner of its exercise, could come from within the political nation—from within a governing class whose vision scarcely reached beyond the idea of a traditional community possessed of traditional liberties.[6]

Elliott, to be sure, advanced this argument in the course of a debate on the meaning of early seventeenth-century political uprisings and in that context it constitutes a useful rejoinder to arguments about the depth and pervasiveness of an alleged general european crisis. He has not considered with equal care the uprisings which accompanied the beginnings of the protestant reformation, early in the sixteenth century. Still he seems to believe that his conclusion applies to the entire early modern period in european history.

I would argue that this conclusion is defective as an explanation of reformation changes because it overlooks one crucial fact: it ignores the role of the clergy in pre-reformation european society. A revolution does not have to be aimed at the power of kings and aristocrats or at the bourgeoisie to be a true revolution. It can also be aimed at other ruling classes. The class against which the protestant reformation was aimed was the roman catholic clergy. In most of Europe before the reformation, the catholic clergy did constitute an important element in most political organization and in social structure, did control a good deal of the property, and were custodians of the predominant social myth. A challenge to the clergy thus had to be a radical challenge, calling for a revolutionary change in european society. It is my contention that the protestant reformation was such a challenge.

Protestants, of course, were not the only enemies to clerical power. Much of the power of the clergy had been attacked and eroded in many parts of Europe well before the reformation, during the renaissance and even earlier. Furthermore clerical power survived the reformation in many areas and in many ways. In some instances it even grew in strength. However protestants, wherever they were active, invariably

[6] Elliott p 55.

Reformation and revolution: the case of Geneva

opposed the catholic clergy, often with considerable vehemence and insistence. The protestant reformation can fairly be called, I believe, an anti-clerical revolution.

To document this conclusion fully would require massive empirical studies of the growth and nature of anti-clericalism all over western Europe during the reformation. That is clearly beyond my present capacity. I would like to provide some indication of the plausibility of my conclusion, however, by presenting one case study. The case I have selected is of the european community in which I have lived and worked the longest and whose history I know best, the canton of Geneva.[7]

Before the reformation Geneva was an episcopal city, part of an episcopal principality.[8] Her temporal and spiritual ruler was a bishop. Occasionally, especially in the early middle ages, she claimed to be a part of the Holy Roman Empire, but as an ecclesiastical principality rather than as a free imperial city. More important by the sixteenth century was the fact that she was then closely connected to the duchy of Savoy. Many of the rural areas and villages surrounding Geneva belonged directly to the dukes of Savoy or their vassals. For several decades before the reformation the bishop of Geneva had always been attached to the court of Savoy. Often he had been a younger son or brother of the duke himself. This arrangement had the advantage for Geneva of securing savoyard support for the city. She could call on the ducal army for defense and her merchants could trade more freely throughout the duchy. It also meant, however, that the bishop was seldom in actual residence within the city. He had to spend a good deal of time at the ducal court. Some of the bishops also acquired charges

---

[7] A good introduction to the early history of Geneva is supplied by the symposium volume edited by [Paul-E.] Martin, *Histoire de Genève [des origines a 1798]* (Geneva 1951). A fine guide to more intensive studies is supplied by Paul-F. Geisendorf, *Bibliographie raisonnée de l'histoire de Genève*, vol 43 in the series *Mémoires et documents [publiés par la Société d'histoire et d'archéologie de Genève]* (Geneva 1966). An important recent contribution to our knowledge of medieval genevan ecclesiastical history is provided by [Louis] Binz, [*Vie religieuse et réforme ecclésiastique dans le diocèse de Genève pendant le grand schisme et la crise conciliare (1378–1450)*], first of a projected two volumes, published as vol 46 in the same series (Geneva 1973). For an excellent introduction in english to the history of Geneva during the reformation, see [E. William] Monter, [*Calvin's Geneva*] (New York 1967).

[8] An interesting contemporary description of pre-reformation Geneva is provided by [François] Bonivard, [*Advis et devis de l'ancienne et nouvelle police de Genève.*] . . . (Geneva 1865). An excerpt, translated by Raymond A. Mentzer, Jr., is appended to the Burgess Press version of this essay. See also Binz, part 2 of the Martin *Histoire de Genève*, and vol 1 of [Henri] Naef, [*Les origines de la Réforme à Genève*] (Geneva/Paris 1936).

V

outside of Savoy. Many acquired ecclesiastical property with attendant responsibilities in France. A few received administrative assignments from Rome. Still the power of the bishop was always felt within Geneva. That power was symbolised graphically by the cathedral of St Pierre on the top of the hill in the center of the old city. It had been splendidly rebuilt and redecorated in the course of the fifteenth century, when the commercial fairs for which the city was famous in that part of Europe were flourishing. It was visible for miles around, even from the high mountains which enclose three sides of the city from a distance. It easily dominated the city physically.

Within Geneva, the bishop's power was exercised by an episcopal council. The most important members of this council were the vicar, who was the bishop's chief representative in the city and presided over the council in his absence, and the 'official,' who supervised the administration of justice, both civil and criminal, for all clerics. This council acted as both an administrative body and an ecclesiastical court. The bishop was further assisted in his rule of Geneva by a cathedral chapter of thirty-two canons. Almost all of them came from prominent savoyard noble families. Each of the canons was assigned a luxurious house near the cathedral. Vacancies in the chapter were filled by the canons themselves, through co-option. Their most important single function was to elect a new bishop on the death or resignation of an incumbent. However they often saw their choice set aside by the pope. Not only did he retain the right to confirm any election of a bishop, but in the case of Geneva he also reserved to himself the right to make his own final selection. Both the chapter elections and the final papal selections reflected heavy political pressure from neighboring secular authorities. This pressure came primarily from the dukes of Savoy but it could also come from the french royal house or the swiss cantons.

For the exercise of his spiritual responsibilities, the bishop depended upon ordained clergymen. There were several hundred of them in pre-reformation Geneva, out of a total population of about ten thousand.[9] They included secular priests, most of whom were attached to one or another of seven city parishes. They also included regular clergy, mostly of the mendicant orders, housed in some seven convents. The newest of these convents had been built in the century before the

---

[9] See Naef, 1, pp 22–5, for a careful estimate that there were four to five hundred clergymen resident in Geneva. See Monter p 2, for an estimate that the total population in 1537 was 10,300.

Reformation and revolution: the case of Geneva

reformation for communities of augustinian hermits and Poor Clare sisters.

For the exercise of his temporal responsibilities, the bishop delegated some of his powers to laymen. Justice for laymen, in both civil and criminal cases, was supervised by an officer with the unusual title of 'vidomne.' Some time before the reformation, a bishop of Geneva had ceded the right to choose this officer to the ducal government of Savoy. The vidomne and his staff lived in a castle on an island in the middle of the river Rhone which cuts Geneva in half. That castle symbolised graphically the power of Savoy within the city. The bishop further allowed the lay population of Geneva to elect certain other officers to share in local government. The most important of these elected officers were four syndics, chosen once a year by the entire body of male citizens in an assembly called the general council. These syndics had the right to act as judges in the more important criminal trials initiated by the vidomne. That right, along with many others, had been spelled out in writing in a charter of liberties of the citizens of Geneva promulgated by a bishop in 1387. Every subsequent bishop was expected to swear to uphold these liberties at the time of his installation. The syndics also chose a small or ordinary council, of twelve to twenty-five men, who met at least once a week to handle local civic problems. They had to see to it that the walls and moats which fortified the city were maintained in good condition, that adequate food supplies were regularly brought into the city and stored with care, that the streets were kept clean. They also had to direct the collection and expenditure of much of the city's money. And they supervised a variety of educational and charitable institutions.

At this last point ecclesiastical and temporal authority overlapped. For most of the educational and charitable institutions were staffed by clergymen. The education of the clergy had been handled within the cathedral establishment for a long time. In the fifteenth century, an independent school for laymen had been established, financed and supervised by the city council, but normally staffed by clergymen. Charity was handled primarily by seven 'hospitals'.[10] Most of them had been founded by the gifts or legacies of wealthy individuals, to provide both for the repose of their own souls and assistance to the poor. A typical 'hospital' would be a converted house, perhaps itself part of the original bequest. Resident in it would be a priest, who would be in

[10] See J.-J. Chaponnière and L. Sordet, *Des hopitaux de Genève avant la réformation*, vol III/2 in *Mémoires et documents* (1844).

charge and would say masses for the souls of the founder and his family. He would be assisted by a *hospitallier* or administrator, who would help the poor. Usually there would be a dozen or so of the poor in residence, a mixture of orphans, the handicapped, and the very old. From the middle of the fifteenth century, many of these hospitals were supervised by a municipal foundation, controlled by the council, which also had supplementary funds to assist the poor who could remain in their own homes. In addition the city maintained a pestilential hospital, outside the walls and near the cemetery, for the victims of serious contagious diseases. It was staffed by a priest, a doctor, and several servants. The city also maintained two small *leprosaria* outside its walls.

The control of public morals should have been the responsibility of the bishop, but he was seldom interested.[11] There were always a good number of prostitutes in pre-reformation Geneva, to service the visiting merchants and clergymen. Seldom was any effort made to drive prostitutes from the city. Instead they were regulated by the city council. At one point they were asked to organise themselves into a kind of guild and elect from their number a 'queen' who would represent them in dealings with the government. The prostitutes were also expected to live within an assigned quarter of the city, wear distinctive kinds of clothing, and limit their solicitation to specified times and places. If a sexual or marital problem required legal intervention, of course, the courts were prepared to act. Most cases of this sort were handled by the court of the bishop.

Geneva's ecclesiastical establishment was supported materially from a variety of sources. Taxes and church property within the city provided some income. A great deal of additional income came from a patchwork of rural properties scattered over the countryside around Geneva and belonging directly to the bishop. These were superintended by episcopal officers who saw to it that order was maintained in each rural village, that local priests served the spiritual needs of the peasants, and that all the rents and taxes due the bishop were regularly paid.

After the reformation Geneva was a secular city-state. The bishop and all his officers had been evicted, including the ones appointed with his permission by the dukes of Savoy. The clergy had all, without exception, been forced either to leave the city or abandon clerical careers. Almost all of the ecclesiastical property, both within the city and in the countryside, had been confiscated by the new government.

[11] See Naef, 1, cap 5, section 1.

Reformation and revolution: the case of Geneva

Many of the social services provided by clergymen had been secularised. A new reformed church had been created to minister to the spiritual needs of the population, but it was completely under the control of the city government. All of this had been engineered by the lay merchants and professional men of Geneva, led by their elected syndics and council members. These changes began in the 1520s, with the whittling away of the bishop's powers. They reached a climax in 1536, with a formal vote by the entire male population to adopt the protestant reformation. They were not fully consolidated until 1555, when John Calvin, the new director of Geneva's spiritual life, finally won a definitive triumph over all local opposition.[12]

It all began as a rebellion against the government of the bishop and his savoyard allies. Step by step the syndics and the city council seized powers that had heretofore been held by the episcopal government as parts of its sovereign prerogatives, until finally nothing remained for the bishop. The first powers to go were those of control over foreign affairs. This crucial attribute of sovereignty had naturally been claimed by the bishop. Now, however, the syndics and city council, on their own initiative, opened formal negotiations with other governments, particularly with those of free city-states within the swiss confederation. These were states with which genevans had long had commercial relations. A struggle developed within the city between merchants with savoyard and swiss interests. When the latter faction won the upper hand, it tried to consolidate its power by negotiating formal alliances with two of the more powerful neighbours to the north, Fribourg and Berne. Fribourg soon withdrew but Berne remained as Geneva's staunchest ally. That alliance was important, for Berne was one of the greatest military powers in the area.

The savoyards protested vehemently against these alliances, arguing that they amounted to usurpation by the city council of a sovereign

[12] There is an excellent but unfortunately incomplete account of these changes in Naef, 2 (Geneva 1968), published posthumously, carrying the story only to 1534, without any documentation for the period 1532–1534. To complete this narrative, the best accounts remain those of Jean-Antoine Gautier, *Histoire de Genève des origines à l'année 1691*, 9 vols (Geneva 1896–1914), esp vol 2 (1501–1537), and [Amédée] Roget, [*Histoire du peuple de Genève depuis la Réforme jusqu'à l'escalade,*] 7 vols (Geneva 1870–1883) which covers the period 1536–1567. See also the contemporary accounts of Michel Roset, *Les chroniques de Genève*, ed by Henri Fazy (Geneva 1894) and Jeanne de Jussie, *Le levain du calvinisme ou commencement de l'hérésie de Genève*, ed Ad.-C. Grivel (Geneva 1865). Excerpts from both of these chronicles translated into english by Raymond A. Mentzer, Jr. can be found following the Burgess Press version of this essay. I have been told that the Grivel edition of the Jeanne de Jussie chronicle is based on an inferior manuscript and that a new edition is consequently needed.

power belonging to the bishop. The incumbent bishop, however, did not support this protest. He had become alienated from the duke, despite the years he had spent in the ducal entourage, and was trying to play an independent game. In 1527, he conceded to the city council the right to sign alliances and tried to make himself a party to the alliance with Fribourg and Berne. The bernese refused to admit the bishop to the alliance and the bishop tried to revoke his concession to the Geneva council. But it was too late.

The next episcopal powers to be seized by the city council were the rights to control justice, another crucial attribute of sovereignty. The syndics had already won much earlier, under the terms of the 1387 charter, the right to sit as judges in certain criminal trials. The council now moved, during the 1527 negotiations with the bishop, to gain control over all civil cases. In granting this request, the bishop was surrendering powers previously exercised by his 'official' and by the vidomne. His cession of the vidomne's powers made the savoyards furious, since the vidomne was appointed by their government. Again the bishop changed his mind and tried to retract the concession, but again he was too late. Instead the city council proceeded to take over even more judicial powers. It blocked all appeals to superior courts outside of Geneva. It transferred to the syndics the right to execute criminal sentences. Finally a new elective magistracy was created, the office of the lieutenant, charged with supervising all criminal justice. By 1530 all the judicial powers once belonging to the bishop and his agents had been transferred over to the elective government of the city. In 1533 the bishop paid one last visit to the city, then left it for good. He soon transferred his entire court to the small neighbouring town of Gex. A number of canons also left Geneva during these years of turmoil.

Meanwhile protestantism had begun to penetrate Geneva. It was introduced with powerful encouragement from Berne, which had itself formally adopted zwinglianism in 1528. The leader of the campaign to convert Geneva to protestantism was Guillaume Farel, who repeatedly visited Geneva during these years in spite of fierce opposition from the local clergy. His inflammatory sermons and public appeals plunged the city into further turmoil. Iconoclastic riots began and catholic services were repeatedly disrupted. Protestants seized certain of the church buildings, most notably the franciscan convent, and began holding services and administering sacraments, in competition with the local priests. Finally a public debate was held in 1535 between

Reformation and revolution: the case of Geneva

a group of protestant pastors and a few of the local priests. The protestants claimed that the debate had resulted in a decisive victory for them, and that the population was now generally convinced of the truth of their point of view. They demanded that the city adopt legislation to establish firmly a truly reformed service of worship. The council responded cautiously by ordering a suspension of the catholic mass.

That step convinced most of the catholic clergy who were still in the city that they could no longer remain. A number had already left. A few had abandoned their religious vocations, had publicly converted to protestantism, had turned to secular occupations, and had even married. In 1535, after the great debate, practically all the remaining catholic clergy left Geneva. This included the bishop's vicar, the remaining canons, most of the parish priests, and most of the friars and sisters. A handful of priests who tried to remain were ordered by the council either to leave or to conform. The few who conformed were relieved of all clerical duties.

Once most of the clergy had left the city, the council seized control over all church property, both within the city and in the country districts heretofore controlled by the bishop's officers. Some of this property was used to pay off a substantial debt to Berne. The rest was allocated to charity. All of the hospitals created during the middle ages were closed. A new hospital-general was established in the building which had been the convent of the Poor Clare sisters. A civilian staff, including a *hospitallier* or administrator, a teacher, a doctor, and servants was assembled and housed in the building. A special committee of the government was created to supervise the activity of this staff. The administration of charity was thus thoroughly laicised and rationalised in Geneva.[13]

As a final assertion of sovereignty, the city council authorised and supervised the coining of money. The new coins carried a slogan which was to become a rallying cry for the reformation: *Post tenebras lux.*

Naturally all of these changes increasingly alarmed the bishop, the ducal government of Savoy, and the savoyard noble families of the area surrounding Geneva. The bishop could see his power and wealth evaporating, the duke could see his claim on the city withering away, the nobles could see their relatives among the canons insulted and exiled. Considerable military pressure was brought to bear upon

---

[13] See [Robert M.] Kingdon, 'Social Welfare [in Calvin's Geneva,'] *AHR*, 76 (1971) pp 50–69.

Geneva to stop this course of events. Armed bands of savoyard noblemen, encouraged by the duke and the bishop, ravaged the countryside, interdicting much of the trade so vital to the city's economy and making it hard for the city to gather in essential food on a regular basis. By 1535 the city was virtually under siege. Geneva persuaded its bernese ally to come to the rescue. A large swiss army came pouring down from the great plain to the north. This army commanded by the bernese effectively conquered all the savoyard and independent territory surrounding Geneva. It even tried to take over the city itself, but the genevans were able to resist that pressure.

With a ring of bernese dependencies around her, Geneva was now free to go all the way to reformation. In a special meeting of the general council held in May of 1536, the final step was taken. It was voted that the city would henceforth live by the gospel and the word of God as it had been preached in Geneva since the suspension of the mass. It was further voted that the 'masses, images, idols, and other papal abuses' would no longer be permitted in the city.[14]

That decision ended the power of the catholic clergy in Geneva. But it did not immediately create a reformed church. It really only left a vacuum, which was unstable and dangerous in an age when almost all europeans felt it necessary to build their lives and their communities around some form of religious ideology. Farel desperately tried to fill this void. He had the great good luck to recruit as his principal assistant a brilliant young french humanist lawyer who happened to be passing through Geneva only a few months after its fateful decision to become protestant. This was John Calvin. He had only recently converted to protestantism and fled from religious persecution in his native country. He was now appointed a public lecturer in theology. For two years, Farel and Calvin worked together to announce the christian truth as they saw it and to give that truth reality within Geneva by developing reformed services and ecclesiastical institutions. They were frustrated at every turn, however, by genevans who did not want to trade catholic clerical tyranny for a new protestant yoke. Finally they were both rather unceremoniously ejected from the city.

Now Geneva was really drifting, without any clerical leadership it could respect. Some thought the city might return to catholicism. Others expected it to drift into some wild and eccentric religious experiment. This period of indecision ended when Calvin, alone, was

---

[14] See [Ioannis] Calvini Opera [quae supersunt omnia], ed by Baum, Cunitz, & Reuss, 21 (Brunswick 1879) cols 201–2, for the full text of this decision of 21 May 1536.

Reformation and revolution: the case of Geneva

invited back to take charge. He was reluctant to return to Geneva and he posed strict conditions, but they were accepted. Finally in 1541 he came back. He remained in Geneva until his death in 1564, and created there a reformed church which proved to be a model for protestants in much of Europe and America.

Calvin accomplished this feat solely by moral suasion. He never possessed even a fraction of the legal power of the deposed catholic bishop. He never commanded even a fraction of the material resources owned by the bishop, or for that matter by any one of the canons. Political power remained solely within the hands of the elected council and syndics. Calvin and the other pastors were only employees of the municipal government, living on salaries paid by the city,[15] most of them in houses owned by the city. They were far fewer in number than the catholic clergy whose places they took. Altogether there were only nine pastors in 1542. The number had risen to only nineteen by 1564, the year of Calvin's death.[16] A few additional men with protestant theological training secured positions as chaplains, teachers, or tutors. But the total of all these men was far short of the hundreds of catholic religious who had served Geneva under the bishop. Furthermore none of these protestant clergymen was allowed to become a full citizen of Geneva. The city had become so suspicious of foreign pressures that it reserved citizenship, with full rights to vote and hold office, to certain native-born residents. All the pastors were immigrants, most of them from France, like Calvin. No native genevan had secured the type of advanced education the council now decided was essential for the position. A few of the pastors became 'bourgeois' of Geneva, an intermediate status which gave a man many political and legal rights, but not full citizenship. Calvin himself was granted the status of *bourgeois*, but only toward the end of his life, in 1559.[17]

This does not mean that Calvin and the other pastors did not

[15] See the excellent study of Jean-François Bergier, 'Salaires des pasteurs de Genève au XVIᵉ siècle,' in *Mélanges [d'histoire du XVIᵉ siècle offerts à Henri] Meylan*, vol 43 in *Bibliothèque historique vaudoise* (Lausanne 1970) pp 159–78. The salaries consisted of both payments in cash and large allocations of grain and wine from the municipal supplies.

[16] There are lists of all the pastors employed by the city in each year from 1542 on, in Roget at the end of each volume.

[17] *Le livre des bourgeois de l'ancienne république de Genève*, ed by Alfred L. Covelle (Geneva 1897) p 266, two variant entries for 25 December 1559. For the distinction between the status of citizen and that of bourgeois, see Bonivard p 25. On the significance of the appointment of foreigners as pastors, see Monter esp pp 126, 221.

exercise considerable political power in Geneva. But their power was always exercised indirectly, usually through preaching or consulting. Calvin used both means effectively. He became an eloquent preacher, who clearly commanded the respect, if not always the affection, of his audience. This was in marked contrast to many of his predecessors both in the catholic clergy and among the earliest protestant preachers. He also became an active consultant to the city government. The council found his skill as a trained lawyer and his first-hand knowledge of the greater world of international politics to be extremely useful. He was often called in for consultation and his advice was usually accepted.[18]

One of the first things Calvin did on returning to Geneva in 1541, was to draft a set of ecclesiastical ordinances, to give institutional shape and legal standing to the newly reformed church. His right to do this had been part of the bargain that led to his return. After some discussion and a few minor amendments, these ordinances were enacted into law by the government.[19] This famous settlement organised the genevan church by creating four categories of ecclesiastical officials and then building institutions through which the work of each could be channelled. The categories were, (1) the pastors who were to preach the word of God and administer the sacraments, (2) the doctors who were to study the word of God and teach, (3) the elders who were to maintain discipline within the community, (4) the deacons who were to supervise the administration of charity.

The pastors were distributed among the parishes created before the reformation both within the city and in the country villages it controlled. There were seldom enough men to staff all of these parishes fully, but arrangements were made so that everyone had access of some sort to a pastor. For organisational purposes, the pastors were grouped into a company, which met once a week to handle routine church business, to discuss theology, and to engage in criticism of

[18] Records of many of these consultations can be found in the *Annales Calviniani* in vol 21 of the *Calvini Opera*. Several of them are discussed further in Robert M. Kingdon, *Geneva and the Coming of the Wars of Religion in France, 1555–1563* (Geneva 1956) for example pp 34–5.

[19] There is a good recent critical edition of these ordinances by Jean-François Bergier in the *Registres de la Compagnie des pasteurs de Genève, au temps de Calvin*, 1, 1546–1553 (Geneva 1964) pp 1–13. There is an english translation, without most of the critical apparatus, in *The Register of the Company of Pastors of Geneva in the Time of Calvin*, ed and trans by Philip E. Hughes (Grand Rapids, Mich, 1966) and a fresh translation of some of them by Raymond A. Mentzer, Jr., appended to my essay in the Burgess volume.

Reformation and revolution: the case of Geneva

themselves and their colleagues.[20] Calvin served as moderator, or presiding officer, of this company until his death. That was his only position of pre-eminence in Geneva. He also served as one of the pastors in the cathedral parish of St Pierre, and occasionally also preached in the nearby parish of the Madeleine. The pastors were all chosen by co-optation, with the existing company deciding on each new appointment. No choice could become final, however, until the candidate had been approved by the city council and presented to the parish in which he was to serve. The council reserved to itself the right to dismiss without notice any pastor who displeased its members. Over the years a number were in fact dismissed, most commonly because they had offended council members by things they said in sermons.[21]

At first Calvin was the only doctor. In addition to his pastoral duties, he spent a good deal of time in writing and lecturing on the bible. His lectures attracted hundreds of eager young intellectuals from all over Europe. This teaching did not get formal institutional shape, however, until 1559, fairly late in Calvin's life. In that year Geneva created a new academy, providing both secondary and university-level training in theology.[22] Calvin, of course, was the star of this faculty. He was joined by a number of his disciples who had been teaching in neighbouring Lausanne but who had recently been driven out by Berne. Material support for this new academy was provided primarily from property confiscated by the council from native genevans who had been expelled from the city in a number of internal upheavals ending in 1555.[23] These ejections had the net effect of eliminating all opposition within Geneva to Calvin and fully consolidating his authority.

The other two orders of ecclesiastical officials, elders and deacons, were laymen, most of whom served in this capacity only on a part-time basis. They were drawn from the same pool of wealthy merchants

---

[20] For a full critical edition of the rather casual records of this body, see the *Registres de la Compagnie des pasteurs de Genève, au temps de Calvin, 1546–1564*, 1 and 2, ed by R.-M. Kingdon and J.-F. Bergier (Geneva 1962–1964); 3, *1565–1574*, ed by Oliver Fatio and Olivier Labarthe (Geneva 1969); 4, *1575–1582*, ed by Olivier Labarthe and Bernard Lescaze (Geneva 1974).

[21] There are several examples of dismissals discussed in Robert M. Kingdon, *Geneva and the Consolidation of the French Protestant Movement, 1564–1572* (Geneva/Madison, Wisconsin 1967) cap 1.

[22] The standard account is Charles Borgeaud, *Histoire de l'Université de Genève*, vol 1, *L'Académie de Calvin, 1559–1798* (Geneva 1900).

[23] E. William Monter, *Studies in Genevan Government (1536–1605)* (Geneva 1964) pp 25 *et seq.*

and professional men as the members of the city council and the city's various governing committees. Near the beginning of every year, a meeting of the general council was called to elect the syndics and council members for the coming twelve months. At the same time members of a number of governmental committees were elected, from slates prepared by the outgoing government. These committees included ones to maintain the city's fortifications, control its grain supply, keep the streets clean, act as courts to judge certain legal cases. Calvin's ecclesiastical ordinances added two new committees to the list: a committee to maintain christian discipline, staffed partly by elected elders; a committee to assist the poor, staffed by elected deacons.

The committee to maintain discipline was called the consistory.[24] It was made up of all the elders and city pastors, with one syndic added as its presiding officer. It acted as a court and met once a week. The elders were chosen so as to represent all of the districts into which the city was divided. They reported to the consistory names of residents whose religious ideas were suspect, who still clung to catholic practices, and who did not behave properly. A high percentage of their cases were of people accused of sex crimes—fornification, adultery, sodomy, rape. The consistory examined each case. If the fault was minor and the accused penitent, he might be let off with a scolding. If the fault was more serious and the accused stubborn, he could be excommunicated. If the accused had done something of a criminal nature that required further punishment, he would be referred to the city council.

This was the most controversial single institution established by the reformation in Geneva. Calvin insisted on its creation when he returned in 1541, and threatened to resign when its power to excommunicate was challenged in later years. Calvin ultimately had his way, the opponents of consistorial excommunication were discredited and driven out, and a moral 'reign of terror' followed.[25] All of this helped to create that particularly austere pattern of behaviour which has come to be labelled 'Puritan.'

[24] See Robert M. Kingdon, 'The Control of Morals in Calvin's Geneva,' in Lawrence P. Buck and Jonathan W. Zophy, *The Social History of the Reformation* (Columbus 1972) pp 3–16, and the works there cited, particularly [Walther] Köhler, [*Zürcher Ehegericht und Genfer Konsistorium,*] 2 (Leipzig 1942). The registers of the consistory have never been edited and merit further study.

[25] For statistics of the dramatic increase in excommunications following Calvin's definitive triumph in 1555, see Köhler p 614, n 544.

Reformation and revolution: the case of Geneva

The deacons worked with the hospital-general.[26] Their positions had actually been created before Calvin's arrival, in the series of events which led up to the final break with catholicism. Calvin simply made room for them in his ecclesiastical ordinances and found biblical warrant for their assignments. In effect he sanctified this office, gave it a special religious character, and in so doing made it a more highly valued and respected feature of genevan society.

The ecclesiastical ordinances required the council to consult the pastors every year when it drew up its slates of nominations for elders and deacons before the elections. This rule, however, was not followed invariably. It was followed more often in the choice of elders than of deacons, and was followed quite scrupulously in the selection of both only after Calvin's power had been fully consolidated toward the end of his life.

This ecclesiastical structure was an outstanding success in consolidating the reformation in Geneva. Much of it persists there down to the present. It helped win for the city its international reputation as a centre of reformed protestantism.

Taken all together, it seems obvious to me that the changes in Geneva between 1526 and 1559 constitute a genuine revolution. They meet every requirement of the definition of a revolution laid down by Neumann which I described earlier. There was a fundamental change in political organisation: a government run by a bishop assisted by canons, chosen according to church law, was overthrown; a new government run by a council of local laymen elected by the people took its place. There was a fundamental change in social structure: several hundred catholic clergymen, a number of savoyard noblemen, and ordinary laymen hesistant to go all the way to calvinism were all driven out of the city; their places were taken by hundreds of immigrants, most of whom were artisans and merchants and most of whom came from France, as had Calvin. There was a fundamental change in economic property control: large amounts of property were confiscated from the old church and its supporters and in effect socialised, put at the disposition of the entire community as represented by its government, rather than being distributed to private individuals. All of these changes were justified and sanctified by the

[26] See Robert M. Kingdon, 'The Deacons of the Reformed Church in Calvin's Geneva,' in *Mélanges Meylan*, pp 81–90; also Kingdon, 'Social Welfare' and the works there cited, particularly Léon Gautier, *L'Hôpital Général de Genève de 1535 à 1545 et l'Hospice Général de 1869 à 1914* (Geneva 1914).

V

most obvious change of all, in the predominant myth of social order. Roman catholic theology was brutally rejected and a new variety of protestant theology was created to take its place.

There remains one final problem that must be explored, however, before we can resolve our problem satisfactorily. We must consider the extent to which the reformation in Geneva was typical. Even if the reformation clearly meant revolution in this particular city-state, it may not have had the same meaning elsewhere. Geneva may have been unique, and thus not a case upon which generalisations should be built.

To resolve this problem would require extensive comparative studies. Even some tentative and preliminary consideration, however, does make one thing clear: the reformation in Geneva was clearly more radical than in many communities. In few places had the power of the catholic clergy remained as strong and as pervasive as it was in pre-reformation Geneva. Cities all over Europe had once been controlled directly by bishops. For example in Germany most cities had been ruled by bishops back in the tenth century. Since that period, however, new secular cities had been founded and many old cities had broken loose from episcopal control. By the time of the reformation only a few german cities remained under the effective control of bishops. Most of the cities of importance had become free imperial cities, acknowledging allegiance to only one sovereign—the holy roman emperor. Remnants of episcopal power remained in most of these cities, but most temporal power was concentrated in elected city councils like those of Geneva.[27]

Furthermore, in many cities services that had previously been performed by the clergy had been turned over to secular institutions well before the reformation. This was particularly true of educational and charitable services. The move to secularisation of these services was especially pronounced in the great italian city-states of the late middle ages. In fact it can be argued that the celebrated culture of the italian renaissance was made possible by the creation of secular schools and academies supported by municipal governments and wealthy laymen in communities like Florence. Similarly the administration of charity had been laicised and rationalised in

[27] Hajo Holborn, *A History of Modern Germany: the Reformation* (New York 1959) makes a special point of noting the remnants of episcopal powers in the free imperial cities for example pp 23, 183. See also Bernd Moeller, *Reichsstadt und Reformation* (Gütersloh 1962) also in french translation (Geneva 1966), and english (Philadelphia 1972).

Reformation and revolution: the case of Geneva

communities like Milan which built and endowed large municipal hospitals for this purpose.[28] Clergy still staffed some of these institutions. But clerical control was gone and clerical participation was reduced if not ended. It can thus be argued that Geneva in the sixteenth century was socially retarded and that she used the reformation to catch up, to introduce changes which had already occurred in other communities.

It is also clear that in few places did the reformation go as far as it did in Geneva. It was not common for the entire body of the clergy in a community to be deposed or ejected. More often catholic parish priests were simply converted to protestantism, with a greater or lesser appreciation of what that meant, and allowed to remain at their work. Only slowly was a body of clergymen fully trained in protestant doctrine developed. This seems to have happened in most of the lutheran principalities in Germany and in England.

Even if the changes accompanying the reformation were seldom as abrupt and as far-reaching as in Geneva, however, there were always some changes. In every single instance, to begin with, a community adopting protestantism rejected the authority of the pope and broke all ties with Rome. And this was not a trivial move. The papacy had long symbolised in a concrete institutional way the unity of all western european civilization. Rejection of its power meant a move to some sort of particularism, often to some type of nationalism, with great consequences for the future.

Another change that almost always came with the reformation was the closing of all monastic communities and the confiscation of their often considerable property. On rare occasions convents or monasteries were simply not allowed to recruit new members, thus going out of existence when all existing members died.[29] But more commonly all the monks and nuns, friars and sisters, were required either to leave or find new occupations. And they lost all of their community property. There is, to be sure, a good deal of debate as to how significant were the resulting massive transfers of property, as english scholars of the period know very well.[30] In many areas

[28] See Giacomo C. Bascapè, 'L'assistenza e la beneficenza a Milano dall'alto medioevo alla fine della dinastia Sforzesca,' part 4 in *Storia di Milano*, vol 8 (Milan 1957) esp pp 405 *et seq* re establishment in 1456 of the Ospedale Maggiore.

[29] For example the two convents of St. Clara and St. Catherine in Nuremberg. See Gerald Strauss, *Nuremberg in the Sixteenth Century* (New York 1966) pp 158, 178.

[30] For a useful summary, see A. G. Dickens, *The English Reformation* (New York 1964) cap 7.

noblemen who already controlled much of a monastery's activities were no doubt able simply to control this property more directly. But changes of some sort had to occur. And they could be brutal and of far-reaching impact.

Yet another change that usually came with the reformation was the collapse of the system of church law and church courts. Appeals to Rome, of course, were always stopped. So at least that element in the catholic legal system invariably disappeared. But a good many further changes usually followed. Church courts were either abandoned completely or their powers and the range of their jurisdiction were sharply reduced. New protestant ecclesiastical bodies were seldom given many legal functions. In at least one aspect of legal practice, most protestant communities went further than Geneva. Before the reformation cases involving marital and sexual problems were normally tried before church courts. Geneva assigned these cases to a semi-ecclesiastical court, the consistory. This court did not, to be sure, use catholic canon law to settle these cases, turning instead to civil law and the relevant parts of the bible as interpreted by Calvin. But clergymen were at least involved in this part of the judicial process in Geneva. In most protestant communities they were not granted this right, and jurisdiction over marital and sexual offences was jealously reserved to secular courts.[31] Both catholic law and the catholic type of court were abandoned.

These three changes—the renunciation of papal authority, the closing of the monasteries, and the dismantling of the catholic legal system—were all of considerable significance. They required some modifications in political organisation, in the social structure, and in the predominant myth of the community. It seems to me that these changes can fairly be called revolutionary. Their full implications, to be sure, become obvious only when one examines an extreme case like Geneva. But they were always present. I would therefore conclude that the protestant reformation was indeed a revolution.

University of Wisconsin

---

[31] For example in Württemberg. See James M. Estes, 'Johannes Brenz and the Problem of Ecclesiastical Discipline,' *Church History*, 41 (1972) pp 464–79. See also Köhler.

VI

Social Welfare in Calvin's Geneva

Between 1520 and the end of the sixteenth century a number of Western European governments made significant new provisions for dealing with social problems. Municipal governments took the lead in this wave of welfare reform. Reforms whose wide influence has been particularly well documented are those of the cities of Nuremberg in Germany (1522), Ypres in the Low Countries (1525), and Lyon in France (1531–34).[1] The welfare ordinances of these three cities were published, in several editions and in several languages, and pamphlets were issued further explaining and justifying them. These reforms, moreover, influenced the policies not only of other cities, but also of royal governments. The imperial edict on poor relief in the Low Countries, promulgated in 1531 by the government of Charles v, was based on preliminary study of the municipal reforms of Mons, Ypres, and Audenaerde, and it in turn stimulated the reforms of other cities such as Brussels.[2] The English statute on poor relief, promulgated by the government of Henry viii in 1536, was based on a draft very likely prepared by the man who translated the Ypres ordinance into English.[3] And

This is an expanded version of a paper read at the joint meeting of the Social Welfare History Group and the American Historical Association in New York, December 30, 1968. Much of the material upon which it is based was gathered while I was in Europe on a research trip made possible by a grant from the American Philosophical Society. I have been assisted in revising the paper by comments and information generously supplied by several friends, notably Natalie Z. Davis, Harold J. Grimm, and E. William Monter.

[1] See, in particular, Otto Winkelmann, "Die Armenordnungen von Nürnberg (1522), Kitzingen (1523), Regensburg (1523) und Ypern (1525)," *Archiv für Reformationsgeschichte*, 10 (1912–13): 242–80; J. Nolf, *La réforme de la bienfaisance publique à Ypres au XVIᵉ siècle*, in *University of Ghent, Recueil de travaux publiés par la Faculté de philosophie et de lettres*, 45th fasc. (Ghent, 1915); Natalie Zemon Davis, "Poor Relief, Humanism, and Heresy: The Case of Lyon," *Studies in Medieval and Renaissance History*, 5 (1968): 217–75.

[2] See Paul Bonenfant, "Les origines et le caractère de la réforme de la bienfaisance publique aux Pays-Bas sous le règne de Charles-Quint," and "La création à Bruxelles de la Suprême Charité," in *Hôpitaux et bienfaisance publique dans les anciens Pays-Bas, des origines à la fin du xviiiᵉ siècle* (Brussels, 1965), 118, 149 ff.

[3] The translator was William Marshall, a propagandist of Protestant sympathies who worked for Thomas Cromwell. This is the plausible hypothesis presented by G. R. Elton in "An Early Tudor Poor Law," *Economic History Review*, 2d ser., 6 (1953–54): 65–66. Elton does not, however, discover close parallels between the Ypres ordinance and the draft act he attributes to Marshall. See also W. K. Jordan, *Philanthropy in England, 1480–1660: A Study of the Changing Pattern of English Social Aspirations* (London, 1959), 84–85.

the royal edicts and ordinances on poor relief of the French crown from 1543 to 1599 reflect the experience of such reforming municipalities as Paris and Lyon.[4]

Two essential principles characterized almost all of these reforms: laicization and rationalization. Practically every reform law vested most of the control of social welfare in the hands of laymen. In some areas this constituted a dramatic break with the current practice of leaving welfare programs in the hands of the Church, but in more areas it simply marked the culmination of a centuries-long shift in the control of welfare from ecclesiastical to secular hands. Practically every reform also established some sort of new institution to centralize and coordinate welfare. Such new institutions sometimes replaced a network of welfare organizations created over the centuries, but more often they simply controlled, coordinated, and supplemented the activities of already existing institutions.

The spread of this movement for laicized and rationalized welfare reform coincided almost precisely with the spread of the Protestant Reformation. Like the Protestant reformers, it challenged practices and institutions dear to many orthodox Catholics. Its spokesmen, the most prominent of whom was the great Spanish Catholic humanist Juan Luis Vives, were men vitally interested in religious reform. In consequence, many scholars have claimed that welfare reform and the Protestant Reformation were connected. Welfare reforms, however, were not limited to areas that became or were to become Protestant. They were adopted not only in Catholic Ypres and Lyon, in countries where Protestant influences were pervasive and strong, but also in cities of Catholic Italy and Spain where Protestant influences were weak. This complication has led to a good deal of debate among historians and has provoked some lively polemic.[5]

In order to unravel the connections between Protestantism and welfare in the sixteenth century, it should be useful to examine an extreme case, one in which the pressures for both kinds of reform were particularly intense and effective in changing institutions. Geneva is an obvious example. Under the leadership of John Calvin this city developed a most thorough and uncompromising reform in church organization. And with Calvin and his associates as spokesmen, it powerfully encouraged governments all over Europe to make similar changes. This encouragement was not without its effects in many countries, including English-speaking lands, and Geneva became a sort of Protestant Rome. A study of social welfare in Calvin's Geneva should, therefore, provide more than simply another example of how social problems were handled in one relatively small and comparatively backward sixteenth-century city. It should also provide a

4 Jean Imbert, "L'Eglise et l'Etat face au problème hospitalier au xvi⁰ siècle," in *Etudes d'histoire du droit canonique dédiées à Gabriel Le Bras* (Paris, 1965) 1: 577–92.

5 A useful summary of the earlier stages of this exchange can be found in Bonenfant, "Les origines et le caractère de la réforme," 115 ff. For a thoughtful recent contribution to the debate, see Davis, "Poor Relief, Humanism, and Heresy."

model of how early Protestants reformed the administration of social welfare, a model that may have had some influence in the period, and that, in any case, should be useful to modern scholars for purposes of analysis.

A study of social welfare in Calvin's Geneva must focus on a single institution, the Hôpital-Général, or General Hospital. It was much more than a "hospital" in the modern sense of the term. It was rather an all-purpose institution that provided "hospitality" to all sorts of people who were recognized to possess needs that they could not meet with their own resources. It maintained a large building in the center of Geneva that housed several dozen children—most of them orphans or foundlings—and a smaller number of older people who were too old, too sick, or too badly crippled to care for themselves. It distributed bread every week to poor households throughout the country and provided shelter and food every evening to visitors who had just arrived in Geneva and could not pay for their own accommodations.

Fortunately a study of this institution is possible. Extensive manuscript records of the operations of the General Hospital of Geneva still survive, particularly for the period after Calvin's definitive return to power in 1541. These records, carefully preserved and beautifully classified in the Geneva State Archives,[6] have been studied by several local historians,[7] but they deserve further study.

The Geneva General Hospital was a creation of the Reformation, but it was not a creation of Calvin. It was established in 1535 in one of the series of measures by which Geneva broke all connections with the Roman Catholic Church and established a Protestant regime. The movement toward social reform and the movement toward Protestantism thus coincide exactly in Geneva. In 1535, however, Calvin had not yet arrived in Geneva. The city was witnessing the culmination of a period of radical ferment stirred by the inflammatory preaching of William Farel. The General Hospital was actually established by the pious laymen who later invited Calvin to Geneva and then protected his Reformation against formidable pressures from many directions. In establishing this new institution, the Gene-

---

[6] These manuscript records are briefly described by Gustave Vaucher, "Archives hospitalières aux Archives de Genève," in *Mélanges offerts par ses confrères étrangers à Charles Braibant* (Brussels, 1959), 523–29. There is a more detailed manuscript inventory in the Archives d'Etat de Genève (hereafter AEG).

[7] Notably by Léon Gautier and E. Joutet, *L'Hôpital-Général de Genève de 1535 à 1545 et l'Hospice Général de 1869 à 1914* (Geneva, 1914). See also [Jean-Jacques-Louis] Odier-Cazenove, *L'Hôpital de Genève, depuis son origine jusqu'en 1842: recherches historiques* (Geneva, 1862), a study largely of the management of the Hospital's financial resources, containing several petty errors and lacunae; and Alice Denzler, *Jugendfürsorge in der alten Eidgenossenschaft: ihre Entwicklung in den Kantonen Zürich, Luzern, Freiburg, St. Gallen und Genf bis 1798* (Zurich, 1925), a study of the care of children by the Hospital and similar institutions in other Swiss cities.

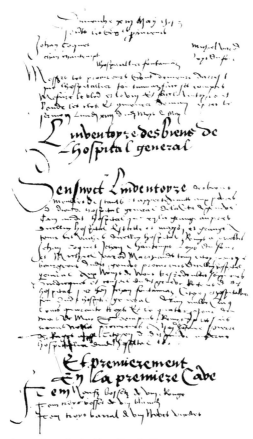

A page from the Archives Hospitalières, Aa1 (1542–50), fol.
48v. Courtesy Archives d'Etat de Genève.

van community endorsed the two principles that had characterized the
movement for welfare reform since 1522: rationalization and laicization.
The General Hospital replaced a number of different and competing earlier
institutions with a single, rationally organized institution, and the direction of this institution was entrusted entirely to laymen drawn from the
group of relatively prosperous merchants who ruled the city-state. Both
principles of organization were innovations in Genevan practice and merit
further analysis.

Trends toward rationalization and laicization of the administration of
social welfare can be discerned in Geneva before the Reformation. In
1535 there were at least eight institutions devoted primarily to coping with
social problems in the city. Seven of them were called "hospitals," while
the eighth was named Pyssis Omnium Animarum Purgatorii, or Box for All

Souls in Purgatory.[8] We know nothing about the establishment of the hospital that was evidently created first, but we do know that all the rest were founded and maintained primarily by the gifts or legacies of wealthy individuals, who were anxious to provide both for the welfare of the poor and the repose of their own souls. Control of these hospitals was vested in different bodies. The one apparently founded earliest, before 1288 and probably before 1269, was supervised by the Geneva cathedral chapter. Another was founded in the fourteenth century by the convent of Great Saint Bernard;[9] two were founded by the city government; one by a lay confraternity; one by the founder's heirs; and one either by a lay confraternity or by trustees of some sort—the record is unclear. Actual administration of each hospital was in the hands of a rector, or *procureur,* named by the governing body. In five of the hospitals the *procureur* seems usually to have been a secular priest who saw to it that mass was regularly said in a chapel attached to the hospital and who administered the hospital's property. In the hospital controlled by the lay confraternity the elected lay prior assumed the functions of the *procureur.* In the remaining hospital, members of the city council assumed those functions.[10] Both of these hospitals directed by laymen arranged for the priests of nearby chapels to minister to the spiritual needs of their inmates. Each *procureur* was usually assisted by a *hospitallier*—a man, woman, or couple—who supervised the actual care of the poor. The *hospitalliers* seem to have been invariably selected and supervised by the city councils and seem also invariably to have been laymen.

It is significant that the two hospitals with lay rectors were, in 1434 and 1452, the last to be created before the Reformation, thus revealing a pronounced trend toward laicization in the mid-fifteenth century. A step toward community-wide, rational direction of these institutions had also been taken with the creation by 1452 of the Box for All Souls in Purgatory. This was a municipal foundation probably established, as its name suggests, to collect money to pay for the saying of masses for the souls of all Genevans in purgatory. But it quickly became an institution concerned primarily with social problems. It controlled two of the hospitals for the city, provided funds for another, and even helped support a fourth hospital in a suburban village outside the city of Geneva. It also provided services supplied by no other institutions: placing foundling children in private homes

---

[8] For an extended analysis of each of these institutions, see J.-J. Chaponnière and L. Sordet, "Des hôpitaux de Genève avant la Réformation," *Mémoires et documents publiés par la Société d'histoire et d'archéologie de Genève,* 3 (1844): 165–471. This study also covers certain related institutions not located within the city itself, notably the pestilential hospital built for Genevans suffering from contagious diseases.

[9] Respectively, the Hôpital de Nôtre-Dame du Pont and the Hôpital Saint-Bernard, founded before 1376. See *ibid.,* 178–207, 239–47.

[10] Respectively, the Hôpital de l'Eucharistie ou des Pauvres Honteux, by far the best endowed of the seven hospitals, and the Hôpital de la Magdeleine, de Saint-Antoine et de Saint-Sébastien. See *ibid.,* 247–70.

and paying for their support and arranging for burial of the poor. In order to support all these activities, the Box collected money and invested surplus funds. The institution was administered by a board of *procureurs,* who, elected by the city government, were apparently all laymen.[11]

The most decisive steps toward laicization and rationalization, however, were taken during the Reformation. Some step of some kind had to be taken at that particular time. Lay confraternities and institutions concerned with purgatory had been discredited by the new theology. All the priests who administered five of the hospitals apparently left Geneva, no doubt partly—as the city councilors had charged—to make off with some of the property that had been in their custody,[12] no doubt also to escape the continuing abuse and physical assaults to which many priests had been subjected, and finally because they strongly disapproved of the religious changes being adopted by the city. Meanwhile, during these same months, the social problems to which these hospitals ministered had almost certainly grown more acute as Geneva fought off armed raids into her hinterland and braced herself for an actual siege from neighboring powers hostile to the Reformation. Something had to be done. The city councils decided to take the drastic step of consolidating all these services. All seven hospitals and the Box for All Souls were abolished. The properties of these institutions were turned over to a new General Hospital. Other properties were also allocated to the support of the new institution, most of them properties confiscated from churches, convents, and confraternities, which had earlier been earmarked for pious uses. They were now turned over, so say the council registers, to "this, the most pious of all uses."[13] One of the most substantial of these new properties was the former convent of Sainte-Claire, a large building that became the headquarters of the new General Hospital. The orphans and other poor people supported completely by the city were housed and fed in its rooms; the loaves of bread granted weekly to the deserving poor who remained in their own homes were doled out from its doors; the cows, work horses, and field equipment belonging to the Hospital were lodged in its stables.

The direction of the General Hospital was turned over entirely to laymen. A full-time *hospitallier* was hired. He was required to move into the headquarters building with his family,[14] and the free room and board

11 *Ibid.,* 341–60.

12 This charge was made in the text of the act by which the General Hospital was established, November 14, 1535. For copies of this act, see Emile Rivoire, Victor van Berchem, and Frédéric Gardy, eds., *Registres du Conseil de Genève* (Geneva, 1900–40), 13: 351–52; Emile Rivoire and Victor van Berchem, *Les sources du droit du canton de Genève* (Aarau, 1927–35), 2: 302–04; and Gautier and Joutet, *L'Hôpital-Général,* 12–14.

13 Rivoire, van Berchem, and Gardy, *Registres du Conseil de Genève,* 13: 352; Rivoire and van Berchem, *Les sources du droit,* 2: 303; Gautier and Joutet, *L'Hôpital-Général,* 13.

14 A detailed set of regulations defining the position was adopted May 12, 1553, at the time Jullian Boccard was named *hospitallier.* It is published in Rivoire and van Berchem, *Les sources du droit,* 3: 13–16, based on AEG, Pièces historiques (hereafter PH) no. 1533. Another manuscript copy can be found in AEG, Archives hospitalières (hereafter Arch. hosp.) Aa2, insert between fols. 39 and 40.

that this arrangement provided the *hospitallier* made the position an attractive one.[15] A number of assistants and servants worked under the direction of the *hospitallier*—one, normally a barber-surgeon, was charged with providing medical care to the poor; another, usually a theology student preparing for ordination as a pastor, was charged with educating the children in the Hospital.[16] The *hospitallier* was in turn responsible to a board of *procureurs*. The principles governing the choice of these *procureurs* and regulating their activities seem to have developed rather casually during the first few years following the establishment of the Reformation. This is at least suggested by the fact that references to them in the municipal records of the period are occasional and brief, and no regular records of their deliberations have survived. By the time Calvin returned to Geneva in 1541 to take full charge of the ecclesiastical establishment, however, the role of the *procureurs* seems to have been fixed. Perhaps it was fixed by some of the reforms that accompanied his return, but this cannot be demonstrated, at least not yet. From 1542 on we have quite detailed records of the deliberations of these *procureurs*[17] and fuller information on how they were selected.

After 1541 these men were chosen in precisely the same way as most other officials of the Genevan Republic. Every February, at the time of the general municipal elections, the retiring small council, the institution that possessed real sovereign power in Geneva, nominated a slate of four or five *procureurs* for the Hospital. This slate normally included two men who would be sitting on the incoming small council and two men who were members of the less important council of sixty and council of two hundred. The slate of nominees, often headed by one of the four syndics who were to be reigning magistrates in the city for the coming year, was then presented to the council of two hundred and to the general council of all citizens for election. These elections were generally pure formalities, however; the real choice was obviously made by the twenty-five members of the ruling small council. The *procureurs* of the Hospital were eligible for re-election and were often, in fact, re-elected, even for several years in a row.

The *procureurs* of the Hospital thus came to constitute a kind of standing committee or department of the city government and were fully equivalent, legally and constitutionally, to the standing committees that supervised the city's accounts, served as courts for adjudicating civil and criminal

---

[15] Among the men who agreed to take on the office during Calvin's lifetime were at least three who also served the city as syndics: Anthoine Chicand, 1540–41; Pierre Jean Jesse, 1550–53; Pernet des Fosses, 1560–61. Other *hospitalliers*, such as Jean Collondaz, 1557–60, and Pierre Sommaretta, 1560, rose to positions on the small council. Several of these men were elderly at the time of appointment and may have looked on the position as a step toward retirement.

[16] A detailed set of regulations on the entire operation of the General Hospital was adopted on March 10, 1552. Duplicate copies can be found in AEG, PH no. 1507 and Arch hosp., Aa2, fols. 1v.–6. Article 35 provides for the appointment of a surgeon; article 38 for the appointment of a teacher.

[17] AEG, Arch. hosp., Aa1, 1542–50; Aa2, 1552–57, 1558–60; Aa3, 1562–63.

cases, and oversaw the city's defenses. The *procureurs* were also fully equivalent to the elders of the consistory, that special court for the supervision of Genevan beliefs and morals that was Calvin's pride and joy and easily the most controversial institution created by the Calvinist Reformation. This fixed constitutional position was not achieved immediately by the *procureurs,* however. The first year in which I find evidence that they were elected in the regular February elections is 1541.[18] Only from 1544 on did the election of hospital *procureurs* become a regular feature of these annual elections, and even then it was not one of the more prominent elections.[19] In fact, in February 1547 the city councils forgot to elect Hospital *procureurs* and had to be reminded in April that something needed to be done.[20] Only from 1552 on did it become customary to choose a syndic as the presiding officer of the Hospital *procureurs,* and even then this did not become an invariable rule. From 1548 on, the selection of the *hospitallier* was ratified at the same time that the *procureurs* were elected. One can generalize by concluding that by 1550 it became an accepted fact of Genevan political life that members of the city's power structure, men from the small group of merchant families who controlled the city, were prepared to take regular turns in personally supervising the single institution that cared for all the city's poor.

This willingness to serve the poor becomes a bit surprising when one discovers just what these *procureurs* of the Hospital had to do. Their most persistent obligation was to attend a weekly meeting on Sunday mornings at 6:00 A.M., before the sermon. In this session the *procureurs* heard the *hospitallier's* report on his work for the week, decided on every proposal he made for special expenditures, and made a decision on every single request from every poor family applying for a weekly ration of bread.[21] This last burden was lightened a bit when it became customary for each of the city's *dizainiers* to screen the requests from the poor in his own *dizaine.* The *dizainiers* were city officials in charge of the subunits into which the city was divided for purposes of defense, and consequently they were in a good position to judge the real needs of the poor families in their own neighborhoods. But the final decision on each grant of bread remained in the hands of the *procureurs.*

The *procureurs* also had many special duties. They were responsible for the care of all the considerable properties allocated to the Hospital. This meant arranging for the cultivation, either by work crews supervised by the *hospitallier* or by lessees, of all of the widely scattered fields and vineyards belonging to the Hospital.[22] It meant collecting rents from lessees of agri-

---

18 AEG, Registres du Conseil (hereafter RC), vol. 35, fol. 64v., Feb. 9, 1541.

19 Recorded every year in AEG, RC, on date.

20 AEG, RC, vol. 42, fol. 75v., Apr. 4, 1547.

21 The *procureurs'* obligations are outlined in some detail in the set of regulations adopted in 1552, described in note 16 above. They are illustrated in copious detail in the registers described in note 17 above.

22 For a list of these properties as of 1542, see Gautier and Joutet, *L'Hôpital-Général,* 37–40.

cultural property and of town houses and loaning cash funds belonging to the Hospital that were not needed immediately.[23] The *procureurs* also had to approve a great variety of legal instruments and contracts. They had to secure approval of legacies bequeathing property to the Hospital, sometimes over the strenuous legal opposition of family heirs.[24] They had to arrange for contracts of apprenticeship, establishing the conditions under which boys in the care of the Hospital were apprenticed out to master craftsmen to learn trades,[25] and they had to approve and finance marriage contracts, setting up the dowries that made it possible for girls in the care of the Hospital to marry.[26] They also were required to represent the interests of the Hospital before the small council, to recommend new appointments of staff members, and to draft new regulations. Above all they had to beg, repeatedly, for supplementary grants of cash to finance adequately all the social programs sponsored by the Hospital.[27]

These obligations, furthermore, were not the only ones the *procureurs* of the Geneva Hospital had to meet. They were all very busy men. Most were merchants with businesses to direct and families to support, and as members of the city's ruling elite they had other governmental obligations. Those on the small council had to attend the almost daily meetings of that body. Many of the *procureurs* were also elected to other standing committees of the city government. From one to three of them, for example, were usually members of the consistory and were therefore obliged to attend that body's weekly meetings and to join in the often venomous tongue-lashings of assorted suspected fornicators, wife-beaters, idolators, and heretics, which constituted the consistory's main activity.

Further reflection on these duties of the Geneva Hospital's *procureurs*, however, suggests rather concrete reasons why, after an initial period of difficulty, it became quite easy to persuade members of the city's power elite to take on these chores. The *procureurs*' management of large amounts of property belonging to the Hospital no doubt brought them information of considerable value to shrewd businessmen. I am not suggesting corruption, for I found no evidence of any.[28] I am merely suggesting that the knowledge of opportunities for good investments and other business deals that came to the *procureurs* as a matter of course may have occasionally proved personally useful to them. Their control of every government ra-

---

[23] Copies of two loan agreements can be found in AEG, Arch. hosp., P, liasse 27, no. 563.

[24] Records of two such legal proceedings can be found in *ibid.*, liasse 56, nos. 1218, 1219.

[25] Copies of apprenticeship contracts were often inserted into the registers of the *procureurs'* deliberations. See, for example, AEG, Arch. hosp., Aa1, fols. 26–29, May–July 1542; and Aa3, fols. 120v., 123v., July 1563.

[26] See, for example, copies of such contracts in AEG, Arch. hosp., Aa3, fols. 7, Apr. 1562; 86v., Mar. 1563; and 100v., Apr. 1563.

[27] AEG, RC, *passim.*

[28] In 1545 the *procureurs* were accused by the city treasurer of mismanaging the Hospital's funds and grain supply, but the accusation was never proved. See E. William Monter, *Calvin's Geneva*.(New York, 1967), 139; and Jean-François Bergier, "La démission du trésorier Amblard Corne," in *Mélanges offerts à Paul-E. Martin* (Geneva, 1961), 456–57, 461–62.

tion of food to every poor family in the city must also have given them considerable political leverage. Although the city's form of government was basically oligarchic, there remained some democratic elements in it. When it came time in the annual elections for all citizens to vote for certain offices in which they could exercise a limited choice—in the election of syndics, for example—a man who had been Hospital *procureur* no doubt had certain advantages over some of his opponents.

It would be possible to demonstrate with considerable exactness the degree to which the *procureurs* of the Hospital were integrated into the ruling class of Geneva, for the Genevan constitution was extremely precise and extremely hierarchical. The surviving records make it quite simple to reconstitute the membership of the interlocking councils that ruled the city and of the standing committees that actually administered that rule, year after year, particularly after the stability following Calvin's return to power in 1541 led to better record keeping. One could establish very precise correlations among memberships in all of these bodies and record the changes over a period of time in these correlations. This work might require the use of statistics, perhaps even of machines, but I doubt that it would prove to be extremely complex, given the small numbers of people involved. Such a study is clearly beyond the scope of this article. Even without it, however, I am reasonably certain that almost all of the *procureurs* of the Hospital were members of Geneva's power elite and that they tended to be more prominent and better entrenched members of that select group as the Reformation regime became consolidated.

Nothing has been said so far about the role of Calvin and other pastors of the Reformed Church in Geneva in the foundation and operation of the General Hospital for the very good reason that there is practically no evidence in any of the voluminous manuscript records of the Hospital that the pastors were involved in its operation in any significant way. One occasionally finds a notice that Calvin or some other pastor had referred a poor man to a *procureur* for consideration for help,[29] but even a notice of this sort is very rare. And one occasionally finds a reference to a request from one of the pastors to borrow equipment from the Hospital—some horses and a wagon, for example[30]—but requests of this sort are even more rare and invariably trivial.

Calvin does, to be sure, occasionally mention the *hospitalliers* and the Hospital *procureurs* in his own writings, most notably in the ecclesiastical ordinances, which he drafted for the city of Geneva in 1541 shortly after his triumphal return from Strasbourg as a constitution for the Reformed

---

[29] See, for example, Calvin to *procureur* Michel Varro, 1542, in Wilhelm Baum, Eduard Cunitz, and Eduard Reuss, eds., *Calvini Opera* (Brunswick, 1863–1900), 11: 482.

[30] See, for example, the request of Pastor de la Faverge, AEG, Arch. hosp., Aa3, fol. 74, Jan. 27, 1563.

Church he was to direct. These ecclesiastical ordinances distinguish four types of ministry within the Church, the fourth being that of the deacons. Calvin further distinguished two types of deacons: those who gather alms for the poor and those who distribute these alms. The *procureurs* of the Hospital filled the first of these functions in Geneva, the *hospitallier* the second. Calvin's ordinances then laid down the method of selection of the *procureurs*, fixed the number of deacons at four *procureurs* and one *hospitallier*, and provided for periodic review of their activity by the pastors and elders of the Church.[31]

Calvin, furthermore, develops principles pertaining to deacons in a number of his writings. There are passages in the *Institutes of the Christian Religion* devoted to the diaconate,[32] and additional comments in some of his other writings, notably in certain of his New Testament commentaries,[33] that help to fill out our knowledge of his views. These statements demonstrate that Calvin felt the diaconate should be a lay ministry devoted solely to aiding the poor. This seemed to him to be the clear sense of the key texts in the Pauline epistles and in the Acts of the Apostles that describe the beginnings of this institution. Calvin frequently coupled his definitions of the diaconate with characteristically vigorous attacks on the Roman Catholic Church for corrupting the institution in its typical way—by making deacons into apprentice-priests and giving them sacramental as well as charitable duties, thus distracting them and the Church from the proper fulfillment of its charitable obligations to society. In developing his definition of the diaconate, Calvin made it quite clear that he believed the key Biblical proof texts revealed that God intended the Church to establish two kinds of deacons: those who would collect alms for the poor and those who would use these alms in helping the poor. It seems quite probable to me that Calvin was thinking of the Genevan arrangement when he developed this distinction. In one of his sermons on 1 Timothy he even uses Genevan language, defining the deacons as *"hospitalliers* and *procureurs* of the poor."[34]

It should be noted that most of these passages were written later in Calvin's career, in the later editions of the *Institutes* and the commentaries, after he had established himself definitively in Geneva and after the Geneva General Hospital had been operating smoothly for many years. I see no evidence that Calvin's arguments had any effect on the creation of this particular Genevan institution. I think, in fact, that there may be some truth

---

[31] For published copies of the relevant parts of these ordinances see Robert M. Kingdon and Jean-François Bergier, eds., *Registres de la Compagnie des Pasteurs de Genève au temps de Calvin* (Geneva, 1962—), 1: 7–8; Rivoire and van Berchem, *Les sources du droit*, 2: 383–85; and *Calvini Opera*, 10a: 23–25.

[32] Particularly 4.3.9, also 4.4.5, 4.5.15, 4.19.22, 4.19.32, of the 1559–60 editions.

[33] See, for example, the commentary on Philippians (*Calvini Opera*, 52: 7–8); on 1 Timothy (*ibid.*, 53: 289–94, 301–03); on Acts of the Apostles (*ibid.*, 48: 122); and 1 Corinthians (*ibid.*, 49: 507).

[34] *Ibid.*, 53: 291.

in the reverse proposition: that when it came to deciding how the Christian community should institutionalize its obligation to help the poor, it was not Calvin who influenced Geneva, but rather Geneva that influenced Calvin.[35]

As for Calvin's role in the later development of the General Hospital, I suspect it was profound but extremely indirect. While he did not in any sense create or direct this institution, he did consecrate it. By making the *procureurs* and *hospitalliers* into deacons he made them into lay ministers of the Christian Church, different in function but not in dignity from the ordained clergy. He presented a warrant for this definition, furthermore, from the Word of God, from the Bible. This consecration of the office may well have had a powerful effect on the members of Geneva's ruling elite. It may well provide yet another explanation for the willingness of a good number of them to take on the chores associated with running the Hospital.

The preceding may seem to provide support for an argument that has found much favor in recent years particularly among conservative churchmen and scholars, an argument that holds that Calvin never entered directly into the political arena, that his energies were concentrated entirely upon preaching the Word of God, and that this constitutes a model that modern pastors would do well to emulate. One can certainly find powerful evidence for this argument in studying the relations between the first Calvinist pastors and the General Hospital, the one institution charged by the Genevan community with meeting all the internal social problems it had to face. This conclusion, however, is not one that really satisfies me. To understand fully the relations between Calvin and the General Hospital in Geneva, one needs to place them in context by looking also at the relations between Calvin and other Genevan institutions. One rather instructive comparison can be gained by examining Calvin's relations with the consistory. This ecclesiastical court was composed partly of elected lay elders who were chosen every February in the same way that the Hospital *procureurs* were chosen. Consequently the consistory could be regarded as yet another standing committee of the Genevan municipal government. But it also included the ordained preachers of the Genevan Church. These preachers, led by Calvin, certainly exercised their right to attend consistory meetings. Calvin was almost always in attendance himself, except when illness or travel kept him away. And he was often one of the most active members, administering the scoldings that were stock punishment with a polemical skill that reduced most of those accused of incorrect belief or immoral behavior to tears and repentance but provoked a few to outright rebellion.

Calvin insisted, furthermore, on a voice in the selection of the lay elders

---

[35] See also the similar conclusion of J. K. S. Reid, in his "Diakonia in the Thought of Calvin," in James I. McCord and T. H. L. Parker, eds., *Service in Christ: Essays Presented to Karl Barth on His 80th Birthday* (London, 1966), 106.

who sat on the consistory. To do this he had to intervene in the Genevan elections, and he did not hesitate to do so. Every February, at the meetings for the annual elections, Calvin was invited to open the ceremonies with prayer. Under the general rules of election, since he was never a voting citizen of Geneva, this might have ended his participation in these meetings. But there were special rules governing the election of elders contained in the ecclesiastical ordinances that Calvin had drafted for the city. These rules provided that the small council, when it drew up its slate of nominees for elders every year, should consult with the city's pastors. They also provided that the elders should normally be re-elected every year, but that such re-elections should be subject to annual review.[36] If an elder's performance was judged satisfactory, he could be re-elected; if not, he was replaced. These provisions gave Calvin extensive rights in the election of elders, rights both to be consulted about, and, in effect, to veto, nominations. It may have taken him some time to make good these rights; the election records are not as precise as they might be on this point. It is clear, however, that "the ministers" were consulted on the selection of elders in 1546 and 1547; that "the ministers . . . through their spokesman, M. Calvin" were consulted in 1552; that Calvin, again representing the entire corps of pastors, was consulted in 1556, 1557, and 1558; that two other pastors reported on the wishes of the company in 1559; and that from 1560 on, the entire company of pastors was invited to the council session at which the year's slate of elders was drawn up.[37] The innovation of 1560 was adopted at the request of Calvin and Pierre Viret.[38] At the same time these two accomplished yet another breakthrough in the selection of elders by persuading the council to nominate a few elders who were not native-born citizens of Geneva but immigrants. The first of these was the Marquis Galeazzo Carracciolo, a prominent Italian convert to Calvinism. This not only marked a rather significant departure from the fixed Genevan constitutional rule that the city offices be limited to native-born citizens; it also increased Calvin's power and maneuverability since many of the immigrants were among his most zealous supporters.

There is no evidence that during all these years Calvin and the other pastors took any similar interest in the annual election of deacons. This was not for lack of legal warrant, since the ecclesiastical ordinances provided that deacons be elected in the same way as elders. But in spite of these provisions, and in spite of the fact that the deacons were technically min-

[36] Kingdon and Bergier, *Registres de la Campagnie des Pasteurs*, 1: 7; Rivoire and van Berchem, *Les sources du droit*, 2: 383; *Calvini Opera*, 10a: 22–23.

[37] AEG, RC, vol. 41, fol. 9, Feb. 8, 1546; vol. 42, fol. 17v., Feb. 11, 1547; vol. 46, fol. 151v., Feb. 11, 1552; vol. 51, fols. 7–7v., Feb. 12, 1556; vol. 53, fol. 7v., Feb. 11, 1557; vol. 54, fol. 77, Feb. 8, 1558; vol. 55, fol. 4v., Feb. 9, 1559; vol. 56, fol. 4v., Feb. 8, 1560; vol. 56, fol. 147, Feb. 13, 1561; vol. 57, fol. 5, Feb. 12, 1562; vol. 58, fol. 5, Feb. 11, 1563; vol. 59, fol. 3v., Feb. 10, 1564.

[38] For the request, see *Calvini Opera*, 21: 726–27, Jan. 30, 1560; for the edict granting the request, see *ibid.*, 727–28, Feb. 1, 1560. For the record of the election itself, see AEG, RC, vol. 56, fol. 4v., Feb. 8, 1560.

isters of the Church, they still seem to have been elected in the same way as the supervisors of the fortresses and the members of the chamber of accounts. Not until 1562 do the annual election records reveal any change in this procedure. In that year the pastors finally intervened openly in the election of deacons, but there is no evidence that Calvin himself was involved in this intervention. In 1560 he and Viret had persuaded the council to consult on elections with the pastors as a body rather than allow Calvin to act as their representative.[39] As he became increasingly distracted by developments in his native France and by problems with his own health, Calvin tended to allow his colleagues to take his place in dealings with the city councils.

In 1562, then, the record reveals that the pastors appeared in a body before the small council to protest that the ecclesiastical ordinances were not being strictly observed in the election of the Hospital *procureurs*. Taking this protest into account, the small council then proceeded to review the performance of the incumbent *procureurs* before proceeding to the election of new ones.[40] A similar review in consultation with the pastors preceded the elections of 1563 and 1564, the last years of Calvin's life.[41] This clerical intervention in the selection of deacons had one very visible, practical result; it meant that more of the same men tended to get elected to both the consistory and the group administering the Hospital. In each of the yearly elections before 1562, from one to three out of the total four or five *procureurs* were also elected elders. Only in 1556 were more than one-third of the total number of deacons also elders. After the 1562 intervention three of the four *procureurs* were elders, constituting a clear majority. The pastors had succeeded in consolidating a power elite of lay supporters; a small group of laymen completely devoted to the pastors held almost all the lay offices in the Church.

It may still be argued that Calvin intervened in politics only when he felt that matters of belief were at stake, that he tried to control elections to the consistory because it controlled religious belief in Geneva, but that he kept hands off the General Hospital because it only ministered to men's bodies. It would be a mistake, however, to conclude that Calvin took no interest in problems of social welfare. This can best be demonstrated by looking at the history of yet another institution created in Geneva during the Refor-

39 *Calvini Opera*, 21: 726–27; AEG, RC, vol. 56, fol. 4v.

40 AEG, RC, vol. 57, fol. 5v., Feb. 12, 1562. The specific protest by the pastors was that the council was ignoring the ecclesiastical ordinances by selecting five *procureurs* rather than four, the number specified by the ordinances. A precedent for consultation with the pastors in the selection of a deacon had been established in 1561. When Pernet des Fosses resigned as *hospitallier*, the small council voted to consult the pastors about his replacement. AEG, RC, vol. 56, fol. 196v., May 29, 1561. Perhaps even earlier precedents could be found in pastors' appeals to the small council to name or replace a *hospitallier*, beginning with Farel's plea, shortly after Claude Salomon's death, that a replacement be chosen quickly. Rivoire, van Berchem, and Gardy, *Registres du Conseil de Genève*, 13: 414, Jan. 28, 1536.

41 AEG, RC, vol. 58, fol. 5, Feb. 11, 1563; vol. 59, fol. 3v., Feb. 10, 1564.

mation, the Bourse française.[42] One social problem, which the General Hospital was not prepared to handle, was how to help the dozens of poor refugees who were now moving into Geneva from other countries as a result of the spread of the Reformation. The Hospital's programs were intended to meet only the problems of native Genevans and transients planning to spend a single night in Geneva. It was not ready to handle the needs of refugees who wanted to settle in Geneva more or less permanently. This created a considerable gap in the Hospital's coverage that Calvin sought to remedy with the Bourse française, which was essentially a large fund of cash. The money was collected from wealthy French refugees to Geneva— from printers like Robert Estienne, lawyers like Germain Colladon, and businessmen like Laurent de Normandie—and distributed to poor French refugees who because of illness, family problems, or the loss of property at home were having trouble supporting themselves. The Bourse française, unlike the Hospital, was a private institution. It was run by laymen bearing the title of deacons, who were elected by the contributors. These deacons collected the money, doled it out, and kept accounts of both receipts and payments. In these respects the Bourse française was much like the Hospital, but it differed in that it attracted Calvin's interest and powerful personal support from the beginning. In fact he may well have founded it. The accounts reveal that in the earliest years he was almost invariably the most generous single contributor, no doubt drawing from his rather large Geneva salary for this charitable purpose.[43] On at least one occasion the deacons of the Bourse française even met in Calvin's house to elect officers for the coming year.[44]

When one considers this wider context, one must conclude, I feel, that Calvin was neither indifferent to the needs of the poor nor unwilling to enter politics to advance a cause he valued. He simply selected with care the particular arenas in which he deployed his formidable energies. If he did not work hard to resolve Geneva's social problems personally, it was probably because he thought they were already being handled by men of competence whom he trusted. I am led to this conclusion partly by a study of the men who actually became *hospitalliers* and *procureurs* of the Hospital.[45] While one can find among them representatives of almost every shade of Genevan political opinion, the great majority and the most active of them were especially devoted to Calvin's leadership. A few examples will help to illustrate this contention. Among the very first *procureurs* of the General Hospital, who were commissioned first to close down the earlier institutions and then to superintend the new one, the man who was easily the most

---

[42] The best study of this institution of which I know is Henri Grandjean, "La bourse française de Genève (1550–1849)," in *Etrennes Genevoises, 1927* (Geneva, 1927), 46–60.

[43] AEG, Arch. hosp., Kg12, fol. 1, Oct. 1550; fol. 7, Nov. 1550; fol. 11, Dec. 1550.

[44] *Ibid.*, Kg15, fol. 1, July 1554.

[45] See Robert M. Kingdon, "The Deacons of the Reformed Church in Calvin's Geneva," in *Mélanges d'histoire du XVIᵉ siècle offerts à Henri Meylan* (Geneva, 1970), 81–90.

active was Claude Bernard.[46] Bernard was also one of the key lay leaders of the entire early Reformation. He had been converted to Protestantism early, probably by his brother, a former priest. He was an enthusiastic supporter of Farel and even provided Farel and Viret with lodgings in his own house during the period when the preaching of these two firebrands was persuading Geneva to abandon Roman Catholicism. Bernard was involved in many of the specific moves that culminated in the break with Rome, and he supported Farel and Calvin strongly when they were established as the principal pastors of the new Reformed Church.[47]

The most active *procureur* of the Hospital in the next few years was Jean Chautemps. Like Bernard, he was also one of the first to renounce Roman Catholicism, having been converted to Protestantism by Farel. He had helped to engineer the break with Rome and supported Farel and Calvin against local opposition. As one of the group who arranged for Calvin's return in 1541,[48] he rose to political power and became a member of the small council in 1542. Throughout the bitter internal controversies that followed he continued to support Calvin.[49]

The leading *procureur* of the Hospital in Calvin's last years was Guillaume Chicand. He had been a particularly active lay member of the consistory since 1546, working closely with Calvin.[50] He vigorously supported Calvin against his last local enemies, the Perrinists, in 1555. Soon thereafter he won positions of considerable political power, joining the small council in 1556 and becoming syndic in 1557.[51] With men like these running the Hospital, Calvin hardly needed to intervene directly in its operations.

A final evaluation of the Geneva General Hospital should attempt to judge its success. I have not studied this problem in any detail, but the evidence that has come to my attention suggests that it suffered considerable growing pains until about 1547[52] and was a considerable success from then on in meeting the social problems faced by the Genevan community. There were, to be sure, occasional complaints about its operation. In 1584, for example, the city's pastors demanded a thorough investigation of the Hospital and suggested a number of reforms in its administration.[53] But complaints of this sort never, in fact, led to a major change in the institution.

[46] See the repeated references to Bernard's appeals for the Hospital in Rivoire, van Berchem, and Gardy, *Registres du Conseil de Genève*, 13: *passim*.

[47] AEG, MSS, Louis Sordet, "Dictionnaire des familles genevoises," 1: 92–93; *Calvini Opera*, 21: 224–25, Apr. 20, 1538.

[48] *Calvini Opera*, 21: 282, Sept. 9, 1541.

[49] AEG, Sordet, "Dictionnaire," 1: 243.

[50] *Calvini Opera*, 21: 400, Mar. 21, 1547; 402, Apr. 15, 1547; 527, Nov. 15, 1552. AEG, Registres du Consistoire, *passim*.

[51] AEG, Sordet, "Dictionnaire," 1: 255.

[52] Repeated complaints from Calvin and the other pastors about the operations of the Hospital in 1547 led to a general review by the small council and the selection of new *procureurs* for 1548. *Calvini Opera*, 21: 404–05, May 24, 1547; 414, Sept. 26, 1547; AEG, RC, vol. 42, fol. 354, Nov. 28, 1547. For the elections, see RC, vol. 43, fol. 13v., Feb. 7, 1548.

[53] Monter, *Calvin's Geneva*, 220.

A final evaluation of the Geneva General Hospital should also attempt to judge its uniqueness and influence. This would require extensive comparative studies. A preliminary survey of published studies of welfare reform in other cities, however, already suggests to me the conclusion that the Genevan reforms were different not in kind but in degree from those of most other contemporary municipalities. They were more thorough, more radical in their break with the past. It was probably Geneva's uncompromising brand of Protestantism that made this radicalism possible.

In many contemporary cities enlightened laymen took the lead in engineering welfare reforms. Their actions were often provoked by famine in the area around their city, famine that was particularly reflected by a sharp increase in begging as starving peasants from the hinterland came into relatively better-supplied cities in a last desperate attempt to stay alive. The welfare reforms in Lyon and Venice, for example, can be related directly to famines in the immediately preceding years.[54] But the lay reformers' actions were also stimulated by altruism, as they sought to do something in a practical way to resolve problems the existing social institutions could no longer handle. The councilors of Geneva were thus following a pattern established elsewhere when they assumed the sole right to organize and direct charity in their city.

The Genevans did not, however, have to face the opposition to reform that the lay leaders of other cities did, opposition that came mostly from the orthodox Catholic clergy. The mendicant orders protested particularly vehemently since attempts to outlaw begging and substitute secular, institutionalized charity threatened their very existence. But opposition also came from bishops, particularly after the Council of Trent later in the century vested all supervisory powers over charitable institutions in the hands of bishops. Thus the burghers of Catholic Ypres had to face attacks from members of the mendicant orders who complained that their welfare reforms smacked of heresy and Lutheranism. The burghers were able to limit such attacks only by an appeal to that bastion of Catholic orthodoxy, the theological faculty of the University of Paris, which gave conditional approval to their reform.[55] And the welfare reformers of Lyon had to face the indifference of the archbishop and the outright hostility of the local inquisitor, who again smelled heresy in their proposals.[56] In Geneva this block to change did not exist. The Catholic clergy and many of its supporters had been expelled from the city before welfare reform was adopted. Their Protestant successors, as we have seen, warmly supported the changes.

[54] Davis, "Poor Relief, Humanism, and Heresy," 228–29; Brian Pullan, "The Famine in Venice and the New Poor Law, 1527–1529," *Bollettino dell'Istituto di Storia della Società e dello Stato Veneziano*, 5–6 (1963–64): 141–202.

[55] Nolf, *La réforme de la bienfaisance publique à Ypres*, xlviii–lx.

[56] For the indifference of the absentee archbishop and the inquisitor's attack, see Davis, "Poor Relief, Humanism, and Heresy," 236, 238, 259–62.

This is not to say that the welfare reformers were invariably Protestant. Sometimes they were and sometimes they were not. There was occasionally some fire behind the smoke of their opponents' accusations, but not always. Welfare reform in the German cities seems often to have developed as it did in Geneva. It was the work of Protestant sympathizers active in a city government at a time before that government had actually committed itself to the Lutheran form of Protestantism, which came to prevail in most of Germany. This seems to have been the case at least in Nuremberg. There welfare reform was enacted in 1522 by a city council that included many humanists of Lutheran sympathies and whose clerk was Lazarus Spengler, a particularly devoted follower of Luther. And welfare reform in Nuremberg became effective partly because it was supported by the provosts of the two parish churches, whose Lutheran sympathies were reflected most strikingly in their choice of Lutheran preachers for their pulpits in these same years.[57] This may also have been the case in Strasbourg. There the welfare reforms were adopted in 1523 and 1524 on the basis of recommendations made late in 1522 by a committee of laymen, two of whom were known for their Lutheran sympathies. These recommendations had been drafted at a time when the community was obviously moving in a Protestant direction, before Martin Bucer, Wolfgang Capito, and Matthias Zell, the three reformers who really made the city Protestant, began to preach in the city.[58]

It seems plausible that these German models influenced the development of welfare reform in other countries. One cannot prove direct influence, however, partly because so many of these other countries remained Catholic and hence would deny or disguise influence that might be labeled Lutheran. The welfare reformers in the Netherlands, for example, acknowledged no German inspiration. Yet the reforms in that country followed so closely on the reforms in Germany, and resemble the German measures so much, that it seems at least possible that the Netherlanders modeled themselves after the Germans. In particular the seminal reforms in Mons and Ypres, adopted in 1525, resemble the Strasbourg reforms of 1523-24.[59] We know that the Strasbourg reform excited the admiration of at least one prominent Dutch humanist in 1526.[60] There were no doubt others like him. Similarly, the re-

[57] See Harold J. Grimm, "Luther's Contributions to Sixteenth-Century Organization of Poor Relief," to be published in the *Archiv für Reformationsgeschichte* (1970). Professor Grimm kindly lent me a draft of his article.

[58] Miriam Usher Chrisman, *Strasbourg and the Reform: A Study in the Process of Change* (New Haven, 1967), 275–83. See also Otto Winckelmann, *Das Fürsorgewesen der Stadt Strassburg vor und nach der Reformation bis zum Ausgang des sechzehnten Jahrhunderts* (Leipzig, 1922).

[59] This was the argument of Otto Winckelmann, developed most fully in his article, "Über die ältesten Armenordnungen der Reformationszeit (1522–1525)," *Historische Vierteljahrschrift*, 17 (1914–15): 187–228; 361–400. It was carefully evaluated and cautiously endorsed, in a modified form, by Bonenfant in "Les origines et le caractère de la réforme," 140–43. It was thus supported by two of the most eminent specialists in this field.

[60] This was Gerard Geldenhouwer of the circle of Vives. See his letter of August 21, 1526, in Henry de Vocht, ed., *Literae virorum eruditorum ad Franciscum Craneveldium, 1522–1528* (Louvain, 1928), 515; noted and quoted by Marcel Bataillon in "J. L. Vives, réformateur de la bienfaisance," *Bibliothèque d'Humanisme et Renaissance*, 14 (1952): 144.

forms in Venice, adopted in 1528 and 1529, followed soon after the reforms in Germany. There were extensive commercial relations between Venice and Nuremberg, and in 1505 Nuremberg had copied Venetian wardship laws. It seems at least possible that Venice returned the compliment when economic crisis forced its government to reform her welfare legislation.[61]

It is hard to stretch the chain of German influence directly to Geneva. While Calvin was personally influenced deeply by the ecclesiastical reforms he observed in Strasbourg, he was not responsible, as we have noticed, for the fundamental change in Geneva's welfare program. It seems much more likely that the merchants of Geneva were influenced by the establishment, in 1531–34, of the Aumône-Général in Lyon. Geneva's merchants were in constant commercial contact with Lyon, and the Aumône-Général was founded just before the Geneva General Hospital and exercised many of the same functions.

In some contemporary cities, intellectuals assumed a role in welfare reform similar to Calvin's in Geneva. In other words, rather than initiating change, intellectuals often justified the changes engineered by the practical business leaders of the community. This is most strikingly the case with Juan Luis Vives, whose *De subventione pauperum* was the most eloquent single plea for the reform of poor relief published in the early sixteenth century. But it was published in the Low Countries in 1526, the year after reform had already been adopted in the cities of Mons and Ypres.[62] It may thus be regarded, like Calvin's *Ecclesiastical Ordinances*, as more a consecration of reform already under way than an impetus to new reform. There are, however, exceptions to this pattern. The most striking that have come to my attention are the eloquent pleas made in Lyon by two crusading Catholic clergymen, Jean de Vauzelles, a humanist priest and doctor of laws, and Santo Pagnini of Lucca, a humanist Dominican theologian. These men were among the leaders in the campaign for the establishment of the Aumône-Général in Lyon.[63] Only more extensive comparative studies can demonstrate which pattern was the more common.

In few cities, however, were the welfare reforms as radical as in Geneva. While laymen were granted the real power of direction everywhere, a role was often reserved to the clergy. Sometimes it involved only exhorting the people to support the new institutions of charity and calling the attention of the lay authorities to poor individuals deserving assistance, as in Ypres;[64] sometimes it meant actually administering the new charities, as in Venice.[65] Rarely was the management of charity reserved to the laity to the same de-

61 Pullan, "Famine in Venice," 143–44.

62 Bonenfant, "Les origines et le caractère de la réforme," 119–23; Bataillon, "J. L. Vives," 141–43.

63 Davis, "Poor Relief, Humanism, and Heresy," 231–36.

64 Bonenfant, "Les origines et le caractère de la réforme," 122, 125. See also references to articles 10 and 11 of the 1525 ordinance in Nolf, *La réforme de la bienfaisance publique à Ypres*, xxx, 23.

65 Pullan, "Famine in Venice," 173–74.

gree as in Geneva. Similarly, while all of these cities created new institutions to rationalize the administration of charity, they seldom abolished all of the older ones, as was done in Geneva. Thus the large Mehrere Hospital and other medieval charitable institutions in Strasbourg survived the reforms of 1522–24;[66] three hospitals in Ypres continued to function after the creation of the Bourse commune in 1525;[67] the Hôtel-Dieu, or hospital of Lyon, already under municipal management, survived the creation of the Aumône-Général in 1531–34.[68] The new institution, therefore, often supplemented and coordinated existing programs. Most often it provided external relief to the poor in their homes, a provision frequently linked with the outlawry of begging. Assistance to the poor without homes, which was also provided by the Geneva General Hospital, was often reserved in other cities to hospitals that were medieval foundations.

The greater radicalism of the Genevan reforms may help to explain their greater permanence, for the Geneva General Hospital proved to be a remarkably durable institution. It continued in operation until the late nineteenth century with only one major interruption, which was caused by the French Revolution. In 1869 it was reorganized and converted into a new institution called the Hospice-Général, with headquarters in the same neighborhood as the old General Hospital. The Hospice-Général is still standing and ministering to the problems of the poor in Geneva in ways that have not changed substantially since 1535. It would appear that there are times in history when radical reform, however painful it may seem at the time, proves to be more permanent than moderate reform.

[66] Winckelmann, *Das Fürsorgewesen der Stadt Strassburg*, 122–67.
[67] Nolf, *La réforme de la bienfaisance publique à Ypres*, xli-xlii.
[68] Davis, "Poor Relief, Humanism, and Heresy," 240–43; Imbert, "L'Eglise et l'Etat," 579–80.

VII

THE DEACONS OF THE REFORMED CHURCH IN CALVIN'S GENEVA *

Among the ecclesiastical institutions which John Calvin found corrupted by the Roman Church of his time and which he wished to reform, was the deaconate. He insisted that the deaconate must be a separate lay ministry, not a sort of apprenticeship for the priesthood. And he insisted that deacons should have only one basic function, that they should be "ceux qu'on ordonne pour avoir le soin des povres, et pour distribuer les aumosnes."[1] He did not believe that they should be expected to assist regularly in the administration of sacraments or to have general responsibility for the management of church property. Calvin consequently made of the deacons social workers, and focused the social concerns of the Church in the institution of the deaconate. Detailed studies of the formation and operation of the Calvinist deaconate should therefore help us to understand more fully what the earliest Calvinists thought were the social obligations of the Christian community and how they thought these obligations should be met.

The earliest Calvinist community was, of course, Geneva. And Geneva served as a kind of model to other communities as the Calvinist Reformation spread. A study of the Calvinist deaconate should logically begin, therefore, with the deacons of Geneva. It is to such a study that this paper is devoted. Fortunately the records of the deacons of the Reformed Church in Geneva during Calvin's ministry there have been preserved, in the *Archives d'Etat de Genève*, and are admirably classified and indexed.[2] They have already been studied by several Genevan scholars, notably Léon Gautier.[3] But they merit further and more extended study. This paper is a first, and somewhat preliminary step toward such a study.

The Genevan deaconate was described most concisely in the Ecclesiastical Ordinances of 1541, which Calvin himself drafted, shortly after his triumphal and definitive return to the city. These ordinances provide for the establishment of four kinds of ministry to supply leadership for the local Church. The fourth kind of

* Most of the material upon which this paper is based was gathered while I was in Europe on a research trip made possible by a grant from the American Philosophical Society, in connection with a study I was asked to prepare by the Social Welfare History Group.

[1] BAUM, CUNITZ, and REUSS, eds., *Calvini Opera* (hereafter cited as CO), LIII, 289, in commentary on I Tim. 3:6-7.

[2] For a brief description of them, see Gustave VAUCHER, "Archives hospitalières aux Archives de Genève", *Mélanges offerts par ses confrères étrangers à Charles Braibant* (Brussels, 1959), p. 523-529.

[3] In Léon GAUTIER & E. JOUTET, *L'Hôpital-Général de Genève de 1535 à 1545 et l'Hospice Général de 1869 à 1914* (Geneva, Kündig, 1914).

ministry was the deaconate.[4] There were to be two types of deacons, one to gathe: and administer property which would be used for the relief of the poor, the other t‹ supervise the actual daily use of this property to help the poor. The first kind o deacon Calvin called a *procureur*, the second he called a *hospitallier*. Calvin developec this distinction of two types of deacons in his later writings, both in the editions of th‹ *Institution de la Religion Chrétienne* and in certain of his commentaries on books of th‹ New Testament.[5] He believed this distinction had warrant in Scripture, particularly in certain proof texts in the epistles of the Apostle Paul.

The Ecclesiastical Ordinances of 1541 also provided some specific recommenda tions on the deacons. There were to be five of them, four *procureurs* and one *hospitallier* They were to be elected every year, by the *Conseil Général* of Geneva, in the sam‹ way as the lay elders who sat on the Consistory. Their work was to be reviewe‹ every three months by the ordained pastors and elders of the city.

In working out these specifications, however, Calvin was not creating a nev institution. He was rather providing a religious warrant, drawn from the Bible, for ‹ program of social work already established. He was giving city officials who wer‹ already at work a special place of honor in the Church. In short, he was consecratin‹ an existing institution.

That institution was the *Hôpital-Général*. It was a product of the Reformation but had been established before Calvin's first arrival in Geneva, in 1535, as one of ‹ series of measures leading to the definitive break with the Church of Rome. It was th‹ work of the same laymen who had been converted to Protestantism by Farel an‹ Viret and who were to welcome and support Calvin in his program of Reformation‹

The *Hôpital-Général* consolidated and organized in one institution programs fo‹ social welfare which had previously been conducted by several institutions.[6] Seve› of these earlier institutions were called hospitals. They were private foundations created by the gifts of wealthy individuals or families, to provide for the repose o their souls and the care of the poor. They maintained buildings in which were provide‹ free food and lodgings for widows, the crippled, those sick of non-contagious diseases poor pilgrims passing through the city, and others. A typical one of these hospitals wa managed by a *rector* or *procureur* who was usually a priest of a chapel attached to th hospital. He was appointed by the heirs of the donor or by some group specified b‹ the donor. He was assisted by a *hospitallier*, who was directly responsible for admin istering help to the poor. The *hospitallier* was usually a layman, often appointed b‹ the city council.

An eighth earlier institution was called the *Boîte de Toutes Ames*. It was a munici› pal foundation, apparently designed, judging from its name, for raising money to pa‹ for masses for the dead, but also designed for service to the poor. It received mone‹

[4] For published copies of the relevant parts of these ordinances, see Robert M. KINGDO‹ and Jean-François BERGIER, eds., *Registres de la Compagnie des Pasteurs de Genève au temps ‹ Calvin*, I (Geneva, Droz, 1964), 7-8; Emile RIVOIRE and Victor VAN BERCHEM, *Les source du droit du canton de Genève*, 4 vols. (Aarau, Sauerländer, 1927-1935), II, 383-385; CO, Xa, 23-2:

[5] See CO, II, 783 and IV, 624-625 (IV.3.9 of the 1559-1560 editions of the *Institut*); XLI> 507 (commentary on I Cor. 12:28); LIII, 291 (commentary on I Tim. 3:6-7).

[6] For an extended analysis of these earlier institutions, see J. J. CHAPONNIÈRE and L. SORDE⸱ "Des hôpitaux de Genève avant la Réformation", *Mémoires et documents publiés par la Sociét d'histoire et d'archéologie de Genève*, III (1844), 165-471.

from the city government for such services as placing orphans in private homes and providing for their support. It was administered by lay *procureurs* selected by the city council.

The legislation which created the *Hôpital-Général* [7] earmarked for its support all the property belonging to these earlier institutions. It also earmarked to the support of the *Hôpital-Général* all that property previously belonging to churches, convents, and confraternities which had previously been allocated for the support of pious uses. While not all of this property remained in the hands of the Genevan state, enough remained to make possible the support of the new *Hôpital*. The large convent of Sainte-Claire, on the rue Verdaine as it enters the Bourg-de-Four in the center of Geneva, was made the headquarters building of the *Hôpital*. Five men were selected by the city council as commissioners, to inventory the property of the earlier institutions and establish a plan for a single hospital. They became the first *procureurs* of the new *Hôpital-Général*. At their suggestion another man was appointed to live in the new institution and superintend its welfare programs. He became its first *hospitallier*. These six men are really the first deacons of the Reformed Church in Geneva, even though they never bore that title, even though they were selected before Calvin arrived.

For the next several years these deacons had to struggle to win acceptance as a regular part of the Genevan community. These were, of course, years of general struggle, often desperate struggle, to establish the Reformation in Geneva. We should not be surprised that city officials were too busy to worry about the problems of the poor or at least to keep records of programs for the poor. The *Hôpital-Général* is mentioned only rarely in the *Registres du Conseil* of the period. Most of the references are to appeals from one of the *procureurs*, most commonly from Claude Bernard, the most active of the first *procureurs*, for supplementary funds or other assistance.[8] There seems to have been no provisions for regular election of deacons.[9] Whenever a *hospitallier* died, or resigned, or was forced out of office, a new one was selected. Whenever it seemed necessary to provide for closer supervision of the *Hôpital*, new *procureurs* were chosen. No regular records were kept, or at least none survive. We have only occasional records of certain *hospitalliers*, notably Claude Magnin.[10]

After 1541, the year of Calvin's definitive return to Geneva, the situation in the city generally and in the *Hôpital* particularly was stabilized. A group of *procureurs* chosen late in 1541, from among Calvin's most ardent supporters, continued in office until 1548, with only one replacement, in 1546, due to a death. A *hospitallier* chosen in 1543, Pierre de Rages, stayed in office until his death in 1550. The frequent changes of the early years were over. These new deacons also began keeping records more

---

[7] Published copies in Emile RIVOIRE, Victor VAN BERCHEM, and Frédéric GARDY, eds,. *Registres du Conseil de Genève*, 13 vols. (Geneva, 1900-1940), XIII, 351-352; E. RIVOIRE and V. VAN BERCHEM, *Sources*, II, 302-304; L. GAUTIER, *L'Hôpital-Général*, p. 12-14.

[8] See E. RIVOIRE, V. VAN BERCHEM, and F. GARDY, *Registres*, XIII, *passim*.

[9] For tabulated information on the election of all the deacons during Calvin's ministry in Geneva, with archival references, see Appendix to this paper.

[10] See the account books in Archives d'Etat de Genève, hereafter cited as AEG; Archives hospitalières, hereafter cited as Arch. hosp., Fe 1 and Fe 2.

systematically, or at least more of their records have survived. From 1542 on, with only a few lacunae, we have records of the weekly meetings of the deacons.[11] They also began to work out standard procedures for administering their programs. By 1552 these procedures were codified, in a set of regulations describing all the principal activities of the *Hôpital*.[12] In 1553, the duties of the *hospitallier* were described in greater detail, in a special set of regulations governing his office.[13]

In the years after 1541, the attention of the city government to the programs of the *Hôpital* also seems to have increased. Its problems are mentioned more often in the *Registres du Conseil*, and more care was taken in the selection of the deacons. It still took several years, apparently, for all the provisions of Calvin's ecclesiastical ordinances to take effect. This can be illustrated by a study of the elections of the *procureurs* and *hospitalliers*.[14] In February of every year, the *Conseil Général* of Geneva gathered for the elections of the officers and councillors who would govern the city in the coming year. The *Registres du Conseil* contain detailed records of these annual elections. I do not find the election of deacons mentioned regularly in these records until 1544, however, and then the decision that was taken was merely to continue the existing *procureurs* in office. A similar decision was taken in 1546. In 1547, the Conseil forgot to elect *procureurs* at the time of the regular February elections, and only in April voted to continue the existing *procureurs* in office. Only in 1548, did the election of deacons become a fixed and regular part of the annual elections in Geneva. In that year a new set of *procureurs* was elected, and it was voted to continue the *hospitallier* in office. From then on a group of *procureurs* was elected every February. The group usually contained several *procureurs* who had held the office earlier, but there were occasional changes. In 1550 and in 1551 it was decided to replace as a *procureur* a man who had just been elected as one of the city's four ruling syndics for the year. But in 1552 it was decided to retain on the board of *procureurs* a man who had been elected syndic and to make him its presiding officer. At the same time the size of the board was expanded by adding a fifth member. It became normal practice every year after that, to elect a syndic as *procureur* of the *Hôpital*. There is only one exception in Calvin's lifetime—1562. It also became normal practice to elect five *procureurs*, until 1562, when the number was cut back to four. There is again one exception—1554.

These developments in the elections of deacons almost surely meant that they were of increasing importance in the city. The fact that their work was subject to annual review and approval, meant that the administration of the program to help the poor had to maintain the support of the entire Genevan population. The fact that the board of *procureurs* came to be presided over almost invariably by a syndic, gave the office more prestige and also more political power. In almost every respect the deacons of the Genevan Church became an administrative department of the Genevan government. Both *procureurs* and *hospitalliers* were chosen by the same people and in the same ways as the other officers of the Genevan state.

[11] AEG, Arch. hosp., Aa 1 (1542-1550), Aa 2 (1552-1560), Aa 3 (1562-1563).
[12] Duplicate copies in AEG, PH No. 1507, and Arch. hosp., Aa 2, fols. IV.-6.
[13] Published in E. RIVOIRE and V. VAN BERCHEM, *Sources*, III, 13-16, based on AEG, PH No. 1533. Another manuscript copy can be found in AEG, Arch. hosp., Aa 2, insert between fols. 39 and 40.
[14] See Appendix to this paper for names and references.

The *procureurs* were chosen in precisely the same way as the members of such other standing committees of the government as the *Chambre des Comptes*, the Consistory, the courts—of *premières appellations*, of *suprêmes appellations*, of *procès criminels*—, and the board of supervisors of the *forteresses*. In each case, the Small Council drew up a slate of nominees for the committee. This slate was presented to the Council of Two Hundred for election, and then to the *Conseil Général* of the entire citizenry for final approval. In almost every instance, the slate presented by the Small Council was elected without change. The board of *procureurs* shared with several of these standing committees the distinction of being chaired by a syndic. It may not have been the most important and prestigious of these bodies, but it came to hold a secure place among them.

The *hospitalliers* were chosen in much the same way as the executive officers of the Genevan government, as, for example, the four reigning syndics. In each case, the Small Council drew up a slate with twice as many nominees as there were positions. From this slate, a more widely representative Council made the final choice. Thus when a new *hospitallier* had to be selected, the Small Council drew up a slate of two names, and then presented it to the Council of Two Hundred which made the final single selection. This procedure was not repeated every February, however, as it was in the election of syndics. A *hospitallier* was elected only when another *hospitallier* had to be replaced—because of death, of departure from the city, or of complaints which convinced the Small Council that a change was necessary. In the general February elections a *hospitallier* was often reelected, when the *procureurs* were elected, but the change to a new *hospitallier* was seldom made at that time.

Records of all these elections of deacons say curiously little about their place in the Church. Calvin and the other pastors of the Church were seldom consulted in these elections. The elections of deacons thus stand in striking contrast to the elections for the lay *anciens* or elders who sat on the Consistory. The Ecclesiastical Ordinances of 1541 had provided in some detail for the election of elders.[15] Every year, when the Small Council was preparing its slates of nominees for the coming year, it was to consult the pastors about the slate of elders. Normally elders were to be reelected for a number of years. But their performance was subject to annual review by the pastors, who also attended the weekly meetings of the Consistory. If any elder's performance for the year was judged to be unsatisfactory, he was to be replaced, again in consultation with the pastors. These arrangements gave the pastors a very considerable voice in the choice of elders—a right to be consulted on every nomination of a new elder, and an informal right to veto the reelection of any present elder.

It is hard to be sure that the pastors exercised these rights in every one of the elections of elders which followed. The election records are unfortunately vague on this point. But we can be sure that the pastors were consulted often. We know that they were consulted in 1546 and in 1547. We know that Calvin, representing the entire group of pastors, participated in the nominations of elders in 1552, 1556, 1557, and 1558. In 1559, two other pastors represented the Company. And in 1560, Calvin and

---

[15] R. M. KINGDON and J.-F. BERGIER, *Registres de la Compagnie*, I, 7; E. RIVOIRE and . VAN BERCHEM, *Sources*, II, 383; CO, Xa, 22-23.

Viret persuaded the Small Council to invite the entire Company of Pastors to the session at which was drawn up the slate of nominees for the coming year. This practice was followed for the rest of Calvin's life.[16]

The Ecclesiastical Ordinances had explicitly provided that the deacons be selected in the same way as the elders. This should have given the pastors a right to be consulted in the choice of every new deacon and to participate in a review of the performance of every deacon considered for reelection. However I can find no evidence that such rights were exercised, until the very last years of Calvin's life. Calvin was often asked, to be sure, to initiate the regular annual election meetings with a prayer, and on occasion he was similarly invited to open a special meeting for the election of *hospitallier* with a prayer.[17] Several times Calvin and other pastors appeared before the Small Council to complain about the ways in which the deacons were performing their duties. A series of such complaints, in 1547,[18] may help explain the 1548 election of an entirely new group of *procureurs*. Occasionally the Small Council consulted pastors about the choice of an individual deacon. In 1561, for example, when Perne des Fosses resigned as *hospitallier*, the Council, in its deliberations on the choice of successor, decided to "en communiquer avec les ministres daultant que loffice est dimportance et quil merite bien y estre pourveu." [19] But not before 1562, do I find any evidence that any of the pastors participated in the annual elections of deacons. In that year, a delegation of pastors appeared at one of the meetings in which slates of officers were established, to protest that the Ecclesiastical Ordinances were not being observed in the choice of deacons. Their specific complaint was over a technicality, however—that the Council had become accustomed to electing five *procureurs* rather than the four specified by the ordinances.[20] The Council nevertheless proceeded to a general review of the qualifications of the previous *procureurs* and drew up the new slate for 1562. In 1563 and 1564, the election of *procureurs* was yoked to the election of elders, with the pastors being consulted by the Council in the drafting of both slates. Until 1562, however, the records of the selection of the Hospital *procureurs* parallel much more closely those of the supervisors of *forteresses* than those of the elders. One gets the impression that the deacons were regarded as secular officers of the state rather than as ministers of the church.

This impression is heightened by other records. The records of the *Hôpital Général* itself, for example, hardly ever mention any participation of the pastors in its activities. There are occasional records of a pastor's referral of a particular poor person

---

[16] AEG, RC, vol. 41, fol. 9, 8 February 1546; vol. 42, fol. 17 v., 11 February 1547; vol. 47, fol. 151 v., 11 February 1552; vol. 51, fols. 7-7 v., 12 February 1556; vol. 53, fol. 7 v., 11 February 1557; vol. 54, fol. 77, 8 February 1558; vol. 55, fol. 4 v., 9 February 1559; vol. 56, fol. 4 v., 8 February 1560; vol. 56, fol. 147, 13 February 1561; vol. 57, fol. 5, 12 February 1562; vol. 58, fol. 5, 11 February 1563; vol. 59, fol. 3 v., 10 February 1564. On the change in 1560, see also CO, XXI, 726-727, 30 January 1560, and 727-728, 1 February 1560.

[17] E.g. AEG, RC, vol. 45, fol. 64 v., 11 August 1550, election of Pierre Jean Jesse.

[18] See CO, XXI, 404-405, 24 May 1547, and 414, 26 September 1547, for two complaints; AEG, RC, vol. 42, fol. 354, 28 November 1547, for yet another.

[19] AEG, RC, vol. 56, fol. 196 v., 29 May 1561.

[20] AEG, RC, vol. 57, fol. 5 v., 12 February 1562.

) the *procureurs* for attention.[21] But these are very rare. Referrals of this sort were much more likely to come from the lay *dizainiers* who had various responsibilities or the people in the *dizaines* into which the city was divided, and were in a position to know which of these people needed assistance. And there are occasional requests from a pastor for the use of equipment belonging to the hospitals.[22] But these are even more rare, and requests of this sort could come from any inhabitant of the city.

Even the title deacon itself is not used in these records. The registers of the *Hôpital-Général* and of the Council both speak of the *Hôpital's* administrators as *procureurs* or *hospitalliers*, never as deacons. When the term deacon occasionally creeps into these records, it refers to one of the administrators of the *Bourse française*, an entirely separate and private institution, set up by the wealthy French refugees to provide financial assistance to the poor French refugees.[23] Only in the Ecclesiastical Ordinances drafted by Calvin is the title deacon applied to the administrators of the *Hôpital*, and there it is applied to them alone.

Our conclusion, therefore, must be that the Reformed deaconate as it developed in Calvin's Geneva was almost entirely a lay institution. It had been created by laymen even before Calvin arrived in Geneva. There is no reason to believe that Calvin had much influence on its early development, even after he arrived in the city. In fact, it might well be argued that in this domain Geneva influenced Calvin more than Calvin influenced Geneva. In other words, in his discussions of the deaconate, Calvin may have been describing an institution which he had seen operating in Geneva, and no doubt in other communities, and which seemed to him to be a successful or at least promising way of handling the Christian community's social obligations. Even when Calvin was at the peak of his power within Geneva, after all his local enemies had been eliminated, there is still no evidence that he and the other pastors took more than an occasional or trivial interest in the deaconate. Only in the last years of Calvin's life, when he himself was distracted by the bloody developments in his native France and by the deterioration in his health, did the Genevan pastors intervene systematically in the choice of deacons. There is no evidence that Calvin led them in this intervention. Clearly the deaconate was the most thoroughly laicized of all Calvinist ecclesiastical institutions. The earliest Calvinist community had decided that its Christian obligations to the poor should be met by laymen, specially chosen for this task by their fellow laymen, not by ordained pastors.

---

[21] E.g., Calvin to *procureur* Michel Varro, 1542, in CO, XI, 482.
[22] E.g., request of pastor de la Faverge for loan of *charette et les chevaux*, AEG, Arch. hosp., a 3, fol. 74, 27 January 1563.
[23] The best study of this institution of which I know is Henri GRANDJEAN, "La bourse française de Genève (1550-1849)", *Etrennes Genevoises*, 1927 (Geneva, Atar, 1927), p. 46-60.

VII

APPENDIX

LES DIACRES DE L'ÉGLISE RÉFORMÉE DE GENÈVE AU TEMPS DE CALVIN

I. *Les procureurs de l'Hôpital-Général*

1535: Conradus Victy (Vity, Vyty, Vytyz)
Claude Bernard
Aymo Vullielmi (Vullielmoz, Vullier-
mo, Vulliermy)
Franciscus Comitis (Conte)
Johannes Amedeus Curtet
(RC, Rivoire & van Berchem ed.,
XIII, 351-352, 14 novembre
1535)

1537: Amy Porral (Porralis)
Jean Bordon (Bourdon)
(RC, vol. 31, fol. 1, 14 juin 1537)

1538: Pierre Tissot
Jean Bordon
(RC, vol. 29/3, fol. 37 v., 1er mars
1538)
(encore procureurs en 1540—
RC, vol. 34, fol. 118, 1er mars)

1541: Jean Bordon
Michel Varro
Jean Pictrod
Aymo Vuilliermoz
(RC, vol. 35, fol. 64 v., 9 février
1541)

1541: (fin de l'année):
Jean Coquet
Jean Chautemps
Michel Varro
Loys du Fort
(PH, 1271, 28 décembre 1541,
Inventaire des meubles de l'hôpi-
tal général de Genève)

1542: Jean Coquet
Jean Chautemps
Loys du Fort
Michel Varro
(Arch. hosp., Aa 1, fol. 1, février
1542)

1543: Jean Coquet, syndic
Jean Chautemps
Loys du Fort
Michel Varro
(Arch. hosp., Aa 1, fol. 4
11 février 1543, et ss.)

1544: Jean Coquet
Jean Chautemps
Loys du Fort
Michel Varro
(RC, vol. 38, fol. 68 v., 8 févri
1544)

1545: Jean Coquet
Jean Chautemps
Loys du Fort
Michel Varro
(RC, vol. 40, fol. 22, 12 févri
1545)

1546: Jean Coquet
Jean Chautemps
Loys du Fort
Michel Varro
(RC, vol. 41, fol. 11 v., 11 févri
1546)
Jean Coquet est mort et a été rem
placé par Anthoine Chicand
octobre
(RC, vol. 41, fol. 219, 12 octob
1546)

1547: Jean Chautemps
Loys du Fort
Michel Varro
(RC, vol. 42, fol., 75 v., 4 av
1547)
Anthoine Chicand, syndic
(Arch. hosp., Aa 1, fol. 26
13 mars 1547, et ss.)

1548: Anthoine Chicand
* Pierre Bonna (Bonnaz)
François Vullens
Jean Leurat
(RC, vol. 43, fol. 13 v., 7 févri
1548)

1549: Anthoine Chicand
Pierre Bonna
François Vullens
Jean Leurat
(RC, vol. 44, fol. 12 v., 5 février
1549)

1550: Jean Phillipin
(Anthoine Chicand
François Vullens
Jean Leurat)
(RC, vol. 44, fol. 323, 13 février
1550)

1551: Michel de l'Arche
(Jean Phillipin
François Vullens
Jean Leurat)
(RC, vol. 45, fol. 195 v., 16 février
1551)

1552: *Jean Phillipin, syndic
Michel de l'Arche
Françoys Vullens
Jean Leurat
*Guillaume Beney (Benôit)
(RC, vol. 46, fol. 157 v., 15 février
1552)

1553: Pernet des Fosses, syndic
Jean Amed Curtet, dit Botellier
*Michel de l'Arche
Jean Balard, le jeune
Jean Lois Ramel
(RC, vol. 47, fol. 12, 13 février
1553)

1554: Michel de l'Arche, syndic
Claude Delestra
Pierre d'Orsières
Jean Amed Curtet, dit Botellier
(RC, vol. 48, fol. 6 v., 8 février
1554)

1555: *Pierre Jean Jesse, syndic
Michel de l'Arche
Jean Amed Curtet, dit Botellier
Claude Delestra
Pierre d'Orsières
(RC, vol. 49, fol. 7, 7 février
1555)

1556: Jean Chautemps, syndic
Pierre Jean Jesse
*Jean Donzel
*François Lullin
*Guillaume Chicand
(RC, vol. 51, fol. 8, 12 février
1556)

1557: *Guillaume Chicand, syndic
Jean Chautemps
*Jean Donzel
Girard Catry
Jean Chrestien, dit de Roquemont
(RC, vol. 53, fol. 8, 11 février
1557)

1558: *Jean Donzel, syndic
*Guillaume Chicand
Jean Chautemps
Girard Catry
Jean Chrestien
(RC, vol. 54, fol. 78, 8 février
1558)

1559: Jean Porral (Porralis), syndic
*Guillaume Chicand
Jean Chautemps
Girard Catry
*Claude Testu
(RC, vol. 55, fol. 3, 7 février
1559)

1560: Jaques Blondel, syndic
Pernet des Fosses
Guillaume Chicand
Girard Catry
Aymoz Plonjon (Plongeon)
(RC, vol. 56, fol. 5, 8 février
1560)

1561: Guillaume Chicand, syndic
Jaques Blondel
Jean Collondaz
Aymoz Plonjon
*Girard Catry
(RC, vol. 56, fol. 147, 13 février
1561)

1562: *Amy Chasteauneuf
Pierre Chappuis
*Girard Catry
*François de Roches
(RC, vol. 57, fol. 5 v., 12 février
1562)

1563: *Bertholome Lect, syndic
Pierre Chappuis
*Girard Catry
*François de Roches
(RC, vol. 58, fol. 5, 11 février
1563)

1564: *(Claude) de la Maisonneuve, syndic
Pierre Chappuis
*Girard Catry
*François de Roches
(RC, vol. 59, fol. 3 v., 10 février
1564)

* Membre du Consistoire au même temps

II. *Les hospitalliers de l'Hôpital-Général*

1. Claude Salomon, dit Pasta
   14 novembre 1535 (RC, Rivoire & van
   Berchem ed., XIII, 351-352)
   28 janvier 1536 (*Ibid.*, p. 414, re sa mort)

2. Lois Bernard
   22 février 1536 (RC, Rivoire & van Berchem ed., XIII, 457)

3. Jean Leurat
   14 juin 1537 (RC, vol. 31, fol. 1)

4. Claude Magnin
   31 août 1538 (RC, vol. 32, fol. 137)
   29 juin 1540 (RC, vol. 34, fol. 314 v.)

5. Anthoine Chicand
   30 juin 1540 (RC, vol. 34, fol. 317 v.)

6. Jean Fontannaz
   21 décembre 1541 (RC, vol. 35, fol. 441)
   2 mai 1543 (RC, vol. 37, fol. 82)

7. Pierre de Rages
   2 mai 1543 (RC, vol. 37, fol. 82)
   28 juillet 1550 (Reg. morts, I, 16)

8. Pierre Jean Jesse
   11 août 1550 (RC, vol. 45, fol. 64 v.)
   12 mai 1553 (Arch. hosp., Aa 2, fol. 41 v.)

9. Jullian Boccard
   12 mai 1553 (RC, vol. 47, fol. 73 v.)
   10 février 1557 (Arch. hosp. Aa 2 fol. 177)

10. *Jean Collondaz
    12 février 1557 (RC, vol. 53, fol. 10)
    18 juin 1560 (RC, vol. 56, fol. 51)

11. Pierre Sommaretta
    18 juin 1560 (RC, vol. 56, fol. 51 v.)
    12 novembre 1560 (mort — RC, vol. 56 fol. 100)

12. Pernet des Fosses
    15 novembre 1560 (RC, vol. 56 fol. 100 v.)
    29 mai 1561 (RC, vol. 56, fol. 196 v.)

13. Pierre Dance
    3 juin 1561 (RC, vol. 56, fol. 198 v.)

* Membre du Consistoire au même temps

VIII

THE CONTROL OF MORALS IN CALVIN'S GENEVA

Calvinism is often thought to be an important source of that drive for moral austerity or asceticism that is commonly labeled "puritanism." Some think this is bad, and blame Calvinism for introducing into modern society a repressiveness that has killed joy and led to many serious problems. Others think this is good, and praise Calvinism for introducing into modern society a measure of discipline that has made it both more cohesive and more productive. But most people who have thought about the matter, seem to think that men formed by the Calvinist tradition have usually set for themselves higher standards of private morality, including sexual morality and morality in business dealings, than the ordinary run of men, and that these Calvinists have had greater success in living up to these high standards. They have thus often set a moral tone that became pervasive throughout our society. This belief, no doubt, has something of the character of a folk myth, and folk myths are often imprecise and have a way of becoming anachronistic. It is obviously a very gross generalization, and could not apply with equal force to every Calvinist in every place at every time. But, like most folk myths, it almost certainly contains a very important kernel of truth. It thus poses an interesting problem in historical explanation. Where did this moral austerity come from? Why have Calvinists been more concerned with morals than other men?

If one tries to explain this phenomenon in exclusively theological terms, it seems to me that one must fail. I do not think that Calvinist theology values the moral life more than other types of Christian theology. Indeed, since it accepts the basic doctrine of

4

all sixteenth-century magisterial Protestantism, of "justification by faith alone," one might well conclude that it values the moral life less than either Catholic theology or certain types of radical Protestant theology. If one could demonstrate that a moral life is a sure sign of election to salvation in Calvinist theology, one could establish an important place for morality as allied to the strong doctrine of predestination so characteristic of Calvinism. Such a link can apparently be discovered in certain varieties of late Calvinist or Puritan theology. But if it is present in the thought of Calvin himself, it is in a highly attenuated form.

Similarly, I do not think that it can be argued that Calvinist theologians taught a different kind of morality than other Christians, except, of course, for the clergy, who are absolved from such special requirements imposed upon them by Roman Catholicism as celibacy. For the generality of mankind, Calvinism taught the same code of morals, derived from such biblical texts as the Ten Commandments and the moral teachings of Jesus, as almost all systems of Christian thought.

The real explanation of the moral austerity that characterized Calvinism from the beginning, lies, it seems to me, in the fact that early Calvinist communities *enforced* morality. And they enforced it by the creation and effective use of a new institution, the Calvinist consistory. The model for this body was the consistory established in Geneva by Calvin himself. It is in the history of this body that one must search, I am convinced, for the essential source of modern moral puritanism. This search, thus, demands the talents not of a historian of thought but rather of a historian of municipal institutions.

The Genevan Consistory was not, of course, created out of a vacuum. It was created in response to a need felt by the Genevan community.[2] For centuries, morals controls in Geneva had been quite lax. Although the city was an ecclesiastical principality, ruled by a bishop, aided by a chapter of cathedral canons, these clergymen had never tried to impose a strict code of morals on the population. What controls were adopted simply tried to regulate moral lapses regarded as inevitable. Prostitution, for example, was accepted and permitted. Repeated attempts were made to limit prostitutes to certain parts of the city, to require them to wear distinctive dress, to organize themselves under an elected or appointed "queen," to limit the times they could enter the public baths where they apparently did much of their soliciting. But no attempt was made to outlaw prostitution. Similarly, illegitimacy was accepted as inevitable. If a father would acknowledge and provide financial support for his illegitimate children, the authorities were content. Even adultery was punished only occasionally and lightly.

Furthermore, there was no institution in medieval Geneva charged with primary responsibility for maintaining morality. The actions that were taken against those who had flouted Christian morality in notorious ways were taken by the city council, an elected group of lay businessmen and professionals, charged by the bishops with the responsibility for maintaining order in the city. But this council had so many other responsibilities more important and pressing to its members that they rarely considered morals cases. They could be assisted in locating and punishing morals offenders by the "official," an officer of the bishop. And their decisions could be reviewed by the bishop's court. But these agents of the church did not seem to be very concerned about morality either.

This rather loose situation began to change early in the sixteenth century. Growing criticism from the general population began to force the authorities to consider ways of controlling morals. This criticism tended to focus increasingly on clergymen found guilty of such moral lapses as frequenting prostitutes, maintaining concubines, and the like. It thus combined with the general tide of rising discontent that led to the ejection of Roman Catholicism and the introduction of Protestantism. The first concrete result of this popular puritanism was the enactment of a number of laws regulating morals on the very eve of the Reformation. These laws were enacted by the lay members of the city council entirely on their own authority. Some of them may have been persuaded to this action by William Farel, the flamboyant Protestant preacher who was actively agitating for the outlawry of Catholicism in the city. But they acted before Farel had been named to any position of authority, and before John Calvin had even arrived in Geneva. On February 28, 1534, the council ordered all fornicators and adulterers to "abandon their wicked life" or be whipped and banished.[3] On April 30, 1534, it ordered the caretakers of the baths to keep all prostitutes out of those establishments.[4] On March 7, 1536, the prostitutes were ordered either to abandon their trade or leave the city.[5] The ordinance establishing the Reformation was not adopted until May 21, 1536.[6] Calvin did not arrive in Geneva until several months after that.

Systematic enforcement of these laws, however, had to wait for several years. The first years of the Reformation regime in Geneva witnessed considerable turmoil. Farel and Calvin became the principal ministers of the Reformed church, but they were forced out of the city in 1538. It was only on Calvin's return, in 1541, that the building of a Reformed society could really begin. One of the first of Calvin's accomplishments was to persuade the city council to establish the consistory. In his very first interview with the council on returning to Geneva, he asked that a consistory be established and that ordinances be drafted describing the nature and functions of this and other Genevan ecclesiastical institutions.[7] A committee made up of all the pastors of the city and selected lay members of the governing councils immediately went to work on this project. After a draft had been prepared and modified in meetings of the councils, the new ecclesiastical ordinances were adopted, about two months after Calvin's return.[8] A few weeks later, the Genevan Consistory met for the first time.[9]

This new institution was at once an agency of both the state and the church. Its members included both elected lay elders and the ordained pastors of the city. The elders were elected annually, in the February elections in which all municipal officials were chosen. In those elections, the entire voting population of Geneva gathered together to select four governing magistrates, called syndics; members of three governing councils, the most important of which, the small council, met almost every day to handle government business for the city and possessed the real sovereign power in Geneva; members of a number of standing committees that handled such problems as the maintenance of city fortifications, the maintenance of city grain supplies, the control of city funds, the judgment of both criminal and civil legal cases. In most of these elections, however, the voters simply ratified slates of candidates prepared by the outgoing small council. In only a few of the elections, in those for syndics, for example, were the voters given a choice between two candidates for each office. The crucial decisions, consequently, were made by the small council, in drawing up its lists of nominees.[10]

The consistory fitted into this constitutional structure as a new standing committee of the government. Its lay members were chosen in much the same way as members of the committees controlling fortifications and grain supplies. Two of them had to be members of the small council itself, and one of these customarily came to be a ruling syndic; four of them had to come from the less important and less active council of sixty; six had to come from the council of two hundred. They were so selected that each geographic section of the city would be represented.[11] The elder who was also a syndic for the year, acted as the presiding officer of the consistory.[12]

Only in one way did the selection of these elders differ from the selection of the members of the city's other standing committees. But that difference was crucial. The ecclesiastical ordinances provided that the small council consult the city's pastors on the nominations it made annually both of the elders and of the deacons, who were responsible for maintaining the city's programs of social welfare. They further provided that the council would decide, at the end of every year, which elders should be reelected and which should be replaced, presumably again in consultation with the pastors. It was expected that an elder who was doing a satisfactory job would normally be reelected for a period of several years.[13] The pastors, headed by Calvin, thus gained an important legal right to share in the selection of elders and deacons.

This right does not seem to have been exercised for some time in the selection of deacons. Not until 1562, only two years before Calvin's death, is there sure evidence that the pastors were, in fact, consulted by the small council when it drew up its annual slate of nominees for the office of deacon.[14] This right may not have been exercised right away in the selections of elders, either.

Election records are not clear on this point. But it clearly was exercised sooner and more forcefully. In 1546 and 1547, "the ministers" were consulted on the selection of elders; in 1552, "the ministers . . . through their spokesman, M. Calvin," were consulted; Calvin, again representing the entire corps of pastors, was consulted in 1556, 1557, and 1558; two other pastors were consulted in 1559; from 1560 on, the entire body of pastors was invited to the small council session at which the slate of elders for the coming year was drawn up.[15]

Until 1560, the elders, like most other elected officials of the Genevan state, were always native-born citizens. In that year, Calvin and his fellow pastor Pierre Viret persuaded the council to permit the election also of members of the council of two hundred who were immigrant "bourgeois," who had obtained that position of legal and political privilege by special action of the council without having been born in the city.[16] In the election which followed this breakthrough, the Marquis Galeazzo Carraciolo, a prominent Italian convert to Calvinism, was made an elder. This change tended to increase the authority of Calvin among the lay members of the consistory, since many of his most fervent supporters came from the large group of religious refugees in Geneva.

The remaining members of the consistory, the ordained pastors, were also technically agents of the Genevan state. They were salaried employees, hired by the small council, on the nomination of the company of pastors, of which Calvin was moderator, but they were considerably more independent of state control. It was clear that it was the company, not the council, that had the decisive role in their initial selection. They normally held office for life. If they were deposed, for bad behavior or incorrect belief, it was normally, although not invariably, at the initiative of the company. If they were released to take positions elsewhere, it was normally the permission of the company that was decisive.[17] Furthermore, none of the pastors were native-born citizens of Geneva, for no Genevans could be found who possessed the requisite education. Most of them became "bourgeois" sooner or later. Calvin, surprisingly, was one of the last to become a "bourgeois," not being elevated to that position until 1559.[18] The number of pastors grew significantly during Calvin's lifetime, from nine in 1542, the first full year of his service after his return, to nineteen in 1564, the year of his death.[19] A few of these men were deputed to serve in small churches in the outlying villages dependent on Geneva, and thus would not have been always present for the weekly meetings of the consistory. But most of them lived and served in the city, and were regularly available for consistory duty. This was the only civic duty to which the pastors were all assigned, and they took it very seriously. The elders often had many other civic duties to which they had to devote attention. Those who sat on the small council had to spend most of their time working for the city government. And many of them held positions on other standing committees of the city. However, the elders also, in spite of these distractions, took their consistory duty seriously. Attendance at the weekly meetings was almost always nearly full, with generally only members who were ill or who had to leave the city on government or personal business being absent.

This seriousness may be explained in part by the fact that both pastors and elders were not only agents of the state but also ministers of the church. Both Calvinist theology and Genevan law are explicit on this point. The Calvinist ministry was made up of four orders: preaching pastors, teaching doctors, disciplining elders, and charity-directing deacons. All were parts of the organization dictated by God and described, if fleetingly, in the New Testament. All were equal in dignity and value, if different in function and length of tenure.[20]

The functions of the Genevan Consistory were various.[21] In the beginning, particularly, it devoted much of its energy to wiping out vestiges of Roman Catholicism. It stopped such practices as the saying of traditional prayers in Latin. It punished those who left Geneva to receive Catholic sacraments. It complained of acts labeled "superstitious" to which Catholic authorities had not objected. For example, a number of Genevans were disciplined for going to a country spring to collect samples of a water believed to have the miraculous ability to cure certain diseases. The consistory also worked hard to uphold the honor of God, of the Reformation of His worship, and of its leaders. Many

Genevans were punished for blasphemies of various sorts; for public insults to the consistory, to the Reformed pastors, above all to Calvin himself; for failure to attend church services or catechism. Occasionally the consistory considered charges of doctrinal error, although the most celebrated of those cases, the trials of Bolsec and Servetus, were handled primarily by other institutions. For our purposes, however, its really important function was to expose and punish immorality of many kinds, particularly sexual immorality. These cases occupied a good deal of its time and energy. In handling them, the consistory came to act like a morals court.

The procedures of the consistory were simple. Its members, both elders and pastors, were supposed to be constantly on the alert for signs of unchristian belief or behavior. If they spotted cases that were not serious, that were perhaps even private or secret, they were to reprimand the sinner involved. If these reprimands did not induce repentance, or if the sins involved were open and serious, the sinner would be referred to the entire consistory. Cases could thus be referred to the consistory by any of its members. They could also be referred by the city council or by the standing governmental committees devoted to judicial matters. They could apparently also be referred by any individual citizen who thought his neighbor's belief required correction or behavior merited discipline. These cases thus reflected a fair amount of spying by the residents of Geneva on each other.

Those summoned before the consistory were sharply questioned. If found guilty, they were subjected to vehement tongue-lashings, at which Calvin was particularly adept. Often this scolding would reduce a sinner to tears and repentance, and be deemed punishment enough. If the sinner proved stubborn, however, or if his sins were deemed sufficiently serious, he could be turned over to the small council for further discipline. The small council could then apply to him its usual summary justice, ending often in secular punishment—ranging from a spectacular public humiliation, to a short prison term, a small fine, or even death, executed in several brutal ways (by burning, drowning, strangling, hanging, or decapitation). The small council could also find the consistory in error, and release the sinner without punishment. It could also find the consistory overly severe, and administer a relatively mild punishment.[22]

The only further punishment that the consistory itself could administer was ecclesiastical. It could excommunicate, bar a sinner from receipt of Communion, a terrible penalty in a day when regular receipt of Communion was regarded as an essential sign of the operation of God's saving grace. This power of excommunication made the Calvinist consistory unusual, setting it apart from many of the institutions to control morals that preceded it in a number of other Protestant cities in both Switzerland and southern Germany.[23] It was also the feature of the consistory's operation that aroused the most vehement opposition among Protestants otherwise disposed to accept Calvin's leadership. It was the root cause of the Erastian quarrel, which first boiled up in the Palatinate, between Erastus and Calvin's student Olevianus,[24] and which later became a serious issue in such other Protestant countries as England. Opponents of consistorial excommunication felt that it usurped powers really belonging to the secular courts, that it put into human hands decisions that should be made by God alone, and that it permitted an intolerable intrusion into human privacy.

Some of this resistance to consistorial excommunication can be found within Geneva itself. It became so bitter, in fact, that it threatened Calvin's position in the city. It suggests that the systematic enforcement of morality was new to Calvin's Geneva, or at least relatively new. The small council was not at all certain that the ecclesiastical ordinances had in fact granted a sole right of excommunication to the consistory. It tried to intervene in the consistory's punishments by lifting sentences of excommunication when it judged those upon whom they were levied to be penitent. There were some particularly important cases of this sort involving Genevans of great prominence between 1553 and 1555. Calvin reacted against this intervention with fury, absolutely refusing to administer Communion to these sinners and persuading the other pastors to join him in this stand, even threatening to leave the city over this issue. In the resulting showdown, Calvin won a complete victory. His enemies were forced to give in completely, or were driven from the city or even put to death.[25]

12

An immediate result of this dramatic victory was a kind of moral reign of terror in Geneva. After 1555, no one could oppose the consistory effectively. There was a sharp increase in the number of morals cases referred by the consistory to the council and then acted upon, perhaps reaching a peak in 1557 and 1558.[26] Complaints were made to the council, but they had no effect. At one point, for example, a delegation appeared before the council to argue that the standards of sexual morality demanded by the consistory were humanly impossible, and to suggest that if the consistory continued to insist on such pure behavior, they feared their wives might all be tied in weighted sacks and thrown into the river (the punishment for flagrant adultery). The delegation was scolded for being frivolous and its leader was imprisoned.[27] Only after 1560, when Calvin and his colleagues began to be distracted by the demands of a tremendous missionary campaign in France, was there any slackening in the consistory's campaign to purify Geneva.

This campaign for morality produced results that were most impressive to visitors. John Knox, for example, who came to Geneva for the first time during these years, reported that in other cities he had found true doctrine preached, but in no other city had he seen such good behavior.[28] It seems to me that one finds in this stern enforcement of morality the essential explanation for the moral austerity of the entire Calvinist movement. Enforcement of morality was not, of course, unique to Calvin's Geneva. One can find analogous enforcement and sometimes even analogous institutions of enforcement in such other places as Savonarola's Florence, several decades earlier, and in the German and Swiss cities influenced by Zwingli, in the years immediately preceding the establishment of Calvin's regime in Geneva. A program of enforcement as strong as Geneva's, moreover, could not be imposed upon every community in which Calvinists were active. But it was imposed on many. And the very fact of its frequent existence in Calvinist communities gave a special sanction to the stern Calvinist education in morality that internalized this austerity and passed it on to succeeding generations. At least, this seems to me to be the most important element in any explanation of Calvinist moral austerity.

The main outlines of the history of the Genevan Consistory during Calvin's lifetime are already known. There are even some rather detailed studies of its operations, perhaps the best of which is Walther Köhler's *Zürcher Ehegericht und Genfer Konsistorium*, a monograph that traces with great skill the development of the Reformed methods for treating sexual and marital problems from Zwingli's establishment of a marriage court for Zurich in 1525 through similar developments in a number of south German and Swiss cities, to the full flowering of the Calvinist consistory in Geneva.[29] Those of us who have worked in the Genevan State Archives, however, know that these studies are far from definitive. They are based, at best, on a random sampling of the records of the consistory's operations. For those records are not only voluminous but also peculiarly difficult to use. There are some twenty manuscript registers in those Archives containing minutes of the weekly meetings of the consistory during the period when Calvin was its most prominent member, and dozens of registers for the succeeding periods. In these same Archives, one can also find hundreds of dossiers of manuscript trial records, which include records of cross-examinations, judgments, even on occasion private papers impounded as evidence, all in the cases of sinners referred by the consistory to the small council and the criminal courts of Geneva. No one, to my knowledge at least, has ever gone through this entire mass of manuscript material. It is not only dismayingly bulky, but its use also poses severe technical problems. These manuscripts were all written by hand, sometimes at top speed, as hearings before the consistory or council were in progress. They are in a French that is not only four hundred years old and includes many abbreviations, but that also contains many peculiar local usages. To read these manuscripts at all requires some training or experience in paleography. Even with experience, the reading of these materials is a slow and laborious process, as I can testify from personal experience. Most scholars who have tried to use these materials have given up in despair. Both Walther Köhler and Emile Doumergue, for example, based their studies of the consistory on a selection of transcribed excerpts from the consistory's Registers, prepared in the nineteenth century by A.

14

Cramer,[30] a local antiquarian who seems to have been the only man in history to have read much of these materials.

Yet a really intensive study of them might well yield some extremely interesting results. It should make possible studies of a much greater precision than can normally be attempted of how morality can be controlled in a community determined to do so. One could develop statistics on the various kinds of moral aberrations brought to the consistory's attention, and with them establish which aberrations were most prevalent in Calvin's Geneva. One could find out how each variety of aberration was treated by the consistory and the council, and thus estimate which aberrations were regarded as serious and which were accepted as petty. One could discover how many cases were handled by the consistory alone and how many were referred to the council, thus fixing the relative role of church and state in punishing moral offenders in Geneva. One could establish how many of the sinners referred to the council were punished as the consistory wished, how many were let off with lighter punishments, and how many were released without punishment, thus measuring in another way the relative weight of the church's moral influence in the community. Finally, one could measure how all these statistics changed over the years, with the annual changes in the personnel of both consistory and council and the shifts in the primary interests of these men, both affecting institutional reactions to moral lapses, and in turn revealing how the climate of opinion in Geneva developed.

At the moment, however, all of these possibilities remain nothing but possibilities. They can only be realized by intensive archival research, which may be beyond the capacity of any one historian, requiring the work of an entire team of scholars. The definitive history of the Genevan Consistory remains to be written. And the full history of the centuries-long devotion to moral austerity that issued from Calvin's Geneva lies still farther in the future.

1. François Wendel, *Calvin: sources et évolution de sa pensée religieuse* (Paris, 1950), pp. 209–10 (hereafter cited as *Calvin*).

2. On the pre-Reformation history of morals controls in Geneva, see Henri Naef, *Les origines de la Réforme à Genève*, 2 vols. (Geneva, 1936), 1:chap. 5

(hereafter cited as *Origines*). See also chap. 2, section 1, on the government agencies to which police powers were attributed.

3. *SD*, 2:300. Noted by Naef, *Origines*, p. 234.

4. *RC*, 12 (Geneva, 1936): 533. Noted by Naef, *Origines*, pp. 229-30.

5. *RC*, 13 (Geneva, 1940):480. Noted by Naef, *Origines*, p. 230.

6. *SD*, 2:312-13; *RC*, 13:576-77.

7. *CO*, 21:282.

8. For copies of the full text, see *CO*, 10a:15-30; *SD*, 2:377-90; *RCP*, 1:1-13.

9. E. Doumergue, *Jean Calvin, les hommes et les choses de son temps*, 7 vols. (Lausanne, 1899-1927) 5:169 (hereafter cited as *Jean Calvin*).

10. This information comes from my own examination of the annual election records in the Archives d'Etat de Genève (hereafter cited as AEG), manuscript Registres du Conseil (hereafter cited as RC), for the period of Calvin's ministry.

11. *RCP*, 1:7.

12. A rule established by custom, not ordinance. See AEG, manuscript Registres du Consistoire de l'Eglise de Genève.

13. *RCP*, 1:7.

14. Robert M. Kingdon, "Social Welfare in Calvin's Geneva," *American Historical Review* 76 (1971):63.

15. Ibid., p. 62, based on AEG, RC, vol. 41, fol. 9, Feb. 8, 1546; vol. 42, fol. 17v, Feb. 11, 1547; vol. 46, fol. 151v, Feb. 11, 1552; vol. 51, fol. 7-7v, Feb. 12, 1556; vol. 53, fol. 7v, Feb. 11, 1557; vol. 54, fol. 77, Feb. 8, 1558; vol. 55, fol. 4v, Feb. 9, 1559; vol. 56, fol. 4v, Feb. 8, 1560; vol. 56, fol. 147, Feb. 13, 1561; vol. 57, fol. 5, Feb. 12, 1562; vol. 58, fol. 5, Feb. 11, 1563; vol. 59, fol. 3v, Feb. 10, 1564.

16. *CO*, 21:726-28.

17. Robert M. Kingdon, *Geneva and the Consolidation of the French Protestant Movement, 1564–1572* (Geneva and Madison, Wis., 1967), pp. 38-39.

18. Robert M. Kingdon, *Geneva and the Coming of the Wars of Religion in France, 1555-1563* (Geneva, 1956), p. 7. On Calvin, see also *CO*, 21:725.

19. Amédée Roget, *Histoire du peuple de Genève depuis la réforme jusqu'à l'Escalade*, 7 vols. (Geneva, 1870-83), supplies lists of the pastors active in every year from 1542 to 1567. For the 1542 list, see 2,2:335; for the 1564 list, see 7, 2:265.

20. Wendel, *Calvin*, pp. 230-31.

21. The analysis that follows is based on my own survey of Genevan records. Cf. the analogous analysis of Doumergue, *Jean Calvin*, 5:189-97; Walther Köhler, *Zürcher Ehegericht und Genfer Konsistorium*, 2 vols. (Leipzig, 1932, 1942), 2:580-88 (hereafter cited as *Konsistorium*).

22. For two examples, dating from shortly after Calvin's death, see *RCP*, 2:109.

23. See Köhler, *Konsistorium*, passim; above all, in his conclusion, 2:661-62.

24. On which see, inter alia, Ruth Wesel-Roth, *Thomas Erastus: Ein Beitrag zur Geschichte der reformierten Kirche und zur Lehre von der Staatssouveränität* (Lahr/Baden, 1954), pp. 43–81.

25. Köhler, *Konsistorium*, 2:604-14.

26. Revealed by the inventories of *procès criminels*, or criminal trials, still preserved in the AEG. Cf. the tabulation of sentences of excommunication, also increasing sharply in these years, in Köhler, *Konsistorium*, 2:614 n. 544.

16

27. See register entries excerpted in *CO*, 21:656 and 657; noted by Köhler, *Konsistorium*, 2:592.

28. John Knox to Mrs. Locke, December 9, 1556, in David Laing, ed., *The Works of John Knox*, 4 (Edinburgh, 1855):240.

29. Walter Köhler, *Zürcher Ehegericht und Genfer Konsistorium*, 2 vols. (Leipzig, 1932, 1942). There are extended reviews of vol. 1, by Jean Adam and François Wendel, in *Revue d'histoire et de philosophie religieuse* 13 (1933): 448-57.

30. AEG, A. Cramer, *Notes extraites des registres du Consistoire de l'Eglise de Genève, 1541–1814* (Geneva, 1853). Cited by Doumergue, *Jean Calvin*, 5:189; Köhler, *Konsistorium*, 2:vii, 568.

IX

Protestant Parishes in the Old World and the New: The Cases of Geneva and Boston

There can be little doubt that for centuries the most important single unit of the Christian church has been the parish. It is surely the most fundamental of the structures upon which the institutional church has been built. Only by studying closely the parish and what goes on within it can we gain a real appreciation of what religion has meant and continues to mean to the average Christian at the grass roots level. It is somewhat surprising, given the general spread of interest in social history among contemporary historians, that there has not been more study of the parish. One can understand the superior appeal of historical theology to the historian who concentrates on ideas, given the range and sophistication of the systems of thought created over the centuries by theologians, but we should not forget that these systems could not even be comprehended by the great majority of Christians. One can similarly understand the superior appeal of ecclesiastical politics to the historian who concentrates on events, given the high drama in which ecclesiastical leaders have often been engaged, but we should not assume that these events necessarily even came to the attention of average Christians. But for the historian of society who is interested in the religious experience of the average man, the parish must be a starting point.[1]

Most of the work undertaken so far on the history of the parish has focussed upon areas which remained Roman Catholic. It is in these areas, of course, that the parish is most clearly an institution of unusual longevity and

This paper was prepared to be read at the meeting of the International Commission for the Comparative Study of Ecclesiastical History in San Francisco on August 25, 1975, as part of the International Congress of the Historical Sciences. I am indebted to Richard J. Ferraro for assistance in its original preparation, particularly in gathering material for the section on developments in Boston, and would also like to acknowledge the bibliographical suggestions of my colleague David S. Lovejoy.

1. We should all be grateful to the Parish Studies Group of the International Commission for the Comparative Study of Ecclesiastical History for its reminder of this basic truth and its stimulating initiative in developing this field of study. I am grateful to Professor Jerzy Kloczowski of the Catholic University of Lublin for introducing me to the work of this group. Brief reports on its activities can be found in the annual chronicle of the work of relevant international organizations in the *Revue d'histoire ecclésiastique* 66 (1971), 1: 1040–1045; 68 (1973), 1: 925–927; 69 (1974), 1: 543–545; 70 (1975), 1: 671–672, 829.

durability. In countries like France, parishes can probably be traced back to units of civil administration established by Roman imperial authorities before the spread of Christianity. In countries like Poland, parishes can be traced back to the introduction of Christianity during the Middle Ages. In both types of countries, parishes have proved more durable than perhaps any other institution except for the family, certainly more durable than any political institutions.

We should not forget, however, that the Protestant Reformation did not abolish the parish. The parish was an administrative subdivision of an established church which held a monopoly over religious practice within practically every community in Europe. The earliest Protestants did not seek to splinter that establishment by creating alternative institutions or deny that monopoly by introducing freedom of religion. They rather sought to take over the entire establishment with its monopoly, and reform it. They never succeeded on the international level, but did succeed within several nations and parts of nations. The result was a number of established churches, each monopolizing religious practice within a defined area, each subdivided into parishes of the traditional kind.

The fact that there were several Protestant establishments may mean that there are more differences among Protestants than among Catholics in types of parish organization. In any event, it surely creates considerable opportunities for significant comparative studies. It is upon one such difference that this article concentrates: the difference between the types of parishes developed on opposite sides of the Atlantic in communities dominated on the intellectual level by Calvinist theology. Briefly and schematically, the difference is this: on the European side of the Atlantic the parish remained a geographic unit, drawing together for worship all the inhabitants of a fixed area in the country or within a city; on the American side of the Atlantic the parish became an ideological or social unit, drawing together people of common ideas or social attachments, with little regard to their places of residence. This difference is so pronounced that it is even reflected in linguistic usage. The *Oxford English Dictionary* points out that the word parish itself means different things on the two sides of the Atlantic. In Britain a parish is primarily "the name of a subdivision of a county: applied to it primarily in its ecclesiastical aspect, but also as an area recognized for various purposes of civil administration and local government." In America a parish is primarily "the body of people associated for Christian worship and work in connexion with a particular local church; a congregation; hence, a denomination."[2]

This difference is also part of the experience of many who have lived for extended periods of time within Protestant communities on both sides of the

2. *Oxford English Dictionary*, corrected re-issue of 1933, s.v. "parish."

Atlantic. It became a part of my own experience when I first moved to
Geneva to begin a year of study. Upon registration with the city government,
I received a written assignment to a particular parish of the National
Reformed Church of Geneva and to a particular pastor within that parish,
solely on the basis of my place of residence. I also soon discovered that rather
sharp differences in theological viewpoint were contained within many of
these Genevan parishes. One can, for example, hear on succeeding Sundays
from Calvin's own pulpit in the parish of St. Peter, sermons both liberal
enough to please an American Unitarian and orthodox enough to satisfy a
conservative American Presbyterian. I have never encountered in American
Protestant communities either this method of assigning a church member to a
parish on the basis of geography alone or this containment within one parish
structure of such a wide range of beliefs.

Both of these parish systems, however, evolved from a single Calvinist
system. It was a system, moreover, with an important ecclesiological

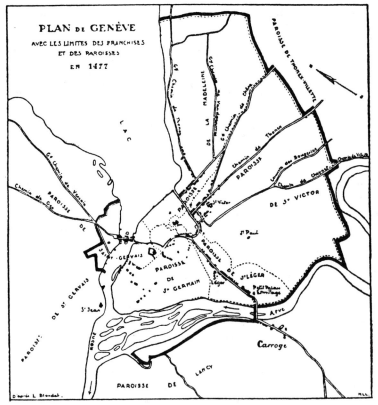

Reproduced from Henri Naef, *Les origines de la Réforme à Genève,* Vol. 1 (Geneva and Paris:
Jullien and Droz, 1936) p. 8.

component. This paper seeks to explain the rather obvious divergence. It does so by comparing the parish systems developed within two Calvinist communities: Geneva, the city whose initial reformation was directed personally by Calvin, and Boston, the largest city in North America settled primarily by Calvin's spiritual descendants.

Systematic study of Geneva's parishes has begun only recently. It was launched most impressively with the publication of Louis Binz, *Vie religieuse et réforme ecclésiastique dans le diocèse de Genève . . . 1378-1450.*[3] While this monumental study strays beyond its announced chronological limits, it really stops before the establishment of the Protestant Reformation in 1536. It also concentrates its attention upon the rural parishes within the rather large hinterland of the medieval diocese of Geneva, and deliberately excludes much examination of the urban parishes within the city itself. It is thus useful for my present inquiry only as background. I shall therefore have to depend for my analysis upon random bits of published source material, because the systematic study the subject deserves has yet to be undertaken.

Geneva on the eve of the Reformation had seven parishes. The violence accompanying the Reformation led to the closing of four. Two were abandoned when the city razed its suburbs and tightened its defensive perimeter, because they lay primarily outside the walls. Two others were abandoned because they were in a part of the city that served the clergy around the episcopal establishment. Once that establishment had been eliminated by the Reformation regime and hundreds of religious had been forced either to leave the city or convert to secular occupations, these churches were no longer needed. That left three parishes: (1), St. Pierre, centering on the old cathedral church up on a hill, a part of the city dominated by its patrician rulers; (2), La Madeleine, extending along the left bank of the Rhone river below the hill, a part of the city which was dominated by commercial interests and contained the houses of merchants and innkeepers; and (3), St. Gervais, extending across the river over bridges and an island to a right bank area, the part of the city which contained most of the city's industrial establishments and artisan population.[4] The status of these three parishes was fixed quite precisely by Reformation legislation. The ecclesiastical ordinances of 1541, which Calvin helped draft as part of the deal that brought him back to Geneva in that year, contain a clause fixing

---

3. Louis Binz, *Vie religieuse et réforme ecclésiastique dans le diocèse de Genève pendant le grand schisme et la crise conciliaire (1378-1450)*, vol. 1, vol. 46 of "Mémoires et documents publiés par la Société d'histoire et d'archéologie de Genève," (Geneva, 1973).
4. For a description of parishes on the eve of the Reformation, including a map, see Henri Naef, *Les origines de la Réforme à Genève* 2 vols. (Geneva and Paris, 1936), 1: 8-10. For a description of the churches after the Reformation was well-established, see E. William Monter, *Calvin's Geneva* (New York, 1967), especially the quotation on p. 1 and the map on p. 116. On the razing of the suburban churches of St. Victor and St. Léger, see Michel Roset, *Les chroniques de Genève*, ed. Henri Fazy (Geneva, 1894), p. 196.

Reproduced from E. William Monter, *Calvin's Geneva* (New York: Wiley, 1967), p. 116, with permission of the author.

the geographic limits and the authority of these three parishes. St. Gervais and La Madeleine retained precisely the boundaries and the central church buildings they had possessed before the Reformation. St. Pierre was constituted from the remnants of four pre-Reformation parishes. Its church building was the old cathedral.[5] Two other church buildings remained

5. There are several editions of these ordinances. One of the best is in Jean-François Bergier, ed., *Registres de la Compagnie des Pasteurs de Genève au temps de Calvin* (Geneva, 1964-), 1: 1-13; see p. 5 for this clause.

within its boundaries; one, the "Auditoire," was adapted for religious lectures and Bible study "congregations," while the other, St. Germain, remained empty until an influx of refugees later created need for a fourth temple.

The ordinances of 1541, furthermore, give these three primitive parishes explicit functions. They were to be the basic units for both the religious education of children and the administration of the sacraments. The text of the ordinance reads: "To send children to catechism and to receive the sacraments, as much as possible the limits of the parishes are to be observed."[6] In short, the pre-Reformation Catholic parish principle was maintained: the town was divided into parishes for ecclesiastical purposes, the parishes were basically geographic units and their integrity was protected.

Later sixteenth-century Genevan ecclesiastical ordinances, however, do not repeat all of this particular clause. The ordinances of 1561, which Calvin again helped draft and which were published, speak of the "three parishes" of St. Pierre, La Madeleine, and St. Gervais, and specify the services to be held in each.[7] But they do not again set the boundaries of each or require explicitly that each resident go to the church of his own parish for catechism and the sacraments. The ordinances of 1576, prepared under the supervision of Calvin's successor, Theodore Beza, have even less to say about the city parishes. In fact they use the word "parish" only to refer to the rural village churches dependent upon Geneva.[8]

What seems to have happened is that the central ecclesiastical institutions of Calvinist Geneva had taken to themselves so many of the powers of decision that the parishes were left with little autonomy. In particular, the Company of Pastors, over which Calvin and then Beza presided as moderator, collectively ordained all pastors and regulated the routines of all city parishes. This has led two very able, young Genevan historians, Olivier Labarthe and Bernard Lescaze, editors of the fourth volume of the *Registres de la Compagnie des Pasteurs de Genève (1575–1582)*, to claim that "the city formed a single parish."[9] They point out that the baptisms and marriages recorded in each of the three churches were not always performed by the pastors assigned to preach in those buildings. It is nevertheless clear that there were three separate sets of ecclesiastical records kept in the city, one in each of three churches. There is also independent evidence that lay Genevans of this period regarded themselves as belonging to only one of these three ecclesiastical units. The same scholars include in their edition a petition

---

6. Ibid., p. 5. "Pour envoyer les enfans au cathechisme et pour recepvoir les sacrements, que en tant qu'il se pourra faire on observe les limites des parroisses."

7. Guilielmus Baum, Eduardus Cunitz, and Eduardus Reuss, eds., *Ioannis Calvini Opera quae supersunt cmnia*, vol. 10/1 (Brunswick, 1871; reprinted 1964), col. 99.

8. Henri Heyer, *L'Eglise de Genève, 1535–1909* (Geneva, 1909), p. 283.

9. Olivier Labarthe and Bernard Lescaze, eds., *Registres de la Compagnie des Pasteurs de Genève*, vol. 4, *1575–1582* (Geneva, 1974), p. 161, n. 24.

from a number of people living around La Madeleine, drafted in 1584 after a period of epidemic had forced curtailment of church services, begging that they be re-established in their building.[10] It seems clear to me that these people regarded themselves as members of a parish.

While the problem certainly requires more intensive archival research in Geneva, the evidence I have seen points to the conclusion that a geographic parish structure survived in Geneva, even if in an attenuated form. That would explain why it was so easy for it to be legally re-emphasized early in this century. The 1908 Constitution of the Geneva National Protestant Church, legislation adopted after a partial disestablishment early in this century, contains an entire section on parishes which states flatly, "The Church is divided into parishes."[11] It goes on to describe in some detail their organization and powers. The writers of the 1908 legislation wanted to decentralize, to reduce the power of the Company of Pastors and other central institutions. It was easy for them to find more localized institutions to which power could be devolved, for the parishes were still there.

Systematic study of Boston's parishes is even more difficult, for they present a complexity which has yet to be faced in its entirety. Much can be pieced together, however, from some rather detailed histories of certain local churches. They reveal a pattern radically different from Geneva's, in spite of the fact that Boston, like most of the other towns in New England, was originally designed quite consciously to be a Calvinist community. It was the hub of the Massachusetts Bay colony, settled largely by Puritan Anglicans from England. Most of these settlers had been members in good standing of parishes of the Church of England and had never joined sectarian "separatist" congregations like their brethren in the slightly earlier Plymouth colony. Their first spiritual leaders in the New World had generally been ordained as priests of the Church of England. They were, to be sure, committed to a purification of the theology, the liturgy, and the ecclesiastical discipline of that church. The royal government, particularly after the accession of Charles I, and the Anglican bishops, particularly after the appointment of Laud as primate, had become increasingly hostile to this program of purification and brought great pressure to bear on these Puritans to conform to the practices of the established church. It was to gain freedom to establish a truly Reformed church that these Puritans came to New England.[12]

John Calvin's thought supplied the most important single ingredient of the

10. Ibid., pp. 261-270, but misdated there as 1578. The correct date was established by a related register entry of July 1, 1584, published in Olivier Labarthe and Micheline Tripet, eds., *Registres de la Compagnie des Pasteurs de Genève*, vol. 5, *1583-1588* (Geneva, 1976), p. 34, with the earlier dating error pointed out in n. 39.

11. Heyer, *L'Eglise*, p. 363. See also pp. 363-364, 366-367.

12. For a good recent introduction to these developments, see David D. Hall, *The Faithful Shepherd: A History of the New England Ministry in the Seventeenth Century* (Chapel Hill, North Carolina, 1972). For background on the earliest Boston community, see Darrett

Puritan's program of reform. Their Calvinism, to be sure, had been modified in the century since the beginning of the Reformation and its passage from the continent to England, notably by the addition of a highly developed convenant theology which owed much to certain other Swiss and Rhenish Protestant theologians. But the works of Calvin were often cited quite explicitly and the main outlines of his thought are clearly reflected in the confessions, the ecclesiastical legislation, and the apologetic books published in Puritan New England. In this body of thought, the ecclesiological component was certainly not neglected. Calvin's basic analysis of the Christian ministry into four offices—pastors, teachers, elders, and deacons—is adopted by practically every code and commentator in New England. In addition to Calvin's thought, Calvinist practice provided models for these Puritans. They were well aware of the ways in which Reformed churches had been organized by Calvinists in Scotland, France, and the Netherlands.[13] Some of them were even aware of the model of Geneva. Among the early settlers were a number of French Huguenots who had actually visited Geneva. One of them, Andrew Le Mercier, pastor of the French Reformed Church in Boston, published in that city a *Church History of Geneva*. It did not appear, to be sure, until 1732, a good century after the foundation of Boston and well after the basic structures of Massachusetts churches had been set. But it suggests a tradition of interest among New England Puritans in their Calvinist roots in Geneva. It speaks of Geneva as "the Head of the Reformed Body." While it does not have much to say about the parish system in Geneva, it explicitly mentions the parish church buildings of the city, noting that four had originally served as Catholic churches before the Reformation and only a fifth had been constructed since then, early in the eighteenth century.[14]

These Puritans, furthermore, were thoroughly familiar with the operations of the parish system in England. They were no doubt aware that it was being introduced at that time, with only a few modifications, into the other main English settlement in North America, Virginia.[15] Their first impulse

B. Rutman, *Winthrop's Boston: Portrait of a Puritan Town, 1630–1649* (Chapel Hill, North Carolina, 1965), especially chap. 5, pp. 98–134, "Toward a New Jerusalem," on First Church in Boston.

13. See, for example, Williston Walker, *The Creeds and Platforms of Congregationalism* (Boston, 1960; reprint of 1893 ed.), pp. 90–91, a 1618 statement of the Plymouth Brethren while still in Leiden: "Touching ye Ecclesiasticall ministrie, namely of pastores for teaching, elders for ruling, & deacons for distributing ye churches contribution . . . we doe wholy and in all points agree with ye French reformed churches, according to their publick confession of faith."

14. Andrew Le Mercier, *The Church History of Geneva* . . . (Boston, 1732) pp. 1, 206–207. I consulted a microfilm of the Newberry Library copy.

15. Guy Fred Wells, *Parish Education in Colonial Virginia* (New York, 1923), chap. 1. Cf. William H. Seiler, "The Anglican Parish in Virginia," in *Seventeenth-Century America: Essays in Colonial History,* ed. James Morton Smith (Chapel Hill, North Carolina, 1959), pp. 119–142, for analysis of some changes in internal parish organization made necessary by the colonial situation.

was to introduce it without change into their own colony. The town, the basic unit into which they divided Massachusetts, was, in fact, a simple transplant of the English parish.[16] It was a unit of both civil and ecclesiastical government. The first towns, to be sure, were small and widely scattered agricultural settlements. Only with the growth of Boston as a major commercial center did New England develop an urban complex so large that it could no longer be served by a single parish church.

Boston's problem of creating several parishes within one community was foreseen before it was met. Among the first to foresee it was John Cotton, a highly educated and articulate minister of the Boston church who, in 1644, published a general defense of the new ecclesiastical polity being created by the Puritans of New England titled *The Keys of the Kingdom of Heaven*. In considering the propagation and multiplication of churches, he says:

> When a particular church of Christ shall grow so full of members, as all of them cannot hear the voice of their ministers; then as a hive full of bees swarmeth forth, so is the church occasioned to send forth a significant number of her members. . . . And for that end they either send forth some one or other of their elders with them, or direct them where to procure such to come unto them.[17]

That suggestion became legislation in 1648, when a synod of ministers called by the General Court of Massachusetts, the legislative assembly of the colony, enacted the Cambridge Platform. This statement was, in effect, the draft of an ecclesiastical constitution for the Puritan churches of New England. In many ways it is comparable to the ecclesiastical ordinances of Geneva drafted by Calvin. While the Platform is designed largely for a polity in which there would be one church in each town, it does foresee a need for expansion in certain settings. It says that a local church "ought not to be of greater number then [sic] may ordinarily meet together conveniently in one place."[18] It provides for the creation of a new church "out of an other, by sending forth such of their members as are willing to remove, & to procure some officers to them," using for illustration Cotton's metaphor of bee swarms.[19]

Only two years later, Second Church of Boston was created. First Church,

---

16. Any transplant, of course, poses some problems. One of the more difficult in this case was the fact that there were variations in the English model and sometimes citizens of a Massachusetts town came from several different types of English parishes. For an extended case study of this problem, see Sumner Chilton Powell, *Puritan Village: The Formation of a New England Town* (Middletown, Conn., 1963). For a stimulating but schematic overview of the parish in England during the early seventeenth century, see Christopher Hill, *Society and Puritanism in Pre-Revolutionary England* (London, 1969), a reprint, chap. 12, pp. 407–428, "The Secularization of the Parish."

17. John Cotton, *John Cotton on the Churches of New England*, ed. Larzer Ziff (Cambridge, Mass., 1968), p. 111. Cf. the slightly expanded version of the same argument in J[ohn] Cotton, *The Way of the Churches of Christ in New England* ... (London, 1645), pp. 109–110.

18. Walker, *Creed and Platforms*, p. 206.

19. Ibid., pp. 232–233.

formed in 1630 by the original settlers in Charlestown where they first landed, within a few months was moved permanently across the Charles River to the middle of the peninsula upon which Boston was being built. As the town grew, more and more people built homes on the northern tip of the peninsula, including many of the most respected and wealthiest of the community. Obviously this new section needed its own church and, accordingly, in 1650, Second Church (which came to be called Old North) was created in that area with the full cooperation of John Cotton of First Church.[20] It looked as if Boston were on its way to building a uniform system of geographic parishes on the European model.

That did not happen. Over the next century the city of Boston grew very fast and its people felt a clear need for additional churches, but they did not establish them in a system of geographic parishes. By 1750 Boston had eleven Congregational churches, of which three had been established in schisms of established congregations. There were also three Anglican churches, two Baptist churches, a Presbyterian church, and a Quaker meeting. Some traces of geographic parish systems can be found among non-schismatic Congregationalists and the Anglicans, but since their two systems overlapped each other, there were many complications. Clearly, a distinctive American type of parish was emerging.

Three factors explain this fundamental change. The most important was a sectarianism more pronounced among the American Puritans than among most European Protestants. A second was the intervention of a royal government hostile to the direction of ecclesiastical development in the colony. A minor factor in colonial Boston, but a major one elsewhere and at later times, was the ethnic diversity of immigrants to America.

Sectarianism is most obvious in Boston in the two Baptist churches and the Quaker meeting created there between 1650 and 1750. Their members were avowedly sectarian and openly scorned any established church supported by a secular government. They had been savagely persecuted in their native England and were initially persecuted in Boston as well. Some of the earliest Quakers there had even been put to death. But both groups eventually won grudging toleration.[21] Sectarianism, however, was probably more significant, if more subtle, within the dominant and established Puritan churches. It was given a chance to develop by a basic organizational principle adopted by the Puritans in New England, the principle which awarded all significant

20. A useful general introduction can be found in Joseph S. Clark, *Historical Sketch of the Congregational Churches in Massachusetts, from 1620 to 1858* (Boston, 1858). On the foundation of Boston First Church, see p. 8; on the foundation of Second Church, pp. 34–35. See also Chandler Robbins, *A History of the Second Church, or Old North, in Boston; to which is added, a history of the New Brick Church* (Boston, 1852), pp. 5–7.
21. Nathan E. Wood, *The History of the First Baptist Church of Boston, 1665–1899* (Philadelphia, 1899); Richard P. Hallowell, *The Quaker Invasion of Massachusetts* (Boston, 1887).

ecclesiastical powers, and especially the primary power to ordain a minister, to each local congregation. Collective bodies, like the synods which adopted the Cambridge Platform, and more informal assemblies of ministers had no powers to coerce individual congregations. Boston never developed an institution with the powers of the Geneva Company of Pastors. Because of their insistence on this principle, New England Puritans came to be called Congregationalists.

The thrust of sectarianism within Congregationalism first became apparent in the creation of Third Church in Boston (which came to be called Old South) in 1669. It was created by the secession of a large minority of members from First Church. The reason for their secession was violent objection to the election of John Davenport as minister to First Church, replacing Wilson and Cotton, its recently deceased, original ministers. There were several reasons for the objection to the elderly Davenport, but the most important seems to have been theological. Davenport rejected the new doctrine of the half-way covenant, which would permit the baptism of children of congregational members who were in good standing, but were not communicant members of the church because they had never provided a public "relation" of a personal experience of spiritual illumination. Davenport and the majority at First wanted to maintain the very high standards for admission to both sacraments, baptism and communion, which had been established at the beginning among Puritans in New England. The minority, along with most of the ministers in other churches in the colony, wanted to relax the standard for admission to baptism. The secession seems to have been encouraged by the ministers of other churches in the area. The new congregation erected for itself a church building only two blocks from First. It clearly meant to appeal to exactly the same geographic area as First and ignored any kind of geographic justification for its existence. It may be considered the first Congregational parish of an ideological rather than a geographic character.[22]

In the decades that followed, two additional schisms led to the establishment of new Congregational churches in Boston. In 1699, a group of dissidents formed Fourth (or Brattle Square) Church. They wished to make certain changes in the liturgy and to relax membership standards still further by waiving the requirement of a "relation" before admission to communion. Their building was also only two blocks from First. They seem to have drawn members principally from Old South.[23] In 1720, another group of

22. Hamilton Andrews Hill, *History of the Old South Church (Third Church), Boston, 1669–1884*, vol. 1 (Boston and New York, 1890), chaps. 1 and 2. For locating the precise sites of church buildings, I have used a map prepared by John Bonner, "The Town of Boston in New England," first printed in 1722, reprinted in 1835, in Boston.

23. Hill, *Old South Church*, p. 312. See also Ellis Loring Motte et al., eds., *Records of the Church in Brattle Square, Boston . . . 1699–1872* (Boston, 1902), especially pp. vii–viii. At least half of its founding members came from Old South. Compare the membership lists in

Reproduction of a map of Boston drawn by Captain John Bonner, first published in 1722.

dissidents created what became New Brick Church by seceding from New North, the fifth of the Congregational churches created in Boston, in a dispute over the selection of a new second minister.[24] Their building was only three blocks from the church they were leaving. Most of the other ministers of Boston opposed the establishment of Brattle Street Church; many of them, however, encouraged the formation of New Brick Church.

These three schisms clearly complicated the parish structure of Congregational Boston. Each took place on an ideological or organizational issue. None could be prevented by a superior church body. Together they weakened seriously the traditional concept of a geographic parish.

But there were further complications. In the 1680s the English crown decided to take more direct responsibility for the government of the colony and dispatched a royal governor to Boston to act as the crown's agent. The first of these governors, Edmund Andros, was a committed Anglican. He insisted that he and his retinue be permitted to worship according to the liturgy of the Church of England, without any of the innovations introduced by Congregationalists, and he forced the members of Old South to permit a newly formed Anglican congregation to use their building for this purpose. This group became the nucleus of King's Chapel, which was formally organized in 1686, and erected its own building two blocks away in 1688.[25]

Later English governors were less arrogant in their treatment of the majority Congregationalists, but continued to support Anglican worship. As the number of Anglicans grew in Boston, the geographic parish system of England was introduced for them; a second church, named Christ Church, was organized in the northern part of the city in 1722, and a third, Trinity, was organized in 1733 and erected its building not far from King's Chapel in 1735.[26] The result of official encouragement was thus the creation in Boston of an Anglican system of parishes which overlapped the already weakening system established by the majority Congregationalists, and was in direct competition with it.

A final complication lies in the organization in 1729 of a Presbyterian church. It was the creation of recent Scotch-Irish immigrants who, though they were in full doctrinal agreement with the majority Congregationalists,

Motte, p. 95, with those in [Hamilton Andrews Hill and George Frederick Bigelow?], *An Historical Catalogue of the Old South Church (Third Church), Boston, 1669–1882* (Boston, 1883), pp. 5–18 and 114.

24. Robbins, *History of Second Church*, pp. 170–181. See also [Ephraim Eliot], *Historical Notices of the New North Religious Society in the Town of Boston . . .* (Boston, 1822), pp. 9–16.

25. Henry Wilder Foote, *Annals of King's Chapel* (Boston, 1882), chaps. 2 and 3.

26. Ibid., pp. 321–325, and chap. 12. See also Henry Burroughs, *A Historical Account of Christ Church, Boston* (Boston, 1874) and *Trinity Church in the City of Boston, Massachusetts, 1733–1933* (Boston, 1933).

subscribing to the same Calvinist Westminster Confession of Faith as their basic creedal affirmation and using similar liturgies, still preferred a more aristocratic form of church government which vested more powers within each local congregation to local elders, and granted more power over the congregation to more broadly based and powerful synods. In addition, the Scots probably preferred to worship with people of their own background. That complication proved to be temporary, for in 1786 this Presbyterian congregation joined the majority as Federal Street Congregational Church. The failure of more Scotch-Irish to settle in Boston obviously made difficult the establishment of a full presbyterial system. One generation later, the ethnic reasons for maintaining a separate church had no doubt also faded away.[27]

These same three factors seem to have been at work throughout the American colonies, but were of differing importance. In New York, the ethnic complication was particularly pronounced. The first Dutch settlers had created a Calvinist Reformed Church on the classical (or presbyterial) model of their homeland. Later English conquerors imposed an Anglican Episcopalian system on top of that, again creating two competing parish structures, and soon other more sectarian groups established themselves.[28] Since royal authority was particularly strong in the southern colonies, many of them established Anglican churches. But these establishments were resented and undermined by large numbers of non-English immigrants, particularly Presbyterian Scotch-Irish, and were finally discredited and collapsed during the turmoil associated with the American Revolution.[29]

By the time of the creation of the American national government, therefore, ecclesiastical structures had been profoundly modified. Established churches claiming a monopoly right over religious practice had collapsed in every colony, and with them, the geographic parish system. America began its national life as a religiously pluralistic society, predominantly divided into ideologically defined parishes. Despite the Calvinist impulse that explains much of the country's first settlement, the Genevan model of an established church divided into geographic parishes had been abandoned. There were, to be sure, attempts to re-introduce geographic parish systems in the nineteenth century. This was particularly true among Roman Catholics who began arriving in great numbers only after the creation of the new nation. They have been successful, to a degree, in certain large urban areas with dense Catholic populations. But in other parts of the country even Catholics have

27. Ezra S. Gannett, *A Memorial of the Federal-Street Meeting-House* (Boston, 1860).
28. Jonathan Greenleaf, *A History of the Churches of all Denominations in the City of New York from the First Settlement to the year 1846* (New York, 1846); Gabriel P. Disosway, *The Earliest Churches of New York and its Vicinity* (New York, 1865).
29. Lester Douglas Joyce, *Church and Clergy in the American Revolution: A Study in Group Behavior* (New York, 1966).

found it difficult to maintain a traditional parish system. Nowhere has a parish structure been created which orders the religious life of an entire population as it once did in European communities. Indeed, much of what religious life still remains vital in Europe, in communities which are now often highly secularized, is still organized on traditional parish lines. America, on the other hand, remains, in organization as in belief, a religiously pluralistic society.

Reprinted by permission from Church History *48 (1979), 290-304.*

X

The First Expression
of Theodore Beza's Political Ideas*

Calvinism supplied one of the roots of modern democracy. The democratic revolutions of the eighteenth century in America and France
drew some inspiration from the English civil war of the mid-seventeenth
century, which in turn was justified partly by arguments developed
during the French religious wars of the sixteenth century in such
Calvinist polemical works as the *Vindiciae contra tyrannos*[1]), the
Franco-Gallia of Francis Hotman, and the *De jure magistratuum* of Theodore Beza. While Beza was not the most original of these sixteenth-
century theorists, his position as Calvin's chief aide and, after 1564,
as Calvin's successor in the Geneva church, meant that his ideas were
particularly likely to be respected by Calvinists. It is therefore important
to find out more about the sources and first expressions of his political
ideas.

The first religious polemic Beza wrote was a defense.of Calvin's
arguments for the burning of Servetus. These arguments had been
attacked by Castellion. Calvin did not answer Castellion directly, but
Beza did in a work that defended the position that governments have
a duty to put dangerous heretics to death, titled *De haereticis a civili
magistratu puniendis*[2]), published in 1554. In developing his position

*) I must thank Professors Garrett Mattingly and Roland H. Bainton for
advice on earlier drafts of this article, and the Rotary Foundation of Rotary
International for a fellowship that made possible some of the research on which
it is based.

[1]) Harold J. Laski, ed., A Defence of Liberty Against Tyrants: a translation
of the Vindiciae contra tyrannos by Junius Brutus (London, 1924), is a modern
reprint of a 1689 English translation. In the long introduction Laski diccusses the
popularity of this book and its influence on many English thinkers.

[2]) Full title: DE HAERETICIS A CI- / uili Magistratu puniendis Libellus,
ad- / uersus Martini Bellii farraginem, & no / uorum Academicorum sectam, /
Theodoro Beza Vezelio auctore. / Oliua Roberti Stephani. / M. D. LIIII.

I must thank Professor Roland H. Bainton of Yale University for the loan of
his personal copy of this book.

Cf. the French translation: TRAITTE / DE L'AVTHORITE / DV MAGI-
STRAT EN LA PVNITION / des heretiques, & du moyē d'y proceder, fait / en
Latin par Theodore de Besze, / CONTRE L'OPINION DE CERTAINS / Academi-

Beza first had to define the nature of government and its basic functions. It is this part of the book which is of special interest to the student of political ideas.

The first political principle Beza enunciates, is that governments are established by social consent, in order to achieve a harmonious social organization. Here is the analysis in his own words:

> Since therefore all councils and assemblies of men joined by oath, which we call cities, have this ultimate goal, to help men live the happiest possible lives; moreover in order to attain this goal, certain laws must be maintained, some men [are] constituted custodians and protectors of these laws, [these men] being called in the general Greek vocabulary *archas* and in Latin the Magistrate. It is well-known, unless I am mistaken, that the Magistrate is he who by the public consent of the citizens is declared custodian of that peace and tranquillity. This peace depends on the observation of laws, which establishes the safety of all the citizens.[3]

Beza's term "consent of the citizens" seems to mean that citizens must participate in the selection of the governors, if a valid government is to be established. His statement is thus a rudimentary expression of social contract. He does not set this consent principle up as a norm of the way government should be established, but rather as a description of the way it actually was established. His description roughly corresponds to the method by which municipal government was re-constituted periodically in the Swiss city-states and in most of the large cities of France.[4] In nearly every one of these cities all those inhabitants

---

ques, qui par leurs escrits soustiennent l' impunite de / ceux qui sement des erreurs, & les veulent exempter de la su / iection des loix. / Nouuellement traduit de Latin en François par Ni- / colas Colladon. / Imprimé par Conrad Badius, / M. D. LX. / There is a copy in the Bibliothèque publique et universitaire de Genève.

Bibliographical information on both editions in Paul-F. Geisendorf, Théodore de Bèze (Geneva 1949), p. 65.

[3]) This and all following translations into English are my own. They are based on the original Latin text. See p. 22 for this passage. Cf. French edition, pp. 31—32.

Pierre Mesnard, L'Essor de la philosophie politique au XVIe siècle (Paris, 2nd ed., 1952), pp. 309—315, takes note of most of these statements, but has overlooked the last and most important statement I quote below. He bases his analysis on the 1560 French edition.

[4]) For France see Gaston Zeller, Les Institutions de la France au XVIe siècle (Paris, 1948), pp. 37—56. Research in the municipal archives of Geneva, Lausanne, and Neuchatel in Switzerland convinces me that the same generalizations apply there. Check such municipal narrative histories as the collectively written

who had either inherited or purchased the privileged position of "bourgeois" met at regular intervals, usually once a year, to elect the governing magistrates or syndics and the other administrative officials. Syndics were usually, but by no means always[5]), chosen from a nominated slate prepared by one of the governing councils. It is this approximate municipal "democracy" which Beza probably had in mind when developing these general statements on the nature of government.

Beza goes on to define the functions of the Magistrate very inclusively:

> Therefore, to define concisely the "Magistrate," let us say that it is he who is constituted in the Republic for the conservation of all things public as well as private, sacred as well as profane, in order that the citizens of the Republic which he superintends live the happiest life possible.[6])

This definition of function also corresponds roughly to the functions actually assumed by Swiss and French city governments at this time.

Up to this point Beza's analysis has been avowedly "secular" and based on sources drawn from classical antiquity. Now he turns to a "spiritual" definition of government, and in so doing indicates that he thinks popular consent is necessary not only to the establishment of valid government, but also to the enactment of valid law. He distinguishes two kinds of law: civil law and custom law. Civil law is relatively universal, custom law is the strictly local, traditional law. Both kinds apparently were derived ultimately from popular consent. But Beza also insists that the popular control of the enactment of civil law must be superintended by the true Church of God, and is in fact one of the reasons for the existence of the Church.

> Furthermore, because it is necessary that these laws first gain the assent of all the citizens, which cannot be done if they are not first made intelligible to them, and moreover a work (to speak properly) is best done by one person; for these reasons the Lord our God who established this Church first of all wished to constitute certain duly constituted interpreters of that civil

---

Alexandre Jullien, ed., Histoire de Genève des origines à 1798 (Geneva, 1951), passim., hereafter cited as Histoire de Genève.

[5]) Histoire de Genève, p. 208, for an example of the selection of a Syndic not nominated by one of the governing councils.

[6]) Beza, op. cit., p. 24. Cf. French edition, pp. 33—34.

law pertaining to the conscience. Their duty in each assembly is to train the consciences of the citizens, partly by word, example, and oration, to lead them to the knowledge and approval of these laws; partly also by dogma and its enforcement by means of the Ecclesiastical Consistory which he himself established, to keep opinion dutiful.[7])

This description of law-formation roughly corresponds to the actual processes of law-formation in Calvin's Geneva.[8])

After a further discussion of the nature of law, Beza finally comes to his "spiritual" definition of government:

Therefore, to express all these things in a few words: in each assembly or Republic of the Christian Church, Magistrates are constituted as representatives of God, to serve as examples to the faithful in the declaring of glory and praise to God.[9])

Beza then goes on to discuss the duty of subjects, and concludes that they are bound to obey the Magistrates in all earthly things. But the Magistrates themselves are bound by the Word of God in spiritual things. This creates problems:

(1) The Church has become, in Beza's thought, an important secondary organ in the processes of law-formation and law enforcement. What will happen if these two agencies, magistrate and Church, conflict? Who triumphs if the enacting and enforcing magistrate and the persuading Church cannot agree on what can and ought to be law? What happens if the magistrate actually goes so far as to defy or suppress the Church?

(2) This whole theory of government is city-centered. The sovereign unit in Beza's political system seems to be the semi-democratic city-state. The city alone gains authority directly from consent of the people and it appears to be sovereign, not only in controlling the political and religious life of its citizens, but also in protecting them against outside threats. Now what happens if the city is actually subject to a superior jurisdiction? The problem was not so obvious in Switzerland, but it was acute in France and Germany where cities owed more or less direct allegiance to King or Emperor. And it was especially acute for Calvinists

---

[7]) Beza, op. cit., p. 26. Cf. French edition, p. 37.

[8]) The Histoire de Genève has enough descriptions of passage of actual laws to illustrate the methods of law-formation in Geneva. Eugène Choisy, La Théocratie à Genève au temps de Calvin (Geneva, 1897), describes at length the extent of clerical activity in the legislative process.

[9]) Beza, op. cit., p. 29. Cf. French edition, p. 41

since so much of their strength was in such cities. In this situation which authority ultimately should determine religious and political policy? What does a city magistrate do when a prince commands him to abandon policies he believes to be divinely inspired? Should divinely instructed obedience to the "powers that be," or obedience to the word of divine writ prevail?

Much later in his argument Beza faces some of these problems. In a later section of the book, in which he is answering one by one the arguments of Castellion, he comes to this one: Many princes abuse their power and therefore should not be trusted with the power to punish heresy. This immediately raised in Beza's mind the problem of conflict between different governmental agencies.

> What then if the Lord grant us princes who either through apparent cruelty or through crass ignorance combat the reign of Christ? First of all the Church should take refuge in prayers and tears, and correct its life. For these are the arms of the faithful for overcoming the rages of the world. However the inferior Magistrate must, as much as possible, with prudence and moderation, yet constantly and wisely, maintain pure religion in the area under his authority. A signal example of this has been shown in our times by Magdeburg, that city on the Elbe . . . [aside against Castellion]. . . . When then several Princes abuse their office, whoever still feels it necessary to refuse to use the Christian Magistrates offered by God against external violence whether of the unfaithful or of heretics, I charge deprives the Church of God of a most useful, and (as often as it pleases the Lord) necessary defense.[10])

In this statement I see an embryonic justification for democratic revolution. To be sure there is much hedging. Resistance to a government can be led only by already constituted inferior agencies of government, deriving their original and continuing legislative power from only a part (and probably a minority) of the subordinate population. These inferior agencies of government and their sustaining populations must be under the supervision of the Church of God. This meant the churches of the Reformed persuasion, to Beza. And these inferior agencies of government cannot act until such other expedients as prayer have already been tried. But despite these qualifications this is one of the

---

[10]) Beza, op. cit., p. 133. Cf. French edition, pp. 207—208.

first justifications of popular right to overthrow tyrannical government ever expressed by a Calvinist. And in historical fact this right of inferior magistrates to revolt was expanded to permit whole populations, even without the benevolent supervision of the Church, to revolt against royal government.

Another qualification: this justification for independent magistral action was aimed primarily against "heretics" such as Servetus. But Beza's addition of the phrase, "the external violence of the unfaithful," shows clearly that he felt these magistral powers could also be used against Catholic over-government. His citation of the example of Magdeburg is especially significant. This imperial city in Germany had used its medieval secular prerogatives in 1524 to reform the city by introducing the Lutheran brand of Protestantism, without consulting the temporal lord, the archbishop, and had in 1548 taken the lead in North German armed defiance of the "Interim," which had been enacted by the Emperor and Electors of the Holy Roman Empire in an attempt to suppress the Protestant worship established by local authorities in many places in the Germanies.[11]) Both times the regularly chosen councilors and hundred-men of the city, pushed by popular clamor, took the measures in defiance of constituted over-authority.

By taking Magdeburg as his example, Beza sanctions resistance against intolerant Catholic government, when it is led by constituted inferior governmental authorities. Beza's thought here may even show direct influence of the Magdeburg *Bekenntnis*[12]), an early Lutheran statement of a religious right of resistance, published by the Lutheran ministers of Magdeburg in 1550. Beza's contemporaries refer to a Magdeburger influence on his thought, but such historians of political thought as J. W. Allen are inclined to discount these stories.[13]) Here

---

[11]) Friedrich Hülsse, Die Stadt Magdeburg im Kampfe für den Protestantismus während der Jahre 1547—1551 (Halle a. S., 1892), pp. 5, 20 ff.

[12]) Full title: Bekentnis Unter- / richt und vermanung der Pfarr- / hern und Prediger der Christlichen / Kirchen zu Magdeburgk. / Anno 1550. Den 13. Aprilis. /

Three Bible quotations fill out the title page. Folio recto Qiii lists the nine signers of the tract, eight of them identified as pastors of specific Magdeburg churches. The succeeding recto folio gives the publisher, Michel Lotther of Magdeburg.

I must thank Professor Roland H. Bainton for allowing me to consult his personal copy of this book.

[13]) J. W. Allen, A History of Political Thought in the Sixteenth Century (London, 3rd ed., 1951), pp. 103—106, analyses the Magdeburg Bekenntnis, and the

we have a positive indication that Beza did indeed know of the Magdeburg example, and that the sources of his resistance theory may hence have ultimate connection to the crude but rarely used resistance theory of certain early Lutherans.

The Magdeburg *Bekenntnis* had vested optional powers of religious resistance in the "untere Obrigkeit" against the "hohe Obrigkeit" or imperial power of Charles V. This appeal to "untere Obrigkeit" was in part an appeal to the Protestant Electors of the Holy Roman Empire whose constitutional position in choosing the Emperor and sanctioning his edicts was already legally defined. But the action of Magdeburg in defying the "Interim" without princely support would indicate that "untere Obrigkeit" could apply to the elected governments of independent cities. Beza thus applies this doctrine of "inferior magistrates" to cities, and thereby adds an important element to developing democratic theory.

The writers of the Magdeburg *Bekenntnis* probably drew on even earlier Lutheran thinkers for some of their ideas, and Beza could conceivably have also been influenced by these men. Luther himself claimed that in certain cases the Princes of Germany could, in the name of the nation, resist the Emperor when he overstepped the boundaries of his imperial power by behaving as a tyrant on religious matters.[14] And a number of publicists at the time of the Schmalkadic war developed even further this theory justifying princely resistance for religious reasons.[15]

Another possible literary source of this idea of Beza's can be found in Calvin's classic *Institute*. At the end of all the editions following that of 1541, Calvin says that inferior governmental authorities like the *ephors* in ancient Greece, the Senate in classical Rome, and possibly the Estates in contemporary Europe might restrain a ruler bent on

---

possibilities of its influence on Calvinist thinkers. He minimizes or dismisses these possibilities. Hereafter cited as Allen.

[14] Karl Müller, Luthers Äußerungen über das Recht des bewaffneten Widerstands gegen den Kaiser, no. 8 in Sitzungsberichte der philosophisch-philologischen und der historischen Klasse der K. B. Akademie der Wissenschaften zu München (Munich, 1915); also in Hans Baron, "Religion and Politics in the German Imperial Cities during the Reformation," English Historical Review, LII (1937), see pp. 422—427.

[15] Oskar Waldeck, „Die Publizistik des Schmalkaldischen Krieges I", Archiv für Reformationsgeschichte, Texte und Untersuchungen VII (1909—1910), 1—55. Cf. Baron, op. cit.

oppression.[16]) Calvin here is more explicit than Beza as to the nature of the inferior authority and less explicit as to the actual nature of the right of resistance.

It is also possible that Martin Bucer, the Strasbourg theologian who influenced Calvin so deeply in so many ways, influenced Beza's political thought either directly or via Calvin. Bucer's ideas on the nature of secular government, expressed briefly as early as 1530 in the second edition of his *In evangelium Matthei enarrationes*, resemble Beza's in many ways, in particular being very city-centered. An edition of Bucer's *In librum Judicum enarrationes*, which contains a few brief anti-monarchic statements, was published in Geneva in 1554, the year of the publication of Beza's *De haereticis*.[17])

But much of this speculation on sources is inconclusive. The only influence that I found could be proved by actual citation in the *De haereticis* to have affected Beza's political thinking is the influence of the Magdeburg example in defying the "Interim."

Speculation on the possible influences of Beza's resistance theory on others is also inconclusive, but nevertheless also important. Let us begin this second set of speculations by examining possible influences of this theory on writers contemporary to Beza.

A first possible line of influence may have led to John Ponet, the exiled English bishop whose book, *A Shorte Treatise of Politicke Power* (1556), contains an important early statement of the right to resist, argued on the same lines as the Magdeburg *Bekenntnis*.[18]) He may have had the opportunity to read Beza. He was an exile in Strasbourg at the time he wrote his book and could very easily have seen the *De haereticis*, published two years earlier.

---

[16]) John Calvin, Ioannis Calvini Opera quae supersunt omnia (Corpus Reformatorum Vols. 29ff., Brunswick, 1863—1900), II, 1116 (1559 Latin ed. of Institute) and IV, 1160 (1560 French ed. of Institute); hereafter cited as CR Calv. opp. See Allen, pp. 58—59, for commentary and information on earlier editions.

[17]) Hans Baron, "Calvinist Republicanism and its Historical Roots," Church History, VIII (1939), 30—42, analyzes Bucer's political ideas and insists that they are the source of Calvin's political ideas, on grounds of philologic similarity and because the 1554 edition of the In Librum Judicum was published in Geneva. Baron does not discuss the possible influence of Bucer on Beza.

[18]) Winthrop S. Hudson, John Ponet (1516?—1556), Advocate of Limited Monarchy (Chicago, 1942), chapter VIII, discusses sources of Ponet's thought at length but does not mention Beza as a possible source. Cf. Allen, pp. 118—120.

It is even more likely that John Knox and Christopher Goodman, the two English-speaking Calvinist exponents of the right to revolt for religious reasons who were later active in Scotland, knew Beza's book. Goodman and a friend both claimed that the leading scholars in Switzerland had been consulted before his inflammatory book was drafted.[19]) Knox is known to have consulted theologians in Geneva and Zurich.[20]) One of the most important roads from Geneva to Zurich passes through Lausanne where Beza was at that time teaching. Perhaps Beza was one of the men who supported the ideas of Knox and Goodman on female government when many other theologians remained dubious.

There is even the possibility that Calvin may have been influenced by Beza's ideas. An obscure reference to Daniel in the *Institute* which has been interpreted as permitting resistance first appeared in the 1559 and 1560 editions.[21]) The other reference of this nature in the *Institute* of course precedes the first publication of the *De haereticis*.[22])

Other pieces of evidence also suggest that Calvin could have supported Beza's political ideas. The Geneva municipal council granted permission for publication of the *De haereticis* by a Genevan printer at Calvin's

---

[19]) Goodman to Peter Martyr, CR Calv. opp., XVII, 295—297, 20 August 1558, relevant part translated in editor's notes, John Knox, The Works of John Knox, David Laing ed., 6 vols. (Edinburgh, 1846—1864), IV, 359. Whittingham of the English congregation in Geneva, quoted in Emile Doumergue, Jean Calvin, les hommes et les choses de son temps, 7 vols. (Lausanne & Neuilly-sur-Seine, 1899—1927), V, 520—525.

[20]) CR Calv. opp., XV, 91—93, a memorandum in Bullinger's hand of questions posed by Knox on the legitimacy of political authority and the Zurich church's answers, a document apparently sent to Calvin with a letter of 26 March 1554. Translated by Laing in The Works of John Knox cited above, III, 221—226. Cf. CR Calv. opp., XVII, 490—492, Calvinus Cicellio, n. d., probably March 1559, for Calvin's account of Knox's conferences with him on these political questions, translated in The Works of John Knox, IV, 357—358. Knox used what was apparently a copy of the Magdeburg Bekenntnis in a 1564 debate in Scotland, and this is therefore assumed to be an important source of his theories, no doubt more important than Beza's book. See The Works of John Knox, II, 453—454.

[21]) CR Calv. opp., II, 1117 (1159 Latin ed. of Institute) and IV, 1161 (1560 French ed. of Institute). Allen, pp. 57—58, does not accept this interpretation; Hudson, op. cit., p. 193, does and cites further evidence from Calvin's sermons.

[22]) See above, n. 16. For full length studies of Calvin's political thought see Hans Baron, Calvins Staatsanschauung und das konfessionelle Zeitalter (Berlin u. Munich, 1924); Josef Bohatec, Calvin und das Recht (Feudingen in Westfalen, 1934); Marc-Edouard Chenevière, La pensée politique de Calvin (Paris, 1937).

personal request.[23]) Furthermore, Calvin probably approved of the later translation of the book into French since it was drafted by his loyal follower and one-time secretary, Nicolas Colladon.[24]) A Genevan printer again published it, and Genevan censorship laws were so strict and so insistent that theological works be referred to the pastoral corps headed by Calvin[25]), that it is difficult to see how the translation could have been printed without Calvin's approval.

The timing of this French translation is also significant and suggests that Beza's political ideas may have influenced not only writers but also men of action. The translation was published in 1560, just following the Conspiracy of Amboise, the ill-fated attempt of a rash group of young Protestant noblemen to kidnap the king and do away with his Guise regents. The translation thus accompanied a host of bitterly anti-Guisard pamphlets from the presses. Some of these pamphlets have been traced to Francis Hotman, another important Calvinist political writer of the period. Some of them are known to have been distributed in France with Beza's help.[26]) Perhaps the translation was released at this time to reinforce the political arguments of the anti-Guisard tracts and to prove again Calvinist Biblical orthodoxy and abhorrence of real heresy.

Reception in France of the general theological arguments of Beza after 1560 is suggested by synodal minutes.[27]) It is logical to assume that the political ideas were carried to France along with the theological arguments. In fact there is proof that a statement of the aims and

---

[23]) Bibliothèque publique et universitaire de Genève, Mss. Dufour, contain quotations from the Geneva Registres du Conseil for July 17, 19, 20, 1554, regarding this publication. Originals of these entries may be checked in the Archives d'Etat de Genève. See CR Calv. opp., XXI, 580 for printed excerpts. I must thank MM. Delarue and Chaix of the Library staff for placing these manuscripts on sixteenth-century printing in Geneva at my disposal.

[24]) On Colladon see Hippolyte Aubert, "Nicolas Colladon et les Registres de la Compagnie des Pasteurs et Professeurs de Genève," Bulletin de la Société d'histoire et d'archéologie de Genève, II (1898—1904), 138—163.

[25]) On the edicts regulating Genevan censorship see Alfred Cartier, "Arrêts du Conseil de Genève sur le fait de l'imprimerie et de la librairie de 1541 à 1550," Mémoires et documents publiés par la Société d'histoire et d'archéologie de Genève, XXIII (1888—1894): Paul Chaix, Recherches sur l'imprimerie à Genève de 1550 à 1564 (Geneva, 1954).

[26]) Henri Naef, La Conjuration d'Amboise et Genève (Geneva 1922), passim., especially the Annexes VIII and XII on these pamphlets. See pp. 489 ff. on Beza's action in sending pamphlets to France.

[27]) Aymon, ed., Tous les synodes nationaux des églises réformées de France ... 2 vols. (The Hague 1710), passim.

purposes of government including its duty to suppress heresy was actually adopted by one provincial synod — the Synod of Montauban, April 8—11, 1561. This synod sent a copy of its minutes to the Geneva Company of Pastors, which certainly must have made the Geneva pastors aware of the adoption of these ideas in France.[28]) The Synod of Montauban did not go so far, however, as to claim in writing a right to revolt.

Though this type of direct evidence of Beza's influence is scanty and scattered, there is proof that the idea of a right of resistance caught hold. John Knox succeeded in 1559 in rousing the nobility and "com monalty" of Scotland to revolt against their ruler. Acceptance of the idea in France came more slowly. In 1560 most French Calvinists had refused to support the Conspiracy of Amboise partly because Calvin himself refused to support it.[29]) But even then there were notable exceptions.[30]) And two years later, when Beza helped the Prince de Condé organize the revolt against the Guise control of the monarchy which became the first war of religion, the Reformed churches of France joined wholeheartedly in the revolutionary effort, this time with the active encouragement of Calvin himself.[31]) Hosts of noblemen rushed to Condé's standard and dozens of cities immediately "declared" for Condé. City magistrates thus put into practice an idea Beza had earlier expressed in theory.

It would be unwise to trace all of these activities back to this particular book by Beza. But the revolutionary trend the activities took and the fact that Beza himself assumed an increasingly important role in actually leading them together suggest that Beza's justification of the right of resistance influenced the Huguenot party deeply.

Thus we see first stated in 1554, then restated and put into action in 1560, then finally widely adopted in 1562, a rudimentary expression of a right of resistance. I think this discovery has real significance. It first of all establishes the fact that Beza developed his ideas of the right to resist tyranny nearly twenty years before the publication of the

---

[28]) Bibliothèque publique et universitaire de Genève, Correspondance ecclésiastique, I—B, fols. 37—38, the copy of the minutes sent to Geneva.

[29]) Naef, op. cit., passim., especially in chap. IX.

[30]) e. g. the Reformed churches of Provence. See ibid., pp. 550ff. For other examples see ibid., passim., especially in chapters VIII and IX.

[31]) For examples of Calvin's many activities on behalf of the Huguenot armies in 1562 see letters in CR Calv. opp., XIX, 505—507. 550—551.

De jure magistratuum, the best theoretical statement of those views and the one studied by the historians of political thought.[32]) This in turn reverses earlier ideas of the relation of theory and practice in the development of the earliest democratic ideas. Such authorities as J. W. Allen say that these early Protestants' theories of a right of resistance were only formally stated after years of actual resistance — that they were issued in the three famous pronunciamentos of 1573—1575, the *Vindiciae contra tyrannos,* the *Franco-Gallia,* and the *De jure magistratuum,* after a full decade of Huguenot revolt against the government, and were provoked by the increasingly brutal Catholic opposition represented by the St. Bartholomew's Massacre — that they were a justification for and a rationalization of a course of conduct that had been adopted long before.[33]) But if we find these theories already expressed in embryo as early as 1554, we have to reverse the causative sequence, and say that the beginnings of religious war were in part at least a rational and deliberate attempt to put into practice a semidemocratic concept. The possibility of severe oppression had been foreseen by Beza and the justification for revolt against it had been briefly stated. Actual revolt can therefore be taken as a deliberate reaction to a foreseen contingency — an attempt to put into practice an existent theory. This sequence therefore gives added weight to the theory that ideas can and should precede action — that men can actually plan the future.

---

[32]) Most recently by A. A. van Schelven, "Beza's De Iure Magistratuum in Subditos," Archiv für Reformationsgeschichte, XLV (1954), 62—83.

[33]) Allen, p. 315, says that in 1574 Beza "... produced an essay in flat contradiction to his master's teachings and in equally flat contradiction of earlier utterances of his own ..." These "earlier utterances" are not specified. For a similar point of view see George H. Sabine, A History of Political Theory (New York, 1937), p. 377; Laski, pp. 22ff.; Georges de Lagarde, Recherches sur l'esprit politique de la Réforme (Paris 1926), pp. 125ff. Cf. van Schelven, op. cit., pp. 78ff. For material on earlier French Protestant political radicalism see Richard Nürnberger, Die Politisierung des französischen Protestantismus (Tübingen 1948).

XI

THE POLITICAL RESISTANCE OF THE CALVINISTS IN FRANCE AND THE LOW COUNTRIES*

It seems to me that much can be learned by comparative studies of the histories of the several European countries, and that this is particularly true of their political histories during the sixteenth century. A stimulating start in this direction was made by H. G. Koenigsberger in an article in *The Journal of Modern History,* titled "The Organization of Revolutionary Parties in France and the Netherlands during the Sixteenth Century."[1] I would like to propose a further exploration of some of the interesting leads presented by Mr. Koenigsberger. For the present, however, I shall avoid attempting to survey the whole field he opens up for us. I shall limit myself to a study of the revolutionary Calvinist parties, and devote most of my attention to the period of their formation.

It was the religious issue which made these parties possible, Mr. Koenigsberger justly observes, and it was "religious organizations from which developed the organization of political parties or which provided the prototype for party organization."[2] Accordingly, one needs to study carefully these religious organizations. That is the first lead which I would propose following.

Material for a study of Calvinist religious organization fortunately still survives in the Geneva State Archives. I have had the opportunity to do some work in these records; others have done even more work and published their findings in books which deserve attention.[3] These records reveal much of the process by which, in each country, before war began, a flexible but highly disciplined network of Calvinist churches was established, under the direction of the Geneva Company of Pastors. Men sent from Geneva manned these networks to a great extent. They occupied key positions of leadership in them to an even greater extent. These missionaries had originally come to Geneva, as students or refugees, to worship God as they saw fit and to learn of the full meaning of their faith. A significant proportion of them studied with Calvin, Beza, and other theologians of Geneva; many of them also served as pastors in minor Swiss charges, and thus gained experience and an even closer acquaintance with the men who then dominated

*This article was originally prepared for reading at the joint meeting of the American Historical Association, the American Society for Reformation Research, and the American Society of Church History, on December 28, 1957, in New York. While preparing it, I benefited from the advice of Dr. Hans Baron of the Newberry Library, my colleague Prof. J. F. Gilliam, Prof. Garrett Mattingly of Columbia University, and Mr. J. J. Woltjer of the University of Leiden. Some of the materials on which it is based were gathered in Europe during a research trip financed by a grant from the Penrose Fund of the American Philosophical Society.

Reformed Protestant thinking. At some point in this apprenticeship, it was common for the Geneva Company of Pastors to examine these men formally, in order to determine their competence and orthodoxy. They were normally sent back to France or the Low Countries only after a formal request from a congregation provided evidence that they were needed and would be both welcomed and protected. They were normally sent with a formal written testimonial, signed by the leaders of the Genevan church.[4] These procedures first take definite shape in 1555, when the first pastor was formally dispatched to France. Two years later, in 1557, the Geneva Company of Pastors made its first formal placement of a pastor in a pulpit in the Low Countries.[5]

Such procedures obviously made it possible for Calvin and his aides to exercise a considerable authority over the Protestant evangelistic campaign. Their control was extended even further, however, partly by the creation of a church organization, partly by Geneva's continuing surveillance of the missionary pastors. The church organization consisted of a hierarchy of synods. Each local church had its own consistory, and, if big enough, its own company of pastors. Each local region had a colloquy or "classe" of pastors, each province a representative synod, and the system was capped by national synods, formed first for France in 1559, in Paris; formed first for the Low Countries in 1571, in Emden.[6] Particularly in the beginning, however, synods could not meet frequently enough, or count on wide enough representation, to govern church affairs systematically. Partly for this reason, and partly because of the substantial prestige of its theologians, Geneva was continually consulted on all kinds of theological and ecclesiastical problems, and even, occasionally, on political problems—by individuals, by local churches, by colloquies, and by synods. The advice of Geneva was always directed at maintaining the ideological and organizational unity of the church it had created. Many of its counsels were aimed at keeping out of the church organization such radical "deviationists" as Anabaptists and Libertines. These suggestions were always listened to with respect, and usually followed.

Geography and linguistic differences probably prevented Geneva's influence from being as strong in the Low Countries as it was in France. Dutch Protestants could also turn for guidance to other centers, nearer home. The church of Emden, from the time of its foundation by John à Lasco, was important in guiding the destinies of Protestantism in the Low Countries. The Dutch churches in London and Cologne played important, if lesser, roles.[7] More Protestant students from the Low Countries went to Heidelberg than to any other single university.[8] Still, the popularity of Calvinist theology, and the prestige of the men sent from Geneva, seem to be enough to justify Beza's proud boast—that the school of Geneva was the "nursery-garden of the ministers of France, . . . of England . . . (and) of Flanders."[9]

The church organizations thus created by Geneva proved to be most useful when the time came when political revolt seemed necessary and possible. That time came very soon. In 1560 and 1561, in the years immediately following the calling of the first French national synod, local synods in south-western France began mustering troops, using colloquies and local churches as the recruiting units.[10] The spread of this practice over France helps to explain the size of the army gathered under Condé's command in 1562 when revolt finally became open, and the speed with which it assembled. In the Low Countries the church organizations were even more ambitious. The united consistories, meeting in Antwerp in 1566, before the formation of a national synod, but following at least three years of regular meetings of provincial synods in Flanders and Brabant, made provisions for the creation of an entire military general staff.[11] It was to be headed by the Prince of Orange, if possible. Failing his consent, Horne and Brederode together, or one or the other of them, were to be offered the command. Under the commander, six gentlemen were to be appointed by the churches to serve as a council. Joined to them were to be six merchants appointed to raise funds for the army of revolt. The subsequent failure of this plan demonstrated the tenacity and strength of Spanish rule; but the very fact that it was proposed must have made it increasingly clear to leaders of undecided religious affiliation, that here was an organization admirably suited to political revolution, no matter what one thought of its theology.

The Calvinist churches had more to offer to these revolutionary parties, however, than just a useful organization. They also offered an important kind of leadership. Supreme leadership of any enterprise that hoped for political success in the sixteenth century really had to come from the high nobility. Only they possessed the experience, the training, and the resources to act effectively in the political arena; only they commanded enough respect from people generally, to serve as real leaders. Every attempt at peasant or burgher action failed, with practically no exceptions. Koenigsberger, in company with most of the historians of the period, has therefore rightly emphasized the leading role played in these revolts by Condé, a prince of the French royal blood, and William, prince of Orange. Both of these men became Calvinist—Condé sooner, William later. Neither was exactly fanatic or even particularly devout in his Calvinism. Both were directly linked to the Calvinist church organization, however, not by some theoretical Machiavellian calculation, but by the actual presence on their staffs of men who were devoted Calvinists. It is the character and activity of these secondary leaders which supplies a second lead I think it important to explore.

The two outstanding examples of these secondary leaders were Theodore Beza and Philippe Marnix van Sint Aldegonde. Both men were noble, both received Calvinist training in Geneva. They were therefore personally well suited to act as links between church and prince. Beza came from a minor noble house established near Vézelay in Burgundy.[12] He had had a nobleman's education in the liberal arts at the usual variety of universities, and in the process apparently acquired the graces expected of a sixteenth-century gentleman. Before his education was finished he had been converted to Calvinism, and fled France, abandoning many of his titles, incomes, and perquisites in the process. In Switzerland, where he sought refuge, he became a Reformed minister of the Gospel, quickly won recognition for his great gifts of character and intellect, and rapidly rose to a position second only to that of Calvin in the Genevan church.

Marnix came from a minor noble house of Brabant.[13] He and his brother took an even more extensive tour of universities in acquiring their education than had Beza. This tour brought them to the newly established University of Geneva at a time when Calvin and Beza were teaching there, probably in 1560. The Marnix brothers became thoroughly attached to the Calvinist cause, and soon returned to their native country to aid in its propagation. Neither became a pastor, yet both devoted much of their time and energy to the spread of Calvinism.

Beza and Marnix won the respect of the Calvinist congregations by their intellectual contributions to the elaboration and spread of the new faith. Both wrote extensively, in Latin and in the vernacular languages of the people to whom they were addressing themselves. Beza's translation of the Psalms into French became one of the most popular and important books of devotion among French Calvinists,[14] and remains so to this day. Marnix's translations of the Psalms into Dutch[15] filled something of the same function among Calvinists in the Low Countries, though they had to face the competition of the earlier translations of Dathenus. Both men were master polemicists. Marnix's *Bijenkorf* (Beehive), and his French revision of that work, the *Tableau des Différands de la Religion,* are among the most effective and biting bits of anti-papal satire written in any country during the Reformation.[16] None of Beza's many anti-papal pamphlets won the enduring fame that did Marnix's.[17] Both men also directed their polemical fire against Protestantism's radical left wing. One of Beza's first polemic writings was a reply to Castellion, in which he defended the use of persecution against heretics of the type of Servetus.[18] One of Marnix's last publications was an attack on the Dutch libertine "fanatics," which attempts to persuade ruling powers to persecute them.[19] Finally, both men published important contributions to theology, in the form both of Biblical commentary and of dogmatic exposition.[20] Beza's theology was of course more sophisticated and authoritative, since he was the professional theologian. But Marnix's must have played a part in popularizing Calvinist orthodoxy in the Low Countries. Calvinist orthodoxy, of course, marked both these men. Throughout their lives they remained devoted to the doctrine taught by their common teacher, John Calvin. Beza, in fact, refined and systematized the doctrine to the point where some think it became more Calvinistic than Calvin's own version.

It was probably talents of a different order, however, which won for these men the respect of the military chiefs of the revolutionary parties which they joined, and which made them so useful to these commanders. Both Beza and Marnix displayed considerable ability as diplomats and negotiators. Beza first had a chance to display these talents when Calvin sent him, with others, to Germany, in 1557, on embassies to the Protestant German cities and princes, to secure intercession at the French court for the Waldensians and for a number of Protestant political prisoners. The intercessory embassies they sought were formed and sent to Paris, but were not particularly successful in their missions.[21] Three years later Beza was approached in Geneva by the young hot-heads who, with Condé's approval, were hatching the daring plot to capture the king and kill the regents, known as the Conspiracy of Amboise. Beza seems to have given considerable encouragement to the plotters, cordially visiting their chief, giving him a copy of his translation of a psalm with a warlike point which was then used to recruit more conspirators, and sending to Paris, in the baggage of a young Calvinist noble minister, a copy of a pamphlet which was to be distributed as justification for the Conspiracy after its success.[22] This plan failed miserably, but Beza's part in it was so well hidden, that his usefulness to Bourbon diplomacy was by no means over. He was soon summoned to the court of Navarre, where another plot was hatched which fell even further short of success than the first.[23] We know nothing about the planning of this plot, so cannot say what Beza's role in it might have been. His presence at the court at that time, however, looks suspicious. He left the court of Navarre when Condé was summoned north to Paris to trial and imprisonment. But when death of the king and the rise to power of Catherine de Medicis as regent gave Condé freedom again, Beza returned to France, this time at the invitation of the royal court, to head a delegation of Calvinist ministers called to debate with the leading Catholic clergy of the realm, at the Colloquy of Poissy. At Poissy Beza presented the Calvinist case with eloquence, took advantage of the opportunity to make conversions among the courtiers, and by his public preaching did his best to strengthen the congregation of the Reformed in Paris which until this time had met in secrecy.[24] When war finally came, Beza was still at Condé's side.[25] He sent out mustering orders to the churches before hostilities began, probably prepared the published justifications of revolts which were issued over Condé's name, and seems to have assumed certain financial duties as well. Soon he was sent as Condé's ambassador to certain of the German princes and the Swiss cantons, to negotiate for financial and military assistance.

Beza, however, did not agree with all of Condé's decisions, and tried to dissuade him from several of them. He grew weary of his political chores and kept at them only because his fellow ministers in the Geneva church insisted upon it. When the first war of religion finally ended, he returned to Geneva to become shortly, on Calvin's death, its ecclesiastical leader. The duties of this new position kept him from engaging too actively in succeeding diplomatic campaigns. He did go to Germany in 1574, at the request of the new Prince of Condé, to help conclude the negotiations that made possible a renewed Protestant attack on the French crown.[26] And he made several trips to France on ecclesiastical business. But most of the time his political role was limited to advice and exhortation from afar.

Marnix, on the other hand, devoted most of his career to diplomatic work for the Calvinist cause.[27] He, like Beza, was implicated at an early stage in a conspiracy against repressive Catholic rule. He and his brother were involved in the plot which issued in the *Compromis des Nobles* of 1565, the first sign of open resistance in the Low Countries, a document announcing the intent of a small group of nobles to resist application of decrees establishing the Inquisition in full force.[28] The *Compromis* was soon followed by an armed uprising led by Jean Marnix de Thoulouze, which was quickly crushed by Spanish troops, partly because of Orange's failure to cooperate. It ended in the death of Jean.

Marnix van Sint Aldegonde, however, reappears at the next crucial stage in the revolt, this time at the side of the Prince of Orange. His summons by Orange in 1568 is one of the first signs of Orange's decision to use the Calvinist party as a popular base for his revolt against Spain. From that time on Marnix served Orange faithfully—too faithfully, many devoted Calvinists thought. He pleaded Orange's cause at the imperial diet, negotiated Orange's alliance with the Duc d'Anjou, became Orange's regent as burgermaster of Antwerp.

Even after the prince's death robbed Marnix of a patron, and his surrender of Antwerp to Parma left him in disgrace with the zealous Calvinists of Zealand and Holland, he came back to render diplomatic aid to the cause of Calvinism and the Seven Provinces, representing them at the courts of Henry of Navarre and Elizabeth I.

Other leaders trained in Geneva served these revolutionary parties in similar ways, but I shall pass them by. What I have said of the activities of Beza and Marnix should provide at least some notion of the extent and importance of the secondary leadership Calvinism supplied to sixteenth-century revolt.

Yet a third Calvinist contribution to the revolutionary parties of France and the Low Countries deserves comparative study, although on this subject Koenigsberger has little to say. That is the theory Calvinist thinkers developed to justify these revolts.

The Calvinist theory of the right of resistance derives in part from theology, in part from a cursory reading of history.[29] It is the creation in part of theologians, in part of Calvinist lay lawyers such as Francis Hotman. Because of its partial derivation from theology, statements of it must be sought not only in the explicitly political pamphlets many Calvinist leaders wrote, but also in theological polemics and even in straight theological studies. Many scholars have noted Calvin's own statement of a resistance theory in the concluding pages of each edition of his monumental *Institutes of the Christian Religion,* beginning with the 1541 edition.[30] Elsewhere I have pointed out that a similar cursory statement of a resistance theory can be found in Theodore Beza's *De haereticis a civili magistratu puniendis.*[31]

The subordination of Calvinist political thought to theology means that it takes many forms. Different writers, and often the same writer in different circumstances, advocated very different forms of government, and presented very different doctrines of the duty of political obedience. One can find Calvinist writers during the sixteenth century defending every form of government from absolute monarchy to democracy. The normal situation of the Calvinists, however, who could hope to find freedom for their form of worship only in alliance with revolutionary political parties led by high nobility, suggested one sort of political theory more than any other. This was a theory which emphasized the role of the "inferior magistrate" in government. The "inferior magistrates" shared with the supreme rulers the prime duty of all government—the maintenance of the "true" religion. When the supreme magistrates failed in this duty, and worse, tried to wipe out the "true religion," the inferior magistrates were allowed to resist their superiors, with force if necessary. This constituted a right of resistance but not a duty of resistance, and foolhardy plots to overthrow government were often rejected by Calvinist ministers when they were obviously impractical and had little hope of success.[32] The Pauline injunction of obedience to the "powers that be (which) are ordained of

God," (Romans 13:1) continues in most Calvinist theory, but is held to apply only to private individuals, not to inferior magistrates.

When it came to define precisely who the "inferior magistrates" were, another practical problem posed itself, but Calvinist thinkers were resourceful enough to think of many answers. The "inferior magistrates" might be representatives of the Kingdom meeting in the Estates-General, with powers similar to the Ephors of ancient Sparta— so Calvin. They might be princes of the royal blood, like the Bourbons in France—so Calvin again. They might be city magistrates—so Beza. And yet other possibilities also suggested themselves.

Running through these theories of resistance I have discovered one thread, which I would now like to follow. It illustrates, I think, not only the need for careful study of the attribution of many of these ideas, but also the need for a study that investigates developments in many different countries. That thread is supplied by the example of the city of Magdeburg. One finds it cropping up again and again at crucial points.

In 1524, the imperial city of Magdeburg in Germany had been re-formed in the Lutheran fashion, without the consent of its temporal ruler, the Archbishop. In 1548, Magdeburg had taken the lead in North German armed defiance of the "Interim," enacted by the Emperor and Electors of the Holy Roman Empire to suppress Protestantism wher-ever it had become established in the Germanies. In each instance, the elected councillors and hundred-men of the city, pushed by popular clamor, had defied constituted superior authority. Here was a dramatic example of armed resistance, led by inferior magistrates against reg-ularly constituted higher authority, and it captured the Calvinist im-agination. The example of the city's defiance was reinforced and publicized by several pamphlets, the most significant of which was written by the principal Lutheran ministers of the city, titled the Mag-deburg *Bekenntnis,* and published in 1550.[33] Many of the Calvinist leaders saw it, and when the time came, they found its arguments most useful.

Beza noted the Magdeburg example in passing, in his polemic against Castellion, in a passage which is apparently his first public statement of a resistance theory.[34] He returned to the Magdeburg example with even more vigor in the avowedly political pamphlet he wrote in 1574, after the St. Bartholomew's massacre. This event had finally persuaded the Huguenots to abandon all pretense of fighting to rescue the king from wicked councillors, and to avow openly the fact that the battle they had been waging for a decade was in resistance to the legitimate superior authority of the crown. This second pamphlet was published anonymously, without indication of place of printing or name of publisher. There is decisive archival proof, however, that

Beza wrote it.[35] In the very wording of his title, Beza deliberately links his arguments to that of the Magdeburg *Bekenntnis*. The title declares the book to be "published by those of Magdeburg in the year 1550, and now revised and augmented."[36]

By these publications, Beza outlined the theory upon which he himself acted while in France, and which he presented to French Huguenots as the justification for their continued resistance.

Now let us turn to the Low Countries to see the influence of Magdeburg there. An early hint of such an influence can be found in a letter written on February 27, 1566, to the younger brother of the Prince of Orange, Louis of Nassau, at that time apparently in Germany. This letter outlines some of the violent plans of a group of impetuous young noblemen who had gathered in Breda, reports on the spread of the Inquisition which was driving them to action, and finally begs Louis to bring back with him, a "treatise which you promised us, touching the causes for which the inferior Magistrate can take arms when the superior sleeps or tyrannizes."[37] Two of the historians who have noted this letter believe the pamphlet referred to is one of the Magdeburg manifestoes,[38] and indeed that seems highly probable. The most systematic expositions of this theory had not yet been published, and the earlier statements of it by Knox, Goodman, and Ponet would probably not have been as readily available to a Dutch nobleman travelling through Germany as the Magdeburg *Bekenntnis,* or perhaps one of lesser pamphlets which accompanied it.

That some statement of the resistance theory was actually received by Dutch Calvinists is suggested by the records of the meeting of the united consistories in Antwerp on December 1, 1566, to which I have already referred. There the question was raised,

> If in the Low Countries a part of the vassals with a part of the subjects can resist by force of arms against their magistrate in case that he breaks and does not observe the privileges, making some wrong or open violence? To which it was advised and resolved that it is licit to do this if one finds good means to execute it.[39]

The consistories, as already noted, immediately proceeded to the finding of "good means," though the disastrous results of the plot must make us question their judgment.

Immediate failure, and the consequent death or exile of most of these plotters, did not kill theories of resistance in the Low Countries, however. We find them in the air again in the 1570's, when, at the initiative of the Sea-Beggars, and under the leadership of Orange, the revolt finally succeeded in maintaining itself. Specifically, in the years when the States-General was preparing for the final open denial of the authority of Philip II, which was made formal by the Placard of

Abjuration in 1581, a Calvinist theory of resistance again raises its head.

John of Nassau, another younger brother of William of Orange, who, like Louis, was a resolute Calvinist, reveals this in a letter to the Duke of Brunswick drafted in March, 1577. A postscript to the letter announces the dispatch of a set of books which he thought Brunswick would find useful. It includes a copy of Machiavelli's *Prince,* an attack on Machiavelli, and the *De jure magistratuum in subditos,* Beza's anonymous exposition of resistance theory.[40] Conceivably these books could have all been in one binding. Machiavelli and Beza were paradoxically included within the same covers in at least one printing.[41]

Yet another piece of evidence that John of Nassau knew of the Calvinist theory of resistance can be found in a letter in which he asks for advice on the religious policy to follow in the newly conquered province of Gelderland, just put under his control.[42] Specifically, he asks whether he should follow the precedents of Holland, Zealand, Magdeburg, or Strasbourg, in suppressing "idolatry" and permitting only one form of religious worship. The answer, interestingly, comes not from the Dutch Calvinists to whom he wrote, but in a general letter written to the Reformed church of the Low Countries from the Geneva Company of Pastors, and signed by Theodore Beza.[43] It advises the Dutch to follow any example but that of Strasbourg, which weakly knuckled under to the imperial *Interim,* and permitted re-introduction of "false" religion. Here the magistrates of Magdeburg are held up, not as exemplars of legitimate resistance, but as defenders of the only true faith. This was taken to be the ultimate duty of all government, and that which we have seen is the only justification for resistance.

Finally, in the *Apology of the Prince of Orange* against the King of Spain, presented to the States-General at the time of the adoption of the Placard of Abjuration, one finds echoes of the Calvinist theory of resistance. Specifically, one finds it in Orange's statement that it is for the great vassals of the realm

> to stand our Dukes in that steede, that the Ephori at Sparta did their Kinges, that is to say, to keepe the kingdome sure, in the power of a good Prince, and to cause him to yeelde equitie, which stood against his othe.[44]

The sentiment expressed here could easily have come from a reading of Calvin.[45] The reference to the Ephors of Sparta certainly suggests that. This time there is no reference to Magdeburg.

Magdeburg, of course, was not the only inspiration for the Calvinist theory of resistance. Hans Baron has argued persuasively in one of his articles for the influence of Bucer on Calvin's original statement of the theory.[46] Other scholars have pointed out other lines of influence. But the tracing of the Magdeburg influence does, I feel, rather neatly illustrate the international development and spread of this theory.

These, then, were important contributions which the Calvinist churches offered to the revolutionary Protestant political parties in France and the Low Countries during the sixteenth century: synodical organization, noble leadership, a theory of resistance. This pattern of analysis could, I feel, be extended to other countries. Scotland is the first example that occurs to me. There John Knox organized the church which was to become Presbyterian, cooperated closely with the noble "Lords of the Congregation" who actually led the revolt against Queen Regent Mary of Guise, and in advance of all this outlined and broadcast a resistance theory, which was apparently derived in part from the Magdeburg *Bekenntnis*.[47] But limitations of space prevent me from pressing the point. I hope that what I have been able to present persuades at least some of you of my conviction: that the revolts of the sixteenth century cannot be viewed solely as chapters in separate national histories; they must also be considered as in part at least the work of a revolutionary international religious organization—the Calvinist Church.

1. H. G. Koenigsberger, "The Organization of Revolutionary Parties in France and the Netherlands during the Sixteenth Century," *The Journal of Modern History*, Vol XXVII, No. 4 (December, 1955), pp. 335-351. Cf. Garrett Mattingly, *Renaissance Diplomacy* (London, 1955), pp. 193-196.

2. Koenigsberger, *op. cit.*, p. 336.

3. Edited copies of much of the archival material relating to the Low Countries can be found in Herman de Vries de Heekelingen, *Genève, pépinière du calvinisme hollandais;* t. I, *Les étudiants des pays-bas à Genève au temps de Théodore de Bèze* (Fribourg, Switzerland, 1918); t. II, *Correspondance des élèves de Théodore de Bèze après leur départ de Genève* (the Hague, 1924). See also the many works of A. A. van Schelven. For discussion of the archival material relating to France, see Robert M. Kingdon, *Geneva and the coming of the wars of religion in France, 1555-1563* (Geneva: Droz, 1956). Hereafter cited as de Vries de Heekelingen and Kingdon, *Geneva.*

4. Not many of these testimonial letters have been preserved. For a good copy of one, see de Vries de Heekelingen, I, 297-298, a transcript of an entry in Geneva, Archives, Register of the Company of Pastors, B2, 1572, fol. 72v.

5. These dates, and much of the information in the paragraph, are taken from the official Registers of the Geneva Company of Pastors, preserved in the Geneva Archives d'Etat, consulted with the permission of the present Geneva Company of Pastors. See Kingdon, *Geneva*, p. 2, and *passim*, for information on the first men officially sent. See *Bulletin de la Société de l'histoire du protestantisme français*, VIII (1859), p. 76, for a list of pastors sent from Geneva, abstracted from these registers, which contains many errors of transcription but does include reliable information about the first man officially sent to the Low Countries.

6. See Kingdon, *Geneva*, p. 46, and *passim*, on the French synod and local church organization. Source references can be found in the notes. On the Emden synod, see F. L. Rutgers, ed., *Acta van de nederlandsche synoden der zestiende eeuw*, in *Werken der Marnix-Vereeniging*, serie II, deel III (Utrecht, 1889), pp. 42-119; note also the articles adopted by an even earlier gathering ("samenkomst") of representatives of the Low Countries' churches in Wesel, 1568, in *ibid.*, pp. 1-41. For information on Calvinist church organization in the Belgian provinces, see E. de Moreau, *Histoire*

de l'église en Belgique, t. V (Brussels, 1952), pp. 215-227. A useful collection of early provincial synodical records can be found in N. C. Kist, ed., ''De synoden der nederlandsche hervormde kerken onder het kruis, gedurende de jaren 1563-1577, gehouden in Braband, Vlaanderen enz.,'' *Nederlandsche Archief voor Kerkelijke Geschiedenis,* IX, in *Archief voor Kerkelijke Geschiedenis inzonderheid van Nederland,* XX (1849), pp. 114-120. Mr. Maurice Edic and Miss Nancy Knapp called my attention to the last two references.

7. For an authoritative study of these refugee churches, see A. A. van Schelven *De nederduitsche vluchtelingenkerken der XVIe eeuw in Engeland en Duitschland, in hunne beteeknis voor de reformatie in de Nederlanden* (the Hague, 1909). On the London church see also J. Lindeboom, *Austin Friars: History of the Dutch Reformed Church in London* (the Hague, 1950).

8. J. de Wal, ''Nederlanders en personen die later met Nederland in betrekking stonden, studenten te Heidelberg en Genève sedert het begin der kerkhervorming,'' *Maatsch. Ned. Letterk. Handelingen & Mededeelingen* (1865), pp. 59-270; J. de Wal, ''Nederlanders, studenten te Heidelberg,'' in *ibid.* (1886), pp. 1-55; cited by de Vries de Heekelingen, I, 188.

9. Geneva, Archives, Registres du Conseil, 5 August 1586, quoted in de Vries de Heekelingen, I, 23.

10. The best documented example of such a muster is that supervised by the synod of upper Guyenne held in Ste.-Foy, in November 1561. See *Histoire ecclésiastique des églises réformées au royaume de France,* ed. by G. Baum and Ed. Cunitz, I (Paris, 1883), pp. 803-804 (original pagination). For further information see Kingdon, *Geneva,* pp. 109 and ff.

11. The relevant text in the synodical minutes is quoted by Bakhuizen van den Brink, in his introduction to R. C. Bakhuizen van den Brink, L. Ph. C. van Bergh, & J. K. J. de Jonge, eds., *Les archives du royaume des pays-bas: recueil de documents inédits pour servir à l'histoire des pays-bas* (the Hague, Leipzig, Brussels, Paris, 1855), pp. 27-28. Hereafter cited as Bakhuizen van den Brink.

12. Paul-F. Geisendorf, *Théodore de Bèze* (Geneva, 1949), pp. 3-4, quotes from the text of the 1551 patent of reintegration into the nobility, granted to his father. See the succeeding pages for further biographical information. For general information on France during this period, see P. Imbart de la Tour, *Les origines de la Réforme,* t. IV, *Calvin et l'Institution Chrétienne*

(Paris, 1935), and Lucien Romier, *Les origines politiques des guerres de religion,* 2 vols. (Paris, 1913-1914); *La conjuration d'Amboise . . .* (Paris, 1923); *Catholiques et Huguenots à la cour de Charles IX . . . (1560-1562)* (Paris, 1924); *Le royaume de Catherine de Médicis . . .,* 2 vols. (Paris, 1922).

13. Albert Elkan, *Philipp Marnix von St. Aldegonde; teil I: Die Jugend Johanns und Philipps von Marnix* (Leipzig, 1910), pp. 7 and ff., discusses the documents which provide proof of Marnix's nobility. One of them was published by Marnix himself. See Alb. Lacroix, ed., *Oeuvres de Ph. de Marnix de Sainte Aldegonde,* t. V. *Ecrits politiques et historiques* (Brussels, 1859), pp. 86-93, originally published as an appendix to text of Marnix's *Response à un libelle fameux nagueres publié contre Monseigneur le Prince d'Orenges* (Antwerp, 1579). This collection hereafter cited as Marnix, *Oeuvres,* Lacroix ed.

14. E. Droz, ''Antoine Vincent: la propagande protestante par le psautier,'' *Aspects de la propagande religieuse* (Geneva: Droz, 1957), pp. 276-293.

15. J. J. van Toorenenbergen, ed., *Philipp van Marnix van St. Aldegonde: godsdienstige en kerkelijke geschriften,* 3 vols. plus supplement (the Hague, 1871-1891), I, l-lxxi, for commentary; 183-438, for text. Hereafter cited as Marnix, *Geschriften,* van Toorenenbergen, ed.

16. Frans van Kalken and Tobie Jonckheere, *Marnix de Sainte Aldegonde (1540-1598): le politique et le pamphlétaire; le pédagogue* (Brussels, 1952), pp. 15-28.

17. Geisendorf, *op. cit.,* pp. 439-441, contains a preliminary list of Beza's works, practically all of which are discussed in his text. A complete bibliography of Beza's works has yet to be published.

18. *Ibid.,* pp. 65 and ff.

19. Marnix, *Geschriften,* van Toorenenbergen, ed., II, ii-xxi, for commentary; 1-240, for text.

20. Geisendorf, *op. cit., passim;* Marnix, *Geschriften,* van Toorenenbergen, ed., *passim.*

12. Geisendorf, *op. cit.,* pp. 82 and ff.

22. Henri Naef, *La conjuration d'Amboise et Genève* (Geneva, 1922), pp. 487-496, 555 and ff., and *passim.*

23. For a detailed description of this plot see Lucien Romier, *La conjuration d'Amboise . . .* (Paris, 1923), pp. 215-231. Cf. Naef, *op. cit.,* pp. 519-521, and Kingdon, *Geneva,* p. 75.

24. Geisendorf, *op. cit.,* pp. 125-166, and *passim.*

25. See Kingdon, *Geneva,* pp. 106-114, for documentation on the succeeding details of Beza's activity.

26. Geisendorf, *op. cit.*, pp. 360 and ff.

27. For information on Marnix's career see van Kalken and Jonckheere, *op. cit.*, and A. A. van Schelven, *Marnix van Sint Aldegonde* (Utrecht, 1939). A good introduction to the general history of Low Countries' diplomacy during this period is P. Geyl, *The revolt of the Netherlands (1555-1609)* (London, 1932; reprinted 1945). See also the works of H. A. Enno van Gelder, e.g. *Revolutionnaire reformatie* (Amsterdam, 1943).

28. Marnix, *Oeuvres*, Lacroix ed., V, 17-22.

29. For general studies of Calvinist political theory, see J. W. Allen, *A history of political thought in the sixteenth century* (London, 1951), pp. 49-72; 103-120; 302-331; also Pierre Mesnard, *L'essor de la philosophie politique au XVIe siècle* (Paris, 1952), pp. 269-385; and for the Low Countries, Ch. Mercier, "Les théories politiques des calvinistes dans les pay-bas à la fin du XVIe et au début du XVIIe siècle," *Revue d'histoire ecclésiastique*, XXIX (133), 25-73.

30. e.g. Allen, *op. cit.*, pp. 58-59; Mesnard, *op. cit.*, p. 294. The original text can be found in John Calvin, *Ioannis Calvini Opera quae supersunt omnia (Corpus Reformatorum*, Vols. 29ff., Brunswick, 1863-1900), II, 1116 and ff. (1559 Latin ed. of *Institutes)* and IV, 1160 and ff. (1560 French ed. of *Institutes).*

31. Robert M. Kingdon, "The First Expression of Theodore Beza's Political Ideas," *Archiv für Reformationsgeschichte*, XLVI (1955), Heft 1, 88-100. Hereafter cited as Kingdon, *Beza.*

32. e.g. Calvin as quoted in Naef, *op. cit.*, pp. 462-463. Cf. Kingdon, *Geneva*, p. 69, and *passim.*

33. A contemporary description of these events can be found in John Sleidan, *The General History of the Reformation of the Church*... (London, 1689), translated from the original Latin), p. 436, and *passim*. The publication of the Magdeburg *Bekenntnis* is described on p. 496. Allen, *op. cit.*, p. 104, n. 2, is wrong in saying that Sleidan misdates the *Bekenntnis*. He actually describes two separate pamphlets; the one which is clearly the *Bekenntnis* is correctly dated. Mr. Elmer L. Lampe, Jr., called this source to my attention. For a more modern account, see Friedrich Hülsse, *Die Stadt Magdeburg im Kampfe für den Protestantismus während der Jahre 1547-1551* (Halle a. S., 1892).

34. Kingdon, *Beza*, 93-94.

35. Relevant sources cited, and some quoted, in Geisendorf, *op. cit.*, pp. 312 and ff.

36. Full title: "*DV DROIT / DES MAGISTRATS / SVR LEVRS SVBIETS. / Traitté tres-necessaire en ce temps, pour ad- / uertir de leur devoir, tant les Magistrats que / les Subiets: publié par ceux de Magdebourg / l'an MDL: & maintenant reueu & / augmenté de plusieurs raisons / & exemples. / (mark) / PSAL. 2. / Erudimini qui iudicatis terram. / M.D. LXXIX. /*" I used the copy in the Newberry Library.

37. G. Groen van Prinsterer, ed., *Archives ou correspondance inédits de la maison d'Orange-Nassau*, series 1 (Leiden, 1835-1847, 8 vols. plus index vol.), vol. II, 37. Hereafter cited as *Archives d'Orange-Nassau.*

38. A. A. van Schelven, "Beza's De Iure Magistratuum in Subditos," *Archiv für Reformationsgeschichte*, XLV (1954), Heft I, p. 63 and n. 3.; Moriz Ritter, "Über die Anfänge der niederländischen Aufstandes," *Historische Zeitschrift*, LVIII (neue folge XXII) (1887), 425. The first article hereafter cited as van Schelven, *Beza.*

39. Bakhuizen van den Brink, p. 27.

40. *Archives d'Orange-Nassau*, series 1, vol. VI, 35.

41. van Schelven, *Beza*, pp. 65-68. The question of the relation between Machiavellism and Protestant social thought is dealt with in broader fashion in George L. Mosse, *The Holy Pretence: a study in Christianity and reason of state from William Perkins to John Winthrop* (Oxford, 1957). He does not mention this physical uniting of the two theories.

42. *Archives d'Orange-Nassau*, series 1, vol. VII, 132.

43. *Ibid.*, p. 254.

44. "*THE APOLOGIE / OR / DEFENCE, OF / THE MOST NOBLE / Prince William, by the grace of God, / Prince of ORANGE,... / Printed in French and in all other languages. / AT DELFT / 1581. /,*" signature H-3 verso. I used a microfilm of copy #30716 in the Huntington Library. The passage is also quoted in Mercier, *op. cit.*, p. 49.

45. It is very likely that a Calvinist wrote the *Apologie* for William. Grotius attributes the authorship of it to Pastor Villiers, who was Orange's chaplain, and, incidentally, served as one of the intermediaries in the correspondence previously noted between John of Nassau and the pastors of Geneva. Others have attributed authorship to Hubert Languet, prominent Calvinist nobleman, diplomat, and publicist. Evidence for both views is discussed in Pierre Bayle, "Hubert Languet," *Dictionnaire historique et critique*, 4th ed., III (1730).

It is, of course, possible that Calvin and the author of the *Apologie* both drew the analogy to the Ephors of Sparta independently from some classical source. The most likely source seems to be Cicero, *De legibus*, III, 16, a passage which draws an analogy between the Ephors and the Roman Tribunes which is much like Calvin's, but omits Calvin's erroneous references to the ''demarchi'' of Athens. For the precise references in Calvin's *Institutes*, see above, n. 30. For evidence that Calvin frequently borrowed ideas from the *De legibus* and other writings of Cicero, see Josef Bohatec, *Calvin und das Recht* (Feudingen in West-

falen, 1934), and *Budé und Calvin: Studien zur Gedankenwelt des französischen Frühhumanismus* (G r a z, 1950).

46. Hans Baron, ''Calvinist Republicanism and its Historical Roots,'' *Church History*, VIII (1939), 30-42.

47. John Knox, *History of the Reformation in Scotland*. The most recent critical edition is that of William Croft Dickinson (London, et al., 1949, 2 vols.). See II, 129-130, for Knox's reference to the ''Apology of Magdeburg.'' For the best examples of his resistance theory, see the David Laing edition of *The Works of John Knox*, vol. IV (Edinburgh, 1895), 349-540.

Reprinted by permission from Church History 27 (1958), 220-233.

XII

Calvinism and Democracy: Some Political Implications of Debates on French Reformed Church Government, 1562-1572

THE idea that Calvinism provided an important source of political democracy was long a popular one in this country. Careful studies of Calvin's own political ideas exploded a part of that theory several decades ago.[1] There remained in some quarters the belief that the Calvinist introduction into church government of some popular participation helps to explain the rise of democratic civil government. Recent studies have cast doubt even on this argument from analogy.[2] There were periods in the early history of the Calvinist movement, however, when the argument from analogy was taken seriously. They deserve further study. One such period was the decade 1562-1572, beginning shortly before Calvin's death in 1564, extending until the St. Bartholomew's massacres in 1572.

During this decade, the Reformed church that Calvin had founded in France was rocked by a bitter running quarrel that assumed significant proportions. One faction within that church argued that Christian church government should be highly decentralized, with local congregations assuming virtual autonomy and with laymen playing a significant role in their leadership. In short, they wanted what we might call congregationalism. Another faction insisted on strengthening the centralizing institutions in Reformed church government, particularly the provincial and national synods, and the peculiarly powerful Geneva mother church, with ordained

---

* The author of *Geneva and the Coming of the Wars of Religion in France, 1555-1563* (Geneva, 1956), Mr. Kingdon is a professor at the State University of Iowa. This paper is a condensed version of two read at meetings of the Pacific Coast Branch, American Historical Association, Los Angeles, August 29, 1962, and the Iowa State College History Teachers in Cedar Rapids, December 1, 1962.

[1] A useful elementary introduction to the substantial literature on this subject is provided by George L. Mosse, *Calvinism: Authoritarian or Democratic?* (New York, 1957).

[2] See, e.g., Leo F. Solt's criticism of application of the argument from analogy to certain seventeenth-century English Puritans in his *Saints in Arms* (Stanford, Calif., 1959), esp. 70-72.

clergymen assuming real leadership at every level. What they wanted is what we would call presbyterianism. Both sides argued vigorously for their views with that blend of arguments drawn from scriptural exegesis, early church history, and prudential political considerations, which was typical of their time and milieu.

The chief protagonists in this debate were Jean Morely, sire de Villiers, and Theodore Beza.[3] Morely was the founder of the "congregational" faction. He was a French Reformed petty nobleman, whose writings reveal him to have been a man of modest education, and whose most important position was as tutor for several months at the court of Navarre, to the young prince who was eventually to become King Henry IV of France. Beza was chief defender of the "presbyterian" position. He was also of a French petty noble family, but was a brilliant product of the best that the French Renaissance educational system could offer and had become Calvin's undisputed successor as ecclesiastical leader of the French-speaking Reformed churches. He served for decades as Moderator of the Geneva Company of Pastors. He influenced key decisions by a number of important French national synods and even presided over the most important of them. And he was the chief ecclesiastical adviser to the great aristocrats who provided political and military leadership to the party.

At first glance, it would seem that a contest between these two men could hardly be an equal one. In the end, Beza did in fact triumph, decisively and completely. But before that end came, Morely had won to his side a number of people who were far more important than he. A look at some of them will help explain the proportions this quarrel assumed.

First and foremost among Morely's supporters were certain of the great Huguenot aristocrats. Their interest in his program lasted only a few months, from 1564 to 1566, but this was time enough for him to form a faction. Of these aristocrats, the one most inclined to defend Morely was Odet de Coligny, the Protestant Cardinal de Châtillon.[4] Odet's even more powerful brother, Gaspard de Coligny, admiral of France, also admitted a passing interest in Morely.[5] And Jeanne d'Albret, queen of Navarre, was impressed

[3] Much of my information on Morely's career, particularly the earlier stages of it, was provided by Henri Naef of Geneva. Some of it was published in his *La Conjuration d'Amboise et Genève* (Geneva, 1922), 438 *et passim*. For information on Beza, see *inter alia*, Paul-F. Geisendorf, *Théodore de Bèze* (Geneva and Paris, 1949).

[4] Bibliothèque publique et universitaire de Genève [hereafter cited as Geneva, BPU], MS fr. 446, contains several pieces mentioning the Cardinal de Châtillon's interest in Morely, e.g., fols. 12–13, 72–73. This entire volume of MSS concerns the Morely affair. Most of them are reports to Beza and others in Geneva about Morely's activities from 1564 to 1566; some are letters from Morely to Geneva begging for reconciliation; a few are drafts of letters from Beza to various people involved in the affair.

[5] Coligny to Beza, Jan. 21, 1567, Geneva, BPU, MS fr. 197b, fols. 123–24.

enough by his intellectual qualities to hire him as a tutor for her son, the titular leader of the entire movement.[6]

By vigorous action, Beza succeeded in persuading these aristocrats to abandon support of Morely, in 1566. Already, however, Morely had won considerable support among the Calvinist clergy, particularly in the provinces surrounding Paris. Of these clergymen, the most prominent was Hugues Sureau, dit Du Rosier. During these very years, Sureau became widely known as a spokesman for the Calvinist position in a series of open debates with certain of the powerful new Catholic controversialists who were posing an extremely serious intellectual threat to Protestantism.[7]

Sureau and his colleagues soon enlisted even more support for the Morely program among lay members of their churches. Of these laymen, the most prominent was Peter Ramus, the royal professor in Paris whose dramatic attacks on Aristotle and other revered authorities of antiquity and whose persuasive proposal of a new system of logic enchanted an entire generation of students and enraged an entire generation of his colleagues. Ramus had been a Protestant sympathizer since about 1561, but became an active lay leader within the movement only from 1568 until his death in 1572.[8] During these years he and Sureau became the really aggressive leaders of the dissident "congregational" faction within the French Reformed church.

Of the many ideas about ecclesiastical polity and discipline debated by these two factions during this decade, one is of particular interest to the historian of political thought. This is the idea that there is analogy between civil government and ecclesiastical government. Not all who were parties to the dispute would even concede the validity of this great analogy. Those who did drew diametrically different conclusions from it. But for those who were willing to pursue the notion of analogy, the concept of democracy became an inevitable part of the debate. The sharpest and most interesting

---

[6] Jeanne d'Albret to Beza, Dec. 6, 1566, published in *Bulletin de la Société de l'histoire du protestantisme français*, XVI (1867), 64–67, a letter promising to dismiss Morely, but reporting that he had been an unusually successful teacher.

[7] For more on Sureau, see Eugène and Émile Haag, *La France protestante* . . . (1st ed., 10 vols., Paris, 1846–58), IX, 329–30, article "Sureau"; Paul Chaix, *Recherches sur l'imprimerie à Genève de 1550 à 1564* (Geneva, 1954), 224; Robert M. Kingdon, "Genève et les réformés français: le cas d'Hugues Sureau, dit Du Rosier (1565–1574)," *Bulletin, Société d'histoire et d'archéologie de Genève*, XII (No. 2, 1961), 77–87.

[8] The most detailed description of Ramus's view on this subject that I have discovered is in a letter (De Lestre to Beza, Mar. 19, 1572), a recent Genevan copy of which I consulted in Geneva, *Musée historique de la Réformation*, Beza correspondence, and which is mentioned in *La France protestante*, 1st ed., VII, 45–46, article "Lestre." A somewhat briefer and more guarded description is in Ramus to Bullinger, Sept. 1, 1571, published in Charles Waddington, *Ramus* (Paris, 1855), 433–35; cf. also the condemnatory acts of the National Synod of Nîmes, May 6, 1572, published in *Synodicon in Gallia Reformata* . . . , ed. John Quick (2 vols., London, 1692), I, 111–13, and *Tous les Synodes nationaux des églises réformées de France* . . . , ed. Jean Aymon (2 vols., The Hague, 1710).

demonstrations of this fact are to be found in the writings of the two chief protagonists, Morely and Beza. Specifically, they are found in certain passages of a book titled *Traicté de la discipline & police chrestienne*, which Morely had published in 1562 and which remained the essential statement of his faction's position even though it was apparently never reprinted,[9] and in certain passages of letters written by Beza in 1571 and thereafter to counter the influence of Ramus, at a time when the length of the controversy and the prospect of complete victory led him to be somewhat more blunt than he had been earlier.

Morely's book was prepared with the idea of an analogy between civil government and ecclesiastical government central to his plan of writing and was to be the first volume in a set of two. It dealt with the form of ecclesiastical government that Morely believed was enjoined by the Word of God as revealed in Scripture, and by the experience of the church. Its successor, apparently never written, was to deal with the form of civil government that similar authorities dictated. The basic argument of the first book was that the government God wants for His church is democratic: specifically that such key functions of the church as the discipline of members who stray from dogmatic standards of truth or moral standards of behavior, and the selection of the lay and clerical leaders of the church (the "elders" and "pastors" to use the terminology of the day), should be in the hands of the entire membership of each local congregation. Obviously this is a form of government that political thinkers of any period would call democratic. To call it democratic in the sixteenth century, however, was to damn it. Centuries of political thought in the Christian West on the possible varieties of government, almost always concluding that a well-ordered monarchy was clearly the variety favored if not actually required by God and by nature, had conditioned most thinking men to instinctive rejection of any form of government in which the people had much share. And this instinctive rejection could only have been fortified by the Renaissance recovery and intensive study of the classical Greek and Roman analyses of the possible forms of government and the relative advantages of each. Both traditions combined to give the very word "democracy" a distinctly negative meaning, to conjure up visions of rule by completely unprincipled and undisciplined mobs subject to no direction but that of occasional vicious and self-serving demagogues.

All of this Morely realized. He was particularly aware of the classical

---

[9] For a full bibliographical description and printing history of this book, see Alfred Cartier, *Bibliographie des éditions des de Tournes, imprimeurs lyonnais* (2 vols., Paris, 1937-38), No. 488, II, 524-25. I consulted the copy in Geneva, BPU, Rés. 277* Dg.

analyses of forms of government, above all of Aristotle's, and he saw that once the analogy between civil and ecclesiastical government was openly admitted, the classical arguments against democracy could be brought to bear against his proposal. At two points in his book he grapples directly with this problem. The first time he denies that the government he proposes is really a "democracy" in the ancient sense.[10] The two great disadvantages of a democracy in the ancients' eyes, he says, are that it has no body of law and no mechanism of administration. Both these essential prerequisites, however, can be found in the form of church government he is supporting. Holy Scripture provides the necessary body of law. Through it God has already done the legislative work necessary to the church of defining doctrine and morals. And in it He clearly provides for the selection of a "Moderating Council . . . composed of Pastors and Elders legitimately elected," which becomes the necessary mechanism of administration.

The second time Morely raises the problem of democracy in church government, he goes even further and leans even more heavily on the principle of analogy.[11] He goes so far as to argue that a "democracy" dominated by law is actually the best form of civil government. He points to the Athenian and Roman Republics as examples of such a government and insists that they in fact provide the models from which all that is good in contemporary civil government derives. And he bolsters this claim by noting that Aristotle observed that just as a banquet to which many bring dishes is better than one prepared by a single person, so a government taking the advice of many is better than a government controlled by few.[12] The conclusion Morely draws from this line of reasoning, of course, is that the natural reasoning embodied in the authors of antiquity reinforces at this point the scriptural revelation that God wants church government to be democratic. It was not then to his purpose to develop further the notion that democracy was the best form of civil government. Whether he would in fact have developed that notion in his second volume probably will never be known. It would have been unusually audacious of him to have done so. And it would almost certainly have cost him the favor of the powerful Huguenot aristocrats who did for a time help him.

Since Morely would have been so vulnerable on this point, it is somewhat

---

[10] Jean Morely, *Traicté de la discipline & police chrestienne* (Lyons, 1562), 32–33. Morely uses the words "ce gouvernement Democratique," at one point, "democratie," at another.

[11] *Ibid.*, 183.

[12] *Ibid.* Morely's precise words: "Car (comme Aristote dit fort prudemment) comme un banquet, auquel plusieurs apportent leur souppe, est mieux fourny, & plus abondant, que ne seroit le banquet ordinaire d'un, ou de peu de personnes, pareillement en une grande assemblee ou chacun apporte librement son advis & jugement, il y a plus de conseil, & prudence, qu'en conseil quelconque de peu de personnes."

surprising that this part of his argument did not draw more fire and draw it earlier. That it did not may be a demonstration that it seemed somewhat peripheral to the fundamental issues at stake in the minds of the antagonists on both sides. But it may also be owing to a tactical decision made by Morely's principal early opponent, Antoine de la Roche-Chandieu, the most prominent of the Parisian Protestant ministers, who was devoted to Calvin and Beza, and who had been charged by the Reformed synods with the task of formally refuting Morely's program.[13] Chandieu based his refutation[14] almost entirely upon an extended exegesis of the Biblical passages that Morely had used. He denied flatly that there could be any analogy between civil and ecclesiastical government and therefore rejected any argument about the form of ecclesiastical government drawn from secular authorities or natural reason. He charged, indeed, that argument from analogy was a fundamental source of the fallacies of Morely's entire program.[15] Since he based so much of his attack upon this charge, he could hardly scold Morely for introducing democracy into the church and tax him with the classical arguments against that form of government. And so he avoided the subject altogether and paid no attention to Morely's statements about democracy.

When Beza turned to his public attack on Morely, however, he did not worry about such logical scruples. He did not really have to. Chandieu had prepared his reasoned and complete refutation to Morely's entire program to win back the man's supporters or any Protestants disposed to waver in France. Beza wrote his letters largely to counter the influence of Ramus abroad, in intellectual centers where the details of the controversy and Morely himself were hardly known. Beza was thoroughly Aristotelian in many aspects of his own thought and was fully aware of the classic use of the term "democracy." He could, furthermore, be quite sure that most of his correspondents, and the wider public for whom he published many of these letters, would share this background and this attitude. He therefore seized upon the charge of "democracy" as a useful polemical point to score

---

[13] Geneva, BPU, MS fr. 446 *passim;* n.b. Rouvière to Chandieu, Mar. 11, 1566, fols. 72–73.

[14] [Antoine de la Roche-Chandieu,] *La Confirmation de la discipline ecclesiastique observee es eglises reformees du royaume de France. Avec la response aux objections proposees alencontre* ([Geneva and La Rochelle,] 1566). There are copies in Geneva, BPU, Bd 865 and Bd 1999. On its printing history, see E. Droz, "Autour de l'affaire Morély: La Roche Chandieu et Barth. Berton," *Bibliothèque d'Humanisme et Renaissance,* XXII (No. 3, 1960), 570–77.

[15] The argument from analogy seems to have been explicitly repudiated by the particularly normative 1571 La Rochelle synod of the French Reformed church. This is suggested by the text of the synod's acts published in *Synodicon in Gallia Reformata,* ed. Quick, I, 92, Article V, and decisively confirmed if we can accept as authoritative the manuscript records of the synod's gloss on its Article 32, preserved in *Staatsarchiv Zürich,* E-II 381, fol. 1310, and Geneva, BPU, MS fr. 405, fol. 20. The Zurich MSS reads: "D'avantage la dicte assemblée ratifiant l'Article trente deuxiesme de la dicte Confession à rejetté & rejette l'erreur de ceux qui veulent abolir la discipline de l'Eglise la confondans avec le gouvernement civil et Politicque des Magistrats. Condamne aussi tous les erreurs qui procedent de telle fausse opinion."

against Morely and his party, employing it again and again. In the most extended of these letters, addressed to Henry Bullinger, leader of the Reformed Church in Zurich and the most influential contemporary Protestant leader of the Zwinglian tradition, Beza charges that Morely has called the French Reformed church government an "oligarchy" or "tyranny" and that he is trying to replace it with the "most troublesome and most seditious democracy."[16] This particular attack had its desired effect. Bullinger replied that he had not heard of Morely before, but suspected he must belong to the dreadful sect of Anabaptists,[17] a condemnation, which, to Bullinger, may well have been the harshest possible. He could not really believe, however, that Ramus could have held such terrible opinions.

In other letters Beza goes further in developing this line of argument. In one, which he later published, he begins by denying that the church should be "democratic" and argues that it should rather be a "monarchy," with Jesus Christ as king. He then briefly discusses the role of different orders of clergy, the possibility of "tyranny" arising within an ecclesiastical organization, and relations between clerical and civil authorities. And he returns to the problem of "democracy" by examining and refuting a number of arguments drawn from Scripture by the proponents of more democratic church government.[18]

Throughout these letters, Beza constantly uses the classic terms for types of government in discussing his ideal of suitable church government, but is not altogether consistent in his use of these terms. Sometimes his ideal is a "monarchy" governed by Christ. At other times it is dominated by the "aristocratic" principle, embodied in the consistory. But never is it a "democracy." That term, indeed, is almost invariably coupled with a negatively weighted adjective or two, and Beza is obviously using it as a polemical weapon.

These are the most considered and extended references to "democracy"

---

[16] "Perturbatissimam et seditiosissimam Democratiam" in Beza to Bullinger, Nov. 13, 1571, *Staatsarchiv Zürich*, E-II 381, fol. 1306v.

[17] Bullinger to Beza, Dec. 4, 1571, published in André Bouvier, *Henri Bullinger, le successeur de Zwingli, d'après sa correspondance avec les réformés et les humanistes de langue française* (Neuchâtel and Paris, 1940), 557–65.

[18] *Epistolarum Theologicarum Theodori Bezae Vezelii, Liber Unus* (Geneva, 1573), 398–403, Letter No. 83, no indication of addressee, date, or place of writing. Cf. Charles Mercier, in "Les théories politiques des calvinistes en France au cours des guerres de religion," *Bulletin de la Société de l'histoire du protestantisme français*, LXXXIII (Apr.–June 1934), 235, for further comment on this letter, and 233–36 for incisive comment on the significance of the whole controversy in the development of Calvinist political thought. Beza's further letters on this problem, most of them addressed to fellow theologians in German-speaking countries, can be found in this 1573 volume or in Geneva, *Musée historique de la Réformation*, Beza correspondence, a set of transcripts collected for preparation of the critical edition of this illuminating correspondence. Henri Meylan and Alain Dufour, who are preparing the edition, graciously granted me access to this collection.

resulting from the entire controversy. They are very nearly the most complete and the earliest (of which I have knowledge) in the entire Reformation period. They make it clear that there were thinkers, in the earlier stages of the Protestant Reformation, who were quite willing to consider analogies between civil and ecclesiastical government and to apply to one sphere arguments drawn from thought about the best form of government in the other sphere. And at least one of these thinkers was convinced that a "democratic" government was best for the church, and might also be best for civil society.

Direct debate between Morely and Beza did not long survive the St. Bartholomew's massacres, for they were most savage in the very areas where Morely had won support and seem to have wiped out his faction. Beza's personal ascendancy within the French Reformed church was confirmed, and with it the synodical or "presbyterian" form of government that has persisted within that church to the present. The ideas developed during this debate, however, were to appear again in other places and at other times. In English-speaking countries, for example, similar debates were soon joined between Congregational and Presbyterian factions of the Puritan movement, and reached a climax in the 1640's, when radical Britain wrestled with the problem of the proper church polity to substitute for that of Charles I and William Laud. Several of the leading polemicists in that battle cited Morely in passing, generally disparagingly.[19] Arguments from analogy like Beza's were used against the threat of ecclesiastical anarchy even by Congregationalists.

In an even later period, when the battle for democracy had become largely secular, Morely's name was mentioned again. It was cited by Jean-Jacques Rousseau, the unhappy Genevan who became the Enlightenment's greatest exponent of political democracy. I have found no evidence, however, that Rousseau knew of Morely's ideas. He discussed the burning of Morely's book in Geneva, but only to argue that the Genevan authorities of his day did not have a similar legal right to burn his *Social Contract*.[20]

---

[19] E.g., John Norton, *The Answer to the Whole Set of Questions of the Celebrated Mr. William Apollonius* . . . (London, 1648), tr. and repub. Douglas Horton (Cambridge, Mass., 1958), 6. Horton has kindly called to my attention references to Morely in quotations from a 1644 pamphlet by William Rathband, and from two of Robert Baillie's 1643–1644 letters, published in order by Benjamin Hanbury, *Historical Memorials Relating to the Independents or Congregationalists: From Their Rise to the Restoration of the Monarchy*, A.D. *MDCLX* (3 vols., London, 1839–41), II, 318, 435, 438. For fuller texts and additional references by Baillie, see *The Letters and Journals of Robert Baillie* . . . , ed. David Laing (3 vols., Edinburgh, 1841–42), II, 115, 155, 165, 179–80, 184, 188, 193. Most of these references are repeated requests for copies of the books by Morely and Chandieu (identified only by his pseudonym "Sadael"), which Baillie apparently had not seen, but whose basic arguments he knew, perhaps from reference by some such contemporary Dutch scholar as Gysbertus Voetius or William Apollonius.

[20] J. J. Rousseau, *Lettres écrites de la montagne* (2 vols., Amsterdam, 1764), I, 190–97, II, 14.

Perhaps further research will uncover yet more evidence of a continuing impact of this sixteenth-century French Protestant dispute. In any event, the quarrel illustrates neatly one of the many perennial problems in relations between state and church. Now we argue less about whether church democracy will lead to a disturbing political democracy, more about whether a beneficent political democracy requires democracy in the church.

XIII

WILLIAM ALLEN'S
USE OF PROTESTANT
POLITICAL ARGUMENT*

O ne of the main themes distinguishing Garrett Mattingly's work
was an abiding appreciation of the fundamental unity of
Western civilization. He emphasized it in his teaching and
he illustrated it in his work. To his students he often made the point
that the American historian, detached as he can be from the bitter
national tensions which so often distract the European historian,
should employ his vantage point to call attention to those international and supranational forces that have created Western unity. To
his readers he pointed out many ways in which the diplomats active
in the Europe of the Renaissance worked to maintain this unity,
often against bitter odds. This same theme can also be illustrated
by studies in the history of ideas, since ideas are particularly fluid,

---

* This essay is a by-product of an edition I am preparing, at the suggestion of Garrett Mattingly, for the *Folger Documents of Tudor and
Stuart Civilization,* of William Cecil, Lord Burghley, *The Execution of
Justice in England* (1583), and William Allen, *A True, Sincere, and
Modest Defense of English Catholics that suffer for their faith* (1584),
hereafter cited as Allen, *Defense.* I have used the Folger Shakespeare Library
copies of both of these books. [Punctuation has been slightly modernized
in some places where clarity was at stake, and the ambiguous contemporary
spelling "then" has been modernized to "than"; otherwise, quotations are
reproduced here as in the editions cited.—Ed.]

hence particularly likely to seep through or wash over the dikes
of nation or confession which have so often been erected to segment
the West. An illustration of this theme emerges, surprisingly, from
a study of English Catholic use of Protestant political argument in
the late sixteenth and early seventeenth centuries. Polemicists like
Father Robert Parsons and Dr. William Allen deliberately crossed
lines of confession and nationality in a search for ideas that would
advance their cause. Perhaps the most striking example can be
found in a book the importance of which Mattingly himself pointed
out, Allen's *A True, Sincere, and Modest Defense of English Catholics that suffer for their faith* (1584).[1]

Allen's *Defense* was designed most obviously to counter William
Cecil's *The Execution of Justice in England* (1583), a semiofficial
pamphlet developing the claim that the Elizabethan government
was putting to death Jesuits and other Catholic missionaries in
England, solely on charges of treason, never because of their religious beliefs. Allen, as the acknowledged leader and principal
spokesman for a militant new party of English Catholics in exile,
felt obliged to answer Cecil's claim, potentially so damaging to the
English Catholic cause in the eyes of the Continental princes upon
whose support it depended. It seems quite clear, however, that Allen
also had a second, less obvious purpose in drafting his *Defense*. He
had been engaged in a series of secret plots to mount an invasion
of England by Continental Catholic armies in order to depose
Elizabeth I and re-establish the Roman Catholic faith.[2] For such an
invasion to succeed, however, the plotters felt it would have to be
supported by a simultaneous rising of those Englishmen within
the realm who remained loyal to Rome. Allen apparently hoped,
with his writings, to prepare these Englishmen, living "under the
cross," for the great revolt to come.

Both purposes led Allen to devote much of his *Defense* to a
justification of the papal right to depose heretic rulers. Cecil had
argued that *Regnans in Excelsis,* the bull by which Pope Pius V
in 1570 had excommunicated Elizabeth and absolved her subjects
of obedience, revealed the Roman Catholic Church to be an international political conspiracy, determined to destroy all governments
which would not bend to its will. Allen argued that the bull was an
occasionally necessary standard method of implementing the pope's

spiritual duty to guide all Christian souls, that right then it was not binding upon English Catholics, but that it could be put into effect whenever the pope decided that circumstances made enforcement appropriate.

In developing his justification of this papal right, Allen appealed to standard Catholic authorities, of course.[3] He quoted St. Thomas Aquinas and such an authoritative contemporary commentator on his work as Francisco Toledo. He referred to canon law, particularly to a decree drafted by the Fourth Lateran Council in 1215. But this part of his argument was relatively perfunctory, since, as he himself acknowledged, it would carry relatively little weight with his adversaries. Most of his argument was based on extended exegesis of key passages in Holy Scriptures, in the writings of early Church Fathers, and in the standard histories of the early church.[4] In this, Allen was employing a technique typical of many Jesuits and other intellectual leaders of the Catholic Reformation. He was debating Protestants on their own grounds, arguing from the authorities they valued most. Much of his exegesis would seem forced or fanciful to modern Biblical scholars. But so would much of that advanced by his opponents. Generally speaking, this Catholic technique seems to have been quite effective in reversing, among intellectuals at least, the great tide toward Protestantism.

Allen, however, carried his polemical counteroffensive one step further. He not only cited the Protestants' favorite authorities. He also cited the Protestants themselves. In a few brief pages of his book, he inserts a set of quotations and paraphrases taken from the works of such great intellectual leaders of the Protestant Reformation as Luther, Zwingli, and Calvin, and from the writings of certain of their respected followers. The Protestant arguments were not, of course, for any papal right to license revolt. But they were for a general right of revolt quite analogous in certain ways to the kind Allen favored. It is upon Allen's use of these arguments that this article will focus. The particular arguments he cites reveal something about the general knowledge then current in informed circles of what early Protestant thinking on politics was. His use of them helps establish with increased precision the ways in which Protestant resistance theories which developed from 1520 until the 1570s can be linked to Catholic resistance theories which developed in the succeeding decades of the late sixteenth and early seventeenth centuries.

Allen established a background, although he introduced it only part way through this section of his argument, with a number of statements from Lutheran writers in justification of political revolt for religious reasons. He realized that they would not carry the same authority among Englishmen as certain other Protestant writers. But he knew that the Lutherans had established the foundation upon which all other Protestants had built, and, in addition, the Lutherans had drawn the main lines of controversy which continued to govern debate between Protestants and Catholics. Allen's examples of Lutheran political thought do not come from the actual writings of the men who stated them. They come rather from Sleidan's *De statu religionis et reipublicae, Carolo quinto, Caesare, Commentarii.*[5] This precise and detailed history of the course of religious politics, primarily in Germany, during the reign of Emperor Charles V, was thoroughly Protestant in its sympathies. It had been widely circulated throughout Europe and was even available in English translation. In the fashion of many histories of that day, it contained entire texts of certain key public statements and manifestoes, and paraphrases or detailed summaries of others. Altogether it served Allen's polemical purposes admirably.

In Sleidan Allen discovered that Luther himself, at the time of the formation of the Schmalkaldic League, had stated that "indeed he was in doubt for a time, whether they might take armes against their Supreme Magistrate or no; but afterward seing the extremitie of thinges, and that Religion could not otherwise be defended, nor themselves, he made no conscience of the matter, but ether Caesar, or anie, waging warres in his name, might be resisted."[6] This particular sentiment had been stated by Luther in 1530, at a conference in Torgau with certain lawyers and other advisers of the Protestant princes who were trying to devise ways to ward off what seemed to be an impending attempt by the emperor to suppress their faith through military action. It marks a critical point in the development of Luther's political thought, since heretofore he had repeatedly and expressly denied any religious right to political resistance. His denials had been particularly sharp after he had seen the bloody results of the use of mad violence by certain Anabaptists in the

Peasants' Revolt and other uprisings. Even at Torgau, however, Luther did not grant the existence of any religious right to revolt. He merely acknowledged the weight of certain legal and constitutional arguments for revolt, and conceded that the Christian tradition had nothing to say either for or against such arguments. The concession was fateful, nevertheless. It was put into writing in a terse note generally called the Torgau memorandum.[7] The memorandum was widely circulated and proved to be of substantial use to the princes organizing the newly militant kind of Lutheranism which supported the Schmalkaldic League.

These new militants among the Lutherans did not find it necessary to resort to war immediately, however. The imperial threat to suppress Lutheranism by force waned. It was not until 1546, as Luther was dying, that the militancy of his followers was put to an armed test, in the Schmalkaldic war. But this time new spokesmen had to be found to announce the Lutheran position. The first of these of whom Allen took note were two of the leading Lutheran princes—the Landgrave of Hesse and the Elector of Saxony. They were now the leaders of the Schmalkaldic League, they rallied some of its forces for military action, and its manifestoes were issued in their name. A manifesto to which Allen paid particular attention was issued on September 2, 1546. It was issued in response to the Emperor's announcement proscribing Hesse and Saxony as rebels and placing them under the imperial ban. The imperial announcement declared that they were being proscribed only for political rebellion, not for their religious views. Consequently they found themselves in a situation analogous to that of Allen and his English missionaries in the 1580s, and their reaction was similarly bellicose. The heart of their argument was that they had been forced to raise armies to defend what they believed to be the only true religion. In the passage quoted by Allen, they concluded: "Forasmuch as Caesar intendeth to destroy the true religion and our ancient libertie, he giveth us cause inough why we may with good conscience resist him, as both by prophane and sacred histories may be prooved."[8] Thus they extended the Protestant grounds upon which revolt may be supported. Now the argument to justify revolt for religion no longer was merely legal and constitutional. It had also become explicitly religious.

A yet more extreme Lutheran justification of revolt was still to come. The early result of Charles V's attempt to crush Lutheran power was smashing victory. Hesse and Saxony were imprisoned and a temporary compromise settlement, the Augsburg Interim of 1548, was imposed upon the entire empire. Most Lutherans, including Luther's close colleague Philip Melanchthon, saw no alternative open to them but acceptance either of this settlement or of some modified version of it. A few resolutely orthodox Lutherans refused to accept the Interim, however, even though it meant defying the assembled might of the entire Holy Roman Empire. The most vocal of these more orthodox Lutherans were gathered in the city of Magdeburg. There both city magistrates and city ministers resolved to defy local promulgation of the Interim, no matter what the cost. They explained and defended their defiance in a series of impassioned printed treatises and manifestoes. Perhaps the most famous of these was the Magdeburg *Bekenntnis* of April, 1550. Allen summarized the contents of this confession, again drawing his information from Sleidan, in these words: "The same writer [Sleidan] reporteth the like of the Ministers of Magdeburge; declaring how the inferiour may defend him self against the superior, compelling him to doe against the truth and rule of Christes lawes."[9] Allen left one really crucial word out of this paraphrase of Sleidan, however, and thus gave a somewhat misleading impression of the Magdeburgers' position. That word was "magistrate." While the ministers of Magdeburg, led by Luther's own disciple Nicolaus von Amsdorf, had advanced beyond Luther's position to one of justifying on religious grounds the right of political revolt, they were not prepared to vest this right in the entire population or in any random fragment thereof. It was to be vested only in "inferior magistrates," regularly constituted agents of government such as princes or city councillors, agents who could lay equal claim with the emperor to having been "ordained of God," and hence were equally charged with the responsibility of protecting the true worship of Him. Here we have come to a more sophisticated statement of Protestant resistance theory. For the Magdeburg *Bekenntnis* specifies not only the causes that justify revolt but also the institutions which may rightfully license it. This Magdeburg position was to be restated in significant and influential ways by later Protestant thinkers, most of them in the Calvinist rather than the Lutheran camp.

Before the Calvinist position jelled, however, even before the Lutherans had reluctantly decided to claim a religious right of resistance, another Protestant position had been stated—that of Zwingli. The general Zwinglian position, as Allen noted several times in his book, had won great favor in England. In fact Allen believed that the entire religious settlement developed by the government of Edward VI, the first really Protestant government of England, was basically Zwinglian. Zwingli's position on the problem of political resistance was much more bellicose than that of Luther, and it was stated at a much earlier point in his career. Zwingli had launched his campaign to reform the city of Zurich by triumphantly winning a public debate on sixty-seven articles of Christian doctrine. Among these articles was a group of ten on the role of government in religion. One of them, article forty-two, flatly justifies a right of resistance. It reads, in Allen's quite accurate translation: "When kinges rule unfaithfullie, and otherwise than the rule of the Gospel prescribeth, they may, with God, be deposed." Furthermore, within a few months after his defense of these articles, Zwingli had published a lengthy defense of each and every one of them. His defense of article forty-two, a part of which Allen also quotes, specifies that kings may be deposed "when they punish not wicked persons, but speciallie when they advaunce the ungodlie, as idle Priests, &c. such may be deprived of their dignitie, as Saul was."[10] While this gloss does mention agents or institutions who may rightfully depose a ruler, it remains rather vague as to who they are.

Zwingli did not abandon this strong view in his later career, even when the excesses of the Peasants' Revolt, which shocked him as they did Luther, must have tempted him to soften its bluntness. Shortly before his untimely death, he repeated the view in a letter to Konrad Sam and Simpert Schenk, ministers of the free German cities of Ulm and Memmingen. The letter was drafted in August of 1530, a few months before Luther was persuaded to sign the Torgau memorandum. It consequently represents a parallel reaction to the same Protestant fear of suppression by imperial arms. But Zwingli's reaction was predictably stronger and less ambiguous than

Luther's. He openly endorsed resistance, and on religious rather than merely constitutional grounds, and he justified his endorsement with yet another appeal to Scripture. His words, again in Allen's translation: "If the Empire of Rome, or what other Soveraigne so ever, should oppresse the sincere religion, and we necligentlie suffer the same, we shalbe charged with contempt, no lesse than the oppressors thereof themselves: wherof we have an example in the fiftenth of Jeremie, wher the destruction of the people is prophecied; for that they suffred their K. Manasses, being impious and ungodly, to be unpunished."[11] This particular letter of Zwingli's was soon published, in a collection of letters written by him and his fellow Reformer Oecolampadius,[12] and so it also became widely known and generally available.

In Allen's eyes the most important of the Continental Protestant positions he cited was the Calvinist one. He frequently argued that the Elizabethan settlement was basically Calvinist, that it had received its theology from the Reformer of Geneva, and that even the precise wording of one of the parliamentary statutes which had created the Elizabethan church had been influenced by Calvin's opinions.[18] In his summary of Protestant resistance theories, consequently, he gives pride of place to Calvin's. The entire summary begins, "And first their grand-maister, Jo. Calvin putteth doune his oracle, as a conclusion approved of their whole sect and confraternitie in thes wordes. . . . 'Earthlie Princes doe bereave themselves of al authoritie when they doe erect them selves against God, yea they are unworthie to be accompted in the number of men: and therfore we must rather spit upon their heades than obey them when they become so proude, or perverse, that they wil spoile God of his right.' "[14] The quotation is from Calvin's commentary on Daniel. It was published in 1561, as tempers in France were rising toward the fever pitch that within a few months was to plunge the nation into nearly forty years of bloody religious war. The commentary on Daniel is preceded by a dedicatory letter to Calvin's followers in France.[15] This letter reminded the faithful that Calvin had repeatedly urged them to avoid any resort to violence. But it also warned the authorities that further persecution of the atrocious sort his followers had had to endure might easily drive them to desperation and revolt. Calvin clearly recognized in the story of Daniel a parable of peculiar relevance to the contemporary situation. The courage and resolution of Daniel and his friends in the face of persecution should provide an encouraging example to his own followers. The dreadful fate of the kings of Babylon who persecuted these servants of God should provide a usefully stern warning to the rulers of France. The particular passage from Calvin's Daniel commentary which Allen chose to cite is remarkable for the vehemence with which it criticizes established authority. It is a peculiarly sharp example of the picturesque language which resulted when Calvin lost his celebrated temper. But it did not justify armed revolt, unless spitting be regarded as a form of revolt. It really justified only passive disobedience of laws which prohibit the exercise of "true religion," a position which Calvin had held consistently for years, and which he developed at length in this particular commentary.

These are nuances which are lost to Allen, however. He hastened on to advance his argument by quoting Calvin's principal lieutenant and successor, Theodore Beza, and he tied this opinion directly to England, to the Queen herself, in fact. He noted with horror, in the 1565 version of Beza's great New Testament, an epistle dedicatory to the Queen of England, proudly dated on an anniversary of the day "that the nobilitie of France (under the noble Prince of Condey) laid the first foundation of restoring true Christian religion in France, by consecrating most happilie their blood to God in the batail of Druze [Dreux]."[16] Clearly Beza was here glorifying a revolt against the laws and lawful king of one of the greatest kingdoms in Christendom. Obviously he thus approved of revolt to advance religion. Elsewhere Allen also noted that Beza accompanied the Huguenot armies through much of this campaign.[17]

Allen concluded his analysis of the Calvinist position by quotation from a yet more definitive authority, the Confession of Faith adopted by the national synod of the French Reformed Church. This statement had a far greater binding force upon the Calvinist movement than any particular commentary or letter drafted by its leaders, since its exact wording had been the result of lengthy deliberation and had been ratified by official representatives of the entire church, several times. Unfortunately for Allen's argument, it does not appear to give him very powerful support. The exact wording of the article he quotes: "We affirme that subjects must obey the lawes, pay tribute, beare al burthens imposed, and susteine the yoke even of infidel Magistrates; so for al that, that the supreme dominion and due of God be not violated."[18] Allen did not explain his construction of this article. Apparently he felt the final clause created a loophole which could be used to justify disobedience of laws, refusal to pay taxes, avoidance of other governmental responsibilities, and revolt.

Finally Allen connected these assorted justifications of resistance directly to England, by quoting two English proto-Puritans, Christopher Goodman and John Knox. And in their writings he found statements which substantiated his case more fully than any he could find among Continental writers. Goodman, in his inflammatory tract, *How Superior Powers Ought to be Obeyed* (Geneva, 1558), published while he was a refugee from Marian persecution in Calvinist Geneva, had called for revolt, preferably revolt led by nobles and others charged with governmental responsibility in the realm, but if necessary revolt led by anyone in the population. He had, in providing an example, praised the abortive revolt of 1554 against Mary's regime led by Sir Thomas Wyatt, in these words quoted by Allen: "Wyat did but his dutie, and it was the dutie of al others that professe the Gospel, to have risen with him, for maintenance of the same. His cause was just, and they al were traitors that tooke not part with him."[19] Knox, in a variety of tracts, developed an argument quite similar to Goodman's. The parallel is particularly striking in the book which contains Knox's most complete argument for resistance, the *Appellation . . . to the Nobility and Estates of Scotland* (Geneva, 1558). From this work, Allen quoted a statement which summarizes neatly the position of these firebrands: "If the people have either rashelie promoted anie manifest wicked person, or els ignorantlie chosen such an one, as after declareth himself unworthie of regiment above the people of God (and such be al Idolators and cruel persecutors) most justlie may the same men depose and punish him."[20] Here the justification for revolt is really constitutional, based on a rough notion of social contract. But the tests of incompetence which justify revocation of the contract remain religious. They are idolatry and religious persecution, two prime characteristics, for Knox, of Roman Catholicism.

These are the specific Protestant political arguments to which Allen alluded in this section of his treatise. Together with the few traditional Catholic arguments he quoted, they led him to this conclusion: "Thus both Schooles and Lawes speake and resolve for the matter in hand: both Catholiques and Protestants agreing, that Princes may for some causes, and especiallie for their defection in Faith and Religion, be resisted and forsaken: though in the maner of executing the sentence and other needful circumstances, Protestants folowe faction and populer mutinie; we reduce al, to lawe, order, and judgement."[21]

The last clause of Allen's conclusion, of course, is hardly fair. It is in fact a caricature of the position held by the most responsible Protestant thinkers. This was quickly pointed out by the polemicist assigned by the English government to prepare a careful refutation of Allen's book. Thomas Bilson, an Anglican divine, had begun working on a refutation of one of Allen's earlier works even before the publication of the *Defense.* He enlarged it to include a partial refutation of the *Defense,* and then, for good measure, added a refutation of much of the gloss on the Reims New Testament which had been recently published by a committee of scholars organized by Allen. The total result was a hefty tome which attacked the Catholic polemicists on several different fronts. Its title reveals its emphasis: *The True Difference between Christian Subjection and UnChristian Rebellion* (Oxford, 1585).[22] In keeping with this emphasis, the very part of Allen's *Defense* upon which it concentrated attention is his defense of the papal power to depose. Most of Bilson's counterattack, of course, was a refutation of Allen's Biblical and patristic exegesis. But he included within it a critique of the very passage which we have been considering, the passage which summarizes Protestant arguments for armed resistance.[23] He pointed out that some of the arguments quoted, *e.g.,* the one from Calvin, really justify only passive disobedience, not armed revolt. He noted that others, *e.g.,* the ones from Luther and Beza, accept armed revolt, but only when it is led by inferior magistrates, such as the princes of the blood royal in France or the hereditary princes of the empire in Germany, men who had a defined legal position within the government of their countries which limited in significant ways the power of the superior authority. Generally his case is plausible and would be accepted by most modern scholars. He had some trouble with Zwingli, whom he made a German, loyal to the imperial tradition of vesting certain powers in inferior magistrates. But the opinions which gave him most difficulty were those of Goodman and Knox. Goodman's opinion, he suggested, was a personal one, later repudiated by its author, not really typical of his party. Knox's opinion he rather rashly suggested might be justified if the Scottish kings were elected, like the German emperors, but he was inclined to reject Knox too, as atypical.

The debate did not end with Bilson. Later references to Protestant political argument figure in later quarrels between Protestant polemicists and Father Robert Parsons, Allen's chief collaborator in the Catholic polemical war on the English establishment.[24] Particularly in Parsons' *A Treatise Tending to Mitigation . . .* of 1607, can one find quotations from Protestant writers supporting a right of religious resistance.[25] But by this time Parsons and his party had become less sanguine. Their hope now was more for toleration of Catholics within England than for any reconquest of their native country for their faith. The particular examples of Protestant political argument used by Parsons are, most of them, quite different from those cited by Allen. Few of them, however, are used with more care.

Even if Allen did not analyze Protestant political ideas with due attention to the differences among them and the nuances in their statement, however, there remains a kernel of truth in his conclusion. Protestants and Catholics did generally agree that governments may be overthrown, sometimes must be overthrown, for religious reasons. Those among them who were most responsible, furthermore, generally also vested the right to license or lead the overthrow in specific established institutions: Catholics in the papacy, Protestants in "inferior magistrates" with constitutional positions within existing governments. Only rarely did either side seek to throw the gates open to popular rebellion. Those on both sides who were most militant stimulated a bloody fanaticism which plunged the West into some of the most appalling wars it has ever seen. But they also encouraged, together, a basic "irreverence about the state"[26] that continues to protect the liberties which are such a rightly cherished part of our common heritage in the West.

N O T E S

1. Garrett Mattingly, "William Allen and Catholic Propaganda in England," *Aspects de la propagande religieuse* (Geneva: Droz, 1957), pp. 333–38.

2. Information about these plots may be found in Albert J. Loomie, *The Spanish Elizabethans* (New York: Fordham, 1963), pp. 22–24, and works therein cited, esp. on p. 269.

3. Allen, *Defense*, pp. 84–88.

4. *Ibid.*, principally in chap. 5.

5. My references are to the Geneva, Badius ed. of 1559 (State University of Iowa Library copy), hereafter cited as Sleidan, *Commentarii*.

6. Allen, *Defense*, p. 79; from Sleidan, *Commentarii*, lib. 8, fol. 119v.

7. For text, see *D. Martin Luthers Werke* (Weimar ed., 1883—), *Briefwechsel*, V, pp. 661–64. For comment on this text, see Karl Müller, *Luthers Äusserungen über das Recht des bewaffneten Widerstands gegen den Kaiser, Sitzungsberichte der Königlich Bayerischen Akademie der Wissenschaften, Philosophisch-philologisch und historische Klasse*, Jahrgang 1915, 8 Abhandlung, pp. 39–52; Hans Baron, "Religion and Politics in the German Imperial Cities during the Reformation," *The English Historical Review*, LII (1937), pp. 423–25.

8. Allen, *Defense*, pp. 79–80; from Sleidan, *Commentarii*, lib. 18, fol. 290. For comment on this manifesto, see Oskar Waldeck, "Die Publizistik des Schmalkaldischen Krieges I," *Archiv für Reformationsgeschichte*, VII (1909/1910), 7–8 (no. 13); p. 27.

9. Allen, *Defense*, p. 80; from Sleidan, *Commentarii*, lib. 22, fol. 359. For an abridged text of the *Bekenntnis*, in English translation, see Roland H. Bainton, *The Age of the Reformation* (Princeton, N.J.: Van Nostrand, Anvil Original, 1956), pp. 172–73. For comment on it and its influence, see Robert M. Kingdon, "The First Expression of Theodore Beza's Political Ideas," *Archiv für Reformationsgeschichte*, XLVI (1955), pp. 93–94; Irmgard Höss, "Zur Genesis der Widerstandslehre Bezas," *ibid.*, LIV (1963), pp. 198–214.

10. Allen, *Defense*, pp. 78–79. For text of article and gloss, see *Huldreich Zwinglis Sämtliche Werke* (*Corpus Reformatorum* ed., 1905—), II, pp. 342–46. For comment on this text, see Alfred Farner, *Die Lehre von Kirche und Staat bei Zwingli* (Tübingen: Mohr, 1930), pp. 65–66.

11. Allen, *Defense*, p. 78; original in *Zwinglis Werke*, *op. cit.*, XI, pp. 68–70. This text was not mentioned by Farner, *op. cit.*, and it suggests a modification of his conclusion, p. 67, that Zwingli's resistance argument was purely theoretical.

12. *DD. J. Oecolampadii et H. Zvinglii Epistolarum, libri quatuor* (Basel, 1536), listed in British Museum Catalogue.

13. Allen, *Defense*, p. 7.

14. *Ibid.*, pp. 77–78; original text in *Ioannis Calvini Opera* (*Corpus Reformatorum* ed., 1863–1900), XLI, pp. 25–26. For comment on this text, see Émile Doumergue, *Jean Calvin, les hommes et les choses de son temps* (Lausanne: Bridel, 1899–1927), V, pp. 497–98; Josef Bohatec, *Calvin und das Recht* (Feudingen in Westfalen: Buchdruckerei & Verlagsanstalt, 1934), pp. 137–38; J. W. Allen, *A History of Political Thought in the Sixteenth Century* (London: Methuen, 1951), p. 57.

15. Text in *Calvini Opera*, *op. cit.*, XVIII, pp. 614–24, "Calvinus Piis Gallis," *n.b.* pp. 619–20.

16. Allen, *Defense*, p. 78. The letter is dated 1564, but printed in the Geneva, Estienne ed. of 1565. I have used the Folger Library copy.

17. *Ibid.*, p. 80.

18. *Ibid.*, p. 78. See the edited copy in John Quick, *Synodicon in Gallia Reformata* (London, 1692), I, xv, article 40. There are many variant copies of these synodical decisions. M. Michel Reulos of Paris is preparing a critical edition of them.

178

19. *Ibid.*, p. 79. For full text, see facsimile edition introduced by Charles H. McIlwain (New York: Columbia University Press, 1931), p. 204. For comment on the entire work, see Charles Martin, *Les Protestants Anglais réfugiés à Genève au temps de Calvin*, 1555–1560 (Geneva: Jullien, 1915), pp. 177–92; J. W. Allen, *op. cit.*, pp. 116–18.

20. Allen, *Defense*, p. 79. For full text see edited copy in David Laing, ed., *The Works of John Knox* (Edinburgh: Thin, 1895), IV, p. 540. For comment on the entire work, see J. W. Allen, *op. cit.*, pp. 110–13.

21. Allen, *Defense*, p. 88.

22. I have used a Folger Library copy.

23. Bilson, *op. cit.*, pp. 509–19.

24. Several examples are cited by Thomas H. Clancy, *Papist Pamphleteers: The Allen-Persons party and the political thought of the Counter-Reformation in England, 1572–1615* (Chicago: Loyola, 1964), especially pp. 65 and n.44. One can also find examples in works which precede Allen's *Defense*, e.g., in Thomas Stapleton's *Counterblast* of 1567. See Marvin R. O'Connell, *Thomas Stapleton and the Counter Reformation* (New Haven: Yale, 1964), pp. 201 ff., particularly p. 207.

25. Parsons, *A Treatise Tending to Mitigation*, pp. 38–51, 113–19. I have used the State University of Iowa Library copy.

26. The phrase is used by Clancy, *op. cit.*, p. 192.

XIV

REACTIONS TO THE ST. BARTHOLOMEW MASSACRES IN GENEVA AND ROME*

The connections between high idealism and extreme violence which are such a sensational feature of the contemporary political scene can also be found in the past. One period in which they can be found in particularly striking forms is the age of the Reformation. This was a time which witnessed some of the greatest and most heroic accomplishments of the human spirit in the entire span of history. But it was also a time which witnessed some of the most appalling atrocities, made all the more appalling because they were committed in complete sincerity in order to advance the "true religion." Of the atrocities which disfigured the period of the Reformation, one of the most dramatic was the St. Bartholomew Massacre. This is a report on the two most extreme reactions to that event.

To make my report fully intelligible, however, I should first draw attention to one basic fact about the St. Bartholomew Massacre: it was actually a combination of two series of atrocities. This point deserves emphasis.[1] It has often been ignored by commentators yet it is very significant. Violence began with a series of political assassinations, almost all of which occurred during the early morning hours of 24 August. It then shifted to a succession of rather indiscriminate religious massacres by mobs of Catholic fanatics. This popular violence began in Paris but soon spread to other parts of France. In September and October about twelve cities witnessed massacres of Protestants by

* This article splices together two papers, one on Genevan reactions to the massacres, read at the Folger Library Conference, the other on Roman reactions, read at the Newberry Library Conference. In revising them for publication, I am indebted to many scholars who read or heard them in their original drafts. I am particularly grateful for the comments of Professor Derk Visser of Ursinus College on the Genevan paper, and of both Father Pierre Hurtubise of Saint Paul University in Ottawa and Professor A. Lynn Martin of the University of Adelaide on the Roman paper.

[1] It is one of the values of Janine Estèbe, *Tocsin pour un massacre: la saison des Saint-Barthélemy* (Paris, 1968), a popular but thoughtful study of the massacres, that this point is emphasized. I have followed her account for much of my general information on the massacres.

Catholic mobs that resembled those in Paris. These cities included
some of the largest in the kingdom – Lyons, Rouen, Orléans. They were
all cities which had had powerful Calvinist minorities living amidst a
predominantly Catholic population. Some had even been controlled
briefly in earlier years by Protestant city governments. In every case
the massacre was the result of mob action, occasionally, as in Bor-
deaux, allegedly egged on by the preaching of a fanatic Catholic
priest. In most cases governmental officials did little either to provoke
or prevent the massacres.[2]

Now assassinations and massacres were not new to sixteenth-century
Europe. They had become regrettably common in France, ever since
the first war of religion had been touched off by a massacre of a
Protestant congregation at Vassy in 1562, and ended with the assassination of a Catholic commander (François duc de Guise) in 1563. But
violence so concentrated and on such a scale was unusual. And
violence at this precise time was unexpected, given the truce just
sealed by a royal marriage. News of these atrocities spread quickly all
over Europe and provoked various reactions, some quite predictable,
some rather unusual. It is upon these reactions that I have concentrated my research for several years. I believe they provide an unusually
revealing index of sixteenth-century European society's fundamental
ideas about the ways in which power should be used in human society.
They are unusually revealing because the extent and unexpectedness
of the massacres provoked unusually strong and spontaneous reactions.

The two most extreme reactions occurred in the city-states which
served as international headquarters for the two versions of Christianity warring for the control of France. Rome, the headquarters of
international Catholicism, was transported with delight. Geneva, the
headquarters of international Calvinism, was plunged into despair.
The best expressions of these two reactions took strikingly different
forms. Thus Pope Gregory XIII, after attending several triumphal
church services in celebration of the massacres, ordered the striking of a
commemorative medal and instructed Giorgio Vasari to include
graphic paintings of the massacres in a set of frescoes being prepared
for the Sala Regia of the Vatican palace.[3] And thus Calvin's successor
Theodore Beza, after presiding over a church service of prayer and
supplication, turned to organizing the composition and publication

[2] Estèbe, chap. ix.
[3] Ludwig von Pastor, *The History of the Popes from the Close of the Middle Ages* (hereafter
Pastor), XIX (London, 1930), 501–07.

of a barrage of pamphlets, denouncing the French government and urging Protestants to resist it with force. The reliance of these two ideological leaders on such different media is both significant and characteristic. The Catholic depended on the visual arts and turned to one of the greatest painters of the day. The Protestant depended on verbal communication and turned to the printing industry. This contrast should not be pressed too far, of course, since there were Catholic publications and Protestant woodcut pictures provoked by the massacres. But I think it contains an important kernel of truth.

I

To illustrate Genevan reactions to the massacres, I have analyzed one of the published treatises they provoked. This is a treatise which has interested me for several years and of which I have prepared a critical edition.[4] It is not one of the polemics printed immediately after the massacres, extolling Coligny as a martyr to his religion and attacking the king, the queen mother, and others responsible for the massacres as the blackest of villains. It is rather a work of political theory, published two years after the massacres, outlining a new political program for the Protestants and others who were radically dissatisfied with the royal government in France. It is one of a series of treatises, sometimes rather imprecisely labelled monarchomach, which is of some importance in the general development of political theory in the West. The title of this work is *Du droit des magistrats sur leurs sujets*, or *On the right of magistrates over their subjects*. It was printed anonymously, without any indication of author, publisher, or place of publication, purporting to be a reprint of a Lutheran political treatise drafted in Magdeburg back in 1550. I have identified ten separate printings of this treatise which appeared in French between 1574 and 1581. Many more printings of a Latin translation appeared in this period and beyond, well into the seventeenth century, sometimes published together with such other political classics of the period as Machiavelli's *Prince* and the *Vindiciae contra Tyrannos*.

Contemporaries suspected that the *Droit des magistrats* was written by Theodore Beza. Although he never published another work of political theory, he had been trained as a lawyer, had been extensively involved in Calvinist political intrigue, and had expressed ideas consonant with

---

[4] Théodore de Bèze, *Du droit des magistrats*, ed. Robert M. Kingdon ("Les classiques de la pensée politique," VII; Geneva, 1971), hereafter cited as Kingdon, *Bèze*.

those of the treatise in rudimentary form in some of his theological writings and in his published letters. That suspicion was proved decisively several decades ago, when scholars found entries in the registers of the Geneva city council, demonstrating that Beza applied as an author for permission to have the work printed in Geneva.[5] Permission was refused, however, at least twice. So the mystery of where the treatise was published remained. That mystery has been partially dispelled in recent years by an expert in sixteenth-century French type faces, Mlle E. Droz of Geneva. She has demonstrated that the first printing of the treatise appeared in Heidelberg, capital of the Palatinate of the Rhine, the most important Calvinist state in Germany. A second printing, deliberately designed to resemble the Heidelberg printing, was illegally published in Geneva. A third printing was published in La Rochelle, center for the most militant resistance to the Catholic government in the years immediately following the massacres.[6] Most of the remaining printings have still not been identified.

The basic argument of the *Droit des magistrats* is that there are times when constitutional resistance to legitimate government is justified, even necessary. This marks an important step forward in the development of political resistance theory in the West. For centuries it had been generally conceded that an illegitimate government, the government of an invader or of a usurper, could be resisted by any means at hand. For centuries it had also been conceded that resistance was possible even to a legitimate government if it had degenerated into a tyranny which was violating the basic purposes for which all government is created. Indeed there were medieval theorists who would even permit individuals to assassinate a legitimate ruler who had become a tyrant. What is new in the *Droit des magistrats*, and in certain other Calvinist political treatises published in the same decade, is that the power to resist a tyrant is located in certain specified political institutions. It is not granted to the community as a whole or to any individual member of the community. Rather it is limited to certain existing political institutions, with already-defined functions in the state. It is thus constitutional. The principal institution to which the *Droit des magistrats* grants a right of resistance is the Estates-General (or its equivalents in other countries – such as the English Parliament, the German Diet, the Spanish Cortes), the deliberative body made of

[5] Reprinted in Kingdon, *Bèze*, annexe 3.
[6] E. Droz, "Fausses adresses typographiques," *Bibliothèque d'Humanisme et Renaissance*, XXIII (1961), 380–86, 572–74; *L'imprimerie à La Rochelle*, vol. III: *La veuve Berton et Jean Portau, 1573–1589* (Geneva, 1960), pp. 42–43.

representatives of every influential class in the population of practically every state in Europe. These bodies were called regularly or irregularly by European governments, primarily to raise taxes but also for other purposes. Beza now insisted that the right to resist the central government was one of those vague other purposes.

Beza faced the obvious practical fact that in many circumstances an Estates-General would not be free to assemble or to act in resistance to a tyranny. In that case, he argued, the right to resist passes to the "inferior magistrates." These were the provincial governors, the elected municipal councils, and the other authorities who actually governed a country on the local level. In this latter form, Beza's argument was of particularly great use to French Huguenots. They did control a significant number of cities in France. A good number of provincial governors and other such authorities belonged to their party or sympathized with them.

In both forms, the theory is of considerable historical significance, particularly in the early modern period of European history. It could be used immediately by the Dutch, to justify the revolt of their Estates-General against the Spanish crown. It could be used a few decades later by the German Calvinist princes to justify their defiance of the imperial government. It could be used again by the Puritan Parliament in England to justify its revolts against the Stuart kings. In somewhat developed and modified forms it could be used in the eighteenth century by leaders of the American and French revolutions. All of these revolutions were constitutional, in that they assigned the power to resist the head of a government to a pre-existing institution or group of institutions which had a settled legal place in that government.

The theory, furthermore, seems to be new in the 1570s. While there are hints of it in a number of treatises and proclamations issued in the earlier course of the Reformation, both in Lutheran and Calvinist countries, it was never fully developed until after the St. Bartholomew massacres. Experts on this theory who know more about medieval thought than I do, also claim that there are no significant earlier precedents for it. There are, to be sure, analogies in the fifteenth-century conciliarists' arguments for resistance to the papacy led by ecumenical councils within the Church. But the analogies between ecclesiastical and temporal resistance do not seem to have been pressed.[7]

[7] Julian H. Franklin, tr. and ed., *Constitutionalism and Resistance in the Sixteenth Century: Three Treatises by Hotman, Beza and Mornay* (New York, 1969), pp. 11–15.

These reflections on the general development of resistance theory have led me quite far from the St. Bartholomew massacres. Perhaps they should. A number of recent experts on Calvinist resistance theory insist that it has very little to do with the massacres. They point to the fact that the important theoretical treatises, including the *Droit des magistrats*, never mention the massacres directly, indeed never say much about contemporary politics in any way. Instead these treatises construct a general theory of resistance, based on appeals to the timeless authorities which undergird most sixteenth-century thinking. These authorities include the Bible, to which Beza in fact appeals repeatedly in the course of his treatise. They include the Roman legal tradition, particularly as it was codified in the *Corpus Juris Civilis*. To this authority Beza appeals in many ways which have not been fully appreciated until quite recently,[8] partly because Beza's allusions to the law are often quite casual, covered by such vague formulae as "natural reason teaches us ...." These authorities include finally history, particularly political and constitutional history, beginning with examples drawn from ancient accounts of the Hebrews and Romans, moving on to a rather exotic and curious collection of examples drawn from medieval chroniclers' descriptions of medieval governments. Clearly Beza felt that the prescriptive power of time, as revealed in political traditions, significantly reinforces an argument based on revelation as recorded in the Bible and natural reason as recorded in law. Given this content to the *Droit des magistrats* and other treatises like it, several experts suggest that they are best studied as the logical fruition of a tradition in political thought, rather than as reactions to the pressure of political events.[9]

While I do see value in the approach to Calvinist resistance theory which places it in an intellectual tradition, I do not think it should exclude the approach which places this theory in a political context. It seems to me that political ideas often can and should be tied to political events before they can be fully understood. I would argue, furthermore, that this is particularly likely to be true of Beza's theory. For Beza was not a full-time thinker in an ivory tower. In addition to being a formidable theologian and Latinist, he was also an ecclesiastical

---

[8] A point emphasized by Ralph E. Giesey, "The Monarchomach Triumvirs: Hotman, Beza and Mornay," *Bibliothèque d'Humanisme et Renaissance*, XXXII (1970), 52–56.

[9] *Ibid.*, pp. 41–42. Cf. the detailed and persuasive application of this approach to another "monarchomach" treatise by Ralph E. Giesey and J. H. M. Salmon in the introduction to their critical edition and translation of François Hotman, *Francogallia* (Cambridge, 1972), esp. pp. 38–52.

statesman. He had been the founding Rector of the Academy of Geneva. He had succeeded Calvin in 1564 as Moderator of the Geneva Company of Pastors. He was in constant correspondence with theologians, ecclesiastical leaders, and leading political figures all over Europe. And he had been deeply involved in political intrigues, mostly in his native France, for more than a dozen years. In 1559, he had been consulted by young noblemen who were plotting to kidnap the king and dispose of his advisers. This abortive coup has come to be called the Conspiracy of Amboise, and it marks the first Protestant attempt to use violence to resolve the problems posed by persecution of the Reformation in France. In 1561, Beza had been invited to the royal court, at the suggestion of the great artistocrats who were assuming leadership of the Huguenot party. He was summoned in order to lead a delegation of Calvinist theologians in a public debate with the Catholic bishops of France, in hopes of working out a compromise that could head off further violence. When compromise failed and religious war began, Beza had joined the staff of the prince de Condé, supreme commander of the Protestant armies, serving him for a year as a speech-writer and negotiator. Since 1563, Beza had lived in Geneva and since 1564, had directed the international Calvinist movement from its headquarters. But he had not lost his interest in political intrigue, particularly in his native France. He had returned to France several times, for meetings of national synods of the French Reformed Church and for other purposes. And he had kept in close touch by correspondence with leaders of the Huguenot movement.[10] Clearly it would be really extraordinary if the St. Bartholomew massacres had not appealed to his taste for political activity.

In point of fact we can demonstrate that Beza was provoked to considerable activity by the massacres. This is revealed by his largely unpublished correspondence, records of the deliberations of Geneva's governing bodies, and a study of some of the pamphlets printed at the time. Beza's first reaction to the massacres was one of dismay and fear. In fact he came nearer to real despair in the first weeks after the grisly news reached Geneva than at any other time in his career. In letters to his good friend Henry Bullinger, leader of the Reformed church in Zurich, Beza says that he may never write another letter, that he thinks more of death than of life. He longs for the day so desired when the Lord will reunite him with the pious souls of his murdered friends. He claims to be so overwhelmed by mourning and tears that he can no

---

[10] On Beza's career, see Paul-F. Geisendorf, *Théodore de Bèze* (Geneva, 1949).

32

longer serve the church, that he can tolerate life itself only in the hope that it will soon end.[11] News of this sort must have come as a particularly severe blow to a man saturated in Calvinist theology – in the Calvinist conviction of the omnipotence of God, of the pervasiveness of divine Providence, of the ways in which God controls every event in this universe. These dreadful massacres may well have suggested to Beza the terrible possibility that God was not a Calvinist after all. This possibility did occur to at least one of the many Calvinist ministers who abandoned their faith and returned to Catholicism in the weeks following the massacres. He was Hugues Sureau du Rosier, and he published a lengthy explanation of his decision to switch, which turned out, incidentally, to be temporary. Sureau had been chafing under Calvinist discipline for several years, and thus had several reasons for abandoning the movement. But his sudden and overwhelming fear that the massacres revealed God's displeasure with the Calvinists seems to have been decisive.[12]

Beza, however, was made of stronger stuff than Sureau. And he was also soon pushed to action by the arrival in Geneva of hordes of refugees, fleeing for their lives from the cities in which massacres had occurred – above all from nearby Lyons – and pleading with him for support of every sort. Altogether there were several hundred refugees, including several dozen Calvinist pastors and a good number of noblemen. Faced with their overwhelming problems, Beza had no more time for reflection and despair.

The first formal step taken by Beza and the other ministers of Geneva was to wait upon the governing city Council. The ministers exhorted the Council to take courage, they assured it that the doctrine they announced was firm and certain, and they asked that a day be set aside for fasting and extraordinary prayers in order to protect the city from the wrath of God.[13] That request was granted, and the result was one of the first in a long series of public fasts proclaimed by the Geneva government in periods of crisis. In the nineteenth century the Genevan Fast became an annual event, celebrated in September, near to the anniversary of the day when news first arrived in the city of the St. Bartholomew massacres.[14] I have been in Geneva on this day several

[11] Qtd., *ibid.*, pp. 306–08.

[12] Robert M. Kingdon, *Geneva and the Consolidation of the French Protestant Movement, 1564–1572* (Geneva and Madison, 1967), p. 117.

[13] Henri Fazy, *La Saint-Barthélemy et Genève* ("Mémoires de l'Institut national genevois," XIV; Geneva, 1879), p. 7.

[14] Olivier Fatio, "Le jeûne genevois, réalité et mythe," *Bulletin de la Société d'histoire et d'archéologie de Genève*, XIV (1971), 391–435.

times, and I must say I find its current celebration a bit bizarre. For days ahead of time one finds advertisements in all the local newspapers in which the better local restaurants list the delicacies they propose to serve in the sumptuous meals which now mark the Genevan Fast.

The next steps taken by Beza are not as easy to follow. For he now plunged into secret and rather tortuous political intrigues. Records of them are extremely guarded, and it is sometimes difficult to find out just what they were about. But their cumulative purpose was clear. It was to revitalize and inspire the remnants of the French Calvinist movement to armed resistance against the entire French establishment.

For purposes of analysis, one can distinguish three parallel intrigues in which Beza was involved more or less directly.[15] A first was aimed at re-grouping French refugee noblemen for renewed war in France; a second was designed to influence the election of a new king of Poland; a third was mounted to protect the city of Geneva from attack by any neighboring Catholic power.

The first set of intrigues involved Beza in direct negotiations with the noblemen who had taken refuge in Geneva and in neighboring towns in Switzerland and in Germany. Beza was well fitted for intrigue of this sort. He was himself of a family of minor Burgundian noblemen, and thus acquainted from boyhood with the style of courtly life in France. And he had been involved in intrigues with French noblemen since 1559, as we have already noticed. It is not surprising, therefore, that one of the messengers who first brought word of the massacres to Geneva, a nobleman named Clermont d'Amboise, made a point of visiting Beza soon after his arrival in the city. The refugees' intrigues did not become serious, however, until it was clear that the massacres were over. At that point, the royal government, fearful of losing control of the population to the fanatic Catholics and the Guises, began to swing again to a mediating position. It proclaimed that it had sanctioned assassinations of Huguenot leaders only for political reasons, and was quite prepared to extend limited toleration again to Protestantism. This turn in policy made the refugee nobles hopeful that they could regain some of the power and status that they had lost in fleeing their homes. They decided to appeal to the French government for two things: (1) release of noble prisoners seized at the time of the massacres, several of whom had been converted to Catholicism, more or less forcibly; (2) return of their own landed property in France, or at least the right to sell that property so that their assets

15 For what follows, see Kingdon, *Bèze*, p. xiv ff.

could be transferred abroad. These appeals were forwarded to the French ambassador in Switzerland. He was accredited to the Swiss cantons in order periodically to negotiate recruitment of the crack Swiss mercenary infantry which had become an important part of the French royal armies. The refugee nobles asked Beza to persuade his Swiss friends to put as much pressure as possible on the French ambassador to get him to secure a favorable response to their requests from the royal court. They even wanted Beza actually to go to the city in which the diet of the Swiss Confederation met, in order to put pressure directly on the ambassador. This suggestion was firmly vetoed by the Geneva city council, which noted that the Swiss Confederation was still half Catholic and met in a Catholic city, hardly a place Beza could prudently visit.

After several months of negotiations, the refugee noblemen received a cautiously favorable response from the royal ambassador. The king was disposed to allow the nobles to recover their property, provided they signed a loyalty oath. A text of a proposed oath was presented to them. It provided that each signatory swear loyalty to the king and affirm that he had left France only to escape mob violence. This proposal was examined in minute detail by a group of forty noblemen meeting in Beza's own house. They drafted a new substitute text of the oath they were to take. It provided that each signatory swear loyalty to the king and his laws and affirm that he had left France only to escape violence. The changes seem minor, but they in fact create significant loopholes. The revised oath left the refugees free to accuse the king, not just the mobs, of violence against their party. And it left them free to resist any action by the king not taken through normal channels of legislation. These changes are thus a tip-off that the refugees were plotting revenge. Beza in fact admitted as much, when he told an irritated city council that the meeting in his house had been kept secret so that the city government could not be accused of sanctioning a just war against the king of France.

The second set of intrigues involved Beza in indirect correspondence with the Calvinist nobles of Poland. The Polish Diet was at that time considering the election of a new king. One of the leading candidates was the duc d'Anjou, younger brother to King Charles IX of France. The French royal family wanted very badly to have Anjou win the Polish crown. A large French embassy, headed by a moderate Catholic bishop, had been sent to present the French case to the Polish Diet as forcefully and as eloquently as possible. An important faction of the

Diet was made up of Calvinists, however, and they wanted to make certain that any new king continued toleration of their form of religion. They had good reason to fear Anjou on this score, because of his deep involvement in the St. Bartholomew massacres. He had been an active member of the council which had decided on the assassinations of Coligny and his associates; he had personally supervised a group of assassins in the streets of Paris that bloody night; and at the time of his suit for the Polish crown he was commanding a royal army which was besieging the Protestant stronghold of La Rochelle, in desperate revolt against the royal government since the massacres. Not all of this was known immediately to the Poles. Beza quickly got in touch with them about Anjou's candidacy to their throne, arranging for several messages to be sent to Cracow by way of Zurich and Nuremberg. A special ambassador was even sent secretly from Geneva to Poland to reinforce personally these messages, but by the time he got there Anjou had already been elected king. I do not know the content of these messages, but it was reported in later years that Beza had worked vigorously to prevent Anjou's election. Very probably he sent to Poland as much damning information as he could collect about Anjou's role in persecuting French Protestants. While he did not succeed in preventing the election, he may well deserve some credit for some significant conditions attached to it. The French ambassador had to swear on Anjou's behalf that there would be no attempt to suppress Protestantism in Poland. He even had to swear that the French government would stop persecuting Protestants in France. This second promise went well beyond his instructions and angered the royal government back in Paris. Further negotiations between Polish ambassadors and the French government modified these agreements in some details before Anjou was finally permitted to ascend the Polish throne. While the French crown was extremely reluctant to grant much formal toleration, these negotiations did result in a perceptible relaxation of pressure on French Calvinists. For example the siege of La Rochelle was lifted.

The third set of intrigues did not involve Beza directly but they conditioned his ability to operate politically. They were between the government of Geneva and members of the Swiss Confederation and were aimed at establishing a multilateral alliance. The massacres had raised in the minds of the Genevan councilors the specter of an invasion by a neighboring Catholic power, most probably its traditional enemy, the duchy of Savoy. Geneva had been protected from earlier Savoyard attacks only by tight alliances with certain of the militarily powerful Swiss cantons, above all with Protestant Berne. The Genevans' immediate reaction on news of the St. Bartholomew massacres was that this probably was a first step in implementing a European-wide Catholic plot, involving the pope, Spain, France, and Savoy, and that Geneva would have to have even more extensive alliances for defense. They immediately set about tightening the Bernese alliance, and on Bernese advice approached the other Swiss cantons. But these Swiss cantons, as we have already noted, were allied to France. The Genevans had to take care, therefore, not to offend France in their negotiations for a Swiss alliance. And the French government was terribly irritated, as the ambassador to the Swiss kept pointing out, by the flood of inflammatory tracts pouring out of Geneva. In fact the ambassador specifically requested the suppression of a number of pamphlets printed in Geneva on grounds that they were insulting to the French royal family and subversive of the French government. Caught between ideology and self-interest, the Genevan government gave in, and agreed to censor all political tracts published in the city. Some of them were permitted to appear anonymously, without any indication of place of publication, but others were banned altogether. Beza and the other ministers complained bitterly about this infringement of a free press, but the government refused to budge.

It was at precisely this point, in July of 1573, nearly a year after the St. Bartholomew massacres, that Beza completed a draft of his *Droit des magistrats*. He presented it for publication permission to the Geneva city council and was turned down flatly. The councilors who read his draft found that it contained only the truth, but they still judged it scandalous and were afraid it would provoke troubles and emotions. They would not even permit its anonymous publication, since they feared that Beza's literary style was so distinctive that it would be easily recognized.[16] Beza then sent a Latin version of the treatise to his friends in Zurich. They liked it and explored the possibility of having it printed in some Swiss German city.[17] That also proved to be impossible, no doubt because of the importance to the Swiss of their alliance with France.

Meanwhile things were becoming hot in France. The Huguenots, having recovered from the shock of the St. Bartholomew massacres, were re-grouping, re-arming, and thinking again of war with the royal

---

16 *Ibid.*, annexe 3, p. 76.
17 *Ibid.*, annexe 4.

government. This would require, as it always did, a justification of their right to resist the royal government with armed force. Such a justification was needed to calm the consciences of loyal Frenchmen being asked to join a revolt against their king. It was also needed to reassure foreign governments, on whom the Huguenots depended for money and troops, that they were not opposed on principle to monarchical government.

Armed resistance had begun in France immediately upon spread of news of the massacres in 1572. It had begun in a few small cities which were already solidly controlled by Protestants and which were determined to protect their faith, above all in La Rochelle and Sancerre. La Rochelle was particularly defiant and refused to deal in any way with the royal government. It would not even accept an offer of a Protestant aristocrat as royal governor. When it was placed under siege by royal armies it grew yet more defiant. The Calvinist pastors in the city suggested the counter-massacre of Catholic prisoners in order to conserve scarce food supplies.[18] And the city hung on grimly until the royal armies finally abandoned the siege and withdrew.

Resistance next spread to the countryside, particularly in the South, above all in the province of Languedoc. There political assemblies of Protestant noblemen began meeting regularly to plot political and military action. More ominous still from the government's point of view, these assemblies occasionally were attended by Catholic noblemen who had become radically discontented with the royal government and persuaded of the futility of religious persecution. Even the royal governor for Languedoc, Henri de Montmorency-Damville, began negotiating with the Huguenot political assemblies and offering them his assistance.

Finally the prince de Condé, one of the two titular leaders of the Protestant party in France, escaped. Both he and his cousin, the king of Navarre, had been confined by the royal government on the night of the massacres. They had both agreed to convert to Catholicism under heavy pressure from the court in their first weeks of captivity, the king of Navarre rather lightheartedly, the prince de Condé with considerable reluctance. Once they escaped the court, both announced . eturn to Calvinist Protestantism and prepared to join the resistance. Condé escaped first and fled to Germany, to the still-German city of Strasbourg, then to Swiss Basel. There he got in touch with the

---

[18] According to contemporary Protestant reports qtd. by E. Droz, *L'imprimerie à La Rochelle*, vol. I: *Barthélemy Berton, 1563–1573* (Geneva, 1960), pp. 109–10.

French noblemen who had fled for refuge from the massacres to Germany and Switzerland. He approached the German princes and cities who had supported earlier Calvinist wars in France with troops and money. And he summoned Theodore Beza from Geneva to assist him in plotting a new war, just as Beza had assisted his father twelve years earlier.

Beza joined Condé in Strasbourg in August of 1574. He then went on to Heidelberg to negotiate with the Elector Palatine on the Huguenots' behalf. He evidently had brought with him a final draft of his *Droit des magistrats*. It was printed in that German Calvinist citadel by a French printer, a refugee from religious persecution in Lyons.[19] The printings in Geneva and in La Rochelle soon followed. Copies were forwarded to Languedoc and circulated among members of one of the political assemblies. A chronicler reports that while the representatives at that assembly were already inclined to fight, it was the reading of three pamphlets circulated among them which inspired them to make the final and fateful decision for war. One of these pamphlets was the *Droit des magistrats*. Thus it played a direct role in provoking the religious war which began in 1574, providing, of course, that the chronicler was accurate in his report. Even if he was not, however, there were other ways in which Beza's political ideas could have reached the delegates to the Languedoc political assemblies. We know that Beza and the other ministers in Geneva, both the local ministers and the refugees from France, were in touch with the political assemblies after November 1573.[20]

Taken all together, these intrigues explain better than ever before the form which Calvinist militancy took in the 1570s, particularly as it is expressed in such theoretical treatises as the *Droit des magistrats*. At least so it seems to me. They certainly explain many of the details of these publications. The *Droit des magistrats* was published anonymously and away from Geneva to avoid compromising that state in its continuing search for defensive alliances. It was published in 1574, because that was an opportune time to re-start religious war in France. The Polish negotiations had forced the royal government to back away from systematic persecution, and had given the Huguenots time to become re-grouped and revitalized. In addition, King Charles IX died in May of 1574, and Anjou had to return from Poland to succeed him as Henri III. This led to a period of transition and weakness in

[19] See above, p. 28.
[20] Kingdon, *Bèze*, pp. xxxv–xxxvi.

royal government and created an ideal opportunity for the Huguenots to attack. The treatise was first published in Heidelberg, because that was an important center of foreign diplomacy in support of a new Huguenot war effort, and was soon published in La Rochelle, because that was an important center of Huguenot resistance within France.

But these circumstances explain more than the details of this particular publication. They also explain the central argument of this and all the other Calvinist resistance treatises published in this decade, the argument for constitutional resistance to a legitimate government. Remember that the St. Bartholomew massacres consisted of two separate series of atrocities. They consisted of assassinations ordered by the royal government, and massacres carried out by fanatic mobs. Together they must have made it perfectly clear to Beza and the other Calvinist leaders in France that if the movement was to survive it would have to resist pressure from two fronts. On the one hand it had to resist frontally the legitimate royal government. Huguenots could no longer argue, as they had for more than a dozen years, that when they went to war they were not resisting the king himself but only such wicked advisers of the crown as the Guises. In 1572 the king had made it very clear that he took credit for personally ordering Coligny's death. But in turning to resistance against the government, the Huguenots could not claim to act in the name of all the people. They did not dare suggest that any group within the population was free to resist its government. That could easily open the gates for mobs, and mobs had slaughtered Huguenots. They thus limited the right of resistance to representative bodies like the Estates-General of the Netherlands and the political assembly licensed by the governor of Languedoc, or to inferior magistrates like the municipal government of La Rochelle and a prince of the blood royal like Condé. All of these authorities, but only such authorities, could resist a legitimate government which had become a tyranny. Armed with these convictions, the Huguenots continued to fight for toleration until they finally won a limited measure of it in France at the end of the century, with the Edict of Nantes. Armed with similar convictions, Calvinists in other countries also went to war for their beliefs, with consequences of considerable importance for the development of modern Europe.

II

The resulting wars of religion would not have been as ferocious as they did in fact become if a militancy parallel to that of the Calvinists had not been rising on the other side. This brings us to Roman reactions to the St. Bartholomew massacres. To illustrate these reactions, I have explored developments in papal diplomacy. I cannot connect them as directly to the massacres as the Huguenot treatises. But I believe there are connections which are significant. The St. Bartholomew massacres occurred, we should remember, at the beginning of the long thirteen-year pontificate of an exceptionally able and energetic man, Ugo Boncampagni, Gregory XIII. They occurred when his pontificate was still in its formative early months, before his policies and practices had had a chance to take definitive shape. Those policies and practices could thus have been influenced significantly by the massacres.

For purposes of analysis, I would like to distinguish two developments in papal diplomacy during this pontificate. One was a development in policy, the other a development in institutions. In policy, it seems to me that the papacy committed itself to greater militancy, to the use of really extreme tactics in meeting the Protestant menace. In the institutional arena, it seems to me that the papacy committed itself to greater professionalism, to the more systematic development of cadres of diplomats dedicated to careers of negotiating with foreign powers.

Looking first at policy developments, we discover that Gregory XIII announced his main policies at his very first consistory, on 30 May 1572. He committed himself to three primary objectives: (1) strengthening of the Holy League against the Turks; (2) resolute opposition to all forms of Protestantism; (3) full reception of the decrees of the Council of Trent.[21] It has been argued that of these three the campaign against the Turks took precedence.[22] A persuasive case can be made for this argument. At the time of the accession of Gregory, the wave of exultation provoked by the smashing victory a few months earlier over a Turkish fleet at Lepanto still had not spent itself. The pope's maneuvers in the first half of his pontificate to assist Spain in the Netherlands, in France, and in Britain, can be viewed as attempts to free Spain from distraction so that it could again assume leadership of a crusade. His maneuvers in the second half of his pontificate with the northern powers in Europe, can be viewed as attempts to persuade a new king of Poland to take leadership of the crusade now abandoned

---

[21] Pastor, XIX, 65. Also see Liisi Karttunen, *Grégoire XIII comme politicien et souverain*, in *Annales Academiae Scientiarum Fennicae*, ser. B. II, 2 (Helsinki, 1911), p. 1.

[22] By Karttunen.

by Spain. It may seem anachronistic to find a late-sixteenth-century pope still campaigning for a crusade, but no one who has studied papal diplomatic records of the period can doubt Rome's continuing commitment to war against the infidel.

Gregory never lost sight of his other objectives, however, and it is these which were significantly affected by the St. Bartholomew massacres. In particular the objective of opposing Protestantism won a higher priority and assumed a different shape after 24 August 1572. These changes can be followed in a number of ways. They can be demonstrated most convincingly by examining the instructions sent by the papal secretariat of state to its agents in France.

For evidence of papal policy before the massacres, I consulted the instructions prepared for Salviati, extraordinary nuncio to France late in 1571.[23] This was some months before the death of Pope Pius V, the predecessor of Gregory XIII. Salviati was instructed in the first place and in most detail to urge the French crown to join Spain, Venice, and the papacy in the Holy League against the Turks. He was to recall the glorious history of the French crown in supporting crusades and he was to try to shame the French from participation in lowly border skirmishes with other Catholic powers. Salviati was not limited to pleading for crusade, however. He was also instructed to complain about a number of developments within France, most of which followed from the peace treaty of St. Germain in 1570. He was to complain about mistreatment of Catholics in many specified parts of the kingdom. He was to complain about power given to Huguenots over Catholics in many areas, and in particular about the power being assumed at the royal court by Admiral Coligny. He was to reject French pleas for papal approval of the projected marriage alliance between the heretic Henri de Navarre and Marguerite de Valois. But he was not asked to seek persecution or suppression of the Huguenots. Their continuing existence is assumed in these instructions. The papacy sought only to deny them any power in the French government. This meant, to be sure, some moderation of Pius V's policy. He had earlier urged resolute military action against the Huguenots.[24]

---

[23] Archivio Segreto Vaticano (hereafter ASV), Pio 131, fols. 2–6, summarized in Pastor, XVIII (London, 1929), 138–39. This draft contains complaints about Protestant mistreatment of Catholics, added to the instructions proper, not noted by Pastor. The principal documents of Salviati's nunciature have recently been edited by Pierre Hurtubise (the 2d vol. in collaboration with Robert Toupin): *Correspondance du nonce en France Antonio Maria Salviati, 1572–1578* ("Acta Nuntiaturae Galliace," XII–XIII; Rome and Paris, 1974).

[24] Ch. Hirschauer, *La politique de St. Pie V en France (1566–1572)* ("Bibliothèque des Écoles françaises d'Athènes et de Rome," CXX; Paris, 1922), esp. chap. ii.

42

For evidence of papal policy after the massacres, I have examined the final instructions prepared for the legate Orsini in November of 1572.[25] Cardinal Orsini's mission had been organized well before the massacres, and in fact he received the cross and final commission for his trip in the same consistory at which news of the Massacre was reported.[26] Orsini was again sent to gain French support for the Holy League against the Turks, support which would require coöperation with the Spanish. He was to suggest a marriage alliance between the two royal houses to ensure this coöperation, specifically a marriage of Henri d'Anjou to one of the infantas of Spain. This part of his instructions continues to implement the policy line worked out in earlier years. But the rest of his instructions in this version are strikingly different. There is good reason to believe that they were added to the original instructions, after the papal curia had had time to collect some information on the massacres. These additions call for persecution of the bloodiest and most thorough sort, designed to eliminate all traces of Protestantism in France.[27] Orsini was to urge the French crown to use full military force to wipe out such pockets of Huguenot resistance as La Rochelle. He was to remind the king of a promise to the papal nuncio in Paris made shortly after the massacres that "in a few days there will not be one Huguenot in all his realm." He was to ask the king to require all bishops to return to their dioceses to supervise the abjuration and integration back into the Catholic Church of the thousands of Protestants who had abandoned their faith in the great shock which followed first news of the massacres. It was regarded as particularly important that bishops be on hand to prevent Protestants from returning "to [their] vomit at least in secret." The legate was to urge the creation of an inquisition within every diocese in France, on the Italian rather than the Spanish model. He was finally to urge formal reception and publication of the decrees of the Council of Trent as the ideal way to make definitive the suppression of Protestantism in France. In these final suggestions, we see an interesting merging of the second and third of Gregory XIII's general policy objectives.[28]

Not all of these suggestions are new. Earlier popes, for example, had recommended extension of the Inquisition in France. But it seems to

[25] ASV, Segreteria di Stato, Francia (hereafter S. S. Francia) 283, fols. 123–25.
[26] Como to Salviati, 8 Sept. 1572, *ibid.*, fol. 52.
[27] Cf. the contribution to this volume by Alain Dufour.
[28] A point emphasized by Victor Martin, *Le gallicanisme et la réforme catholique* (Paris, 1919), pp. 109–12.

me that taken together they are more concerted and more extreme. They represent a new peak of militancy in the Counter-Reformation papacy. They reflect a heightened conviction in Rome that violence is an effective way to handle Protestant opposition, that war, massacre, and assassination are justifiable tools for advancing Christian truth. There are a number of reasons for this flare-up of militancy. A full decade of religious war in France, marked by a good deal of sacrilege, brutality and murder perpetrated by Protestants, had clearly angered and frustrated and alarmed the papacy. Additional experience with militant Protestant opposition in other countries had intensified these feelings. But it was the St. Bartholomew massacres that triggered this frighteningly savage reaction in Rome. Apparently the massacres persuaded the members of the Roman curia that God was truly on their side and that violence works. There is little evidence that anyone in Rome thought violence might be counter-productive. However it must be noted that curial animosity was directed mostly to the heretic leaders and to those who had seduced others. Ample provisions were made for reintegrating the seduced rank-and-file Christians into the Church of Rome.[29] Faculties were immediately granted to all the bishops in France to absolve heretics who were clearly aware of their errors and fully penitent.[30] In these provisions we see an example of the striking pastoral concern which also fills much of the diplomatic correspondence of Gregory XIII's pontificate.

Part of the savage excitement in Rome stemmed from a natural belief that the French government had fully committed itself to the eradication of heresy by force. It gradually became clear to Rome, however, that the French crown had made no such commitment. This must have first been suggested by the detailed and perceptive reports of the papal nuncio in France, Antonio Maria Salviati, who was clearly of the opinion that both the court-ordered assassinations which touched off the massacres and the court's post-massacre policy were motivated not by religious zeal but by complex intrigues among courtiers and other political considerations.[31] It must have become unmistakably clear when the Orsini mission failed completely. To

---

[29] This view is expressed very concisely in instructions to the cardinal-legate St. Sixtus for his negotiations with Henri III in 1574 (ASV, Misc., Armadio II, 130, fol. 129). He is instructed to tell Henri III to treat Huguenots like this: "Castigarli senza remissione, massime li capi, et quelli che seducono gli altri, perdonando sola a la plebe sedutta et mostreranno vero pentimento."

[30] The correspondence between Como and Salviati in the fall of 1572 (ASV, S. S. Francia 5 and 283) refers to these faculties several times.

[31] In ASV, S. S. Francia 5, fol. 133ff.

44

begin with, the French government refused for months to give Orsini permission even to enter the country. When he was finally permitted to visit the court, he found the king and queen mother completely inflexible. In his lengthy report back to Rome,[32] he indicates that he followed his instructions in formulating his proposals. Negotiations centered on the papal suggestions for a Franco-Spanish marriage alliance to prepare the way for a crusade against the Turks, but the proposals for eradicating Protestantism in France were also discussed. Orsini was rebuffed at every single point, sometimes in ways which seem derisive. His plea that all Huguenots be eliminated from the kingdom, for example, was referred to Damville, the governor of Languedoc and *politique* spokesman. But Damville had been in touch with the Huguenots for some time and was soon to join forces with them against the crown.

Frustration at this point did not lead Gregory XIII's curia to abandon militancy, however. The pope's own celebrated obstinacy and optimism may help to explain this. Instructions to later nuncios to France make it clear that whenever the French crown was considering a choice between peace and internal religious war, the official representative of the papacy was to urge war. Paragraphs containing this recommendation, in almost identical words, are to be found in the instructions prepared for Castelli in 1581,[33] and Ragazzoni in 1583.[34] Furthermore militancy can be observed in other areas of papal diplomacy. Thus the nuncios in Spain and France, along with papal diplomats in other areas, worked closely with English Catholics in plotting against the government of Elizabeth I, and Rome provided money and troops for an unsuccessful invasion of Ireland. Gregory XIII even indicated that he would approve the assassination of Elizabeth I, in response to an English query relayed to him through the nuncio in Spain.[35] Similarly the papal diplomats in Germany helped organize the army which successfully drove Gebhard Truchsess von Waldburg from the archbishopric of Cologne, when he had tried to turn Protestant and make of that archdiocese a hereditary principality.

[32] *Ibid.*, fols. 289–95 (7 Dec. 1572).

[33] Robert Toupin, ed., *Correspondance du nonce en France Giovanni Battista Castelli (1581–1583)* ("Acta Nuntiaturae Gallicae," VII; Rome and Paris, 1967), pp. 97–98.

[34] Pierre Blet, ed., *Girolamo Ragazzoni, évêque de Bergame, nonce en France: correspondance de sa nonciature (1583–1586)* ("Acta Nuntiaturae Gallicae," II; Rome and Paris, 1962), p. 137.

[35] Arnold Oskar Meyer, *England and the Catholic Church under Queen Elizabeth* (London, 1967; reprinting of a 1914 ed.), pp. 269–72.

Turning now to institutional changes, we discover that Gregory XIII endorsed professionalism in his very first appointments following his election as pope. He chose as his domestic secretary, with full power to receive and sign all diplomatic correspondence, Ptolomeo Gallio, the cardinal of Como. In doing this he broke with a powerful custom of appointing a cardinal-nephew to this key position. He turned instead to a thorough professional, with extensive experience in handling diplomacy for the papal curia. Gallio had worked intensively in the papal secretariat under Pius IV and had come to be the chief assistant of Carlo Borromeo, the cardinal-nephew who had general charge of all diplomacy in that pontificate. Toward the end of that reign, in fact, when Borromeo moved to Milan in order to begin directing personally the affairs of his diocese, Gallio seems to have taken over real direction of diplomacy. It was apparently on Borromeo's recommendation that Gregory XIII appointed Como to this key position.[36]

Once he had picked the man who was to serve in effect as his secretary of state, Gregory then began selecting the nuncios, who would serve as resident ambassadors to the major Catholic governments of Europe. He proceeded somewhat more slowly in this, avoiding the wholesale turnover one sees in the diplomatic appointments of certain popes of the century. Within a few months he had selected new nuncios for the most important posts in the papal service – Spain and France. The choice of nuncio for France was particularly shrewd. Antonio Maria Salviati was personally related to the queen mother Catherine de Medici. They were second cousins. His uncle, Bernardo Salviati, had earlier been close to Catherine, had even served as her personal chaplain. Antonio Maria, furthermore, already knew France well, having served as papal agent to the French court on several earlier occasions. In addition he was non-resident bishop of St. Papoul, a diocese in southern France which had been passed on from one member of the Salviati family to another.[37]

At this point the St. Bartholomew massacres intervene. Several months later, in 1573, the papacy began a major reorganization of its entire diplomatic apparatus. To understand this change we should

---

[36] P. O. von Törne, *Ptolémée Gallio, cardinal de Côme: étude sur la cour de Rome, sur la secré-tairerie pontificale, et sur la politique des papes au XVIe siècle* (Helsingfors and Paris, 1907), chaps. ii, iv; Pastor, XIX, 29.

[37] On the Salviati family relationships, see *Grosses vollständiges Universal-Lexicon aller Wissenschaften und Künste*, XXXIII (1742), cols. 1252, 1253, 1257, 1258. I am indebted to Father Hurtubise for further information on Antonio Maria. On his diplomatic career, see also Henri Biaudet, *Les nonciatures apostoliques permanentes jusqu'en 1648*, in *Annales Academiae Scientiarum Fennicae*, ser. B. II, 1 (Helsinki, 1910), p. 284 (hereafter Biaudet).

first take a look at the shape of that apparatus before the accession of Gregory XIII. The modern papal diplomatic service, built around a network of permanent resident embassies (known as nunciatures) is a creation of the late fifteenth and early sixteenth centuries. First steps toward it had been taken by a number of activist popes, notably Alexander VI and Julius II, and it had been decisively expanded and organized by the first two Medici popes, Leo X and Clement VII.[38] Then there had been a pause in its development, as the great popes of the Catholic Reformation busied themselves with the direction and implementation of the work of the Council of Trent. Now Gregory XIII was to expand and develop this service further, bringing it close to its most highly developed form.

Gregory XIII began by shifting appointments at four of his nine nunciatures.[39] He had, of course, already shifted his nuncios to Spain and France. In some cases he simply switched an appointee of his predecessor, Pius V, from one post to another. But in every position he made a change. Further general changes occurred in 1577–1578, in 1580–1581, and in 1583–1584. Clearly the papacy was moving to a system of frequent reassignments of ambassadors, probably modeled on the Venetian system. This system had the advantage of training diplomats who could take a broad view of the papacy's international policies, rather than becoming narrowly specialized in its dealings with only one nation.

Gregory XIII had already established a regular salary schedule for all of the nuncios, graded according to the importance and expense of their missions, but completely independent of the individual nuncio's social position and other financial resources.[40] Until this pontificate most nuncios had had to support themselves from family funds, from the income of benefices they had accumulated, or from ecclesiastical income assigned to them in the country to which they were accredited. Now most nuncios received a precise and regular salary, based on their work, not upon their needs. At the top of this diplomatic service were the legates, ambassadors sent to a government for an important special mission, like Orsini's to France in 1572. A legate had to be a cardinal. He was paid 500 *scudi d'oro* a month. Next in rank came the nuncios, ambassadors accredited to Catholic powers with whom the papacy maintained permanent diplomatic relations. The two most

---

[38] Garrett Mattingly, *Renaissance Diplomacy* (London, 1955), pp. 154–55.
[39] Most of what follows is derived from Biaudet, p. 27 ff.
[40] Tabulated, *ibid.*, p. 78.

important nunciatures were those of Spain and France, and those nuncios accordingly received the highest salaries, 300 *scudi* a month. The nuncio to Spain's salary came from funds he gathered as a papal collector in that kingdom. Then came other nunciatures which were labeled first class, as were those of Spain and France. These first-class nunciatures of the second rank were located in Poland, Venice, the German Empire, and southern Germany. Each nuncio in these posts received 200 *scudi* a month. The remaining second-class nunciatures were located in Savoy, Florence, Graz (Austria), Cologne, and Switzerland. Each nuncio in these posts received 100 *scudi* a month, excepting the nuncio to Florence who received only fifty. A nuncio in Portugal received a first-class salary derived from income as papal collector. A nuncio in Naples received a percentage cut of income as papal collector. Almost all of these nuncios were bishops. Most of them were assigned small bishoprics in Italy. This would seem to be in flagrant violation of the Tridentine requirement of residence of all bishops, and is rather ironic in view of the fact that many of these nuncios demanded repeatedly that bishops in the countries to which they were accredited be required to reside in their dioceses. But the papacy felt that prestige required use of men of episcopal rank. The modern dodge of appointing a man bishop of a non-functioning diocese *in partibus infidelium* was not as yet regularly used. At the lower ranks in Gregory XIII's diplomatic service came a number of agents sent for temporary negotiations of a less important or delicate sort than those handled by legates. They were called extraordinary nuncios, internuncios, or apostolic delegates. At the lowest level came the secretaries and cipher clerks who had to accompany every diplomat.

Taken all together these changes made of papal diplomatic service a real professional career. Regular lines of advancement became clear. A man could thus ascend in this diplomatic service from secretary, to extraordinary nuncio, to nuncio, to cardinal legate. Antonio Maria Salviati took just this route to power in the Church, and so did many others. Some rose by this route all the way to the top, to election as pope. That, in fact, is a route still open to leaders of the Catholic Church.

In addition, there was a significant extension in the geographic coverage of the papal diplomatic service during the pontificate of Gregory XIII. At his accession there were nine nunciatures. When he died there were thirteen, an increase of almost 50%. Furthermore, diplomatic relations of a more informal sort were opened with distant governments which had heretofore had very little contact with Rome.

Thus Antonio Possevino was sent by Gregory XIII not only to Poland, but also to Protestant Sweden and Orthodox Muscovy.

Now to return to the St. Bartholomew massacres. Were there any connections between them and the growth of professionalism in the papal diplomatic service? I suspect there were, but they are not obvious. There are other possible explanations of this growth of professionalism. One explanation can be found in the background of the pope. Gregory XIII was a skilled lawyer. He had been a successful professor of law at Bologna before entering the service of the papacy, and he had worked for the Church as a lawyer, for example in drafting texts of some of the final decrees of the Council of Trent, and as a diplomat. One would expect from a pope of this background more interest in matters of organization than from popes trained in theology, such as his predecessor, Pius V, and his successor, Sixtus V. And changes toward professionalism in the papal service do begin before the massacres. Another explanation of this growth can be found in the papal campaign for a crusade against the Turks. Wholesale reassignments of nuncios follow both the withdrawal of Venice from the Holy League against the Turks in 1573, and the withdrawal of Spain in 1579.

But I think a full explanation requires attention to the perceptible rise in papal militancy which followed the St. Bartholomew massacres. This is best suggested by the rapid expansion of papal diplomacy in Germany, where the number of nunciatures was increased by Gregory XIII from one to four, accounting for most of the total increase in the papal diplomatic service during this pontificate. It seems quite clear that this German expansion was not merely a result of a commitment of the pope to professionalism, since there was no evident professional reason for concentrating expansion in one country. Nor can this expansion be explained as part of a move to meet the Turkish threat, since that threat was still felt primarily in the Mediterranean. Clearly the pressing problem faced by the Catholic Church in Germany remained the threat posed by Protestantism, for example in Cologne whose prince-archbishop, Gebhard Truchsess von Waldburg, attempted to convert his state to a Protestant secular principality during these years. The successful campaign of papal nuncios to organize a German army to depose Waldburg and substitute a committed Catholic in his place, is a prime example of the kind of assignment given to papal diplomats in Germany.

How could a policy of militancy have led the papacy to see a need for professionalism in diplomacy? To start with, such a policy required really reliable political information as its essential starting point. I believe the St. Bartholomew massacres gave the papacy dramatic new evidence that it could obtain reliable information only through its own professional diplomats. I am led to this conclusion by comparing the various reports Rome received of the massacres and their meaning. Clearly the papacy would have been misled, indeed it was somewhat misled at first, by the reports of the French in Rome. The reports of the French royal ambassadors to the papal court prove to be vague and tendentious and contradictory. They contain deliberate misstatements and were intended to deceive. The stories circulated in Rome by the cardinal of Lorraine and other prominent French ecclesiastics were extravagant and self-serving. They were also quite unreliable. In striking contrast stand the reports of the papal nuncio, Salviati. They are remarkably frequent, detailed, and perceptive, and include shrewd predictions of the future development of French royal policy. Reports of this type were elicited from Salviati by Como, who constantly badgered the nuncio for more information. For example Como scolded Salviati sharply for his failure to send Rome precise advance information on the plot to assassinate Coligny and the other Huguenot leaders, reminding the nuncio that he had been given a cipher to pass on information of just this kind.[41] The more reliable information supplied by Salviati thus made the papacy aware of just where it stood in France, of which policies were feasible and of which were not.[42]

In summary it seems to me that the St. Bartholomew massacres encouraged militancy on both sides of the ideological fence. Violence bred more violence as it so often has in history. Geneva encouraged the violent dismantling of existing governments into their constituent parts, in the hope that one or another of these parts could protect Protestantism from the persecution of a unified government. Rome used a more and more professional diplomatic service to mobilize and stimulate Catholic powers in attempts to crush Protestantism completely. Both developments reached a peak in the next century, early in the Thirty Years' War, then began slowly to fade away. The terrible intolerance which gave motive power to these institutional developments has by this time nearly disappeared in Geneva and Rome. Unfortunately it still lingers on in certain other parts of the world.

---

[41] ASV, S. S. Francia 283, fols. 53ᵛ–54, noted by Pastor, XIX, 498.

[42] Cf. Pierre Hurtubise, "Comment Rome apprit la nouvelle du massacre de la Saint-Barthélemy," *Archivum Historiae Pontificiae*, X (1972), 188–209, for an independent but somewhat similar conclusion.

XV

THE POLITICAL THOUGHT OF PETER
MARTYR VERMIGLI*

The intellectual leaders of the Protestant Reformation necessarily
found themselves forced to grapple with problems in political
thought. As they all discovered, sooner or later, their challenges to
papal direction of the Christian Church and their calls for new
ecclesiastical structures carried political consequences of great significance. The institutions of the Roman Catholic Church had become
so intimately intertwined with the institutions of secular government
that a challenge to Catholicism inevitably entailed a challenge to
existing political arrangements. This inescapable fact was accepted
more readily by some leaders than others. Protestant lawyers were
more likely to prepare sophisticated political statements than Protestant theologians. And leaders of the Calvinist and Jesuit communities
were more likely to deal seriously with politics than spokesmen for
less militant religious groups. But not even a theologian as wholeheartedly committed to the pure study of theology as Martin Luther
could avoid political judgments altogether.

Of the statements of early Protestant political thought, the most
original, the most sophisticated, and the most studied by modern
scholars were a number of political treatises. The best known among

* I am indebted to Marvin W. Anderson for giving me an unpublished seminar
paper, "Iudicium Domini: Peter Martyr on Moral and Idolatrous Magistrates," which
helped me in locating many of the texts upon which this paper is based. I have,
however, studied them independently and, on a number of points, do not find myself in
full agreement with Professor Anderson. I am also indebted to my colleagues Frank M.
Clover and Raymond B. Waddington for help on specific problems I faced in working
on this paper.

them were almost certainly three treatises published by Calvinists shortly after the St. Bartholomew's massacres of 1572: the *Franco-Gallia* by Francis Hotman, the *Du droit des magistrats* by Theodore Beza, and the anonymous *Vindiciae contra tyrannos*. Together they articulated a fresh and highly sophisticated justification for armed resistance to tyrannical governments if led by inferior magistrates. They had a demonstrable impact on the politics of the sixteenth century and on political thought in later centuries.

I suspect, however, that for the statements of early Protestant political thought which had the greatest influence in the period of the Reformation itself, we should look not at these political treatises but rather at those sections of manuals of theology which deal with politics. Let me make this point first by citing two statements of the political ideas of Theodore Beza. Beza is best known to modern students of political thought for his *Du droit des magistrats*, first published in 1574. This pamphlet of several dozen pages develops a closely reasoned argument for political resistance based on an intricate combination of appeals to Scripture, ecclesiastical and secular history, and Roman law. Beza had already sketched this political point of view, however, in the forty-fifth article of his *Confession of the Christian Faith*, in the version he revised in 1560. This article is titled "On the obedience which is due to magistrates," and it supplies in a few pages a neat capsule version of the argument for political resistance Beza was to elaborate in 1574.[1] The version in the *Confession* was surely better known to Beza's contemporaries. To begin with, there were more copies available. The *Confession* appeared in thirty-nine separate editions in six different languages, plus a number of further editions in larger collections.[2] The *Du droit des magistrats* appeared in about nine separate editions in three different languages, plus a number of further editions in larger collections.[3] Furthermore, the editions of the *Confession* all bore Beza's name, making it clear that this was the opinion of one of the most respected leaders of the international Reformed community. The editions of the *Du droit des magistrats*, on the other hand, were all anonymous, and while some suspected that Beza was its author few could be sure. Finally the *Confession* by its very nature was designed for intensive study by laymen and clergy, while the political treatise was designed more for specialists in political thought.

---

[1] For an edited text of this article, see annexe 2, in my critical edition of the French version, Théodore de Bèze, *Du droit des Magistrats* (Geneva: Droz, 1971): 70-75.

[2] Frédéric Gardy and Alain Dufour, *Bibliographie des oeuvres théologiques, littéraires, historiques et juridiques de Théodore de Bèze* (Geneva: Droz, 1960): 62-80.

[3] *Ibid.*, 162-65, supplemented by the lists of French editions in my edition, xliv, and of Latin editions in the critical edition by Klaus Sturm of the Latin version, Theodor Beza, *De iure magistratuum* (Neukirchen-Vluyn: Neukirchener Verlag des Erziehungsvereins, 1965): 21-22.

Among these early Protestant manuals of theology, the most developed and the most important for the education of clergymen were the collections most commonly titled *Loci communes*, or *Common Places*. These works survey all theology systematically and generally conclude with a consideration of the human institutions through which the divine message was mediated, specifically the church and the state. The format for these collections was set by Philip Melanchthon, whose *Loci communes* was the first and most influential of the genre. In its earliest 1521 edition in Latin, the next to last section is a very brief analysis of magistrates, both ecclesiastical and secular. The page or so on the secular magistrate provides a first statement for general circulation of Melanchthon's point of view on political problems. In its final 1555 edition in German, Melanchthon extended considerably this part of his general analysis. Now there are several chapters on the church and a concluding chapter, "Of Worldly Authority," containing a considerably developed analysis of secular government alone.

This format was adapted for the Reformed branch of the Protestant movement by John Calvin, in his celebrated *Institutes of the Christian Religion*. Now an entire book, the last of four, is devoted to the human institutions through which God works his will. In the final 1559 Latin edition of that work, some nineteen chapters of the fourth book deal with the church; only one, again the last, deals with secular government. This last chapter contains, in its thirty-first section, Calvin's well-known if brief and cryptic defence of political resistance.

Of the several later versions of this basic type of reference prepared for the Reformed community, very likely the most important was the *Loci communes* of Peter Martyr Vermigli. It was not, of course, compiled by Vermigli himself. It was rather the work of his disciples, encouraged by Beza and Bullinger, the surviving leaders of the movement. The *loci* which make it up, however, are clearly the work of Vermigli, for they are selected from among the short systematic treatises on set theological topics with which he laced his Biblical commentaries. The general organization of Vermigli's *Loci communes* resembles that of Calvin's *Institutes*, with a fourth part again assigned to human institutions. But there is now an important shift in proportions. For Vermigli's analysis of politics is not limited to one concluding chapter, as in Melanchthon and Calvin. It rather fills chapters thirteen through twenty (or twenty-one—depending on the edition) of Part Four, eight (or nine) full chapters. There are, in addition, some passages of political analysis in other chapters, devoted primarily to the church or other subjects.

To me this constitutes the most important justification for a study of the political thought of Peter Martyr Vermigli. His political ideas

124

are not strikingly original or unusual. But they are presented in an unusually extended and systematic form in an important reference work of the period. At least fourteen editions of Vermigli's *Loci communes* are known to have been published between 1576 and 1656: three in London, two in Zurich, three in Heidelberg, four in Geneva, one each in Basel and in Amsterdam-Frankfurt. For much of the late sixteenth and early seventeenth centuries this work was clearly a reference of fundamental importance to Calvinists. Several generations of Reformed clergymen in England, Switzerland, and Germany learned much of their theology from it. They also, I would argue, learned much of their political thought from the same source. This influence in many cases was surely reinforced, furthermore, by study of the many editions of the individual Biblical commentaries containing these *loci*, in the contexts within which Vermigli had written them. Of these Biblical commentaries, the most important for *loci* on politics, as we shall see, was the one on Judges. It went through six editions, four in Zurich, one in London, one in Heidelberg. The other Biblical commentaries from which political *loci* can be drawn went through between three and eight editions each, again in Zurich, Basel, London, or Heidelberg. They all clearly reached much the same market as the collected *Loci communes*.[4]

Most of Vermigli's *loci* on political matters came from commentaries on the Old Testament. He prepared more commentaries on books of the Old Testament than of the New, and he insisted on the equal authority of the two testaments in many domains, for example in opposing the arguments of pacifists who claimed that the New Testament's law of love superseded the Old Testament's calls for vengeance. The most important of these *loci* came from Vermigli's commentary on the book of Judges. This commentary was based on lectures delivered during his second stay in Strasbourg, from 1553 to 1556, and was prepared for publication by Vermigli himself after his arrival in Zurich. The first edition appeared in Zurich in 1561.

The content of Judges itself helps to explain the number of political *loci* in this commentary, since much of the book is devoted to recounting the history of the tribes of Israel during a period of political turmoil when there was considerable debate about the appropriate form of government for the community. But Vermigli's decision to lecture on Judges and then to prepare these lectures for publication, complete with these political *loci*, may well reflect his own circumstances. When he arrived in Strasbourg for the second time,

---

[4] These tabulations of Vermigli editions come from the Vermigli bibliography John P. Donnelly and I are preparing for publication. We have published a short-title list of these editions as an appendix to my edition of Vermigli's political *loci*.

Vermigli was in flight from the newly Catholic government of Mary in England. Many of his close associates were English Protestant exiles who were eagerly hoping and working for an overthrow of the government of Mary and an early return to a Protestant government. Several of those exiles even followed him to Zurich. Vermigli arrived in Strasbourg, furthermore, when it was reestablishing its own shaky Protestant settlement, thanks to the stubborn resistance of Protestant cities and princes within the Holy Roman Empire to the efforts of the imperial government to enforce a general return in all Germany to Roman Catholicism. This resistance achieved final success only in 1555, while Vermigli was in residence, with the adoption of the Religious Peace of Augsburg. Vermigli should have heard, finally, while preparing this book for publication, of the growing determination of the Reformed in France to resist royal efforts to wipe them out.

Whatever the reasons, the most important *loci* on political subjects included in Vermigli's *Loci communes* are drawn from his commentary on Judges. Two of them are of particular importance. The longer of them is "De Magistratu," an extended scholium on Judges 19, defining government with precision and vigorously attacking extreme Catholic arguments for temporal power of the clergy. It makes up all of chapter thirteen in part four of the *Loci communes*. The other is "An subditis liceat contra suos principes insurgere," which is Vermigli's most extended and most measured consideration of political resistance theory. It makes up the last of several *loci* on Judges 3 and sections twelve and thirteen of chapter twenty (twenty-one) in the final part of the *Loci communes*. The political matters covered there are then rounded out with the inclusion of a number of other *loci*, of varying lengths. Among the more important are a scholium on 1 Corinthians 5, on excommunication, in the chapters of the church, and *loci* on more strictly political topics drawn from II Samuel 2, I Kings 18:17, II Kings 11, and Genesis 34. The *locus* from I Kings 18:17 is actually a development and refinement of an earlier one, "De Seditione," from the commentary on Judges 12:1-6.

These seven *loci* make up the heart of Vermigli's political argument in its most widely circulated form. Their comment can be further illuminated, however, by exploration of certain *loci* which were not included within the collection. The scholium on Judges 3 dealing with resistance theory, in particular, can be better understood by examining *loci* on Romans 13:1-4, Judges 1:36, and Judges 8:22-23. It is primarily upon these ten *loci* that my analysis rests.[5]

---

[5] In preparing this paper, I used microfilm copies of the *Loci communes* in Latin of 1583 (S.T.C. 24668), the *Common Places* in English of 1583 (S.T.C. 24669), the Romans commentary in English of 1568 (S.T.C. 24672), the Judges commentary in English of 1564 (S.T.C. 24670), all published in London, and the Judges commentary in

Peter Martyr Vermigli was widely respected in his own century for the great clarity of his thought. That clarity is still obvious to the modern reader, distinguishing the writing of Vermigli from the frequent emotionalism of Luther and the evasive convolutions of Bucer. It even surpasses the clarity of Calvin, another master of lucid prose, who nevertheless permitted his strong temper to colour his expression on occasion. The technical reason for Vermigli's superior clarity probably lies in his judicious use of concepts and methods drawn from Aristotle. Vermigli had been thoroughly educated in the use of Aristotle, both in philosophy and theology, at the University of Padua, when it was among the world's greatest centres for the study of Aristotelian thought. And, unlike Luther, Vermigli never saw any reason to abandon the use of Aristotle after his conversion to Protestantism. This use of Aristotle makes of Vermigli, as Professor Donnelly has demonstrated, an important contributor to the development of Protestant Scholasticism.

In his political *loci*, Vermigli used Aristotle both for structure and for substance. He used him for structure by employing Aristotelian terms and logical categories in developing a pattern of analysis. A typical political *locus* would begin with a definition of a term—for example: the magistrate, war, sedition. That term would first be examined linguistically, in good humanist fashion, with explanations of its meaning in Latin, Greek, and Hebrew, ornamented with examples. But it would then be explored logically, often at considerable length. The definition of sedition in chapter twenty (twenty-one) of the *Loci communes*, for example, begins in section two and runs through section eight where it finally is encapsulated into what even Vermigli himself calls a "very full definition." The definition runs, in its English translation: "Sedition is a voluntary action, whereby there is contention among many, as well touching civil things as matters of religion. And there is brought in a privation as well of order as of unity, by reason of the inclination of the mind to the making of strife, or for anger for receiving of an offence, or for desire of glory, or of pleasures, or of gain, and most of all, for the diversity of faith, or else for too much plenty or poverty, and that to the overthrow of good ordinances, and that godly men may shine more and more by the occasion thereof." Each one of the terms in this definition has already

Latin of 1571, published in Zurich. References to the *Loci* are to chapter and section numbers in the Latin text, part four, with variant numberings in the English text in parenthesis. References to the commentaries are to the Bible verses glossed. My quotations are from the sixteenth-century English translations, with spelling and punctuation modernized. I have prepared a critical edition with commentary of most of these texts, entitled *The Political Thought of Peter Martyr Vermigli: Selected Texts and Commentary*, published by the Librairie Droz of Geneva, 1980. It documents more fully and refines much of the argument of this paper.

been carefully analyzed and explained by this point, using typically Aristotelian categories and vocabulary. The term "action," for example, is justified by explaining that sedition belongs "to the predicament of action" (4: 20:3). Quite often these definitions use the four Aristotelian categories of causation as a pattern for analyzing a key term. The definition of war in chapter sixteen (seventeen) of the *Loci*, uses this tactic. In its section one, Vermigli first supplies his definition of just war as a "hostile dissension whereby through the Prince's edict mischiefs are repressed by force and arms, to the intent that men may peaceably and quietly live by justice and godliness." He then points out that the definition "comprehends" the four kinds of Aristotelian causes: "The form is hostile dissension; the matter are the mischiefs which ought to be repressed; the efficient cause is the magistrate; the end is that we may live justly and godly."

Vermigli's use of Aristotle for the substance of his political argument depends, as one would expect, primarily on the *Politics*. His most striking use of that work is his adoption of Aristotle's analysis of the types of government into six categories, according to the *locus* of sovereignty in each: three good types—monarchy, aristocracy, and polity—matched by the three bad types into which they tend to degenerate—tyranny, oligarchy, and democracy. Vermigli applies this pattern of analysis both to church and state. He applies it to the church in section nine of chapter five, on the discipline and government of the church, to argue that the church in reality conforms to the classic ideal of a mixed government, incorporating the best features of the three good types. It is monarchic in that Christ is its King and remains its supreme legislator, even though he is in heaven. It is aristocratic in that it is ruled by "bishops, elders, doctors" and others, chosen by merit rather than by wealth, favour, or birth. It is popular in that some of its most important decisions, for example as to whether to excommunicate a notorious sinner, should be "referred unto the people."

Elsewhere this pattern of analysis is applied even more closely to the secular state. Section two of chapter thirteen, the *locus* of the magistrate, begins with a statement which is close to a quotation from Aristotle: "the form of magistrates is not of one sort but manifold: as *monarchy* (the government of one), aristocracy (the rule of many good men), and polity (politic government). Or else tyranny (where one rules for his own commodity), oligarchy (where a few be in authority), and democracy (when the people bear the sway)." While Vermigli does not refer specifically to the passage in the *Politics* (III.v. i-iv) which contains the same analysis, he does give an explicit credit to ancient thinkers by following his own analysis with this comment: "the descriptions and natures of which forms Plato, Aristotle, and other philosophers have elegantly described." This six-part analysis of the forms of government recurs again and again in Vermigli's political *loci*.

If use of Aristotle explains much of the structure and some of the substance of Vermigli's political thought, most of that substance comes from other sources. The most obvious of those sources is the Christian tradition, most importantly as it is summarized in the Bible. All of these *loci*, we must not forget, were first written as glosses on specific verses of the Bible, and even though Vermigli could wander quite far from his text, he seldom forgets it completely and he often analyzes it quite closely. Vermigli furthermore followed common Protestant practice in using Scripture to interpret Scripture. There are frequent marginal references to other Biblical verses, in both old and new testaments, to support nearly every step of his argument. Discussions of resistance theory, for example, inevitably carry a cross reference to the first verses of Romans 13. In developing his interpretation of Scripture, furthermore, Vermigli relies heavily on the Church Fathers, using patristic writers as authoritative explanations of what specific verses really mean. He relies with particular frequency on St. Augustine, quoting him lavishly, usually with approval, although occasionally in disagreement. In his discussions of resistance theory, he uses very often, in company with other sixteenth-century commentators, the homily number twenty-three by St. John Chrysostom on the first verses of Romans 13.

Vermigli's dependence on the Bible and on the Church Fathers is obvious and has been noted by every other scholar. His reliance on another body of authority has not been looked at closely by others, yet it is particularly important for an understanding of his political thought. So I want to emphasize it. This is the Roman law. Vermigli had an extraordinary command of Roman law, as it had been codified in the *Corpus Iuris Civilis*, the basic textbook used by all sixteenth-century students of the law. Copies of both the *Codex* and the *Digests* from the corpus, with marginal annotations in Vermigli's own hand, have been uncovered by Professor Ganoczy in the Geneva University Library.[6] And he used them frequently to buttress his political arguments. It is startling to find Vermigli using allegations from the Roman law so much more frequently and confidently than Calvin, who after all held a degree in law. His use resembles that of Beza, who also held a law degree, and Hotman, who was a professional jurisconsult. At one point in his career, Vermigli clearly studied the law carefully and apparently committed a good deal of the *Corpus Iuris Civilis* to memory. Political arguments based on Roman law were

---

[6] Alexandre Ganoczy, *La bibliothèque de l'Académie de Calvin* (Geneva: Droz, 1969): 273, nos. 341, 342. Note also no. 322, pp. 266-67, Vermigli's copy of Aristotle's *Politics*.

quite pervasive in the period, as Professor Giesey and his students have recently pointed out.[7] It should therefore come as no great surprise that they are also pervasive in the political thought of Vermigli. The fact has not been pointed out, to my knowledge at least, by other students of Vermigli, however, and I confess this was my greatest surprise in reading his political *loci*.

Let me provide one example of a Roman law used by Vermigli. This is the Roman law of treason called the *lex Iulia maiestatis*. It was enacted either by Julius Caesar or Augustus and defined treason as conspiracy against the life of the emperor, libel and slander of the emperor, and adultery with a member of the emperor's family.[8] Two chapters containing summary statements of this law, under the heading "*Ad legem Iuliam maiestatis,*" can be found in the *Corpus Iuris Civilis*, in the *Digests*, 48:4, and in the *Codex*, 9:8. In going through Vermigli's political *loci*, I have found five citations of this law, in chapters fourteen, sixteen (seventeen), and twenty (twenty-one). It was used for an example of executive clemency, in chapter fourteen, 28, where Vermigli pointed out that Augustus Caesar used one of its provisions to waive the normal death penalty for treason. It was used with other legal allegations to establish the authority of a prince to wage war and punish the wicked, in chapter sixteen (seventeen), 2. It was used obviously enough to define treason, again with other legal authorities and also patristic and classical authorities, in chapter sixteen (seventeen), 29. It was again combined with other legal, Scriptural, and classical authorities, to justify the death penalty for sedition in chapter twenty (twenty-one), 9. And it is alluded to in the *locus* on resistance by inferior magistrates in chapter twenty (twenty-one), 13.

At times Vermigli also supports his arguments with references to the canon law of the Catholic Church, sometimes using it even more frequently and decisively than the civil law. He was obviously using that classic compilation known as the *Corpus Iuris Canonici*, including the *decreti* of Gratian and certain other generally received texts, but he used an edition with a distinctly anti-papal gloss. It was almost certainly an edition prepared by Gallican jurists in Paris.

Occasionally Vermigli supports a political argument with evidence from yet another category. This is evidence drawn from contemporary political practice. It does not loom as large in his thought as it does in that of Machiavelli or of most modern theorists. But it is not totally absent. In discussing the right of resistance by inferior magistrates, for example, he alludes several times to the Electors of the Holy Roman Empire.

---

[7] Ralph E. Giesey, "The Monarchomach Triumvirs: Hotman, Beza, and Mornay," *Bibliothèque d'Humanisme et Renaissance* 32 (1970): 41-56.

[8] *The Oxford Classical Dictionary*, 2nd ed., article "maiestas," 640-41.

130

If Vermigli based his political arguments primarily on appeals to classical philosophers, pre-eminently Aristotle, and to the Holy Scriptures, particularly to the actual texts as he understood them, and to secular law, as codified by the Romans, how did he measure the relative importance of these authorities? It is tempting to reply that he always preferred a proof from Scripture. This is surely what he himself would have said, in common with almost all Protestant theologians of the sixteenth century. The principle of *sola scriptura*, after all, was one of the most fundamental of the Reformation and was held to apply in practically every branch of thought, including political. A close look at Vermigli's arguments, however, reveal that this obvious conclusion does not always hold. At times he actually balances the different types of argument against each other, but he does not always reach the predictable conclusion. In his discussion of political resistance by inferior magistrates in chapter twenty (twenty-one), 13, for example, he points out that in ancient times the pagans "appointed rewards for such as killed tyrants," yet feels that "godliness and the Holy Scriptures allow not the same," and so he cannot approve of tyrannicide. In his discussion of the right of inferior magistrates to resist their superiors in his scholium on Judges 1:36, on the other hand, Vermigli refuses to find a ground for this resistance in the Bible. He rather insists that contemporary constitutional arrangements justify resistance:

> But thou wilt say: by what law do inferior princes resist either the emperor or kings, or else public wealths [republics], when as they defend the sincere religion and true faith? I answer by the law of the Emperor, or by the law of the king, or by the law of the public wealth [republic]. For they are chosen of emperors, kings, and public wealths as helpers to rule, whereby justice may more and more flourish. And therefore were they ordained according to the office committed unto them, rightly, justly, and godly to govern the public wealth. Wherefore they do according to their duty, when in cause of religion they resist the higher power.

His more widely circulated argument for resistance by inferior magistrates, in chapter twenty (twenty-one), 13, of the *Loci communes*, similarly rests ultimately on an appeal to constitutional arrangements, not to Scripture.

My analysis of the material from which Vermigli built his theory of politics should already have given you some idea of its content. But let me turn now to a more systematic analysis of that content. Let us begin with the starting point of any system of political thought, its definition of government, or of "the magistrate," to use the term most common in Vermigli's milieu. He faces this problem right at the beginning of his *locus* on the magistrate, defining him as "a person chosen by the institution of God, to keep the laws as touching outward discipline, in punishing of transgressors with punishment of the body, and to defend and make much of the good." Much of the rest of that *locus*, chapter thirteen of Part four in the *Loci communes*, is an elaboration of that definition. Note that he insists on the divine institution of the sovereign power within government. He is quick to add, however, that not all leaders chosen by God are magistrates. Ministers of churches are also chosen by God and are to keep his word and his law, but have nothing to do with outward discipline. Much of the rest of the *locus*, in fact, is devoted to distinguishing the powers of magistrates and ministers, with a very evident anti-Catholic goal in view. He insists that the clergy cannot claim any temporal power, and spends a great deal of space, here and elsewhere, refuting the claims of plenary temporal power advanced by Pope Boniface VIII in his bull *Unam sanctam* almost two hundred years earlier. He would not deny to the clergy the duty of seeing to it that the magistrate meets his Christian responsibilities, but that duty must never be exercised with force, only through preaching and censures. He would not even deny to the clergy the possibility of personally using force, in a war, but only in cases of extreme emergency, when, for example, there are not enough able-bodied men to defend a city fighting for survival. Normally, however, a clergyman should have nothing to do with warfare or the usual political routine. In another *locus* (4: 16:11), he repeats and documents this point, drawing from Aristotle's *Politics* the maxim that "two offices must not be committed to any one man, because no man can be fit for both the functions, seeing either of both requireth a perfect and whole man" and concluding that it is not lawful for a clergyman to bear arms.

The succeeding chapters in Vermigli's *Loci communes* then award to this divinely instituted magistrate all of the powers normally claimed by contemporary governments. To do this they develop many quite strenuous refutations of the contrary arguments of Anabaptists. One extended chapter, fourteen, is devoted to the argument that magistrates must administer justice and cannot shrink from punishing evil-doers, even when this requires capital penalties. A short section of this chapter, detached as a separate chapter fifteen in at least one edition, considers the utility of exile and banishment as alternative forms of punishment. Another extended chapter, fifteen (sixteen), is devoted to the argument that it is lawful for an individual Christian to use the secular courts of law for the redress of grievances. Contrary advice, drawn from the Bible and the early history of the Christian community, applies, Vermigli argues, only to Christians under a pagan rulers and even in that circumstance is not an invariable rule. The apostle Paul, he notes a number of times, did not hesitate to appeal from the judgment of a Jewish court to a pagan emperor, and was certainly justified in doing so. An even longer chapter, sixteen (seventeen), is devoted to a consideration of war. The power to make war in a just cause, Vermigli insists, is a necessary attribute of sovereign authority. He uses a good deal of space to refute the pacifist arguments advanced by Anabaptists, based on the precepts of the Sermon on the Mount and other New Testament passages, arguing that these rules apply only to private individuals, not to public magistrates. This is followed by some shorter chapters, seventeen to nineteen (eighteen to twenty), including *loci* on whether captives taken in war should be kept or put to death, on the morality of duelling, on the social values of a class system headed by a noble class and resting on a caste of bond servants, and finally on the morality of monopolizing a commodity in trade.

A final political problem is reserved for the very last chapter, twenty (twenty-one), of Vermigli's *Loci communes*. It is the problem, which interests me particularly, of resistance, of whether citizens are ever justified in resisting with force the government to which they are subject. The basis for Vermigli's argument on this topic is prepared by his earlier analysis of forms of government, borrowed from Aristotle. That analysis, you will recall, distinguished six forms of government: three good—monarchy, aristocracy, and polity; three bad—tyranny, oligarchy, and democracy. In the ecclesiastical sphere, you will recall, Vermigli had argued that the guiding principles of each of the three good types should be combined. The church would thus approximate a mixed government, a type admired by many ancient thinkers. Vermigli did not insist, however, on a similar ideal form of secular government. Any one of the three good types would do. There was sound precedent in the Old Testament for each. And any one of these types would be preferable to any one of the three bad types.

That left open the problem, however, of what the citizen was to do who finds himself living under a bad form of government. The specific form in which the problem was normally posed was of how a citizen should cope with tyranny, since that seemed the perversion most common in the sixteenth-century context. A number of thinkers, following ancient and medieval precedents, attacked this problem by first distinguishing two types of tyranny: the tyranny of the usurper, who invaded a country or illegally seized power, and the tyranny of a legitimate ruler who misuses power. Julius Caesar, to cite a common example, was often called a usurping tyrant; his successors, on the other hand, were legitimate tyrants. Many theorists thought that resistance to an invader or usurper posed no problem, that a subject had no duty to obey a tyrant of this sort. Resistance to such a tyrant, therefore, was thoroughly legitimate and could proceed even to his assassination, to tyrannicide, by anyone who could manage it, even a private citizen.

Vermigli was aware of this distinction between two types of tyranny and of the corollary argument for resistance to the usurper. He was not comfortable with the corollary, however, and his resolutions of the problem are not consistent. In his scholium on Judges 3, in chapter twenty (twenty-one), 13, of the *Loci communes*, for example, he says: "Though also it be lawful to resist tyrants which assail a kingdom, yet when they have obtained the same and do bear rule, it seemeth not to belong unto private men to put them down." But in the same section, he will not accept the assassination of Caesar by Brutus and Cassius as legitimate, even though Caesar was a usurper, since Brutus and Cassius had not in any way given Caesar his power and thus could not be licensed to take it away. Opposition to resistance to a usurping tyrant is expressed even more emphatically in section nineteen of this chapter, drawn from a scholium on Genesis 34. It makes the classic distinction between two types of tyranny, stating that it may be imposed "either by invading unjustly, or by ruling the dominion naughtily." But it does not draw the classic deduction, rather concluding that "such a wicked prince must godly men suffer, seeing they be private persons, and have no authority over him."

In one area of government, however, Vermigli would not accept the absolute authority of the secular magistrate. This was the area of religion. In common with every Protestant, he argued that commands to participate in false worship or abstain from true worship must be disobeyed. No private individual should obey such laws. And no inferior magistrate, in a subordinate position in the usual chain of governmental command, should attempt to enforce them. Both private individuals and inferior magistrates were thus required to resist, passively, in that situation. Inferior magistrates, in fact, were forbidden to take the easy way out by resigning from office, and rather were expected to use all their powers to frustrate the application of such laws.

Vermigli freely conceded that passive disobedience of this sort could lead to severe retaliation from a government. In that situation, the true Christian as a private individual only had two choices: he could evade the jurisdiction of the unjust government, as Vermigli himself had done in fleeing Italy back in 1542; or he could accept unjust punishment, even if that meant martyrdom, in the expectation of an eternal reward. Vermigli clearly wanted to avoid any hint of sanctioning popular revolt or tyrannicide. He had no doubt been distressed by tales of the excesses of Anabaptist rebels in Germany and in Switzerland. And he had also been personally upset by the popular western rising against the Protestant establishment of Edward VI in England. He had even helped Cranmer prepare sermons denouncing that revolt.

But Vermigli was not prepared to make this prohibition of active resistance absolute. He did not trust God to defend the Protestant cause without any human help. Like almost all orthodox Protestant

leaders, he did in the end accept an argument for resistance to tyrannical government if led by legitimate inferior magistrates. In his commentary on Romans 13:1-4, probably drafted while he was still in
England, although published for the first time only after his final
move to Zurich, he first develops the case, in these words:

> I speak not this, that I think that superior powers cannot be put down by
> inferior magistrates, or that they cannot be constrained to do their duty
> of those which are appointed either keepers, or authors, or electors of
> princes, if they transgress the ends and limits of the power which they
> have received. As in times past at Rome the Senate and people of Rome
> were wont to do, and at this day in Germany, the Electors of the Empire
> use sometimes to do.

This argument for resistance by inferior magistrates is refined
and developed somewhat in Vermigli's scholium on Judges 3, which
is included in the *Loci communes*, 4: 20:12-13. Here is the revised
wording: "But there be others in the commonweale, which in place
and dignity are inferior unto princes, and yet in very deed do elect the
superior power, and by certain laws do govern the commonweale, as
at this day we see done by the Electors of the Empire, and perhaps the
same is done in other kingdoms. To these undoubtedly if the prince
perform not his covenants and promises, it is lawful to constrain and
bring him into order, and by force to compel him to perform the
conditions and covenants which he had promised, and that by war
when it cannot otherwise be done." Here we see not only a striking
statement of a theory justifying resistance by inferior magistrates but
also a contract theory for resistance, reminiscent of those developed
by the *Vindiciae contra tyrannos*, and even later by the theorists of the
English and American revolutions. Vermigli supports this argument
with three additional examples of permissible revolts: (1) the ancient
Romans sometimes forced a consul, whom they had elected, to leave
office; (2) the Danes of his own time had deposed and imprisoned a
king; (3) according to Polydore Vergil, the English sometimes forced
kings to render account of misspent money. These Danish and English
examples are interesting, as among the few rare references in all of
Vermigli's writings to contemporary politics. But they are not fitted
very convincingly to the general theory, since no evidence is provided that in either Denmark or England was resistance led by inferior
magistrates with powers of election who had actual installed their
kings in office.

This argument is developed even further in other scholia on the
book of Judges, among them several not included in the *Loci communes*. Of particular interest are two sentences in the scholium on
Judges 1:36, on whether it was lawful for a Christian to live with
infidels, published separately as a pamphlet in English while Ver-

migli was still in Strasbourg.[9] One of them appeals to Roman law to
justify resistance, in terms reminiscent of the appeal to the Roman *lex
digna*, which had often been used to justify resistance over the centuries. In Vermigli's words: "The Emperor testifieth in the Code, that
his mind is not that any of his decrees should take place in judgments
against right, but that they ought to be made void and of no force, if
that peradventure they be known to decline from justice." The other
repeats a quotation often attributed to the Emperor Trajan, who reportedly delivered his sword after his election to one of the officers he had
just appointed, saying, "If I rule justly, use it on my side; but if I rule
unjustly, use it against me." It is striking to find these two arguments
in Vermigli. The Trajan anecdote is used again and again by resistance theorists of the sixteenth century and so is the appeal to the *lex
digna*. Both are prominent, for example, in Beza's *Du droit des magistrats*.[10] By using them, Vermigli places himself securely within the
main tradition of Protestant argument for political resistance.

Fitting Vermigli with precision into that Protestant tradition,
however, is not an easy task. It requires a meticulous study of the
entire development of Protestant political thought in the sixteenth
century, particularly of thought on the resistance problem, and that
study has yet to be completed. My own judgment at this point is that
Vermigli's political position was basically a Lutheran one. He did not,
on other words, develop a political position as radical as that of his
fellow exiles from England or the more militant French followers of
Calvin, in spite of the fact that he agreed with them more than with the
Lutherans on matters of pure theology. The fact that early Lutherans
developed an important theory justifying political resistance may still
not be appreciated by non-specialists, although it has been demonstrated with increasing force and growing documentation by a
number of recent articles.[11] The traditional distinction between politically passive Lutherans and politically militant Calvinists simply
does not fit the facts of early sixteenth-century history. It is probably
an anachronism, read back into that period from times in which it did
seem to fit. Early Lutheran resistance theory was developed in the
chancery of the state of Saxony, by jurists seeking to form a pan-
German alliance of Protestant powers designed to resist, with force if

---

[9] On this separate treatise, see Marvin Walter Anderson, *Peter Martyr: A Reformer in Exile (1542-1562)* (Nieuwkoop: de Graff, 1975): 394ff.

[10] See in my edition 21, 49 on the *lex digna*; 21-22 for the Trajan anecdote.

[11] See particularly W. D. J. Cargill Thompson, "Luther and the Right of Resistance
to the Emperor," in Derek Baker, ed., *Church, Society, and Politics* vol. 12 in *Studies in
Church History* (Oxford: Blackwell, for the Ecclesiastical History Society, 1975): 159-
202; Richard R. Benert, "Lutheran Resistance Theory and the Imperial Constitution," *Il
Pensiero Politico* 6 (1973), 17-36, and Cynthia Grant Shoenberger, "The Development
of the Lutheran Theory of Resistance," *Sixteenth-Century Journal* 8 (1977), 61-76.

necessary, the imperial government's attempt to enforce legislation requiring all citizens of the empire to accept Roman Catholicism as the only true form of Christianity. The theory was fully developed by 1530, and in that year Luther himself was persuaded with some reluctance to sign a memorandum endorsing it. The theory was given more public expression by theologians close to Luther like Philip Melanchthon and Justus Menius.

This early Lutheran theory of resistance was based on an interpretation of the German constitution. The emperor who served as chief executive of the government then controlling all of Germany was chosen not by inheritance, as in the kingdoms of Western Europe, but by election. And the election was limited to seven great princes, four of them secular and three ecclesiastical, called *Kurfürsten* or Electors. One of these Electors was the ruler of that part of Saxony in which the Reformation began and to which Luther and his associates were subject. The Electors, these theorists argued, create the emperor by their election of him. They furthermore establish guidelines within which he must rule by requiring him to sign a set of agreements called the "electoral capitulations" before the election becomes final. Any emperor who fails to abide by these agreements loses his claim to supreme power. And the Electors who created this power had the obligation to resist its wrongful use.

Obviously this is a theory ideally suited to justify a rebellion like the Schmalkaldic wars, led by the Elector of Saxony within the Holy Roman Empire. But it was not of very general use. It even left other Protestant states within Germany uncomfortable, so they attempted to broaden the definition of "inferior magistrates" to include not only prince-Electors but also other units of government. Thus Martin Bucer broadened it to include city governments, to justify the participation of the city of Strasbourg in the revolt led by the League of Schmalkalden. And John Calvin broadened it to include the Estates-General, a representative body of an entire kingdom, to justify resistance to the French crown. And Calvin's French followers broadened it to include aristocrats with a permanent claim to a place in royal government, and city governments, and provincial estates, when it became clear that it would take a coalition of that sort to resist the king of France. And Calvin's Dutch and Scottish followers similarly broadened the term to fit the situations in their home countries

Vermigli, however, did not participate in this broadening. He restricts the right of resistance to inferior magistrates who hold a special constitutional place within their government, like the Electors of the Holy Roman Empire. In the same scholium on Judges 3 in which he makes his most developed case for this kind of resistance, he specifies that it cannot be justified in other types of government. Resistance to the Biblical kings of the Jews, for example, was never justified, Vermigli claimed, for those kings "were not chosen by noble men, but the posterity of that family which God had appointed did govern by succession." This precedent would seem to bar any resistance in a hereditary kingdom. Vermigli did, to be sure, in this same passage approve of the imprisonment of the Danish kings by their subjects and of the English practice of compelling kings to account for misspent money. But he did not explain that approval any further.

The classical examples used by Vermigli in support of his arguments for resistance, furthermore, could have come from Lutheran sources; Melanchthon, for example, in 1530 had compared the Electors of the Empire to the ephors of Sparta, magistrates who controlled the king of that ancient city-state.[12] Vermigli also mentions the Spartan ephors as examples of inferior magistrates upon whom superior power depends, in 4: 20:12. (His description of the ephors' role is more exact, incidentally, than Calvin's famous reference in *Institutes*, 4: 20:31). Luther, Melanchthon, Menius, and other Lutherans had all recited the story about the emperor Trajan giving a sword to an aide and telling him to use it for his master only when he ruled justly and to turn it against his master if he used it unjustly.[13] The anecdote seemed to fit the German situation nicely. Vermigli, as we have noted, also used this story.

The broader outlines of Vermigli's political position could also have come from Lutheran sources. The heavy reliance on Romans 13, as interpreted by the Church Fathers, is reminiscent of Luther. And the extensive use of Aristotle is reminiscent of Melanchthon, who even published a commentary on Aristotle's *Politics*.

Quite how Vermigli would have absorbed Lutheran political arguments, I am uncertain. He could, of course, simply have read them in the works of Melanchthon and other prominent Lutherans. During the time he was composing his lectures on Judges, however, Vermigli was unlikely to have been well disposed to Lutherans. He was then engaged in bitter argument on matters of sacramental theology and predestination with Marbach and the other hard-line Lutheran leaders in Strasbourg. My hunch is that he picked up many of these ideas from Johann Sleidan. Vermigli and Sleidan were both teaching in Strasbourg between 1553 and 1556. Neither was comfortable with the direction in which Lutheran orthodoxy was pushing the city and both decided to leave in 1556. (Sleidan died before that year was over.) Sleidan had been a civil servant and a diplomat earlier in life and during these years was composing a monumental history of Germany under the emperor Charles V. He was fascinated by the armed resistance to the emperor first organized by the Schmalkaldic League and

---

[12] Benert, "Lutheran Resistance," 29.
[13] *Ibid.*, 28.

XV

carried on by a variety of the "inferior" governments which ruled in Germany. He included in his history detailed descriptions of the arguments advanced to justify resistance, including entire texts of relevant documents. He was composing this history during the very years Vermigli was composing his lectures on Judges. I suspect a connection.

The limitation of Vermigli's argument for political resistance to a context designed for Lutherans may explain why it did not have a greater influence in later periods. Vermigli's *Loci communes* were reprinted several times during the early seventeenth century in Heidelberg, when that capital of German Calvinism was preparing itself for the monumental conflict that came to be called the Thirty Years' War. Many of the militant Calvinists who formed policy in Heidelberg, therefore, were well acquainted with his ideas. But for specific political ideas, these men could turn to theologians more nearly contemporary to their period, notably to one of the professors in the Heidelberg Academy, David Pareus.[14] And when religious revolt spread from Germany to England, it was more likely to be justified with arguments articulated by men like Althusius and Pareus than by Vermigli. John Milton, the great theorist of the Puritan Revolution, read extensively in earlier resistance theory. He discovered Vermigli's scholium on Judges 3, and carefully summarized its contents in his Commonplace book, in which he made notes of readings he thought might be useful to him in the future.[15] He was particularly impressed by Vermigli's cursory application of the resistance argument to England. But when Milton came to draft his classic apology for the deposition and execution of Charles I, *The Tenure of Kings and Magistrates*, he did not use Vermigli extensively. That book contains a documentary appendix quoting passages from the works of famous theologians in support of Milton's argument. It quotes at length from Luther, as reported by Sleidan incidentally; from Pareus, and others. It reproduces much of the argument of Christopher Goodman's inflammatory treatise on resistance, written in defiance of Mary Tudor back in 1558, against the advice of Vermigli and others. But it refers to Vermigli's scholium on Judges 3 only in passing, as yet another authority in support of Milton's position.[16]

---

[14] On whose political thought, see Daniel John Toft, "Shadows of Kings: The Political Thought of David Pareus, 1548-1622," Ph.D. dissertation (University of Wisconsin-Madison), 1970.

[15] *Complete Prose Works of John Milton*, vol. 1, ed. by Ruth Mohl (New Haven: Yale University Press, 1953): 455-56. See also Ruth Mohl, *John Milton and His Commonplace Book* (New York: Ungar, 1969).

[16] *Ibid.*, vol. 3, ed. byMerritt Y. Hughes (New Haven: Yale University Press, 1962): 220-21, 247. See also Merritt Y. Hughes, "Milton's Treatment of Reformation History in *The Tenure of Kings and Magistrates*," *Ten Perspectives on Milton* (New Haven: Yale University Press, 1965): 220-39.

Even if Vermigli's doctrine of political resistance was not of great practical use to later generations of the Reformed, however, it nevertheless prepared the way for doctrines which were more useful. And it was embedded within an important intellectual context, as a part of a general exposition of political thought which was itself but a part of a general exposition of an entire theology. It is for a further appreciation of that context that Vermigli's political thought deserves to be studied.

XVI

THE FUNCTION OF LAW IN THE POLITICAL THOUGHT
OF PETER MARTYR VERMIGLI*

One of the great values of the monumental edition of
Calvin's *Institutes of the Christian Religion* superintended by
John T. McNeill and containing the felicitous translation and
the splendid indexes prepared by Ford Lewis Battles is that it
helps place that theological masterwork within its sixteenth-
century context. Its critical apparatus reminds us of the
significant fact that Calvin's *Institutes*, as important as it
was, was not written or used in isolation. It was accompanied
by the works of many other Reformed theologians which helped
to elaborate, document, and occasionally even to modify
slightly the message of the greatest leader of Reformed Protestantism. Of these other works, I suspect the most important
was the *Loci communes* of Peter Martyr Vermigli. It was not
the work of Vermigli himself but was rather a compilation of
many of the short treatises and pericopes scattered throughout
his Biblical commentaries. It was prepared by Robert Masson,
a French minister in London and was deliberately arranged to
follow the same organizational pattern as the *Institutes*.
Editors and publishers of the two works clearly expected them
to be used together. The first Latin edition of the *Institutes*
to appear in England, the Vautrollier edition of 1576, was
even keyed to the *Loci*, with dozens of marginal cross-references. All of these valuable cross-references are tabulated in
the author and source index to the McNeill-Battles edition of
the *Institutes*. In fact Augustine is the only author allowed
more space than Vermigli in that index.[1]

Vermigli's most important contribution to Reformed theology was probably in the field of eucharistics. He developed a
highly subtle eucharistic theology in the course of debates
with Catholic spokesmen at Oxford and he further refined it in

later publications from Strasbourg and Zurich. Calvin appreciated Vermigli's insights on eucharistics and seems to have used them in his own later writings. The cordial letters which the two exchanged, when they go beyond reports of news, tend to dwell particularly on this branch of theology.[2]

But Vermigli made an additional contribution, whose significance is only now winning attention, to yet another branch of Reformed thought. This is the field of Reformed thought on politics.[3] The space given politics in Vermigli's *Loci communes* reflects an extraordinary expansion of attention to this domain. Some rough comparisons will make this point clear. The classic form for Protestant collections of Common Places was set, of course, by Philip Melanchthon. This collection systematically surveys all theology and concludes with a consideration of the human institutions through which the divine message is mediated, specifically the church and state. In the earliest edition of his *Loci communes*, of 1521, this consideration is limited to a single section, the next to the last, which considers both ecclesiastical and secular magistrates, allowing only a page or so for secular authorities. In the last edition of this work which he prepared, of 1559, this part of the general analysis is substantially expanded. Now there are several chapters on the church and a full chapter, toward the end, containing a considerably developed analysis of secular government alone.[4] This same format was adapted for the Reformed branch of the Protestant movement by Calvin in his *Institutes*. Now an entire book, the last of four, is devoted to the human institutions through which God works His will. But of these institutions, the church clearly interests Calvin more than the state. In the final edition of the *Institutes* which he saw through the press, the French edition of 1560, some nineteen chapters of the fourth book deal with the church while only one, the last, deals with secular government.[5] When one turns to the *Common Places* of Vermigli, however, one finds a quite startling shift in proportions. This collection ends, like the *Institutes*, with a fourth book on human institutions. But now eight (or nine) of the twenty (or twenty-one) chapters are devoted to secular government, often, to be sure, in its relation to the church, rather than the one chapter of Melanchthon and Calvin. The Vermigli collection thus devotes several times as much space to politics as the two earlier collections to which it is most comparable. Not all of Vermigli's *loci* on politics, furthermore, are included in the *Common Places*. There are additional ones in several of his published Biblical commentaries, particularly in his commentary on Judges, which was printed in several independent editions.[6]

To me this constitutes an important justification for a

study of the political thought of Peter Martyr Vermigli. His
political ideas are not strikingly original or unusual. But
they are presented in a much more extended and systematic form
than in most of the comparable reference works of the period.
Clearly the political ideas of Vermigli were among the most
developed of those widely circulated in the Reformed community
of the late sixteenth and early seventeenth centuries.

Another important justification for a study of the political thought of Peter Martyr Vermigli can be found in their
form. All of his *loci* are documented with unusual precision.
We can discover not only the precise sources Vermigli used to
develop his argument, on occasion we can even discover the
relative weight he attached to each.

For purposes of analysis, one can distinguish three main
categories of authority upon which Vermigli built his political arguments: ancient philosophers, particularly Aristotle;
the Bible; law, particularly as codified by the ancient Romans
and by the Roman Catholic Church. The use of Aristotle and
the Bible runs through all of Vermigli's writings and has been
pointed out by every other specialist. But the frequent use
of law in his political *loci* has not been pointed out until
very recently[7] and came as a real surprise to me when I began
work on these writings. This paper is an exploration of that
use.

But first let me describe the general form of Vermigli's
political argument. A typical political *locus* begins with the
definition of a term. Examples include the magistrate, war,
sedition. The term is first examined linguistically, in good
humanist fashion, with explanations of its meaning in Latin,
Greek and Hebrew, ornamented with examples. The term is then
explored logically, often at considerable length. The definition of sedition, for example, runs through seven sections of
a chapter in the *Common Places,* and is finally encapsulated in
a summary definition which even Vermigli himself admits is
"very full" (L. C. IV:20, 2-8). By this point, each term
within the definition has been carefully analyzed and explained, typically using Aristotelian categories and vocabulary. Quite often these definitions use the four Aristotelian
categories of causation for a pattern of analysis. Vermigli's
definition of just war, for example, is summarized in these
words: "hostile dissension whereby through the Prince's edict
mischiefs are repressed by force and arms, to the intent that
men may peaceably and quietly live by justice and godliness."
It is then immediately followed by the observation that the
definition "comprehends" the four kinds of Aristotelian cause:
"The form is hostile dissension; the matter are the mischiefs
which ought to be repressed; the efficient cause is the magis-

trate; the end is that we may live justly and godly" (L. C. IV:
16, 1).

After developing a definition, Vermigli then proceeds to
flesh out an argument. The argument is often explicitly anti-
Catholic, frequently attacking a position developed in the
canon law of the Roman Catholic Church as codified by Gratian.
Vermigli clearly knew the *Corpus Iuris Canonici* very well and
used it constantly, both as an authoritative source of official
statements of the Catholic position and as a useful collection
of relevant quotations from the church fathers and other authorities. The substance of his argument to counter the Catholic position is drawn primarily from the three types of authority I have already indicated.

His material from Aristotle is taken largely, as one
would expect, from the *Politics*. Probably Vermigli's most
striking use of that work is his adoption of Aristotle's
analysis of the types of government into six categories, according to the locus of sovereignty in each: three good types--
monarchy, aristocracy, and polity--matched by the three bad
types into which they tend to degenerate--tyranny, oligarchy,
and democracy.[8] This pattern of analysis is applied to both
the church and the state. The church, Vermigli argues, conforms closely to the classical ideal of a mixed government,
incorporating the best features of the three good types. It
is monarchic in that Christ is its King and remains its supreme legislator, even though He is in heaven. It is aristocratic in that it is ruled by "bishops, elders, doctors," and
others, chosen by merit rather than by wealth, favor, or
birth. It is popular in that some of its most important decisions, for example as to whether to excommunicate a notorious
sinner, should be "referred unto the people" (L. C. IV:5, 9).
This church, of course, is the one Vermigli believes to be the
only true church, the Reformed church. Vermigli does not insist that the secular state, on the other hand, be mixed or
conform to any one type. There are three possible models for
the state, each equally valuable, and three possible corrupt
forms, each equally dangerous. What is important to him is
that the state, however it is organized, be good (L.C. IV:13,
especially 2).

If material from Aristotle supplies much of the substance
of Vermigli's political thought, even more comes from the
Christian tradition, primarily as it is expressed in the Bible.
All of these *loci*, we must not forget, were first written as
glosses on specific verses in the Bible, and even though Vermigli could wander quite far from his text, and would occasionally go on for pages without mentioning it, he seldom forgot it completely and often analyzes it quite closely. Vermigli

furthermore followed common Protestant practice in using
Scripture to interpret Scripture. There are frequent marginal
references to other Biblical verses, in both the old and new
testaments, to support nearly every step of his argument. Discussions of political resistance theory, for example, inevitably carry a cross-reference to the verses of Romans 13, the
locus classicus of all Christian discussion of that subject.
In developing his interpretation of Scripture, furthermore,
Vermigli relies heavily on the Church Fathers, using patristic
writers as authoritative explanations of what specific verses
really mean. The particular passages from the Fathers which
he uses are often very well-known ones, clearly lifted from
the *Corpus Iuris Canonici* or some collection of that sort.
But they are sometimes not as obvious, and suggest some independent reading in the Fathers. Vermigli relies with particular frequency on St. Augustine, quoting him lavishly, usually
with approval, although occasionally in disagreement. This
should come as no surprise in a man trained as an Augustinian
religious, particularly given the fondness for Augustine displayed by most of the early Protestant Reformers. Another
Father Vermigli often quotes is St. John Chrysostom. In his
discussions of resistance theory, for example, he uses, in
company with other sixteenth-century commentators, Chrysostom's
homily number 23 on the first verses of Romans 13.

Material drawn from Aristotle and the Christian tradition
did not exhaust Vermigli's supply of documentation. He also
included material drawn from law. By this he most often meant
the Roman civil law, as codified in the *Corpus Iuris Civilis*,
particularly in the *Codex* and the *Digests*. He frequently
cited passages from these compendia, usually with considerable
precision. One law which he cites with particular frequency
and which he uses in ways I find especially intriguing, is the
Roman law of treason called the *lex Julia maiestatis*. This
law was enacted either by Julius Caesar or Augustus and defined treason as conspiracy against the life of the emperor,
libel or slander of the emperor, or adultery with a member of
the emperor's family. Two chapters containing summary statements of this law can be found in the *Corpus Iuris Civilis*, in
the *Digests*, 48:4, and in the *Codex*, 9:8. In going through
Vermigli's political *loci*, I have found at least five citations
of this law, generally drawing from both chapters. It is used
for an example of executive clemency, when Vermigli points out
that Augustus Caesar relied on its provisions to waive the
normal death penalty for treason (L. C. IV:14, 28). It is
used, along with other allegations, to establish the authority
of a prince to wage war and punish the wicked (L. C. IV:16, 2).
It is used, obviously enough, to define treason, again with
legal allegations and also patristic and classical sources

(L. C. IV:16, 29). It is again combined with other legal,
Scriptural, and classical authorities to justify the death
penalty for sedition (L. C. IV: 20, 9). And it is alluded to
in Vermigli's most important *locus* on the obligation of inferior magistrates to lead resistance to a tyrannical government
(L. C. IV:20, 13).

Vermigli also drew material from other bodies of law. He
could use allegations from the canon law of the Roman Catholic
Church in constructive ways, as well as to build straw men for
demolition. And he refers a few times to contemporary constitutional law, in ways which I find particularly interesting.
These references become really crucial, in fact, when he discusses the right of inferior magistrates to lead resistance to
tyrannical governments.

This leads me to consideration of the relative importance
of these three sources of documentation to Vermigli's political
argument. How did he measure the relative value of appeals to
classical philosophers, pre-eminently Aristotle, to the Holy
Scriptures as interpreted by the Church Fathers, and to secular law, primarily as codified by the Romans? It is tempting
to guess that he always preferred a proof drawn from Scripture.
This is very likely what he himself would have said, in common
with almost all Protestant theologians of the sixteenth century. The principle of *sola scriptura*, after all, was one of
the most fundamental of the Reformation and was held to apply
in practically every branch of thought, including politics. A
close look at Vermigli's political *loci*, however, reveals that
this obvious conclusion does not always hold. It is particularly instructive to look at passages in which he actually
balances different types of authority against each other, not
always reaching the predictable conclusion. This is especially
striking in his discussion of the resistance problem. I would
like to supply several examples. In the first Vermigli is
discussing tyrannicide as the obvious solution to the problem
of tyranny. He concedes that in ancient times pagan leaders
"appointed rewards for such as killed tyrants." But he cannot
accept this argument based on classical authority, pointing
out that "godliness and the Holy Scriptures allow not the
same," citing the usual verses from the New Testament requiring obedience even to an evil government (L. C. IV:20, 13).
In my second example Vermigli is discussing the legitimacy of
resistance to a tyrant if led by duly created inferior magistrates. He concedes at the beginning that this sort of resistance cannot be justified by an appeal to the Bible. But he
nevertheless concludes that it can indeed be justified by an
appeal to contemporary constitutional arrangements. Let me
quote his conclusion: "But thou wilt say: by what law do
inferior princes resist either the emperor, or kings, or else

public wealths [republics], when as they defend the sincere
religion and true faith? I answer by the law of the Emperor,
or by the law of the king, or by the law of the public wealth.
For they [the inferior princes] are chosen of emperors, kings,
and public wealths as helpers to rule, whereby justice may
more and more flourish. And therefore were they ordained according to the office committed unto them, rightly, justly,
and godly to govern the public wealth. Wherefore they do
according to their duty, when in cause of religion they resist
the higher power" (*Judges* 1, 36). In my final examples, Vermigli becomes even more precise and practical, naming types of
inferior magistrates who may legitimately lead resistance to a
tyrannical prince. The type he finds most persuasive is drawn
from contemporary German constitutional theory. Specifically
he argues that the Electors of the Holy Roman Empire are legally entitled to lead resistance to the Emperor. One finds
this argument in two of his political *loci*, on Romans 13 and
on Judges 3. The latter form of the argument is more extended,
is the one included in the *Loci communes,* and is the one for
which Vermigli became best known. Here is the heart of that
argument: "There be others in the commonweale, which in
place and dignity are inferior unto princes, and yet in very
deed do elect the superior power, and by certain laws do
govern the commonweale, as at this day we see done by the
Electors of the Empire, and perhaps the same is done in other
kingdoms. To these undoubtedly if the prince perform not his
covenants and promises, it is lawful to constrain and bring
him into order, and by force to compel him to perform the
conditions and covenants which he had promised, and that by
war when it cannot otherwise be done." Here we see not only a
striking statement of a theory justifying resistance by inferior magistrates, resting on an analysis of the German constitution; we also see a contract theory of resistance, reminiscent of those developed later and at more length by theorists in France and England. In the *locus* Judges 3, incidentally, Vermigli goes on to line up additional precedents for
legitimate resistance, drawn from classical Roman practice,
recent Danish practice, and medieval English practice as reported by Polydore Vergil. None of these additional precedents, however, is analyzed as fully, as confidently, and as
rigorously as the argument from the German constitution (L. C.
IV:20, 13).

These examples should make it clear, I hope, that for
Vermigli legal arguments on political questions could be decisive, superseding arguments based on appeals to Scripture.
There remains the problem of explaining how Vermigli came by
his knowledge of law and his respect for its authority. It is
becoming increasingly obvious to American specialists that the
law and its study were of pervasive importance during the

Reformation. William Bouwsma has demonstrated the importance of lawyers in European society throughout the early modern period.[9] Donald Kelley has demonstrated the importance of legal thought in the rise of modern historiography during the sixteenth century.[10] Ralph Giesey and his students have demonstrated the importance of legal principles in political thought of the period, particularly thought on the problem of resistance.[11] The importance of legal training in forming several of the most prominent intellectual leaders of the Protestant movement has been known for some time. Martin Luther was beginning a course of study in law when he decided to transfer to theology and become a monk. John Calvin finished a course of study in law and later used his legal talents to draft ordinances for the city of Geneva. Theodore Beza, Calvin's chief assistant and successor, was also trained as a lawyer. None of these theologians trained as lawyers, however, retained great respect for the authority of the law. Luther and Calvin both tended to insist that the law must conform to Scripture and that only holy writ could have ultimate authority in human argumentation. Vermigli agreed. But how did he occasionally come to a different conclusion?

Vermigli's position is a particular surprise in view of the fact that he, unlike Luther, Calvin, and Beza, had not received formal training in the law. In fact it remains something of a mystery to me where Vermigli did acquire both his considerable knowledge of law, particularly as it is revealed in his precise citations of the Roman civil law, and his considerable respect for the authority of the law. From the posthumous biography drafted by his friend Simler, in consultation with Vermigli's personal secretary, we know something of his early studies in Italy.[12] At Padua he studied both philosophy, of the Aristotelian type then favored there, and theology, primarily as systematized by Thomas Aquinas and Gregory of Rimini.[13] Although the biography does not mention this, I think it likely that he learned the canon law as a part of his course of study in theology. The biography also reveals that he made informal arrangements outside the curriculum to learn ancient languages, Greek in Padua, Hebrew in Bologna. It says nothing, however, about any study of civil law. Bologna, to be sure, was an important center for the study of both laws. Conceivably Vermigli first began reading law there.

My own theory, however, is that Vermigli taught himself law in Strasbourg, during his second stay there, from 1553 to 1556. I can find no decisive evidence for this theory, but a number of facts point me in this direction. The most extended and the most sophisticated of the political *loci* of Vermigli come from his commentary on the book of Judges. That includes both the most important of those included in the *Common Places* and a number that were left out. This commentary on Judges was based on lectures delivered in Strasbourg between 1553 and 1556, prepared for publication by Vermigli himself in 1561, after he moved to Zurich.[14] His choice of Judges as a subject for commentary marked a departure from his practice at Oxford which had been to focus on the books of the New Testament which were general favorites of the Protestant Reformers, particularly on Pauline epistles such as the ones to Romans and Corinthians. This choice was dictated in part by the curricular needs of the Strasbourg Gymnasium in which Vermigli was teaching. It needed a professor of Old Testament and had asked him to lecture on its books during his earlier stay in the city. The Gymnasium now wanted him to return to this subject matter. This does not explain, however, why Vermigli chose Judges from among the books of the Old Testament for his commentary in 1553. I suspect that this choice may have been suggested in part by the political situation in which Vermigli found himself teaching. The book of Judges lends itself much more than most parts of the Bible to reflection on political problems, since so much of it recounts the history of the tribes in Israel during a period of political turmoil when there was considerable debate about the appropriate form of government for the community. And there were many within Strasbourg, among Vermigli's students and colleagues, who were unusually concerned about political matters in 1553. Local citizens were concerned about the politics of the Holy Roman Empire, of which the city was a member, as a free imperial city. Strasbourg was then still recovering from the attempts of the imperial government to force upon all of Germany the compromise settlement knows as the Interim. The city was soon to benefit from the efforts of resisting princes when a new Emperor granted full toleration of established Lutheran churches in the Religious Peace of Augsburg in 1555. In Strasbourg Vermigli was surrounded, furthermore, by exiles from other countries determined to promote resistance at home. A number of his English students and friends had followed him from Oxford, and were busily conspiring to overthrow the Catholic government of Mary Tudor, justified and rationalized by the tracts of men like John Ponet. A number of French scholars, increasingly upset with the French crown's repression of Protestantism, also joined Vermigli's circle in Strasbourg. The best known of them is Francois Hotman, who was later to develop in his *Franco-Gallia* one of the sixteenth-century's most influential appeals for political resistance to a tyrannical government.[15]

At about the time Vermigli began lecturing in Strasbourg on Judges, we know that he obtained a number of law books.

After he died, his entire library was offered to Geneva, to establish the initial core of the library of its new Academy. Most of Vermigli's books which were sent to Geneva are still there, in the rare book collections of the *Bibliothèque publique et universitaire,* and have been examined recently by several scholars. Among these books are a copy of the Justinian *Codex* published in Paris in 1550 and a copy of the *Digests* also published in Paris, 1548-1550, both containing marginal annotations in Vermigli's own hand.[16] The dates and place of publication of these books suggest that he obtained them on his return to Strasbourg in 1553. It seems to me quite probable that he obtained them for use in his lectures on Judges.

We also know that Vermigli was associated with a number of prominent legal scholars in Strasbourg during these years. Among his colleagues at the Gymnasium were the irenic French Protestant François Baudouin and the militant French Calvinist François Hotman, who were named successively to the chair of law there in 1555 and 1556. More important for the shaping of Vermigli's thought, I suspect, was yet another colleague, the historian Johann Sleidan. Sleidan was also trained as a lawyer, in Orleans, in the same faculty where Calvin and Beza studied. He then became a diplomat, accepting a number of assignments in both France and Germany, following closely the development of religious policy in the period of tension between the Schmalkaldic League and the imperial government. He spent the last years of his life in Strasbourg, on diplomatic assignments for the city government and writing an extended history of Germany under Charles V. These years coincided closely with Vermigli's second stay in the city. Vermigli's biography reports briefly that Sleidan was one of the friends who welcomed him back to Strasbourg in 1553.[17] Sleidan's *History* includes towards its end a sympathetic account of Vermigli's departure from Strasbourg, under pressure from militant Lutherans.[18] Those same militants apparently also provoked Sleidan to leave the city, only a few months before the publication of his masterwork and his death.

Finally, although Sleidan's *History* is never cited in Vermigli's political *loci,* on at least one crucial question I see the strong possibility of its direct influence on his thought. Sleidan was fascinated by the development of Lutheran resistance to the imperial government. He describes it in considerable detail in his *History*, inserting the texts of relevant documents in support of his account. He follows the development within the Saxon chancery of the argument that the Electors, of course including the Elector of Saxony, choose the emperor and choose him conditionally, stipulating that he must abide by certain rules and maintain certain rights. This

argument was then used to support the claim that Charles V had
violated the conditions of his election by seeking to force
Saxony to return to Roman Catholicism, and that this violation
made it possible for the Elector to lead armed resistance to
the imperial government. Sleidan even describes the dramatic
meeting at Torgau in 1530, when Luther himself had been persuaded to accept this argument. Until this time, Luther had
always insisted that the Bible, in particular Romans 13, made
any resistance to legitimate government impossible. He
specifically included within this prohibition resistance by
inferior magistrates. The Christian oppressed by a tyrant,
according to Luther, can only pray for divine deliverance,
accepting martyrdom if that be necessary. Armed resistance is
never justified. At Torgau Luther listened to the arguments
of lawyers who held that the German constitution permitted
resistance in certain circumstances, if led by an Elector. He
finally agreed to sign a memorandum conceding that in these
circumstances the rules drawn from the Bible did not apply
and that statesmen would have to decide on legal grounds
whether or not resistance was justified.[19]

In his *loci* on resistance, Vermigli in effect adopts the
position of the Saxon lawyers, illustrating the point with the
example of the Electors of the Holy Roman Empire. He concedes,
like Luther, that the New Testament does not allow any sort of
armed resistance to a legitimate government. But he argues
that this prohibition does not apply in states whose laws,
like those of the Holy Roman Empire, permit resistance if led
by duly constituted inferior magistrates. This position was
first stated by Vermigli in a rather rough and tentative way
in his commentary on Romans, based on lectures he delivered
at Oxford shortly before returning to Strasbourg, but published
in a version he prepared himself after he settled in Zurich.[20]
It was elaborated, refined, and stated several times in his
commentary on Judges, delivered in Strasbourg while he was in
touch with Sleidan, although again published only after he
settled in Zurich.[21] It is my contention that the influence
of Sleidan is quite probable on the argument as developed in
the Judges commentary, and even possible on the argument as
developed in the Romans commentary.

My main conclusion, then, is that human law, as codified
by the Romans and as further described by contemporary custom
lawyers, fills a function of critical importance in the political thought of Peter Martyr Vermigli. It is my further conclusion that Vermigli probably learned to appreciate and use
arguments drawn from law in Strasbourg, between 1553 and 1556,
perhaps from Johann Sleidan.

NOTES

* This is a revised version of a paper first read at the spring meeting of the American Society for Reformation Research, held as a part of the Fourteenth International Congress on Medieval Studies at Western Michigan University, Kalamazoo, May 6, 1978. It is a sequel to a paper, "The Political Thought of Peter Martyr Vermigli," hereafter cited as Kingdon, "Political Thought," prepared for a conference on Vermigli and the cultural impact of Italian Reformers organized at McGill University by Joseph C. McLelland, September 27-30, 1977, and scheduled for publication in a symposium volume of papers read at that conference.

1. John T. McNeill, ed., *Calvin: Institutes of the Christian Religion*, vols. 20 and 21 in *The Library of Christian Classics* (Philadelphia, Westminster, 1960), I, xlviii; II, 1526, 1628-1632. See also the publisher's letter to the reader in S. T. C. 4414, the 1576 Vautrollier edition of Calvin's *Institutio*.

2. Joseph C. McLelland, *The Visible Words of God: An Exposition of the Sacramental Theology of Peter Martyr Vermigli, A.D. 1500-1562* (Grand Rapids, Michigan: Eerdmans, 1957), pp. 278-281.

3. Marvin W. Anderson, "Royal Idolatry: Peter Martyr and the Reformed Tradition," *Archive for Reformation History*, 69(1978), 157-201, hereafter cited as Anderson, "Royal Idolatry," provides an admirably detailed introduction to Vermigli's writings on politics, based on his exceptionally complete knowledge of the entire corpus of Vermigli's work. I am indebted to Professor Anderson for providing me with an advance copy of this article. My own conclusions are based on an independent reading of Vermigli's political writings.

4. In Robert Stupperich, ed., *Melanchthons Werke in Auswahl*, see vol. 2/1-2 (Gütersloh: Bertelsmann, 1952-1953), Hans Engelland, ed., *Loci communes von 1521*, pp. 158-161, "De magistratibus," and *Loci praecipui theologici von 1559*, pp. 689-732, "De Magistratibus civilibus et dignitate rerum politicarum."

5. See the fine critical edition of Jean-Daniel Benoît, *Jean Calvin: Institution de la Religion Chrestienne* (Paris: Vrin, 1957-1963), 5 vols., especially vol. IV.

6. In preparing this paper, I used microfilm copies of the *Loci communes* in Latin of 1583 (S. T. C. 24668), hereafter cited as L. C.; the *Common Places* in English of 1583 (S. T. C. 24669); the *Romans* commentary in English of 1568 (S. T. C. 24672); the *Judges* commentary in English of 1564 (S. T. C. 24670)--all published in London. I have also used a copy of the *Judges* commentary in Latin of 1571, published in Zurich. References to L. C. are to chapter and section numbers in the Latin text, Part IV. Occasionally I have added variant numberings from the English text in parenthesis. References to the commentaries are to the Bible verses glossed. My quotations are from the sixteenth-century English translations, with spelling and punctuation modernized. I have prepared a critical edition with commentary of many of these texts: Robert M. Kingdon, *The Political Thought of Peter Martyr Vermigli* (Geneva: Droz, 1980).

7. By Anderson, "Royal Idolatry," *passim*, e.g. pp. 190-191, and by Kingdon, "Political Thought."

8. Aristotle, *Politics*, III, v.i-iv.

9. William J. Bouwsma, "Lawyers and Early Modern Culture," *The American Historical Review*, 78 (1973), 303-327.

10. Donald R. Kelley, *Foundations of Modern Historical Scholarship: Language, Law, and History in the French Renaissance* (New York and London: Columbia, 1970).

11. See, *inter alia*, Ralph E. Giesey, "The Monarchomach Triumvirs: Hotman, Beza, and Mornay," *Bibliotheque d'Humanisme et Renaissance*, 32 (1970), 41-56. See also the dissertations and articles of Richard R. Benert, Lawrence M. Bryant, William F. Freegard, Richard A. Jackson, and Sarah H. Madden.

12. *Oratio de vita et obitu. . .Vermilii. . .Iosia Simlero*, in unpaginated forematter to L. C. and in unpaginated appendixes to the English translation, hereafter cited as Simler, *Oratio*.

13. See the extended commentary on his studies at Padua in Philip McNair, *Peter Vermigli in Italy: An Anatomy of Apostasy* (Oxford: Clarendon, 1967), chapter IV, pp. 86-115.

14. Simler, *Oratio*.

15. On Vermigli's second stay in Strasbourg, see Marvin Walter Anderson, *Peter Martyr, a Reformer in Exile (1542-1562)* (Nieuwkoop: de Graaf, 1975), chapter IV, pp. 161-209, hereafter cited as Anderson, *Martyr*.

16. Alexandre Ganoczy, *La Bibliothèque de l'Académie de Calvin* (Geneva: Droz, 1969), items 341 and 342. See also John Patrick Donnelly, *Calvinism and Scholasticism in Vermigli's Doctrine of Man and Grace* (Leiden: Brill, 1976), pp. 208-217, an appendix which reconstitutes Vermigli's library from Ganoczy and other sources, especially p. 217 for Vermigli's law books.

17. Simler, *Oratio*. On Sleidan's career, see the biographical article in the Herzog-Plitt-Hauck *Real-Encyklopädie für protestantische Theologie und Kirche*.

18. Quoted in Anderson, *Martyr*, p. 379.

19. Johann Sleidan, *De statu religionis et reipublicae Carolo V. caesare, commentarii* (Geneva: Badius, 1559), and other editions in several languages. On the Torgau episode, see lib. 8, fol. 119v. For the text of the Torgau memorandum and some commentary, see the Weimar edition of Luther's *Werke* (1883--), *Briefwechsel*, V, 661-664. For a useful survey of the copious literature on Luther's ideas on resistance, see W. D. J. Cargill Thompson, "Luther and the Right of Resistance to the Emperor," in Derek Baker, ed., *Church, Society and Politics*, vol. 12 in *Studies in Church History* (Oxford: Blackwell, 1975), pp. 159-202.

20. Vermigli's commentary on *Romans* 13:3, "For rulers are not a terror to good works, but to the evil."

21. Vermigli's last *locus* on *Judges* 3:29-30, included in L. C. IV:20, 12-13.

XVII

Patronage, Piety, and Printing in Sixteenth-Century Europe*

Scholars have devoted much study to early printers as technicians, as humanists, and as agents of propaganda. They have devoted comparatively little to early printers as businessmen.[1] Yet they were, of necessity, men of business and occasionally ones of considerable astuteness and vision. Surviving records of their business activities are not as complete as one might wish. Some can be found, however, and they merit more intensive and more technical study than they have yet received. Two sets of these records have attracted my own attention: one scattered among the manuscript collections of the State Archives of Geneva, Switzerland, the other in the Plantin-Moretus Museum of Antwerp, Belgium. The collections in Geneva include notaries' copies of contracts and the minutes of judicial sessions of city councils relating to the affairs of a number of local printers. Of these Genevan printers, two interested me particularly: Henri Estienne, the great publisher of humanist texts, and his brother François. The museum in Antwerp preserves the actual account

* This essay is a revised version of one I read to the Humanities Society of the State University of Iowa in 1958. I thought it appropriate to this volume, because of Mr. Artz's interest in early books and their printers, an interest which helped stimulate my own first work on this subject. Part of the research upon which this essay is based was made possible by a grant from the Penrose Fund of the American Philosophical Society.

1. Among the more important exceptions to this rule are the suggestive synthetic study of Lucien Febvre and Henri-Jean Martin, *L'apparition du livre* (Paris, 1958), and the technical articles of Raymond and Florence de Roover on the business operations of Christopher Plantin: Raymond de Roover, "The Business Organization of the Plantin Press in the Setting of Sixteenth Century Antwerp," *Gedenkboek der Plantin-Dagen, 1555-1955* (Antwerp, 1956), pp. 230-46 (volume hereinafter cited as *Plantin Gedenkboek*); Florence Edler [de Roover], "Cost Accounting in the Sixteenth Century: The Books of Account of Christopher Plantin, Antwerp, Printer and Publisher," *Accounting Review*, XII (1937), 226-37.

books and the business correspondence of Christopher Plantin, who operated what was probably the largest publishing business of the time.[2] Comparison of the business operations of several small-scale printers of Calvinist Geneva with those of a single large-scale printer of Catholic Antwerp suggests to me several interesting generalizations. They concern certain relations among patronage, piety, and the printing industry.

Many, perhaps most, of the really well-known printers of the early modern period depended on patronage. The most generous patrons available were kings and princes. The Estienne firm secured its significant contemporary reputation with materials the purchase of which was financed by subsidies from the kings of France. The link between the two was first made strong during the career of Robert Estienne the elder, father of the Henri Estienne upon whose activities we shall focus.[3] Robert had won subsidies for his publishing house in Paris from King Francis I, who was particularly interested in encouraging the new humanistically oriented classical scholarship inspired by the Renaissance in Italy. He used these grants to commission the manufacture of some of the finest types the world has ever seen, not only fine Latin types, but also Greek and Hebrew ones. One of his most important uses of these materials, however, got him into serious trouble. An edition of the Bible which he published with his own annotations aroused the fury of the members of the Sorbonne faculty, the intellectual guardians of the Catholic orthodoxy of that day. Their persecution goaded Robert Estienne into giving free rein to certain of his own growing religious inclinations. He turned Protestant and fled to Calvin's Geneva, successfully smuggling much of his invaluable equipment along with

2. The standard study of the Estiennes is Ant. Aug. Renouard, *Annales de l'imprimerie des Estienne* (2nd ed., 2 vols.; Paris, 1843; recently reprinted without date by Burt Franklin, New York). The standard study of Plantin is Max Rooses, *Christophe Plantin: imprimeur anversois* (Antwerp, 1883). Both have been supplemented but not replaced by more recent studies cited below. Another important source of information on Plantin is the *Correspondance de Christophe Plantin*, ed. Max Rooses and J. Denucé (9 vols.; Antwerp and other cities, 1883-1918), and M. van Durme, *Supplément à la correspondance de Christophe Plantin* (Antwerp, 1955). Hereinafter cited as Renouard, *Estiennes*; Rooses, *Plantin*; Plantin, *Corr.*

3. Elizabeth Armstrong, *Robert Estienne, Royal Printer: An Historical Study of the Elder Stephanus* (Cambridge, 1954), provides the most complete scholarly study of his career.

him. This decision robbed Estienne of his patron, but he was well enough established by now to carry on his business without much difficulty until his death in 1559.

His son Henri, however, did have to face the patronage problem. Henri Estienne had been superbly educated and was even more of a scholar than his father. His contributions to the editing and analysis of Greek texts still demand scholarly attention. The fact that he published so many works of erudition, however, and published them in provincial Geneva, made his financial problems even more difficult than those of his father. The city possessed no one with wealth and interest enough to become the patron required by the needs of Henri Estienne's business. He could not, furthermore, leave Geneva. His father's printing equipment had been willed to him on condition that he never move it from that city. If he ever did decide to violate this condition, the equipment would revert to the city government for use in ways that would support municipal charities. The pious deacons and councilors of Geneva were constantly on the watch to see to it that Estienne did not try to move anything out of town. More than once he was called before governmental councils and forced to submit to exhaustive questioning on rumors that he had planned to leave the city.[4]

Fortunately for scholarship, Henri Estienne did find patrons willing to subsidize his publishing business, even though it remained in Geneva. Two of them were especially important: Ulrich Fugger and King Henry III of France.

Ulrich Fugger of Augsburg, the only member of that fabulously wealthy family of international financiers to develop Protestant leanings, had decided to collect a library that would contain the best examples of every author, every subject, and every language. To house this library, he arranged to purchase one of the finest houses in the city of Geneva, for the very large sum of 2000 écus. To fill this library and to secure for it personal parchment editions of works he particularly treasured, Fugger contracted with Henri Estienne to become "his printer." This

4. For a more detailed and documented account of these quarrels, see Robert M. Kingdon, "The Business Activities of Printers Henri and François Estienne," *Aspects de la propagande religieuse* (Geneva, 1957), pp. 258-75; hereinafter cited as Kingdon, "Estiennes."

agreement was reached in 1558, even before the death of Estienne's father. It provided that Estienne was to receive an annual stipend of 300 livres outright, supplies of parchment, and a loan of 1500 livres at a rate of interest not specified. In return Fugger was to receive one copy in parchment of every book printed by Estienne. To see to it that Estienne kept his part of the bargain, Fugger sent to Geneva a personal agent—Henry Scringer, a noted Scottish humanist and lawyer.[5]

Fugger's patronage provided the financial basis for much of Estienne's most important work. Unfortunately it lasted only a decade. Relatives of Ulrich Fugger, motivated perhaps by alarm at his heavy expenses, perhaps by jealousy, perhaps by religious orthodoxy, soon secured a court order restraining him from spending money for cultural purposes. By 1568 the Fugger subsidies had stopped. Estienne spent much of the rest of his life trying to regain them. He seems finally to have reached some sort of agreement with Fugger's heirs, but only toward the end of his life, too late to do him any good.

Estienne, meanwhile, had turned to a grandson of the patron who had made his father's reputation—to Henry III. The king was a decadent and frivolous man who lacked the religious fanaticism that dominated so many of his contemporaries. This made it possible for a Protestant like Estienne to visit the royal court. In doing so he succeeded in impressing or at least amusing the king, who, in 1579, agreed to grant him an annual pension of 300 livres, to be paid through the royal ambassador to the Swiss Leagues. The king also promised Estienne a special grant of 100 écus, but this the printer never did collect because he unwisely neglected to bribe a corrupt royal treasurer.

Christopher Plantin managed to tap an even richer vein than did Henri Estienne. His principal patron was Philip II, King of Spain and also ruler of a vast empire including all of what is today the Netherlands and Belgium, much of present-day Italy,

---

5. For more on the Fugger patronage of Henri Estienne, see Kingdon, "Estiennes," and sources therein cited; also Paul Lehmann, *Eine Geschichte der alten Fuggerbibliotheken* (2 vols.; Tubingen, 1956-1960), *passim*.; E.-H. Kaden, "Ulrich Fugger et son projet de créer à Genève une 'librairie' publique," *Geneva*, N.S. VII (1959), 127-36 (valuable for texts appended to it); Henri Delarue, "A propos du différend Ulrich Fugger-Henri Estienne en 1561," *Mélanges offerts à M. Paul-E. Martin* (Geneva, 1961), pp. 497-502.

parts of France, and a good deal of Latin America. Plantin insinuated his way into the king's graces with the help of two friends, both of whom came to hold key positions at the royal court. One was Antoine Perrenot de Granvelle, Bishop of Arras, Cardinal of the Roman Catholic Church, who became Philip's regent for the Low Countries, then his ambassador in Italy, finally his first minister.[6] The other was Gabriel de Zayas, one of the royal secretaries—not the most important of them, he was too lazy for that—but the one who managed to stay in favor the longest. Both had known Plantin when he was still a minor bookbinder and then a one-press printer in Antwerp. He had filled special commissions for each, and must have made a favorable impression on both.[7]

The project with which Plantin and his friends won the attention of the Spanish court was a proposal to publish a new polyglot Bible.[8] The Complutensian Polyglot of Alcala, a multilingual text of the Bible in Latin and the original languages of Greek and Hebrew, prepared by a group of scholars under the organizational direction of Cardinal Cisneros de Ximenez, had long since gone out of print. Scholarly interest in the text of the Bible had, however, grown with the controversies rising out of the Reformation. Plantin, therefore, proposed to produce a revised and improved version of this pioneer work. For such a project he needed subsidies. To be executed properly it required the assistance of a group of scholars with competence in Latin, Greek, and Hebrew. It required fonts of type in each of those languages. It required access to the best available Biblical manuscripts, many of them in the custody of the Vatican. To complicate matters further, Plantin proposed the addition of a "Chaldean" or Aramaic text wherever one was available. All these factors necessitated an enormous initial expense. The return could not be expected to be great, since the Polyglot would be

6. On Granvelle's patronage of Plantin, see the studies of M. van Durme, e.g., "Granvelle et Plantin," *Estudios dedicados a Menendez Pidal,* VII (Madrid, 1957), 225-72.

7. On Zayas' early relations with Plantin, see the document published in Rooses' *Plantin,* pp. 392-93, and *passim.* Other aspects of their relationship are illuminated by the many letters between them published in Plantin, *Corr.*

8. For a good recent discussion of this project, see Colin Clair, *Christopher Plantin* (London, 1960), chap. iv, pp. 57-86. Hereinafter cited as Clair, *Plantin.*

of use only to scholars with competence in the several Biblical languages.

In 1566 Plantin ran off a few sample proofs of his proposed Polyglot and took them to the internationally famous Frankfort Book Fair to sound out the market. Several German noblemen reportedly expressed considerable interest in subsidizing the project. Meanwhile, however, Plantin had written to friend Zayas in Spain. Zayas persuaded his royal master to follow the glorious example of his predecessors in subsidizing Biblical scholarship, in the process overcoming the suspicion of some of the more conservative Spanish religious—that editions of this sort undermined orthodoxy. Philip II agreed to grant subsidies large enough to cover all the expenses of the project. As in all the enterprises that attracted his attention, he insisted on close supervision. To effect this, he sent to Antwerp a learned Spanish doctor, B. Arias Montanus, to work with Plantin in directing the project. Plantin welcomed Montanus into his home, wined and dined him, became his bosom friend, and won another useful contact with the Spanish crown.

The Polyglot Bible was not a commercial success. Plantin published only 1200 copies for general sale, and he never did sell them all. Some remained in the stocks of his books inventoried after his death. But the book nevertheless made his reputation. It was a scholarly and artistic triumph. It confirmed Philip II in his initial high opinion of Plantin's abilities, and led to the establishment of a continuing and profitable connection between the two. The king awarded Plantin several large printing commissions. He also appointed Plantin to the newly created post of "Proto-typographer," a royal agent charged with supervising the printing industry throughout the Low Countries. Plantin or assistants he selected were to investigate the competence and religious orthodoxy of every printer working in that area. Each printer was required to submit affidavits from ecclesiastics who could testify to his piety and orthodoxy, and from magistrates who could testify to the soundness of his moral reputation. Plantin himself was responsible for testing each man's technical competence and knowledge of languages. This measure obviously served the double purpose of enforcing standards of competence and religious conformity. It also placed Plantin in a position of power that could not be challenged by any of his business rivals.[9]

With this new office Plantin also won the right to publish proclamations, both of the king and of local governmental and ecclesiastical authorities. For example, when Philip II decided to circulate a version of the new Index of Prohibited Books suggested by the Council of Trent, Plantin was given the job of printing and distributing copies throughout the Low Countries.

These prosperous relations between Plantin and his sovereign were rudely interrupted by the turn of political events in the area, in particular by the horrifying sack of Antwerp in 1576, commonly called the Spanish Fury. Plantin later bitterly accused the king of failing to honor his agreements.[10] While it is clear that the volume of printing Plantin did for the king fell off after 1576, there is reason to suspect that this accusation was not entirely sincere. It was released to the public at a time when Plantin was keeping some of his presses running by accepting commissions from heretic Dutch Calvinists, thus scandalizing all good Catholics. He had even done work for the Estates-General of the Northern Provinces, the institution then in nominal charge of the full-fledged revolt against the authority of Philip II.

Even Plantin's accusations and Spanish suspicions about his devotion to orthodoxy could not dissolve the connection between the Spanish crown and the Plantin firm. His heirs established ever more cordial relations with the successors to Philip II, and orders continued to pour into Antwerp. The Plantin press maintained its respectable prosperity for centuries following, down practically until the time the steam press and the linotype machine rendered its equipment hopelessly archaic.

These capsule accounts of the search by Estienne and Plantin for patrons should suggest the extent to which a large-scale, successful, sixteenth-century printer had to become a politician. Expanded versions of these accounts would make it even more obvious that complicated and devious intrigues were necessary

9. Plantin as king's proto-typographer see Clair, *Plantin*, chap. vi, pp. 105-12.

10. In a public letter issued from Leiden in 1583, published in Rooses, *Plantin*, pp. 410-17.

forerunners to the substantial wealth and international reputa-
tions these men acquired. Research into the careers of other
printers might well confirm this pattern. In this connection, study
of the Aldine press of Venice, which with the Estienne press and
the Plantin press is often reputed to be one of the three greatest
of the century, would probably prove particularly interesting.
For a time at least, this press gained much of its working capital
from the papacy. Paul Manutius, the second of the Aldines and
the one contemporary to the men we have studied, moved his
operations for a while to Rome, where he could work more closely with the great reforming popes who were his patrons.[11]

The second main generalization I want to advance is even
broader. It can be applied, I believe, to almost all the printers
of the sixteenth century, not just to the well-known and powerful. It deals with the relation between printing and religion.
This relation seems to me to be a close one, and one of great
importance to both. I would even go so far as to suggest that
the rise of a printing industry in the West with all its enormous
consequences in creating mass literacy, mass education, mass
government, and mass participation in a highly organized economy, is a consequence of certain peculiarities in the Christian
religion that have dominated the Western ethos. Christianity has
long been distinguished by the peculiar importance it places on
written Scripture as an ultimate source of truth—hence a persistent demand for many copies of the Bible and of devotional
books based wholly or partly on the Bible, such as the breviary
and the psalter. This demand may well have stimulated Gutenberg's crucial invention of movable type. The book that is generally held to have earned him the reputation of founder of the
printing industry was, after all, a Bible. This demand, furthermore, would logically have been tremendously increased by intellectual developments during the late fifteenth and the early
sixteenth centuries. First many scholars of the Renaissance, then
the religious leaders of the Reformation, renewed and strengthened the Christian emphasis on the importance of Scripture.

11. Ant. Aug. Renouard, *Annales de l'imprimerie des Alde* (3rd ed.; Paris,
1834; reprinted Bologna, 1953), especially pp. 442-50 for Manutius' arrangements with the papacy.

These religious leaders, in addition, stimulated a continuing demand for versions of the Scripture in the vernacular languages. All these developments may well account for the impressive growth of the printing and publishing industry in the course of the sixteenth century.[12]

The straws in the wind pointing me toward these conclusions are fragmentary statistics of the number of copies in sixteenth-century editions. By modern commercial standards these editions were quite small. An average edition for Plantin consisted of 1250 to 1500 copies. Books that were popular or widely used he might publish in editions of 2500 copies, as he did, for example, with his Virgil. Books that were costly or of limited interest he published in smaller editions of a few hundred copies. And Plantin was one of the giants of the industry. This state of affairs is hardly surprising, given the relatively primitive state of printing technology, the relatively small size of the literate public, and the high cost of some of the raw materials that went into books. Paper in particular was very expensive. The stocks of paper for a book would sometimes cost twice as much as the money wages for all the men engaged in composing and printing it.[13]

I have found, however, three great exceptions to these general rules on edition size, one in Geneva, two in Antwerp. All were of books strikingly alike. They were the Huguenot psalter, which was published by a syndicate of printers in Geneva and various other cities, and the Roman missal and Roman breviary, whose publication was superintended from Rome but engrossed for the Spanish Hapsburg domains by Plantin. Let me dwell on two— the Huguenot psalter and the Roman breviary. (Arrangements for the publication and distribution of the Roman missal were almost identical to those for the breviary.)

A vernacular psalter was an essential for practically every literate member of the Protestant congregations being formed all over Europe in the course of the sixteenth century. The singing

12. Cf. the somewhat different but not necessarily incompatible theories on printing and intellectual developments advanced by Walter J. Ong, S.J., in his *Ramus, Method and the Decay of Dialogue* (Cambridge, Mass., 1958), pp. 307-14, and in several of his recent articles.

13. For sample figures of edition sizes and printing costs, see de Roover in *Plantin Gedenkboek*, pp. 235-36.

of the Psalms by laymen and clergy together, in their native tongue, was a part of the service of divine worship which the Reformers believed to be recommended by the Bible itself. Among French-speaking Protestants, the psalter which became most popular was based on translations prepared by the poet Clément Marot and the powerful Calvinist minister Theodore Beza, set to music by Louis Bourgeois and others.[14] Versions, translations, and excerpts of it still provide an important guide to worship for Protestants of the Calvinist tradition all over the world.

The largest early editions of this psalter were prepared in 1561-62, the years of partial toleration of Protestantism in France that made possible the peak of the Calvinist campaign to reform Christianity in that country. Arrangements for their printing were supervised by author Beza, who during this period spent most of his time away from his regular charge in Geneva, guiding the formation both of the Reformed Church of France and of the Huguenot party. For technical help, Beza turned to Antoine Vincent, a prosperous Calvinist printer and publisher, whose business centered in Lyons, but who spent much of his time superintending the operations of a branch in Geneva. Vincent and his son undertook to arrange the publication of the Huguenot psalter by a multitude of printers in many of the cities serving the French market. Eight per cent of the costs of these editions was to be turned over to charitable work, either directly or through the Vincents. This 8 per cent was regarded as an author's right, and may thus have been one of the first percentage royalties in history, even though based on cost of production rather than on sales. The essence of these arrangements was confirmed by a royal "privilege" or copyright, granted for ten years by the King of France, late in 1561. Several months later Vincent licensed more than a dozen printers of Paris to proceed with the production of these psalters—this in the city which was not only the political capital of France but also the historic intellectual center of religious orthodoxy in western Christendom. Soon

14. For a comprehensive study of this subject, see O. Douen, *Clément Marot et le psautier huguenot* (2 vols.; Paris, 1878-1879). The whole subject is now being reworked by Pierre Pidoux of Territet, Switzerland.

afterward, Vincent concluded a licensing agreement with an Orleans printer. It is obvious that he also concluded similar agreements with printers in Lyons and Geneva. Apparently he even recruited Plantin for his syndicate. In 1564 Plantin, still a relatively unknown Antwerp printer without any royal connections, obtained a four-year local "privilege" from the regent of the Low Countries for the printing of this psalter. Other printers in other cities also entered the syndicate.[15]

Information on actual production of these Huguenot psalters is difficult to find. There seem to be no Protestant printers' records as complete as those of Plantin. Scattered records in Geneva, however, make it clear that the printing of the psalter in that city was handled by a local syndicate. When its members squabbled among themselves, a newly established municipal regulatory commission, charged with many of the same responsibilities for protecting orthodoxy and technical competence that Plantin was to exercise as royal "Proto-typographer," stepped in to bring order to local arrangements. The commission allocated quantities of psalters among competing printers, fixed common prices, and regulated the quality of printing and paper used in the books. Printers not meeting minimum standards of quality were forced to cut back operations, and in some cases were driven entirely out of business.

The records of this dispute reveal that during the peak years of 1561 and 1562, the Genevan members of this syndicate produced 27,400 copies of the Huguenot psalter. Of this total, 10,800 copies were produced in a second set of editions allocated by the printing commission.[16] Since this total of 27,400 copies was only a fraction of the entire number published, obviously the total of all these editions must have been really immense for the period. It seems entirely possible that members of Vincent's syndicate ran off more than 100,000 psalters altogether.

Information on distribution of these Huguenot psalters is also

---

15. On all these arrangements, see E. Droz, "Antoine Vincent: la propagande protestante par le psautier," *Aspects de la propagande religieuse,* pp. 276-93.

16. For more information on these figures, see Robert M. Kingdon, *Geneva and the Coming of the Wars of Religion in France, 1555-1563* (Geneva, 1956), p. 100. On Genevan printing during this period in general, see Paul Chaix, *Recherches sur l'imprimerie à Genève de 1550 à 1564* (Geneva, 1954); hereinafter cited as Chaix, *Recherches.*

difficult to find. Many of the Genevan printers, notably Henri Estienne, regularly attended the international book fairs in Frankfort. But they seem to have looked to Frankfort primarily as an outlet for their classical and scholarly books. Wholesale booksellers clearly did distribute tremendous quantities of books. The most important of them seems to have been Laurent de Normandie, a French emigrant who established his business in Geneva. He must have arranged for distribution of a good part of the psalters published in that city. The inventory of his property prepared following his sudden death in 1569 has recently been uncovered and published.[17] It reveals that De Normandie carried several thousand copies of this psalter in a stock of almost 35,000 volumes. These and other records make it clear that itinerant book peddlers called "colporteurs" handled much of the actual retail distribution of the Huguenot psalters.

The size of the market for psalters had many interesting economic consequences for the printing industry. One of the more striking can be found in a number of contracts drafted for François Estienne, a poor younger brother of Henri Estienne, who was also a master printer in Geneva.[18] François never was able to tap the rich patronage that financed his brother's operations. In fact, he does not seem to have had much money or capital of any kind. Henri tried to transfer some of his equipment to François, but the Geneva Council, at the urging of Fugger's agents, blocked this transfer, for fear it was a trick to evade the paternal will, which required that all the Estienne property remain in Geneva. François, therefore, had to depend on his own resources. He managed to finance his operations by using stocks of testaments and psalters which he had already printed or was planning to print, as collateral to obtain loans and stocks of paper. This expedient kept him going for about ten years. Then his business failed and he left Geneva. Of all the books he published he normally used only the testaments and psalters as collateral. Apparently only they commanded a market wide and steady enough to persuade other businessmen to extend him

17. By Heidi-Lucie Schlaepfer, in pp. 184-230 of her "Laurent de Normandie," *Aspects de la propagande religieuse*, pp. 176-230.
18. See Kingdon, "Estiennes," *passim*.

necessary credit. If it can be demonstrated that this method of carrying on business was widespread, it would surely be obvious that most of the printing industry depended on religious staples. The average small printer, who could not make the contacts that won wealthy patrons, must often have been obliged to print or obtain stocks of a popular religious book in order to keep the rest of the business going.

The approximate Catholic equivalents to the Protestant psalter are the breviary and the missal. The breviary is perhaps the closer equivalent since its heart is the Psalms of the Old Testament. Its use is perhaps more limited, since it is normally used only by priests, only rarely by laymen. On the other hand, its use is almost certainly more intensive, since every priest in those days was normally expected, and is nowadays obliged, to use a breviary for the saying of his offices every single day. It is a rare Protestant who sings many hymns every single day.

Breviaries had, of course, been printed before the sixteenth century. But the Catholic Counter Reformation provided a tremendous stimulus to the breviary trade.[19] This stemmed not only from an undoubted increase in priestly piety, but also from an important change in the breviary text. One of the many reforming demands that faced the Roman Catholic Church in that period of confusion and strife was for a single authoritative standard of devotional practice, and wide enforcement of that standard. After several false starts, in two of which Plantin participated, this task was finally accomplished by the liturgical decrees of the Council of Trent. In this, as in so many other fields, the Tridentine Fathers repudiated reforms that seemed modernizing, particularizing, or of a Protestant tendency, and repaired to a more antique and universal standard. The nature of that standard had been suggested by the plan for liturgical reforms proposed by members of the conservative Theatine order. In the Council's concluding decrees of 1563, the job of drafting the actual text of the reformed breviary was entrusted to the Vatican. The specialists hired by the Vatican finished work by 1568, and the official

19. Two general histories of the Roman breviary which contain useful chapters on the Tridentine reforms: Pierre Batiffol, *Histoire du Bréviaire romain* (Paris, 1893); Dom Suitbert Bäumer, *Histoire du Bréviaire*, trans. fr. the German with useful additions by Dom Réginald Biron (2 vols.; Paris, 1905).

text was then released to the printers. At the same time a papal bull banned use of any other breviary, excepting only those that won explicit papal approval or that could claim a prescriptive right of use over a period of two hundred years.

This touched off a mad scramble for the right to publish the new breviary. The printers who won out were Paul Manutius, of the famous Aldine press, and Christopher Plantin.[20] Manutius, as papal printer, got the copy of the official text and a papal "privilege" theoretically granting him the sole right to publish the book. Plantin, thanks to some shrewd bargaining and pressure brought to bear by his old friend and patron, Cardinal Granvelle, won a license to print the new breviary in the Low Countries. It was agreed that a tenth of Plantin's production would be sent to Manutius to pay him for this concession. This was soon commuted to cash payments equivalent to a tenth of the value of Plantin's production. He printed more than seven thousand copies of the Roman breviary under the terms of this agreement.

After a few years, however, Plantin began looking for ways to evade further payments to Manutius. It was not only the expense that irked him. It was also the bother. In those days transferring large sums of cash over great distances involved arrangements that could become complicated or slow. He finally found a safe method of evasion in a new arrangement with the King of Spain. Philip II had already decided to promulgate in his realms a breviary with a text slightly different from that prepared for the Vatican. With the help of Zayas, Plantin persuaded Philip to place orders with him for mammoth quantities of these breviaries and other devotional books, enough to supply the needs of all the clergy in Spain. Since the text of these breviaries was not to be quite the same as the text promulgated in Rome, Plantin felt himself released from his agreement with Manutius and ceased making his payments.

The text of the new Spanish breviary was the personal work of the king. He felt it was slightly more orthodox and slightly more grammatical than the pope's text. Since Roman Catholi-

20. For a documented account of what follows, see Robert M. Kingdon, "The Plantin Breviaries: A Case Study in the Sixteenth-Century Business Operations of a Publishing House," *Bibliothèque d'Humanisme et Renaissance* (1960), pp. 133-50.

cism then depended heavily on the secular support of the Spanish crown, there was little the pope could do but approve these changes. He granted the clergy of Spain special permission to use the royal breviary. That these changes were accurately incorporated into the volumes Plantin published was guaranteed by the king's close personal supervision of their publication. One of the most psychologically revealing sets of manuscripts preserved in Antwerp is a set of printers' proofs for this breviary. They had been sent to Spain by Plantin. They were returned with marginal corrections in the hand of some royal scribe but with additional corrections and comments in the spidery hand of Philip II himself.[21]

The order for Spanish breviaries, and the other Spanish orders for devotional books which quickly followed it, constituted a major business coup for Plantin. This was not only because they released him from his obligations to Manutius. The size alone of these orders was enough to guarantee the prosperity of any printer. In the five years during which the agreement remained in effect Plantin delivered 15,505 breviaries to agents of the Spanish crown. He apparently delivered even more missals and in addition thousands of psalters, antiphonaries, diurnals, and books of hours. He also printed or purchased for sale to the king quantities of other books for the royal library. Most of these books were supplied to the king at retail prices. Plantin offered his royal customer few of the wholesalers' discounts he normally offered to those who bought from him in quantity. This must have made his profits truly impressive. It is no wonder that during this period he was able to expand his printing plant from one that was merely among the biggest in Europe to one that had at least four times as many presses as the plants of such rivals as Henri Estienne and Antoine Vincent.[22] It was also during this period that Plantin acquired the tremendous stock of types, type matrices, and punches that was to serve his descendents for the next three hundred years. One expert typographer estimates the

21. Museum Plantin-Moretus, Archives, No. 122, "Missale et Breviarium," p. 146, *inter alia*.

22. On the controversial question of how many presses Plantin actually operated, see de Roover in *Plantin Gedenkboek*, pp. 240-41, and Clair, *Plantin*, p. 283. Sixteen is the minimum estimate. The number of presses allocated to each Genevan printer is revealed by a text published in Chaix, *Recherches*, p. 32.

34

Plantin stock to contain three times as many sixteenth-century type matrices as the other three surviving collections of real size combined.[23]

This high prosperity, we have already noticed, was ended by the Spanish Fury of 1576. Relations between the Plantin-Moretus press and the Spanish crown, however, continued for centuries thereafter. The most important element in this trade, moreover, continued to be the supply of breviaries and other devotional books to the Spanish market. That market soon grew to include not only Spain proper but also her overseas colonies. Traces of the impact of Plantin's devotional books can even be found in Latin American art of the colonial period.[24]

Altogether Plantin sold at least twenty-two thousand breviaries during the first eight years of his production of them. When we realize that he was only the most important of dozens of printers who were publishing this volume (the Manutius "privilege" had been ignored or violated all over Europe), it becomes clear that the Roman breviary, like the Huguenot psalter, was one of the best sellers of the century.

The channels through which Plantin distributed his breviaries are clearly revealed by his records. In general, all of his books were distributed through four main ones: (1) retail sale through his own shop in Antwerp, (2) wholesale distribution through sales to booksellers, publishers, and other buyers at the semi-annual international book fair in Frankfort, (3) wholesale distribution through booksellers doing business in the Low Countries, northern France, parts of southern England, and the upper Rhineland, (4) quantity sale to patrons who arranged their own methods of further distribution.

Most of the breviaries were distributed by the third and fourth of these methods. By the time his business had grown to sizable proportions, Plantin was selling only a small percentage of his books in his retail shop. The records of those sales reveal, however, that an important percentage of them were of breviaries and other devotional books, particularly in the years immediately

23. Harry Carter, in "Plantin's Types and Their Makers," *Plantin Gedenkboek*, pp. 253-54.
24. For an interesting example, see Pál Kelemen, *Baroque and Rococo in Latin America* (New York, 1951), p. 213, plates 139 and 191.

following the release of the Tridentine texts. At the Frankfort book fairs Plantin also sold a few breviaries, but only a few. As we have already noted, the Frankfort market was apparently mostly for scholarly classical volumes of international interest.

Booksellers seem to have distributed most of the breviaries Plantin printed under the Manutius contract. Many of them were also printers and publishers on their own account, and most of them also sold books to Plantin. Barter appears to have been common in the sixteenth-century book trade. None of these other traders could operate on the same scale as Plantin, however, so practically every account was settled by cash payments to him. On almost all of these accounts Plantin allowed a substantial discount, averaging about 15 per cent, although it varied considerably and seems to have been negotiated separately with the settling of each individual account.

Patrons distributed the rest of Plantin's breviaries. By far the most important of these, of course, was Philip II. He set up his own elaborate distribution network within Spain under the direction of a religious order that maintained headquarters in the royal palace. Plantin also had other patrons. Many of them were bishops or abbots, who probably distributed the devotional books sent to them directly to clergymen under their jurisdiction.

These two generalizations on the sixteenth-century publishing industry suggest a third. For both of them tend to de-emphasize the role in society of the humanist and to emphasize the precariousness of his calling. Such a conclusion may disappoint those who are dedicated today to the pursuit of the humanities. It was commonly believed in the sixteenth century that really thorough training in the languages of classical antiquity was the hallmark of an educated man, and this belief was held more widely and was subject to much less challenge than it is today. It was also accepted that the printing industry could contribute to this training by its production of classical texts. The printers we have considered did make contributions to this cause. The Greek texts of Henri Estienne and the Polyglot Bible of Plantin provide proof of that. And yet careful study of the business operations of these same men makes it clear that these prestige editions did not pay their own way. The market for books of scholarship, then as now, was narrowly restricted and widely scattered. These publications were subsidized, either by the generous patronage of men of power or by profits gained by catering to the popular thirst for religious consolation. Plantin sold at least twenty, possibly thirty times as many breviaries as he sold Polyglot Bibles. Henri Estienne depended on profits from the sale of Bibles and on outright gifts from patrons to underwrite the production of the Greek texts for which he is famous. Piety and patronage made scholarship possible.

Reprinted from "Patronage, Piety and Printing in Sixteenth-Century Europe", by Robert M. Kingdon, pp. 19-36, in A Festschrift for Frederick B. Artz, *edited by David H. Pinkney and Theodore Ropp. Copyright 1964 by Duke University Press.*

XVIII

THE BUSINESS ACTIVITIES OF PRINTERS
HENRI AND FRANÇOIS ESTIENNE *

The printing industry of the sixteenth century has long been recognized as an essential element in the propagation of the religious ideas that agitated that century so greatly. But the printing industry, like any other fairly well developed medium of publicity, could not have been effective without business ability in the men who superintended it. In fact an unusually great amount of business skill was necessary in those days. Censorship laws made it unusually difficult to sell freely the printed products of the inevitably controversial theological debates that then dominated human thought.

For these reasons, it seems to me that a study of the business activities of a few of the prominent religious printers of the period might be useful. Such a study might not only explain the organization of material resources that made possible the quantity production of religious propaganda; it might also help us judge the importance of religious propaganda in the growth of the printing industry.

Much light has recently been shed on the economics of the sixteenth century printing industry by Paul Chaix's fine monograph, *Recherches sur l'imprimerie à Genève, de 1550 à 1564* (Geneva : Droz, 1954). Yet more illumination might be gained by a detailed study of two firms from their foundation to their dissolution. Two firms whose business histories seem to me to be particularly revealing were established by the brothers Henri and François Estienne in the city of Geneva, half way through the sixteenth century, when that city had become the world center of the peculiarly militant brand of Protestantism known as Calvinism. The firm of Henri Estienne won success, wealth for a time, and a permanent European-wide reputation among scholars for its quality editions of Greek classics. The firm of François Estienne was poor and obscure, more or less failed in Geneva, was not much more successful when re-established elsewhere.

Henri Estienne has attracted numerous writers; François Estienne but few. Both have been studied, however, largely from the point of view of the bibliographer and the scholarly student of the classics. Practically nothing has been done by economic historians. Yet the material for a study of these two men as businessmen fortunately still exists. Numerous contracts they had drawn up and notarized have been preserved and are readily available in the Geneva Archives d'Etat. Numerous references to their business activities can be found in the registers of the Small Council which watched over nearly every aspect of the business of the sixteenth century Geneva community [1].

* I must thank the Teaching Staff Research Council of the University of Massachusetts for a grant which helped finance part of the research for this study.

I must thank for help in doing the archival research upon which this study is based, M. Gustave Vaucher and Prof. Paul-F. Geisendorf of the Geneva Archives d'Etat (hereafter cited as AEG); MM. Paul Chaix and Alain Dufour of the Geneva Bibliothèque publique et universitaire (hereafter cited as BPU). Particularly useful as research guides were the Mss. Dufour on printing of the BPU, which the latter two scholars arranged for me to consult. I must also thank for making available printed reference works, Prof. Newton McKeon of the Converse Memorial Library of Amherst College, and Mr. Benton Hatch and others on the staff of the Library of the University of Massachusetts. The standard

CAPITAL

Henri and François Estienne were born into a family of printers. Their father, Robert Estienne, had been printer to King Francis I, and was famous all over Europe for his quality editions of the classics and his edition of the Bible. This last had gotten him into trouble with authorities at the Sorbonne. He then moved his family and plant to Calvinist Geneva, where he spent the rest of his life working at his trade. Robert saw to it that all of his sons were educated in the use of Latin, Hebrew, and Greek. Henri was given considerable opportunity to travel and thus became acquainted with printers and scholars of many countries. During Robert's last years in Geneva, Henri had taken on himself the heaviest part of the work of the press—the job of correcting copy. He had already become a master-printer with several fine editions of the classics to his credit, when his father died. François Estienne was still being trained at that time.

Robert Estienne left to his sons not only knowledge and skill, but also the fixed capital that made it possible for them to maintain themselves as master printers. Henri was particularly well provided for. In his last will and testament, Robert made Henri his " universal heir," for the specific purpose of keeping the entire printing works together and avoiding any possible division and discontinuation of its work [1]. No specific inventory of the printing property is contained in the will itself, but other documents reveal that it included the printing presses, the fonts of type, the house that served as printing shop, store, and living quarters for the Estienne family, and the stock of books on hand at the time of Robert's death. Henri himself estimated that the bulk of the value of the estate was in the stock of books [2].

Robert's large bequest of property to his eldest son was not made, however, without conditions. Two of them affected his sons' future business operations. One rather unique clause required Henri to remain in the printing business and to keep his establishment in the city of Geneva, as long as its religion remained Reformed. The estate was to revert to one of Henri's Protestant brothers or sisters, or to city charities, if Henri did not remain Protestant and in Geneva. This clause was to bring Henri much pain. Geneva was not a major business center and therefore hardly an ideal place for

---

reference on the Estiennes is Ant. Aug. RENOUARD, *Annales de l'imprimerie des Estienne ou histoire de la famille des Estienne et de ses éditions* (Paris, 1843, 2nd ed.). Cf. Léon FEUGÈRE, *Essai sur la vie et les ouvrages de Henri Estienne* (Paris, 1853); Louis CLÉMENT, *Henri Estienne et son oeuvre française* (Paris, 1898). For the father of these two Estiennes, see Elizabeth ARMSTRONG, *Robert Estienne, Royal Printer* (Cambridge, 1954). For general information on the printing industry in Geneva during Calvin's heyday, see Paul CHAIX, *Recherches sur l'imprimerie à Genève de 1550 à 1564* (Geneva : Droz, 1954), and the chapter on printing in Robert M. KINGDON, *Geneva and the Coming of the Wars of Religion in France, 1555-1563* (Geneva : Droz, 1956). All these books will hereafter be cited by the author's last name.

[1] RENOUARD, pp. 578-582, edition of testament of Robert Estienne in Geneva, AEG, Notaire Ragueau, III, 185-191, 5 September 1559 (hereafter cited as Ragueau). Cf. ARMSTRONG, 255-259, for a discussion of this testament.

[2] Henri STEIN, " Nouveaux documents sur les Estienne, imprimeurs parisiens (1517-1665)," *Mémoires de la Société de l'histoire de Paris et de l'Ile-de-France*, XXII (Paris, 1895), 23-25, arbitration agreement of dispute between Henri and François Estienne over their father's will, contains Henri's estimate. The original is in Geneva, AEG, Ragueau, III, fols. 245-249, 30 October 1559. See also Geneva, AEG, Registres du Conseil, LVI, fol. 286, 1 January 1562 (hereafter cited as RC), for a report of a Council inventory of most of the printing machinery in Henri's possession. FEUGÈRE is mistaken when he supposes (p. 38) that the family of Robert Estienne did not contest his unusually large bequest to his eldest son. The two arbitration agreements Stein publishes, pp. 20-23 and 23-25, prove that.

a big printing establishment. And the naming of city charities as possible beneficiaries gave the city governing authorities an unusual interest in regulating Henri's business.

A second significant clause of the will of Robert Estienne provided that Henri must take care of his young brother François, and set aside for his use the sum of 2000 livres tournois. The profits of this sum were to be turned over to François every year until he reached the age of twenty-five. The principal was then to be given to him in cash or in the form of a stock of several kinds of books priced at the merchants' price, i.e., minus the quarter of the sales' price usually reserved to the book-sellers. This was to be done only after the ministers of the city had testified to François' probity and piety. The will also instructed François to turn to his brother Henri for advice should he want to get married.

After the death of Robert Estienne, François protested that this cash grant was less than the " legitimate fourth " of the father's estate to which he should be entitled. A group of arbitrators, headed by minister Jean Calvin, decided against breaking the Estienne will by requiring division of property, but ruled that Henri would have to pay François 3000 livres tournois in books or cash, rather than 2000, when he reached the age of twenty-five [1].

François began business operations even before he came into this inheritance. In 1562 he won permission to become a master-printer [2]. Even earlier he had tried to buy printing equipment from his elder brother. Henri sold him between 1200 and 1500 livres worth of printing tools and instruments. But the Council quashed this sale on grounds that it violated their father's testament [3]. By 1563, he had somehow obtained a single press of his own and was operating independently [4]. In 1564, when he finally reached the stipulated age and passed the test of piety, the 3000 livres inheritance Henri duly turned over to him [5], could help the growth of an already established printing firm.

These handsome inheritances helped the Estienne brothers get started, but they did not guarantee them financial success. As Henri pointed out to the arbitrators adjusting his father's will, the business of selling books was notoriously risky. A wise publisher tried to tap some outside source of wealth to maintain himself. Any publisher had to make some kind of arrangement to meet his expenses in the long intervals between publication and sale of books.

Henri had already found a Maecenas to subsidize his publications. He had persuaded Ulrich Fugger of Augsburg, the only member of this fabulously wealthy family of international financiers with Protestant leanings, to subsidize his firm in a regular way. From 1558 to 1568, many of Henri Estienne's books carried the legend, *Huldrichi Fuggeri Typographus*, and prefaces reveal that Fugger provided Estienne with financial support and let him have manuscripts and rare books from his fine collection as well [6].

---

[1] STEIN, *op. cit.*, pp. 23-25.

[2] Geneva, AEG, RC, LVI, 2 January 1562, fol. 286v.

[3] *Ibid.*, fol. 285v., 30 December 1561. Cf. Geneva, AEG, Registre des particuliers, XII, 2nd part, fols. 146 and 149v., 5 January and 2 February 1562 (hereafter cited as RP), for measures Henri took to recover the property he had transferred to François and to secure his services.

[4] CHAIX, *op. cit.*, p. 32, copy of Geneva, AEG, RC, LVIII, fol. 69v., 25 June 1563.

[5] Geneva, AEG, Ragueau, VII, 14-16, 6 March 1564.

[6] See P. COSTIL, " Le mécénat humaniste des Fugger," *Humanisme et Renaissance*, VI (1939), 165-172, for more information and bibliography.

The specific nature of Fugger's support is revealed by records dealing with a suit brought to force Henri Estienne to maintain his printing works in Geneva under his personal direction rather than turning their management and selling much of the equipment to his brother François. The suit was argued by Henry Scringer, a Scottish humanist and lawyer, who came to Geneva as Ulrich Fugger's personal agent [1].

Scringer reported to the Geneva Small Council that Fugger had collected from many countries a library of the best examples of every author, every subject, and every language, and had decided to install this library in Geneva [2]. To this end, Fugger had bought one of the most beautiful houses of the city for the large sum of 2000 ecus [3]. Partly to better maintain this library, and partly to secure parchment editions for himself, Fugger had contracted with Henri Estienne to make him " his printer." Estienne was to receive an annual stipend of 300 livres outright [4]. In return he had only to send Fugger one copy in parchment of each book he produced. Fugger would supply the parchment. Finally, Fugger had loaned Estienne the sum of 1500 livres, at a rate of interest not specified.

These substantial gifts and loans surely go far to explain how Henri Estienne accumulated his operating capital. Unfortunately, he was not able to tap this source all his life. Relatives of Ulrich Fugger, motivated perhaps by jealousy, perhaps by religious orthodoxy, secured a court order restraining him from spending his money for cultural purposes, sometime around 1568. Henri Estienne reported to friends that he was trying to get the Fugger relatives to honor earlier promises made to him, in the 1570's [5]. A dedication of one of his books to Marc Fugger in 1594, suggests that he finally reached some sort of agreement with other members of the Fugger clan, but by then it was too late to do him much good [6].

When Fugger support failed, Henri turned to other leaders of the contemporary world for financing. In 1572 he extracted from the Holy Roman Emperor a vague promise of a grant to finance some of his publications, but he had difficulty getting much from that source [7].

A rich friend, J. Sambucus, gave Henri several gifts to subsidize the printing of a specific book. But Sambucus died before the book was finished, and it was never published [8].

---

[1] On Scringer, see Françoise de BORCH-BONGER, " Un ami de Jacques Amyot : Henry Scringer," *Mélanges offerts à M. Abel Lefranc* (Paris : Droz, 1936), pp. 362-373.

[2] Geneva, AEG, RC, LVI, fol. 284, 26 December 1561. For further action on this suit see *ibid.*, RC, LVI, fols. 285v., 286, 286v., 30 December 1561-2 January 1562, and RP, XII, 2nd part, fols. 144, 144v., 146, 22 December 1561-5 January 1562.

[3] At this time the ecu was worth about 4 florins, 10 sols, or 2 livres tournois, 10 sols. See Natalis de WAILLY, " Mémoire sur les variations de la livre tournois depuis le règne de saint Louis jusqu'à l'établissement de la monnaie décimale, " *Mémoires de l'Institut Impérial de France, Académie des inscriptions et belles-lettres*, t. XXI (Paris, 1857), 254; and Emile DOUMERGUE, *Jean Calvin, les hommes et les choses de son temps* (Lausanne & Neuilly-sur-Seine, 1899-1927), III, 452.

[4] COSTIL, *op. cit.*, and RENOUARD, p. 381, make this figure 150 thalers or ecus, a total not too far from 300 livres tournois. They base this figure on evidence of a much later date.

[5] RENOUARD, pp. 381-382; COSTIL, *op. cit.*

[6] RENOUARD, p. 437.

[7] CLÉMENT, p. 30, n. 1.

[8] RENOUARD, p. 426.

Finally, Henri Estienne turned to Henri III, King of France. He spent some time at the court, and succeeded in impressing the King with the quality of his work. The king, in 1579, granted him an annual pension of 300 livres per year, to be paid through his ambassador to the Swiss Leagues. Henri III also promised Estienne a grant of 1000 ecus, as reward for a particular book he had published. This princely sum, Estienne never could collect, however, because he unwisely failed to grease the palm of a corrupt royal treasurer[1].

Henri Estienne was nearly unique in his age in having the talent and the address to win financial supporters for his printing from among both the richest bankers and the most powerful rulers of his day. Other printers, like his brother François, had to find homelier expedients to finance their business activities.

Most of the contracts François signed reveal that he financed the operations of his firm by pledging books he had on hand or was about to print. He obtained the loan of fifty pounds tournois from a Geneva book-seller, for example, by promising to sell him five hundred copies of the New Testament, with Psalms, prayers, catechisms and calendars included[2]. This was a standard volume for which the merchant could be quite sure of finding a market.

François also handled some of his business transactions without use of cash at all. He would barter books for paper, for example. This, however, brings us to a second basic business problem the sixteenth-century printer faced : the problem of obtaining supplies.

SUPPLIES

The supply a printer needed in the greatest quantity was paper. Good paper, paper of the quality to which Parisian printers were accustomed, was hard to come by in Switzerland. Henri Estienne, fortunately, inherited from his father a traditional arrangement for the purchase of paper. This he hastened to confirm within two months after his father's death.

Antoine and François Vualiatz of Allamogne, a little village not far from Geneva, had apparently supplied the bulk of Robert Estienne's paper. In November 1559, Henri Estienne signed an eight-year contract with them which engrossed their entire production[3]. They were to deliver to him 8000 reams of paper, 1000 reams each year for the next eight years. Type, weight and price of the paper were carefully specified. Estienne was given the option of changing the type of paper if he so desired, and in that case variant weights and prices were specified. With certain kinds of paper under this option, the Vualiatz brothers agreed to supply 1300 reams instead of the 1000 of the more standard varieties. To make clear the quality he wanted, Henri had included in the contract mention of the fact that he had shown them a sheet of the paper on which his *Aeschylus* was printed, to serve the paper-makers as a guide.

This substantial quantity of paper had already been paid for. The Vualiatz had received 2800 florins from both the defunct Robert Estienne and his son Henri,

---

[1] See CLÉMENT, pp. 55-64, which corrects in some details the version of RENOUARD, pp. 418, ff.

[2] Geneva, AEG, Notaire Bernard Neyrod, IV, fol. 10v., 1 January 1568.

[3] *Ibid.*, Ragueau, III, 278-282, 26 November 1559.

since May 1, 1551. Henri was to collect a rebate of 300 florins on the paper that came to him. Apparently the Estienne had invested their own capital in this paper-making firm, and were getting their return in paper.

Another clause of the contract provided that the Vualiatz brothers had to promise that if they built another wheel and paper mill, or somehow made a greater quantity of paper than that specified in the contract, the surplus paper also was to go to Henri Estienne at the prices per sheet already specified, granting Henri always his rebate.

Paper already in Henri Estienne's possession, was specifically excluded from the totals the Vualiatz had yet to deliver. Paper that was broken or cracked Henri could buy at his own discretion at an unspecified low price his father had also paid.

This arrangement seems to have provided Henri with paper for the better part of the first decade of his activity. Perhaps it even provided him with more than enough, and he found himself able to sell some paper to other printers. In a 1562 Council Register entry Henry was listed as among the paper-merchants summoned to hear the reading of a new edict regulating the quality of paper sold in Geneva [1]. The year following, however, Estienne was no longer included in a similar group of paper-sellers [2]. The Vualiatz were not included in the group either year, probably because their paper was not available on the open market.

Henri Estienne secured a second hold on the Vualiatz paper production in November 1559, by renewing his father's agreement to cover a 700 florin loan made to the Vualiatz brothers by a third party. This sum the Vualiatz henceforth owed directly to Henri Estienne [3].

When the eight years of the original contract were up, Henri Estienne had to make new arrangements for the purchase of his paper. This time, in 1567, he decided to work through a third party—paper-merchant Estienne Chappeaurouge, during that year one of the reigning Syndics of the city of Geneva [4]. Chappeaurouge agreed to supply Estienne with 1600 reams of paper a year for two years. Type, weight and price were again carefully specified. The reams were to be delivered either every three months or every month at Chappeaurouge's discretion. The paper was to be made by the Vualiatz brothers who contracted to sell their entire production to Chappeaurouge [5]. Chappeaurouge was to pay the brothers partly in cash and partly also in rags, the essential raw material for paper making. Chappeaurouge's control of the rag supply is apparently what made it possible for him to horn in on this deal. Previous contracts between Henri Estienne and Vualiatz were specifically annulled. Again Henri Estienne was very explicit in specifying the quality he wanted. One type of paper had to be just like the kind Thomas Grasset had made for his recently printed book on Herodotus. The reference to Grasset makes it clear that the Vualiatz brothers were not Henri's only source of paper. But the contracts he drew up with them are the only ones that have been preserved.

The problem of obtaining paper was an even more difficult one for François Estienne. Even though he required smaller amounts, he apparently could not raise the

[1] Geneva, AEG, RC, LVI, fol. 304v., 5 February 1562, cited by CHAIX, p. 45.

[2] *Ibid.*, RC, LVIII, fol. 71, 28 June 1563, cited by CHAIX, p. 45.

[3] *Ibid.*, Ragueau, III, 283-285, 285-286, 26 November 1559.

[4] *Ibid.*, Ragueau, IX, 197-199, 29 March 1567.

[5] *Ibid.*, Ragueau, IX, 200-202, 29 March 1567.

capital necesary for outright purchase of what he needed. Instead he normally pledged part of his future production of books in payment for the paper he was buying. This at least is what he did twice when he secured paper from Estienne Chappeaurouge. Early in 1568, Chappeaurouge agreed to send him forty-three bales of paper, worth 1204 florins, on condition that François Estienne deliver to his house 4600 New Testaments with calendar, Psalms, prayers, catechisms, and confession. The books were to be delivered to Chappeaurouge day by day, sheet by sheet, as soon as the sheets were dry. François Estienne could have these books back by paying the sum of 1204 florins [1]. Late in 1568, François secured from Chappeaurouge promise of delivery of three hundred reams more of paper, this time in return for 150 florins plus 900 books bearing the title, „ La maison rustique de Mr Charles Estienne docteur en medecine " [2]. Again the books had to be delivered sheet by sheet as they were printed. Chappeaurouge apparently did not trust Estienne very far.

In the year previous to these transactions, François had obtained paper through another third party, Laurent de Normandie, who was probably the most prominent book merchant in Geneva of this time and whose affairs are discussed at greater length in another chapter of this book. De Normandie bought from François Chautemps, a prominent local citizen and paper merchant, 25 bales of paper of specified type, size and quality [3]. This entire consignment was to be delivered to de Normandie or François Estienne within four months. Chautemps had already received an advance of 160 livres tournois from de Normandie, and was to receive the rest of the purchase price upon delivery of the paper. What François was to return to de Normandie is not revealed in this contract. An obvious possibility, however, is that François Estienne produced books for de Normandie to sell. It is therefore probable that François' normal method of obtaining paper was to pledge delivery of quantities of books of a standard, easily salable sort, rather than promising cash payment.

Type was another important supply needed by all printers. The House of Estienne is justly famous for its types, in particular for the Garamond type made especially for them by a Parisian type-maker. Henri Estienne did his best to maintain the family standards. Gaspard Dehus was a type-maker who did some work for Henri in Geneva [4]. In 1569 Dehus agreed to supply Henri both with more Garamond type and with " Greek of the great text," in return for a quantity of books worth 395 florins, 13 sols [5]. Henri had the option of requesting yet another kind of Greek; the " Greek of the great text " had to be finished by a certain date or the type-maker would be penalized. The same contract also provided that a cash sum Henri had previously paid Dehus for a specified kind of Greek type, could be used to make any kind of type Henri wanted.

Note that in this contract Henri Estienne was turning to the business methods of his brother—using books as a pledge to secure supplies. Perhaps the switch is explained by the fact that his Fugger subsidy had just been cut off.

I have not been able to find any information about the ways in which François Estienne secured his type. He could have turned to Dehus, but he hardly ever needed

---

[1] Geneva, AEG, Notaire Aymé Santeur, I, 77, 31 January 1568.

[2] *Ibid.*, Notaire Aymé Santeur, III, fol. 19, 23 November 1568.

[3] *Ibid.*, Ragueau, IX, 195-197, 28 March 1567. For more information on Laurent de Normandie, see below, pp. 176, ff.

[4] CHAIX, pp. 168-169, lists Dehus as a printer, and as a type-maker in Lyons in 1580, but ignores his type-making in Geneva.

[5] Geneva, AEG, Notaire Aymé Santeur, VI, fols. 104v.-105, 26 August 1569.

the fine Greek type Dehus had made for his brother. He might have gotten type from Michel du Boys, a type-maker somehow connected with the Estiennes' sister Catherine [1].

There is similarly very little information on how the Estiennes obtained other supplies. We know that ink was made in Geneva. At least one ink-maker was operating in the 1550's [2]. But we do not know that he supplied the Estiennes.

EMPLOYEES

Printing in the sixteenth century was still a relatively small-scale industry. But a printing firm was more than a one-man operation, and both Henri and François Estienne needed help. Not much evidence survives to indicate the specific kind of help they did get. Generally speaking, the Genevan printing industry, seems to have followed the pattern developed for most other industries of the period. Boys were taken in as apprentices to learn the trade; after a certain number of years they became " compagnons " or journeymen; when they had achieved skill and maturity and if they could assemble the necessary capital, they could apply to the city council for permission to become independent master-printers. In addition to these regular types of employees, the printing industry required numbers of highly educated " correctors", capable of reading proof. Correctors might be trained in the shop; they might be recruited from the ranks of already-educated intellectuals or students. Some of the most distinguished intellects of the sixteenth-century worked for long periods as printers' correctors; e.g., Erasmus for Froben.

The Estienne press had required a considerable number of employees. In the Paris days, Henri Estienne reports that his father Robert, " entertained in his own household ten men employed by him as correctors on his press, or in other parts of his business. These ten persons, all of them men of education; some of them were of considerable learning; as they were of different nations, so they were of different languages. This necessitated them to employ Latin as the common medium of communication " [3]. Presumably the Estienne press still required the same kinds of employees when it was re-established in Geneva.

Record does survive of an apprenticeship agreement between François Estienne and Marcellin Chasand of Riez en Provence [4]. Marcellin's son Claude was apprenticed to François Estienne, to learn the art of printing. François Estienne agreed not only to teach Claude printing, but also to nourish and support him for two years, and to pay him a small sum of pocket money each week, the allowance to be somewhat higher the second year than the first. The arrangement seems to be quite typical for the Genevan printing industry, probably for industry generally at this period.

Henri Estienne seems to have had an unusual amount of trouble with his employees. One suspects that the charge of irascible temper so often levied against him was at least

[1] Geneva, AEG, Notaire Jean Jovenon, III, fols. 92-95, 7 November 1573, a testament including a bequest of a sum from Michel du Boys' daughter to Catherine Estienne.

[2] CHAIX, pp. 38-39.

[3] Mark PATTISON, " The Stephenses," *Essays by Mark Pattison, Series I* (London & New York, n.d.), p. 60, translation by Pattison from Henri Estienne's letter to his son Paul in the dedication to *Aulus Gellius*, 1585.

[4] Geneva, AEG, Notaire Aymé Santeur, I, fol. 131, 6 April 1568. Cf. apprentice contracts in CHAIX, pp. 233-234.

partially true. A wild temper would inevitably have been most obvious to his employees, and could explain their alienation. The most notorious example of trouble between Henri and an employee is his break with his scribe, Jean Scapula. Scapula published simultaneously with Estienne's master-work, his *Thesaurus Graecae linguae*, a handy abridgment of the book. Scapula's abridgment sold much better than Henri Estienne's complete work, and therefore hurt Henri considerably financially [1]. The *Thesaurus* had been an exceedingly expensive book to produce.

On at least one occasion Henri lost the services of a corrector who was called into the ministry in France. He protested, and tried to get the corrector, a man named Urbain Chauveton, to fulfill his contract. The combined pressure of the Church of Beaune which had called Chauveton to serve them, and the candidate himself, was enough to decide the city council against Henri, and Chauveton left his employ. He had earlier promised to secure Henri another corrector [2].

Finally Henri Estienne faced on one occasion a problem many masters met with in their employees—petty thievery. In 1564 one of his "worker-printers" was condemned by municipal authorities to three days in jail on bread and water for having stolen from Henri's shop a copy of Thucydides and a copy of Athenagoras, *De resurrectione mortuorum*, translated from Greek into Latin [3].

SALES

Selling can be a difficult problem for any manufacturer and it must have been a particularly difficult one for sixteenth-century Genevan publishers. Their logical market was the large cities of France, but these cities were far from Geneva and at times closed to them by royal edict. And other markets—in Germany and Italy—must have been even more difficult to reach with quantity merchandise, because of transportation difficulties.

Henri Estienne nevertheless made the attempt. Much of his production was probably sold at the annual Frankfort book fairs. We know that he visited them often from references in the Geneva Council registers to his departures from town, and from references in his letters [4]. We know that he shipped sizable quantities of books to Frankfort. In 1575, he revealed to a friend that the wreck of a boat carrying his books, in the river Aar near Soleure in Switzerland, had really embarrassed him [5]. We know finally that he was well received and highly appreciated the facilities that Frankfort afforded him, from his book on the Frankfort fair, the *Francofordiense Emporium* which was dedicated to the authorities who sponsored the fair [6]. This book contains one of the best contemporary descriptions of the Frankfort fair, the biggest and most important center for trading books during the sixteenth century. And Estienne's

---

[1] Renouard, pp. 402-404.

[2] Geneva, AEG, RC, LXXI, fols. 81v., 83, 11 and 12 June 1576.

[3] *Ibid.*, Procès criminels, No. 1229, 4-5 September 1564.

[4] RENOUARD, pp. 406-407; 436. See also below, p. 273, n. 1, and *passim*.

[5] Letter of 25 March 1575, quoted in part in CLÉMENT, p. 30, and n. 3. Cf. PATTISON, *op. cit.* p. 78.

[6] James Westfall THOMPSON, *The Frankfort Book Fair; the Francofordiense Emporium of Henri Estienne edited with historical introduction, original latin text with english translation on opposite pages and notes* (Chicago : the Caxton Club, 1911).

description helps us understand what drew him to the fair. The city authorities provided special facilities and legal services. The location was good. Book-sellers, printers and writers from all over Europe frequented the fair. It was a good place to find a new manuscript, to check on competitors' production, and to sell books for European-wide distribution.

Henri Estienne's books may have had a peculiarly large sale on the Frankfort market, since those of them in Greek and Latin would sell equally well in scholarly circles in any country, and since the name Estienne was known internationally by now. And Henri's substantial financial resources may have made it possible for him to subsidize trips that other printers could not afford.

The Frankfort fair did not absorb all of Henri Estienne's production, however. Some of his books he sold through third parties, professional book-sellers who served as brokers for books. In November 1566, Laurent de Normandie, the prominent Genevan book merchant, contracted to buy a substantial percentage of one of Henri Estienne's editions [1]. He agreed to buy a full half of an edition of the New Testament in octavo, with the notes of Theodore Beza. This edition was to run to at least 2800 copies, and de Normandie was to pay eight francs a sheet. A few months later the two agreed that de Normandie would buy an additional quarter of the total edition. Preserved with these contracts in the de Normandie family archives, is a list of the payments made to Estienne. They are strung out from January 13 to September 13, 1567. The payments for the additional quarter of the total edition are not listed. It obviously took Estienne the better part of the year to complete this sizable edition, though it is doubtful that he devoted all his time and facilities to turning it out.

Perhaps Henri Estienne sold most of his expensive and probably smaller editions of Greek classics at the Frankfort book fair; and sold to men like de Normandie most of his more popular religious publications.

François Estienne depended even more heavily on professional book-sellers for the sale of his merchandise. De Normandie was one of the principal merchants he turned to. Two contracts which have been preserved reveal this. In one, drafted in August 1566, François agreed to sell to de Normandie 863 Bibles in octavo for eight sols a piece [2]. Most of the sum had already been paid; the books were to be delivered as soon as they were finished. Forty livres of the entire purchase price was withheld. This sum was finally paid to François Estienne in October of that year, when he delivered a final 200 copies of the Bible. The rate of printing revealed here, is probably no faster than the rate of the Henri Estienne edition, since François had fewer presses, and, probably, fewer editions being produced at any one time. Apparently attached to these Bibles, or perhaps included in a package deal between the two men, were several " alphabets " or " calendars " which François was paid for separately.

The other contract between de Normandie and François Estienne, dating from only a few months after the first, provides for an even bigger sale. On March 24, 1567, François agreed to sell de Normandie 12,000 Psalms and red and black calendars for the total price of 500 livres tournois [3]. However François didn't receive any of this

[1] Geneva, AEG, Archives de Familles, 1ère série, de Normandie, 1-2, contains the original contract, 2 November 1566.

[2] See *ibid.*, for the original contract, with additions in the hand of François Estienne. Cf. Ragueau, VIII, 404-405, 15 August 1566, for notary's copy, without the additions.

[3] Geneva, AEG, Archives de Familles, 1ère série, de Normandie, 1-2, 24 March 1567.

in cash. De Normandie cancelled a debt of 200 livres which Estienne owed him; he agreed to buy 24 bales of paper for this edition at the specified price of 195 livres and 17 sols, from paper-maker François Chautemps; and he agreed to deliver to Estienne 123 livres worth of books of many sorts, excepting however books printed by his brother Henri Estienne.

The latter contract reveals, I think, that François was operating on a shoestring. He seems to have depended on de Normandie for capital, for purchase of his most important supplies, and for a stock of books he could use to keep his own book-shop running. He apparently got a discount on one of these items, since the total of the declared values is obviously well over 500 livres tournois.

François Estienne made similar arrangements, on a somewhat more modest scale, with other book-sellers. In December 1568, for example, he agreed to sell 200 books in quarto entitled *La maison rustique de Mr Charles Estienne*, to a certain Maturin Prevost [1]. We have already noticed that François Estienne traded substantial quantities of popular religious works to Estienne Chappeaurouge, in return for the paper he needed.

CONTENTS

The bulk of the books printed by the Estienne brothers were popular religious books– Bibles, Testaments, Psalms, Catechisms. We have already seen that quantities of them were used to gain operating capital and supplies. They were apparently the only books printed in really big editions, the only ones whose sale was so sure that they could be sold to book merchants in big lots, even in advance of actual publication.

The most famous of the religious books published by the Estiennes was, of course, the great annotated Bible which had been Robert Estienne's chief pride and torment. After his arrival in Geneva, he had naturally continued to publish this Bible, with revisions and changes, and had jealously guarded his copyrights to it [2].

These copyrights were inherited by Henri Estienne. He immediately went to work to see to it that they were carefully guarded. Less than a month after his father's death he applied to the Geneva Council for permission to print the New Testament in French, as collated and corrected from the Greek by Calvin and Beza. He also asked for a " privilège " or copyright, granting him monopoly rights to print and sell the book for a term of years. The next day he secured from the Council a *privilège* for three years, not just for the New Testament alone, but for the entire Bible, " in many forms " [3].

The following spring a group of Genevan printers headed by Henri Estienne's chief competitor, Jean Crespin, tried to break some of these monopoly rights. The

---

[1] Geneva, AEG, Notaire Aymé Santeur, III, fol. 42v., 11 December 1568.

[2] Geneva, AEG, Procès criminels, No. 743, 13-17 June 1558. Cf. Procès criminels, 2nd série No. 1208. They are the records of an action against printer Nicolas Barbier for publishing the New Testament as translated by Theodore Beza, to the prejudice of Robert Estienne. See ARMSTRONG Appendix B, pp. 275-288, for critical editions of parts of these records and other documents pertinent to the case.

[3] Geneva, AEG, RC, LV, fols. 121 and 122v., 5 and 6 October 1559. See John CALVIN, *Ioannis Calvini Opera quae supersunt omnia* (Brunswick, 1863-1900, eds. Baum, Cunitz & Reuss), XXI, col. 721 and 722 for partial copies (hereafter cited as CO).

ere willing to leave to Estienne right to print the Old Testament as translated by his ther. But they felt that the New Testament text should become public domain, ecause it had been translated by the ministers of the city, and because in the past obert Estienne had shared some of his work with other printers of the city [1].

Henri Estienne must have had some warning that this complaint was about to be led. A few days earlier he had presented copies of his Bible to every one of the Counlors and to the municipal Library, in rather belated return for the *privilège* granted him. He had at the same time begged the authorities to maintain his monopoly [2].

The Council, after hearing both sides, decided on a compromise arrangement. stienne's three-year *privilège* for the entire Bible was confirmed. But the other printers ere allowed to begin printing separate New Testaments on April 1, 1561, just about ie year after the date of complaint. They were not to finish printing and begin selling efore August 1, 1561. This in effect gave Estienne a one-year *privilège* for the New estament. In addition the other printers were required to pay Henri within fifteen ıys, one hundred ecus of his total production cost of 107 ecus [3].

In the years that followed, Estienne took care to protect as well as he could rights this Bible. In 1568 he applied again for permission to print the Bible " with the mmentaries of his deceased father " [4]. In 1573, he applied with Eustache Vigneron r Vignon), a fellow printer [5], for permission to bring out a new edition of the Bible formerly printed in Paris by Robert Estienne deceased father of Henri, and since then this city with the annotations of Vatable " [6]. In 1582, Henri Estienne seconded by ieodore Beza, asked the city Council for a letter of favor to the rulers of Basle, to event an unauthorized printing there of the New Testament as edited by Beza [7].

Other books for the religious book market were also produced by Henri Estienne. e printed short Scripture texts—for example his 1562 edition in Latin of Genesis [8]. e printed editions of the Genevan scholastic ordinances—though he lost monopoly ght to that within two years to printer Artus Chauvin. Estienne claimed that Beza ıd told his father that he would receive full *privilège*. But Beza was absent from Geneva ıd therefore could not confirm this promise and written records were inadequate [9]. stienne also asked for permission to print popular pamphlets, for example telling ' the death of the Prince of Condé [10], or presenting epigrams composed by Beza d by Henri himself [11].

Beautiful editions of Greek classics won for Henri Estienne his most enduring fame. ie best known is his Greek *Thesaurus*. But he also printed important early or first itions of Plato, Herodotus, Plutarch, Diogenes Laertius, and many others. This

[1] Geneva, AEG, RP, XII, 2nd part, fol. 53v., 2 April 1560.
[2] Geneva, AEG, RC, LVI, fol. 24, 28 March 1560.
[3] Geneva, AEG, RC, LVI, fol. 26v., 4 April 1560.
[4] Geneva, AEG, RC, LXIII, fol. 126, 5 November 1568.
[5] Chaix, p. 227, under " Vignon."
[6] Geneva, AEG, RC, LXVIII, fol. 99, 4 May 1573.
[7] Geneva, AEG, RC, LXXVII, fol. 110v., 8 June 1582.
[8] RENOUARD, p. 120. Publication of this book had been authorized in 1560. See Geneva, AEG, ٢, LVI, fol. 121v., 24 December 1560.
[9] Geneva, AEG, RC, LVI, fols. 266v. and 267v., 21 and 24 November 1561.
[10] Geneva, AEG, RC, LXIV, fol. 110v., 25 July 1569.
[11] Geneva, AEG, RC, LXV, fol. 15v., 27 January 1570.

side of Estienne's production is well known to bibliographers and students of Greek scholarship, however, so I will not go into it in any detail[1].

The production of François Estienne followed a similar pattern. Most of his time and energy were spent in publishing religious books that would command a sure market. One of the first of these was a grammar, or " ABCD," prepared for children and containing some elementary religious instruction. It was first printed by Vincent Bres and later by Michel Blanchier and François Estienne. This was the book which achieved notoriety in 1563 when ministers Calvin and Beza discovered in it a " damnable heresy touching the divinity, wishing to infer that Jesus Christ is not God " Their complaint led to examination of the stocks on hand and, eventually, to the drafting of the regulatory ordinances of 1563 which brought the whole Genevan printing industry under more systematic municipal control[3].

Even more important may have been the editions of Scripture François Estienne published. We have already noted that in 1568 he agreed to deliver to Estienne Chappeaurouge 4600 New Testaments with calendar, Psalms, prayers, catechisms, and confession, partly in return for supplies of paper[4]. Later that same year he agreed to deliver to Chappeaurouge 11200 Psalms in 32mo, with prayers, catechisms, confession of the churches, calendar red and black, again partly in return for supplies of paper There is some reason to doubt, however, that these two large contracts were ever fully filled[6].

Sporadically François Estienne tried to publish other kinds of books. His branching out into other fields began with a request for permission to print a medical book it was rejected, however, on grounds that the book was badly translated and contained faults in medicine[7]. In 1566, and again in 1568, François asked for permission to print Plutarch's *Lives*[8]. There was trouble about this the first time, since another printer had previously requested a Plutarch permit. In 1567, François asked and won permission to print a commentary of Jehan Argeilier on " Galien penale "[9], and in 1568 he asked for permission to print Augustine's *De civitate dei*[10]. Then followed a ten-year lapse in new publications.

François Estienne's publication activity began anew in 1578. In that year he asked the Council for permits to publish a history of Portugal[11], and a triple edition of the works of Cicero, in three formats, 16mo, octavo, and quarto[12]. For the Cicero ed

---

[1] See RENOUARD, pp. 115-160, for a fairly complete list, supplemented by later writers already cited For an abbreviated list of the period see Geneva, AEG, RC, LXV, fol. 59v., 13 April 1560.

[2] CO, XXI, col. 802, 17 May 1563, partial copy of Geneva, AEG, RC, LVIII, fols. 53-53v.

[3] For copies of these ordinances and commentary, see CHAIX, pp. 32, ff.

[4] See above, p. 264, and n. 1.

[5] Geneva, AEG, Notaire Aymé Santeur, I, fols. 263v.-264, 24 September 1568; confirmed in *ibid* VI, fols. 124-124v., 25 September 1569. This deal was exceedingly complicated and involved François wife and brother-in-law as pledges.

[6] RENOUARD, p. 490, notes " eleven years of inaction," of François' press, from 1568-1579. C below, p. 274.

[7] Geneva, AEG, RC, LVII, fols. 180 and 192; 4 and 29 January 1563.

[8] Geneva, AEG, RC, LXI, fol. 120, 5 December 1566; LXIII, fol. 100, 3 September 1568.

[9] Geneva, AEG, RC, LXII, fol. 111, 22 September 1567. Not listed by RENOUARD.

[10] Geneva, AEG, RC, LXIII, fol. 35v., 15 April 1568. Not listed by RENOUARD.

[11] Geneva, AEG, RC, LXXIII, fol. 170, 26 August 1578.

[12] Geneva, AEG, RC, LXXIII, fol. 231v., 16 December 1578. RENOUARD, p. 160, lists a history Portugal dated 1581, but doesn't mention any Cicero editions.

tions he wanted a *privilège* of five years. The following year François gained permission to print *Traicté contre les danses* [1]; he also asked for permission to print the *Traicté de l'Eglise* of Philip de Mornay [2]. In 1580 he won permission to publish Daneau's translation of St. Basil's *l'Exameron* [3].

Renouard believes that soon after this flurry of activity, François Estienne moved his printing works from Geneva to Normandy and ended his career there. One curious piece of evidence, however, indicates that he returned to Geneva at least long enough to persuade the Council to grant him permission to print the Bible in German [4].

The archival records do not always indicate whether François got the permission he requested. They do not prove that these books were actually published. Nevertheless they suggest that he published many more editions than Renouard and other students of the Estienne family have realized [5].

GOVERNMENT CONTROL

By now it must be clear that enterprise in Geneva was not exactly free. The governing Small Council regulated many aspects of business activity, and printing was watched with special care. Various ordinances regulating printing were more or less codified in June 1563. They even listed the number of presses each printer was allowed to operate. Henri Estienne was given permission to use four presses, and this ranked him with Jean Crespin and Antoine Vincent as one of the three biggest publishers in the city. Printer Claude de Huchin could operate two presses when working for Henri; this gave him a total of six he could plan on using. François Estienne was one of a substantial number of small printers who were allowed only one press [6]. Exceptions were soon made to these rigid limitations. One of them was made in favor of François Estienne, who early in 1564 was permitted to operate a second press to print his *'Harmonie des quatre livres de Moise* [7].

The 1563 ordinances also provided for careful regulation of book content. Probably ever since the introduction of printing to Geneva, and certainly since the establishment of the Calvinist Reformation, censorship of every book published had been the rule. Publishers were supposed to submit manuscripts to the Council or to the ministers of the city. Usually they petitioned the Council not only for a license to print, but also for a *privilège* or copyright, giving them monopoly right to publish the book for a stated number of years. Actual printing was to begin only after an official Council license had been granted, and this usually had to follow approval of certain of the leading ministers. Bound copies of each completed book were to be presented to each Councilor and to the city's newly created library. In 1560 a commision on printing was appointed to enforce these rules systematically. Beza was its most prominent member. From now on the printing industry was regulated in yet greater detail.

---

[1] Geneva, AEG, RC, LXXIV, fol. 99, 4 June 1579; RENOUARD, p. 160.

[2] Geneva, AEG, RC, LXXIV, fol. 127v., 21 June 1579; RENOUARD, p. 160.

[3] Geneva, AEG, RC, LXXV, fol. 111v., 23 June 1580. Not listed by RENOUARD.

[4] Geneva, AEG, RC, LXXXIII, fol. 246, 31 December 1588. Cf. RENOUARD, p. 491.

[5] RENOUARD, pp. 489, ff.

[6] CHAIX, p. 32, copy of Geneva, AEG, RC, LVIII, fol. 69, 25 June 1563.

[7] Geneva, AEG, RC, LVIII, fol. 145v., 11 January 1564; partial copy in CO, XXI, col. 811. Cf. RENOUARD, pp. 159, 489.

Labor disputes were adjudicated by the commission and the Council. Quality of the books—the paper used, the margination, the quality of type—was checked. And censorship continued in a yet more systematic fashion [1].

Practically every printer in Geneva ran afoul of these regulations at one time or another in his career, and the Estiennes were no exception. In fact, Henri Estienne seems to have met with more than his share of punishment. Some of his encounters with authorities were fairly minor. One of the regulations that irked him was the requirement that bound copies of every book printed be presented to the Councilors and the library. In 1566, he presented some books for the library without bindings. The Council considered punishing him for this offense, but decided to excuse him from the requirement for once, because he had contributed much for the moats [2]. Years later Estienne was one of a delegation of printers who petitioned for modification of the requirement. They found presentation of an individual copy to each Councilor to be unreasonable, and asked the Council to rest content with a smaller number of copies, perhaps just enough for the library and the governing Syndics. The Council found this request full of " pricks and calumnies," and rejected it for its " impertinence " [3].

Henry Estienne had even more trouble with the licensing regulations. Three examples will serve to illustrate this. In 1566, when he applied for permission to publish his *Apologie pour Hérodote*, he was required to excise several " propos vilains'. This he did, but he also added, without permission, a Table and Advertisement. This addition made the Council furious. He was tried, found guilty, and fined by the civil court of the city, in a trial running from April 29 to May 9, 1567. And the ecclesiastical court of Geneva, the Consistory, then took on the case and excommunicated him for a short period of time [4].

In 1577, Estienne was again hailed before the Consistory and then sent to the Council. This time he had printed without license, a letter of Cicero with a letter to a Pope which called him Vicar of Jesus Christ, " and other imposture." For this he was scolded and ordered to reprint the letter with the offending phrases left out [5].

The greatest furor was created by Henri's printing of the *Deux dialogues du nouveau langage françois italianizé* in 1580. This fight assumed the proportions of a international incident. The book had been written, after a stay in court, partly to please King Henri III of France who did not look with favor on the italianizers among his courtiers. The manuscript was again approved in advance, but no sooner did the book appear, than it was charged that Henri Estienne had made extensive additions. Two of the ministers of Geneva examined the book and found that there were indeed unauthorized and " scandalous " additions, and even " profanations of the Holy Scripture " in the published text [6].

---

[1] See CHAIX, pp. 63-86, for a documented analysis of municipal controls of the printing industry.

[2] Geneva, AEG, RC, LX, fol. 142, 11 January 1566.

[3] Geneva, AEG, RC, LXXVIII, fols. 114 v., 115v.-116, 30 July and 2 August 1583.

[4] P. Ristelhuber, ed., Henri ESTIENNE, *Apologie pour Hérodote* (Paris, 1879, 2 vols.), I, Introductio viii-xxx, contains transcripts of the relevant archival materials on this case, copied from Geneva, AEG RC, Procès criminels, and Registres du Consistoire.

[5] Geneva, AEG, RC, LXXII, fol. 67v., 10 May 1577.

[6] Geneva, AEG, RC, LXXIII, fol. 180, 12 September 1578; LXXV, fols. 16 and 68v., 22 January and 12 April 1580. For copies of these and all other materials relevant to the case, in Geneva, AEG RC, RP, Registres du Consistoire, Pièces historiques (official letters), see P. Ristelhuber, ed., Henri ESTIENNE, *Deux dialogues du nouveau langage françois italianizé* (Paris, 1885, 2 vols.), I, Introductio xviii-xxx.

Henri was hailed before the Consistory for a scolding, but this time he lost his temper, and said a number of unpleasant things to the ministers instead of taking his reprimand meekly. As a result he was excommunicated and immediately remanded to the Council for more temporal punishment. The Council threw him in prison. He was released after only six days, and several months later reconciled himself with the Consistory and was admitted again to Communion.

Meanwhile ambassadors of the King of France bombarded the government of Geneva with letters. Letters asking safe-conduct preceded his return to Geneva. And letters expressing considerable dismay at his treatment arrived in Geneva two weeks after his imprisonment. But the letters do not seem to have affected the course of Genevan justice, unless they perhaps tempered its rigors.

The Council had one hold over Henri Estienne which it did not possess over other printers. It lay in the unique clause of his father's will which we have already noted; he was required to keep the printing works in Geneva. If he failed to do so, city charities might eventually receive the property, and so the Council watched carefully to be sure it stayed in Geneva. This clause had provided the basis for the Fugger suit to force Henri to continue active printing. It may have caused some of the severity in the city's enforcement of censorship laws on Henri; there seems at times to have been reason to fear that he hoped to move his printing establishment back to Paris near the royal court. And this clause was the legal ground for the final and harshest action the city of Geneva took against Henri Estienne. In 1597, when he was old and rascible, perhaps even approaching senility, the city confiscated all of his property.

From 1594 on, the Council had heard numerous complaints that Henri Estienne was neglecting his work and leaving his family in poverty, to voyage rather aimlessly about Germany [1]. Most of these complaints came from the ministers. In 1595 they suggested that the business be turned over to his well-educated son Paul Estienne. Paul agreed to take over the business, but only until his father's return. In 1596, Henri did return, but after a month was preparing to leave again. Beza talked to him, and reported that he was " not in good sense." Finally in October 1597, the Council decided to take drastic action. All of Estienne's property was confiscated and inventoried. The furniture and household utensils were turned over to his wife. The books, presses, fonts, type and all printing instruments, were turned over to his son Paul. The confiscatory clause of the Robert Estienne will was the explicit legal basis for this action [2]. Only a few months later, Henri Estienne, again off on his travels, died a pauper in the hospital of the city of Lyons [3]. Thus ended the career of one of the greatest scholarly printers of the sixteenth century.

François Estienne was subject to the same laws that so annoyed his brother Henri. But there is less record that they caused him trouble. We have already noted that his 1563 request for permission to print a book of medicine was denied; most of his later requests were apparently granted.

François ran into trouble of a serious sort, but not at the hands of the Genevan government—rather at the hands of an ineluctably severe economic system. In 1568,

---

[1] For these complaints see Geneva, AEG, RC, LXXIX, fol. 91v., 24 June 1594; XC, fols. 58v., 52, 209v. and 211, 25 March, 11 August, 1 and 3 December 1595; XCI, fols. 11v., 144, 160, 9 June, 7 July, and 20 August 1596. This incident has been ignored by all the studies of Estienne I have checked.

[2] Geneva, AEG, RC, XCII, fols. 133v.-134, 3 October 1597.

[3] RENOUARD, pp. 438, ff.

the year of his greatest activity, he was apparently not able to meet all of his business obligations. He lost all of his printing property in an auction, to printer Bastian Honorat[1]. The auction, which was apparently called to satisfy his creditors, is not fully explained in the remaining records. Fortunately for François, a clause in the sale made it possible for him to buy the property back in a certain period of time. His brother-in-law at this critical juncture came to his aid and bailed him out—buying back the printing property from Honorat and standing guarantee for the Psalm and New Testament editions Estienne agreed to provide to Estienne Chappeaurouge to get paper and to begin production again.

We have a precise idea of the nature of at least some of the property Honorat received because it was inventoried in an agreement by which Honorat loaned it out to yet another printer, Jehan Barbier[2]. It consisted of (1) a case of notes weighing 26½ pounds, (2) a case of nonpareil Italic letters weighing 21½ pounds, (3) a case of nonpareil letters weighing 42 pounds, (4) two forms of nonpareil letters with their woods and " chasses " weighing 86 pounds, (5) a walnut " post " loaded with page of composition and a " gallere " loaded with three pages weighing 50 pounds, (6) a " post " of fir of distribution letter, weighing 20 pounds, (7) a " post " of fir and a basket loaded with broken distribution letter and some wood weighing 15 pounds, and (8) 61 pounds of letters in page.

The good deed of François Estienne's brother-in-law does not seem to have had very permanent effects. In August 1569, Laurent de Normandie, the wealthy book-seller who had helped François in so many ways, died suddenly of the plague. His business records reveal that he and printer François Perrin had jointly arranged to buy François Estienne's printing works for 1317 livres tournois, apparently in 1569[3]. François Estienne thus was forced by business difficulties clear out of the printing industry. This explains the hiatus in his production from 1569 to 1578, and perhaps why the production even after that was so desultory.

Both the Estienne brothers ended as failures. Politics and flaws of character brought Henri low after a relatively glorious career that won him international reknown. Business difficulties of a rather obscure sort ruined François. Perhaps a comparison of the two firms may indicate some of his troubles. François from the beginning lacked the financial resources of his brother. His inheritance was smaller and he could tap no important vein of wealth for his operating expenses. François also lacked the international contacts that made it relatively easy for Henri to sell his books. He perhaps could not afford frequent trips to Frankfort. In any case, he had to rely on others to sell his books. Both were probably hurt by a steady shrinkage of the market for their books[4]. The wars of religion in France pretty clearly had direct effects on

---

[1] The relevant documents can be found in Geneva, AEG, Notaire Aymé Santeur, I, fols. 84v. 85-85v., 111-111v., 142-142v., 10 February-27 April 1568; IV, fols. 61-63, 64-65, 9 December 1568 VI, fol. 124v., 25 September 1569.

[2] Geneva, AEG, Ragueau, XI, 61-62, 26 January 1569.

[3] Geneva, AEG, Archives de Familles, 1ère série, de Normandie, 1-2.

[4] One piece of evidence demonstrating that this shrinkage did occur : the card catalogue of new book titles published in Geneva during each year of the sixteenth century, recently compiled by the librarians of the BPU, shows that the number of titles declined markedly and fairly steadily, from 156? on.

the sale of Protestant books in French.   Not only were they proscribed by the monarchy in its fits of persecution of the Huguenots; the chaos caused by war must have made sale of books difficult even when royal power was lenient or weak.

My chief conclusion from this study is that printing prosperity and religious propaganda were inextricably tied together for the Estiennes at least (and probably for many more sixteenth-century printers).   Their biggest public was the French Protestant party; their best sellers were the books the French Reformed felt most necessary for their form of worship ; and the absorption of the French Protestant party in the rude task of self-preservation is the probable fundamental cause for their final decline.

XIX

THE PLANTIN BREVIARIES: A CASE STUDY IN THE SIXTEENTH-CENTURY BUSINESS OPERATIONS OF A PUBLISHING HOUSE[1]

The business history of the publishing industry could interest a wide variety of scholars. Knowledge of the technical side of its operations is absolutely essential to the bibliographer. Knowledge of its products is important to the variety of scholars who seriously interest themselves in the historical study of ideas. Knowledge of the ways in which it has been used could be of interest to students of politics and the management of public opinion. Information on the business operations of the industry could illuminate all these specialties, and in addition provide material of intrinsic interest to the economic historian.

A particularly rich source of information on the early history of the publishing industry can be found in the records of the Plantin-Moretus press. A quick look at the firm's own history and that of its records will explain why this is so[2]. The Plantin-Moretus press was founded in 1555 by Christophe Plantin, a recent immigrant to Antwerp from France, who had been a bookbinder by trade. He soon won the favor of the supreme ruler of the Low Countries, King Philip II. Royal patronage made it possible for Plantin to expand his operations greatly, and his appointment by Philip II to the new post of Prototypographer elevated him to a position of supremacy over all the other printers of the area. At its sixteenth-century peak, the House of Plantin may have been the largest publishing establishment Europe had ever seen. It was certainly many times bigger than houses in Basle, Geneva, and London, whose size we can estimate

---

[1] Most of the material upon which this article is based was gathered in the Museum Plantin-Moretus of the city of Antwerp, Belgium (hereafter cited as MPM). I would like to acknowledge the award of a grant from the Penrose Fund of the American Philosophical Society which made possible my work there, and the helpful advice of Professor and Mrs. Raymond de Roover of Boston College; Dr. Voet, Dr. Vervliet, and Mr. de Belser of the MPM staff; M. l'abbé Carlo de Clercq, president of the " Genootschap voor Antwerpse Geschiedenis ".

[2] The most important published materials on the Plantin press are Max ROOSES, *Christophe Plantin: imprimeur anversois* (Antwerp, 1883), hereafter cited as Rooses, and *Correspondance de Christophe Plantin*, ed. by Max Rooses and J. Denucé, 9 vols. (Antwerp, et. al.: Maatschappij der Antwerpsche Bibliophilen, 1883-1918), hereafter cited as PLANTIN, *Corr.* Both are full of valuable detail, but neither meets the highest scholarly standards. The biography lacks annotation, the correspondence edition is incomplete, and both contain occasional factual errors.

134

precisely from figures on the numbers of presses they owned [1]. It may have been surpassed in size by the German house of Koberger, but the evidence for this claim is not substantial [2].

After the death of Plantin the press continued to operate under the direction of the founder's son-in-law, Jean Moretus, and his descendants. They carried on the business until the second half of the nineteenth century. The press was finally closed down and the entire plant, with its building, presses, foundry, types, stocks of books, and business records, was sold to the city of Antwerp and turned into a municipal museum. The Plantin-Moretus Museum archives, therefore, possesses a practically complete set of account books and business correspondence for about three hundred years of continuous successful operation.

Beginning with Plantin himself, and continuing with his heirs, the firm made its most substantial profits from the sales of Roman Catholic devotional books, above all of Roman breviaries and Roman missals. Plantin printed an impressive number of books on other subjects, but the fragmentary statistics on edition size which have been compiled so far, make it clear that none of the other editions ever approached anything more than a fraction of the totals reached by the various editions of breviaries and missals.

This article will concentrate on the production and sale of breviaries. Total volume of sales of the breviary appears to have been slightly less than that of the missal, but the breviary line was launched first and contains more varieties of editions. This article will also concentrate on the years of Plantin's own career, 1555-1589, because it was in these years that the pattern of breviary production and sale was set.

The breviary Plantin produced in greatest quantity was the breviary of the Council of Trent, the one still used by Roman Catholic clergymen all over the world. He had printed earlier breviaries. At least two editions of the reformed version of Cardinal Quignonez came from his presses, one in 1557-1558 [3], and the other

---

[1] Elizabeth ARMSTRONG, *Robert Estienne, royal printer: an historical study of the elder Stephanus* (Cambridge University Press, 1954), p. 46-47.

[2] G. W. K. LOCHNER, ed., *Des Johann Neudörfer Schreib- und Rechenmeisters zu Nürnberg Nachrichten von Künstlern und Werkleuten daselbst: aus dem Jahre 1547...*, vol. X in *Quellenschriften für Kunstgeschichte und Kunsttechnik des Mittelalters und der Renaissance* (Vienna, 1875), p. 173 and ff., a biographical sketch of Anton Koberger, written 34 years after his death, reporting that he used 24 presses and hired 100 employees.

[3] Bibliographical information on this edition may be found in C. RUELENS & A. DE BACKER, *Annales Plantiniennes: première partie, Christophe Plantin (1555-1589)* (Brussels 1865), p. 14 (hereafter cited as RDB); in Hanns BOHATTA, *Bibliographie der Breviere, 1501-1850* (Leipzig: Verlag Karl W. Hiersemann, 1937), no. 222 (hereafter cited as Boh., *Brev.*); in *Bibliotheca Catholica Neerlandica Impressa, 1500-1727* (the Hague: Martinus Nijhoff, 1954), no. 2630 (hereafter cited as BCN); in *The British Museum Catalogue of Printed Books*, XXXII, Liturgies, col. 74 (hereafter cited as BM Catalogue). The title page is dated 1557, the colophon 1558. BCN misdates the edition as of 1558, on the basis of a copy in the Koninklijke Bibliotheek, the Hague, whic h has the title

in 1561 [1]. In 1561 he had also printed copies of the Breviary of the Benedictines of Cologne, acting as subcontractor for printer Materne Cholin of that city [2]. None of these early editions, however, seems to have been big enough to distinguish Plantin from other publishers of that period. In any case, we know very little about the circumstances of their production and distribution. It is upon the Tridentine breviary, therefore, that we must concentrate.

In its liturgical reforms, as in so many other fields, the Council of Trent repudiated earlier reforms which seemed modernizing, particularizing, or of a Protestant tendency, and repaired to a more antique and universal standard. During the discussions on the reform of the breviary, members of the Council attacked the Quignonez version, and urged adoption of a more conservative revision along lines suggested by the Theatines. In its concluding decrees of 1563, the Council entrusted the Vatican with the job of compiling a single authoritative breviary of this type. The job was completed by 1568 and the text released to the printers. A papal bull was promulgated requiring its use, with only a few exceptions, and reserving to the papacy power to control its printing [3].

Paul Manutius was the printer to whom the text of the new breviary was released. He managed the famous Aldine press which had been established in Venice, but which had been moved in part to Rome in 1561 when Manutius became the papal printer. To make sure that Manutius would recover his investment, the Vatican granted him a " privilege " or monopoly right to print the book for a term of years. The granting of such privileges by governmental authorities had become usual practice throughout Europe.

Since almost every clergyman remaining loyal to Rome would need a copy of the new breviary, the demand for it was bound to be tremendous. Manutius obviously could not handle the entire edition with his own facilities, and he was therefore authorized to license other printers to handle parts of the job, subject to approval of the Vatican. Months in advance of the official announcements of these arrangements, Plantin decided to apply for license to print and sell the new breviary in the Low Countries.

---

page torn off. The Quignonez breviary was also called the breviary of S. Crucis, after the cardinal's title, Holy-Cross-in-Jerusalem. M. l'abbé Carlo de CLERCQ " Les éditions bibliques, liturgiques et canoniques de Plantin ", *Gedenkboek der Plantin-Dagen, 1555-1955* (Antwerp : Vereeniging der Antwerpsche Bibliophielen, 1956), p. 296 and ff., skillfully surveys Plantin's publication of breviaries but includes what I believe to be mistaken information from RDB. This volume hereafter cited as *Gedenkboek*.

[1] RDB, p. 30 ; Boн., *Brev.*, no. 243 ; BCN, no. 2742 ; BM Catalogue, *loc. cit.*

[2] Boн., *Brev.*, no. 1054.

[3] Pierre BATIFFOL, *History of the Roman Breviary*, trans. fr. the 3rd French ed. (London, et al.: Longmans, Green, 1912), p. 194 and ff. ; Dom Suitbert BAUMER, *Histoire au Bréviaire*, trans. fr. German and revised by Dom Réginald Biron, 2 vols. (Paris : Letouzey et Ané, 1905), II, 191 and ff. The papal bull, *Quod a nobis*, 9 July 1568, may be found in full or in an abridged form in the front matter of any copy of the Tridentine breviary.

An application of this sort was not a simple business transaction, however. It involved negotiation not only with the papal printer but also with the highest authorities of the Roman Curia to win a regional privilege, plus further negotiation with local governmental authorities to make sure the privilege would be enforced. Fortunately Plantin was able to find an advocate in Rome with the power and the will to help him gain what he wanted. This was Cardinal Granvelle, a minister to Philip II, one of the shrewdest and most powerful statesmen of the day. Plantin had sold him books and printed various works at his request, when he had been stationed in the Low Countries.[1] He was now in Rome and thus in an ideal place to help Plantin. Conferences were arranged between Manutius and representatives of Granvelle and the Vatican. After the negotiations had been opened, Plantin began corresponding directly with Manutius.

Manutius at first wanted Plantin to pay 500 ecus in cash for a local privilege. Granvelle persuaded him to lower the offer to 300 ecus[2]. Plantin hesitated to risk even that much capital before he had had a chance to judge the size of the market. He countered with two alternative suggestions: either he would pay the 300 ecus in installments of 25 ecus for each 1,000 copies he actually printed in return for a privilege which would cover all "the Germanies" (no doubt including the Low Countries), or he would send Manutius a tenth of all the breviaries he published in return for the privilege[3]. Manutius accepted the second suggestion[4]. It was agreed that, on completion of the printing of each 1,000 copies of his breviaries, Plantin would send 100 copies to Manutius, charging him for packing and shipping expenses but for nothing more. In return Manutius granted Plantin a license. A papal brief confirmed the arrangement by granting Plantin the privilege for "Flanders," providing he submitted his copy for correction to a learned canon of the Antwerp Cathedral[5]. Plantin immediately made it clear that he interpreted the term "Flanders" to mean all the Low Countries under the rule of the King of Spain.

Plantin then applied to the royal council of the Low Countries in Brussels for ratification of this monopoly right[6]. Here he had

[1] PLANTIN, Corr., I, 16-17, 10 October 1561, on the book sales; Rooses, p. 44, an unidentified quotation from one of Plantin's business registers for 1562, for a commissioned printing.

[2] M. VAN DURME, ed., Supplément à la correspondance de Christophe Plantin (Antwerp: Nederlandsche Boekhandel, 1955), p. 46-48, Granvelle to Plantin, 30 August 1567. Hereafter cited as PLANTIN, Corr., Supplement.

[3] PLANTIN, Corr., I, 199-202, 18 October 1567, Plantin to Manutius.

[4] Ibid., I, 220-221, either December 1567 or January 1568, Plantin to Granvelle.

[5] Copies of the papal brief, dated 22 November 1568, can be found in every Plantin Tridentine breviary. A minute of the original has been preserved in MPM, Archives, no. 7, fol. 110v.

[6] PLANTIN, Corr., II, 31-32, 34-39, letters of application.

a scare. A young Antwerp competitor, who had some support from the city's church authorities and other men of influence, had somehow succeeded in getting a privilege only a little while before Plantin filed his application. The superior authority of Plantin's credentials and the power of his patrons, however, made it possible for him to have the other grant quashed without difficulty [1].

Now the way was cleared for actual publication of the breviary of the Council of Trent. Plantin began with the octavo format, a somewhat bigger size than the one he had used in his Quignonez breviaries, but one still intended for individual use of the average clergyman. Before 1569 was over he had three octavo editions of 1,050 copies each completed and one more underway. The first three were almost identical. The fourth was quite different. It was an expanded, large-type, two-volume version. He also produced an edition of the cheaper 16mo format in 1569, this of 1500 copies [2].

Further negotiations settled the way in which Manutius collected his payment. It was decided not to ship the promised " tenth " physically, but to remit the cash equivalent. Plantin accordingly sent 100 ecus to Rome by a bill of exchange obtained from a Zurich businessman, payable by a Flemish merchant in Rome [3]. Later payments were remitted in the same way, though through different intermediaries. Altogether Manutius and his successors got 210 ecus according to Plantin's accounts, 232 according to Plantin's letters [4], in either case a good deal less than the 300 that Manutius originally felt he had to have.

Before long Manutius and his successors began to complain that Plantin was violating the agreement by selling in areas not covered by its terms—specifically in Spain and Portugal. Plantin stoutly denied this in letters to them [5]. That there was some substance to this charge is revealed, however, by letters Plantin wrote to men on Granvelle's staff [6], and by an arrangement he soon made to supply liturgical books to the Spanish crown, an arrangement which he insisted superseded and voided the contract with Manutius.

The chief intermediary in negotiating this new agreement was Gabriel de Zayas, one of Philip II's powerful Secretaries of State. Plantin had dealt with him, as with Granvelle, when he was still

---

[1] Ibid., II, 22-23, 10 December, 1568, Plantin to Malpas, a report of the incident.

[2] MPM, Archives, no. 16 " Grand livre 1568-1573 ", fols. 115v. and 116r. Cf. PLANTIN, Corr., II, 90, 26 November 1569, Plantin to Manutius ; II, 71-72, 17 September 1569, Plantin to Granvelle ; ROOSES, p. 157-158.

[3] PLANTIN, Corr., II, 111, 18 February 1570, Plantin to Manutius.

[4] Ibid., III, 331-334, 27-29 May 1573. Both sources agree that the number of florins due Manutius was 465.

[5] Ibid., II, 120-121, 25 February 1570, Plantin to Manutius.

[6] Ibid., II, 112, summary of 18 February 1570 letter to M. de Goneville ; II, 235, 25 August 1571, Plantin to Morillon.

138

stationed in the Low Countries [1]. He had already helped to win Plantin royal subsidy for his Polyglot Bible, a multi-lingual edition which was a scholarly triumph though not a commercial success. Philip II had characteristically insisted on close supervision of the printing of the Polyglot Bible. He had dispatched to Antwerp as his personal representative, a learned Spanish linguist, Dr. B. Arias Montanus, who quickly became a close friend of Plantin [2]. Zayas and Montanus now helped Plantin persuade Philip II to order printing of enormous quantities of liturgical books for distribution to the clergy in all the many lands controlled by Spain.

Breviaries were the first liturgical books printed for this huge order. The text of these breviaries, however, was not supposed to be precisely the same as the one authorized by the Council of Trent. Philip II had his own strong ideas about the exact form the breviary should follow, and had petitioned the Vatican for permission to use a text that incorporated his own minor revisions. Permission, of course, was granted. Philip's changes in the text provided Plantin with his excuse for breaking the Manutius contract. There is reason to believe, however, that this was not the only type of breviary he actually delivered to Spain. Of the original copies of breviaries published in the years Plantin was working primarily for the Spanish crown, which are preserved in the collection of the Plantin-Moretus Museum, only one is specifically labelled a Spanish breviary [3].

Production was now on a much larger scale, and Plantin had to adapt his facilities to this fact. He obtained additional housing for his equipment and his workers. He bought several new presses. He hired new workers and made new arrangements with old. Two specific examples will illustrate the nature of these new labor arrangements. Henricus Alsens, who had been a compositor for Plantin and was now in business on his own, became what might be called a subcontractor for breviary printing. Plantin's accounts list payments to him for batches of specified sheets of the breviary, running from February 1570, through 1571, well into 1572 [4]. On a humbler level, Clas (for Nicholas) van Linschoten, one of Plantin's journeyman printers, was made a breviary-printing specialist, and remained one for the better part of his life. Plantin's accounts list piece work wage payments to him for work on breviaries in 1558, 1571-1575,

[1] ROOSES, pp. 20-21, quoting from a ms. biographical minute of Plantin, prepared by his grandson in 1604 ; full text on pp. 392-393.

[2] ROOSES, ch. VI, pp. 109-148 ; PLANTIN, Corr., I, 48-52, 19 December 1566, Plantin to Zayas ; PLANTIN, Corr., Supplement, pp. 30-31.

[3] MPM, A-1244, copy of one of two octavo breviaries of 1572.

[4] MPM, Archives, no. 31 " Livre des ouvriers, 1563-1574 ", fols. 35, 91, 100, 101v., 102.

1577, 1579-1589 [1]. He occasionally was also paid for work on other books, usually liturgical, whose production was alternated with breviaries, especially after 1575.

In order to meet the Spaniards' needs, Plantin also increased the variety of breviaries he produced. In addition to the editions in octavo and 16mo, which he was now publishing in great quantity, he began printing breviaries in quarto and folio. The folio breviaries were luxury products, exquisitely illustrated, expensively printed, costing much more than the smaller formats. They were no doubt intended for use by the royal chaplains, leaders of the Spanish hierarchy, and the more important monastic houses in land controlled by Spain.

Details of all these editions were carefully regulated from the royal court. Sample sheets and then proofs were sent by courier to Spain. They came back copiously marked and accompanied with sheets of suggestions. The suggestions covered all sorts of matters: kinds of paper, varieties of type, proper alternation of colors in the rubrics and elsewhere, and many minor typographical corrections and changes. Many of these sheets have been preserved in the Plantin-Moretus Museum. Some of the proof corrections are apparently in the hand of the king himself [2]. Certainly this would be characteristic of his almost ludicrous attention to detail. The printers, of course, were particularly careful to incorporate all of the royal suggestions into the final texts.

Work on this huge order of liturgical books occupied much, but not all, of the time and the resources of the Plantin press from 1571 to 1575. In 1576 the Spanish Fury destroyed much of Antwerp. Plantin managed to bribe himself free from destruction. But the subsequent business decline and the Calvinist occupation of the city naturally forced him to restrict his trade with Spain. This did not, interestingly, mean total cessation of the publication of Tridentine breviaries. New editions kept appearing all during these years, continued to appear when the city was reoccupied by Farnese and reconverted to Catholicism, and were still appearing when Plantin died in 1589 [3]. Large orders were still placed by the Spanish crown

---

[1] *Ibid.*, fols. 120v.-122; MPM, Archives, no. 32 " Livre des ouvriers, 1580-1590 ", accounts no. 5, 46, 73, 97, 115, 131, 151.

[2] MPM, Archives, no. 122 " Missale et Breviarium ", p. 416 inter alia.

[3] Further verifiable editions include :

1577, in 8° (MPM, A-1256, a copy ; BOH., *Brev.*, no. 313).

1578, in 16 mo (BOH., *Brev.*, no. 316 ; MPM, Archives, no. 32, Livre des ouvriers, 1571-1579, fols. 237, 281v.-282, 274-275 ; PLANTIN, *Corr.*, VI, 21 and 42, Plantin to Zayas, and other letters in *ibid.*).

1579, in 8° (BOH., *Brev.*, no. 321 ; PLANTIN, *Corr.*, VI, 89, Plantin to Zayas).

1580, in 16 mo (BOH., *Brev.*, no. 327 ; RDB, p. 215 ; MPM, Archives, no. 33, Livre des ouvriers, 1580-1590, fols. 4v. and 11v.).

1583, in 8° (BOH., *Brev.*, no. 333 ; BCN, no. 3792 ; MPM, Archives, no. 33, fols. 45v.-46v., 64v., 67, 72v.-73, 74, 86v., 91v.).

during these periods. Even after Plantin's death, these printings continued. Indeed, under the management of his heirs, breviaries and other liturgical books absorbed an even greater percentage of the resources of the press and became a religious staple for the devout, not only in Spain and her Netherlands, but also in her growing New World colonies.

These were the ways in which the Plantin breviaries were produced. Now let us turn to an analysis of the ways in which they were sold. In this, as in most of Plantin's business, four principal channels of distribution can be distinguished. They are : (1) direct retail sales through the shop attached to his plant in Antwerp ; (2) sales at the Frankfurt book fair, the biggest entrepôt of the book trade during the sixteenth century ; (3) wholesale sales to other booksellers ; (4) sales in large lots to individual buyers who arranged their own methods of further distribution.

Even at the height of his career, Plantin maintained a small retail business, selling books in separate copies or small lots to individuals who came to his retail shop. Details of this business are revealed by two surviving account books, which contain weekly or biweekly summaries of these sales. The first was kept from 1565 to 1569, the second from 1569 to 1576 [1]. Together they cover the period of Plantin's greatest production of breviaries. They permit several general observations about Plantin's retail business.

Before the publication of the Tridentine version, retail breviary sales were quite sporadic. Rarely were more than one or two copies sold. There were no sales at all for long periods. Several entries make it clear that at least some of the breviaries sold were published by Plantin himself. These must have remained in stock for several years, since the last Plantin breviary edition for which there is sure evidence, previous to the opening of these account books, was his 1561 Quignonez version [2]. Other entries, by including such place

---

1585, in 16 mo (MPM, Archives, no. 33, fols. 88, 90v.-91, 96v.-97 ; Boн., *Brev.*, nos. 344 and 345 are to other formats, 4º and 12 mo, for which I can find no further evidence).
1587, in 4º (MPM, A-1565 I & II, a copy ; Boн., *Brev.*, no. 351 ; BCN, no. 3923 ; PLANTIN, *Corr.*, VII-IX, *passim*, under 1586).
1588, in 8º (MPM, A-1240, a copy ; Boн., *Brev.*, no. 355 ; RDB, p. 307).
1589, in 16 mo (MPM, A-221 & A-1285, copies with different kinds of illustrations, perhaps separate editions ; Boн., *Brev.*, no. 360).

[1] MPM, Archives, no. 43-IV " Vente à la boutique, 1565-1569 ", and no. 43-III " Vente à la boutique, 1569-1576 ".

[2] I can find no sure evidence for reports of Plantin breviaries in 1562-1563, 1565, and 1568. RDB, p. 34, lists one for 1562 ; MPM, Bibliographie Plantinienne, lists one for 1563. The alleged example, MPM, R43.6, is a Quignonez breviary published in Venice. Evidence for a 1565 edition is supposedly contained in MPM, Archives, no. 1, accounts 31 and 54, but these are clearly references to a collation, not an entire edition. Reports of a 1568 edition can be found in RDB, p. 78 ; Boн., *Brev.*, no. 269 ; Rooses, p. 154. The alleged example, MPM, K-55, lacks title page and colophon, and contains 1568 front matter identical to that found in all of Plantin's Tridentine breviaries, of any date.

names as " Paris " and " Venetiis," suggest that at least some of
the breviaries Plantin sold were printed by other men. Perhaps he
had acquired them by the barter of books which seems to have been
constant in the trade. When format is specified it is almost always
octavo or 16mo. When copies were gilded or bound, an extra charge
was levied on the customer.

After the publication of the breviary of the Council of Trent,
retail sales immediately shot up and remained high through 1569
and well into 1570. Many sales were now of small lots rather than of
single copies. There were a number of orders for thirteen copies,
sold for the price of twelve. Some of these lots may have gone to
church or monastic officials, buying for a group of clergymen. Others
went to men who can be identified as booksellers. A simple but definite
price policy can now be discerned. Each one-volume octavo breviary
normally sold for one florin; each 16mo breviary for 16 patards or
stivers [1]. These were still the only formats. Discounts of a tenth or
a twelfth for large orders were common, but by no means invariable.
An extra charge was again levied for gilding or binding.

A decline in retail breviary sales coincides with the beginning of
work on the huge Spanish order. Perhaps the local market was
becoming saturated; perhaps Plantin could not spare copies for the
retail market. Most of the time sales remain better than they had
been in the earliest period, but they are no longer large enough to
provide a significant source of revenue. The price policy remains the
same. Only the smaller formats are sold here. Though Plantin was
now producing large-format breviaries in quantity, he apparently
made no effort to sell them in his retail shop.

The Frankfurt fair provided Plantin with a second channel for
distributing his books. It was a bi-annual international book trade
fair, held during Lent and again in September in the city of Frankfurt
on the Main [2]. It provided vital services in co-ordinating the European
book trade during the sixteenth century and beyond. Both of these
fairs were attended every year, perhaps from 1565, surely from 1567,
either by Plantin or his son-in-law Jean Moretus, the two of them
together, or some other important member of the firm [3].

An impressive variety of business was carried on at Frankfurt.
On different occasions, Plantin and Moretus arranged for the purchase
of paper, of woodcuts, and of type; arranged book shipments;
negotiated for the cashing of bills of exchange; collected news about

---

[1] Patards is the Flemish name, stuivers the Dutch, stivers the English. Twenty
of them equalled one florin.

[2] Dr. Aloys RUPPEL " Die Bücherwelt des 16. Jahrhunderts und die Frankfurter
Büchermessen ", *Gedenkboek*, p. 146-165. Cf. James Westfall Thompson, ed., *The
Frankfort Book Fair* (Chicago: the Caxton Club, 1911).

[3] PLANTIN, *Corr.*, III, 3, 26 February 1565, Plantin to Masius; Plantin, *Corr.*,
Supplement, p. 260-262.

political events which affected sales, such as the St. Bartholomew's massacre; met with learned authors and possible patrons; released announcements or displayed proofs of major publishing projects such as the Polyglot Bible [1]. Probably the most important kind of business carried on at these fairs, however, was the buying and selling of books. This was particularly true for the publishers and sellers of classical works, which of course enjoyed enormous prestige in the sixteenth century, but which apparently sold to a rather small and widely scattered international market.

Surviving records of Plantin's purchases and sales at Frankfurt are not as complete as we might wish. They consist of a series of " carnets " running from 1571 to 1644, giving the record of his accounts with other publishers there, but unfortunately not naming the titles of the works bought and sold, with the exception of one carnet. They are supplemented by a series of " cahiers " running from 1579 to 1631, which do give more detailed information about his transactions, but unfortunately for a period after his biggest breviary editions.

The overwhelming majority of the books Plantin sent to Frankfurt were in Latin. A few were in French. Most of them were editions of the classics or books by humanists. Works of the great Flemish neo-Stoic Justus Lipsius were among the house's best sellers at these fairs. There was a sprinkling of religious books, especially Bibles. In return Plantin bought books from a variety of places. He was particularly interested in books printed in Basle, Cologne, Venice, Geneva, and Lyons [2]. His biggest single account was almost always with Georgius Willerus, a bookseller of Augsburg.

Breviaries were sold at Frankfurt but their sales were rather limited. Two samples can serve to demonstrate this. For the Lenten fair of 1579, the cahier reveals that Plantin shipped two kinds of breviaries to Frankfurt, 75 copies of a two-volume breviary in 16mo, and 50 copies of the octavo breviary " ad long." He recorded sales at the fair in two ways, by account with named booksellers in some quantity, and by day in small amounts, no doubt to individual retail buyers. During this particular fair, Plantin sold 29 of the two-volume 16mo breviaries by account, 10 by day, for a total of 39; 26 of the octavo breviaries " ad long " by account, 5 by day, for a total of 31; 13 breviaries in 16mo with copper-plate illustrations by account, 5 by day, for a total of 18. Altogether he sold 88 breviaries, not a very good percentage of the 125 he had brought along with him.

---

[1] PLANTIN, *Corr.*, I, 51, 19 December 1566, Plantin to Zayas; III, 178-182, 6 and 12 September 1572, Moretus to Plantin; and *passim* in *ibid.* and in PLANTIN, *Corr. Supplement.*

[2] MPM, Archives, no. 849 " Carnet de Francfort, 1571 ", contains a list of cities from which he had purchased books, at the end.

He regularly stored books between fairs in a strong-box which was left in Frankfurt. In the inventory of books left behind after this fair are listed four of the two-volume 16mo breviaries with copperplate illustrations, 22 octavo breviaries, 34 two-volume breviaries in 16mo, altogether a small fraction of a stock of several thousand volumes [1]. It will be noticed that the figures for sales and storage total more than the number brought to Frankfurt. Perhaps Plantin already had copies in a stock left from earlier fairs.

The cahier for September 1586 corroborates this pattern. At that fair Plantin sold 128 breviaries in 16mo, 14 copies of a one-volume quarto breviary, and one copy of an octavo breviary. At the Lenten fair of 1587, he sold four copies of the 16mo breviary. At the Lenten fair of 1588 he sold 38 breviaries in quarto and 60 breviaries in 16mo, even though there were no breviaries listed in his inventories of books sent to Frankfurt or stored after the fair. Perhaps they were obtained by barter; perhaps physical transfer of them came later. In the next two fairs there were again no breviaries in the inventories of books sent to Frankfurt [2].

It seems clear that the Frankfurt fairs were not a major outlet for Plantin's breviaries. This would be a more conclusive generalization if the records of transactions at the fairs were more nearly complete, but it nevertheless seems reasonably safe. Perhaps Frankfurt's proximity to Lutheran territory explains this. Perhaps it is explained by the peculiar requirements of the trade in liturgical books.

More importance can be attached to the third channel for distribution of the Plantin breviaries, wholesale purchase by other booksellers. Because of their importance, Plantin from the beginning kept careful records of his accounts with these customers. They are kept in simple single-entry ledgers, and arranged by individual bookseller. On the debit side are listed separate sales, specifying book title, quantity, unit price, and total price. On the credit side are listed periodic cash payments and, often, book purchases by Plantin. He normally sold far more books than he bought. The accounts, therefore, almost always had to be balanced by cash payments. At the time an account was balanced, Plantin would normally credit the other bookseller with a substantial trade discount. The rate of discount varied a good deal, and seems to have been negotiated with each individual. It averaged about 15%, but occasionally ran as high as 40% [3]. When the account was balanced, it

---

[1] MPM, Archives, no. 962 " Cahier de Francfort, Quadregesima Anno 1579 ".

[2] MPM, Archives, nos. 963, 965, 966, 967 " Cahiers de Francfort ".

[3] ROOSES, p. 254. Cf. Colin CLAIR " Christopher Plantin's Trade-Connexions with England and Scotland ", The Library (Fifth Series, Vol. XIV, No. 1, March 1959), p. 41-42.

144

was normally closed, and a new one with the same bookseller would be begun when he made his next purchase.

A good example of a set of bookseller accounts is the series recording Plantin's transactions with Arnold Birckmann, de la Poulle Grasse, of Antwerp [1]. Debit items in these accounts invariably ran into hundreds of florins, rising from a first entry of 156+ florins in the first of three accounts for 1565, to 1102+ florins in the first of three for 1571. They then declined until Birckmann's assets were all transferred to Arnold Mylius of Cologne, a transaction completed in 1584. Against these Birckmann was credited with smaller amounts for books purchased by Plantin, generally less than 100 florins, fluctuating from 55+ florins in the opening account, to 224+ florins in the first of five 1569 accounts. Periodically there was a settlement that always involved a cash payment to Plantin, a variable trade discount, and occasionally more books supplied by Birckmann. For example, the 1575 account was settled for 401 fls. 10 d$\frac{1}{4}$ in books (about 31%); 240 fls. 8d in discount (about 18%); 657 fls. 12d$\frac{1}{2}$ in cash (about 51%); discharging a total debt listed as 1301 fls. 13d$\frac{3}{4}$ [sic].

Most of the accounts were a good deal smaller than this one, and many of them did not last more than a few years, perhaps indicating a high percentage of business failures among the smaller booksellers. The account with Jacob Peetersen (Paets) of Amsterdam, for example, ran from 1576 to 1588 and then was stopped [2]. The account with Iacobus Plancius of Bruges was begun in 1565, became inactive in 1568, and was closed in 1579 [3]. On the other hand, business success is revealed by the account with Jan Bogaerdt of Louvain and Douai, who seldom bought as much as 200 florins worth of books while he remained in Louvain, but who regularly purchased 500 florins worth and more after his move to Douai in 1576 [4].

The growth and the geographic spread of Plantin's business is revealed by a survey of all of these bookseller accounts. In the 1566-1569 period he had dealings with 98 booksellers in 37 cities. In the 1568-1578 period he dealt with 200 booksellers in 61 cities. In the 1575-1593 period the firm dealt with 258 booksellers in 65 cities. The period of most rapid growth obviously coincides with the publication of the Tridentine breviaries and other liturgical books.

Most of this business was centered in the Low Countries. The overwhelming majority of Plantin's bookseller clients lived in cities

---

[1] MPM, Archives, nos. 40 " Libraires A, 1566-1569 "; 17 " B, 1568-1578, Grootboek Boekhandelaars "; 41 " Libraires d'Anvers, signé D, 1577-1580 "; 19 " Grand livre signé C, 1572-1589 "; under account numbers as indexed.

[2] MPM, Archives, nos. 17; 110 " E, 1575-1593, Libraires hors d'Anvers "; under account numbers as indexed.

[3] MPM, Archives, nos. 40, 17, 110; under account numbers as indexed.

[4] *Ibid.*

under the jurisdiction of Philip II, including many in areas since annexed to France, and others in areas at that time joining in the revolt which was to form the independent Netherlands. Of these cities, his native Antwerp provided Plantin with by far the most customers. Louvain, intellectual center of the Low Countries and site of the famous Catholic University, provided the next biggest number during the earlier years of Plantin's career. It was later superseded by Douai, whose new Jesuit University was rapidly winning it a place as an intellectual center, and by the industrial city of Ghent.

TABLE [1]

City	Number of bookseller clients		
	1566-1569	1568-1578	1575-1593
Antwerp	15	27	47
Louvain	11	16	12
Douai	2	7	16
Ghent	4	9	13

While Plantin also maintained relations with a few booksellers in other parts of Europe, including such important printing centers as Paris, Lyons, and Venice, his accounts with most of them were quite small and reveal a rather sporadic trade. There are no accounts at all with booksellers in the important Swiss Protestant publishing centers of Basle, Geneva, and Zurich. Other records reveal that he occasionally did deal with booksellers from these cities, but this business seems to have been reserved mainly for the Frankfurt fairs.

It would require a good deal of space and time to trace all the breviary transactions in the bookseller accounts. Generally it may be said that during 1569 and 1570, the years when the Tridentine breviary was first produced, almost every dealer with whom Plantin then conducted business bought copies. The number of copies per order varied a good deal. A common pattern was sale in lots of either 6 or 7, or 12 or 13, every month. Most of these orders were for the 16mo and octavo formats, and were presumably, therefore, destined for the retail trade. Some of the orders were smaller, some larger. Arnold Mylius, Birckmann's associate, bought 100 breviaries on 20 July 1569, and paid for them in two installments, one on the purchase date, the second on 29 October of that year [2]. A decade later Mylius again placed a big order, this time for 250 breviaries in 16mo on 24 July 1579 [3].

Most of the breviary sales to booksellers stopped quite abruptly in 1571. The bulk of Plantin's ever-increasing production of these

---

[1] Tabulated from MPM, Archives, nos. 40, 17, 110 and 41. Cf. table in Rooses, p. 406-410.

[2] MPM, Archives, no. 17, account 21.

[3] MPM, Archives, no. 19, account 121.

books was now obviously being shifted to his fourth channel of distribution—sales in large lots to individual buyers, above all to the King of Spain. The details of the huge Spanish order for breviaries were worked out in the course of the year 1571. Following Plantin's suggestion, it was agreed that he would first supply quantities of readily salable octavo breviaries. Later when the exact form of the text had been established and the arrangements for publication had been worked out, Plantin would begin producing the lavish folio breviaries dear to the king's heart. He persuaded the king to forego the printing of large numbers of breviaries in parchment, partly because of their tremendous cost, but more because of the practical difficulty of obtaining enough parchment in a limited time [1].

Before the year was out, Plantin had begun shipping breviaries to Spain, to the Library of " St. James of Spain." Further distribution was the responsibility of the Spanish crown, and seems to have been handled for the most part through shops set up by the Jeronymite friars who maintained a headquarters establishment in Philip's favorite palace, the Escorial. Careful records were kept of Plantin's shipments, in several copies and in both French and Spanish, from 1571 to 1575 [2]. Altogether he shipped some 15,505 breviaries during these years, plus a few specially decorated presentation copies. They were printed in four different formats: 2400 in 16mo; 8739, more than half, in octavo; 2200 in quarto; 2166 in folio. The octavo format was begun first and production of it continued through 1574. A first printing of folio breviaries was produced in 1573; the rest were published in 1575. The quarto breviaries were all produced in one big printing in 1574. Publication of the 16mo breviaries was handled in 1572 and 1573.

Prices for these breviaries were fixed by negotiation between Plantin and Dr. B. Arias Montanus, the king's scholarly agent in Antwerp. They vary considerably according to format. Reason for these substantial variations can be found in the fact that, in the sixteenth century, paper costs far exceeded direct labor costs for composition and printing combined [3]. Formats requiring greater quantities of paper naturally commanded substantially higher prices. Precise figures can make this clearer. The octavo breviaries sold on

---

[1] PLANTIN, *Corr.*, II, 196-201, n.d., minute of document prepared for Philip II. Cf. II, 169-170, n.d., minute of Plantin to Philip II; III, 335-338, 29 June 1573, Plantin to Aguilar.

[2] MPM, Archives, nos. 19 and 22 " Envois de livres à Philippe II, 1571-1576 ", contain the most complete records. For partial duplicates see nos. 5 " Biblia Regia; Missel; Compte du Roi d'Espagne, 1568-1578 (in Spanish) " and 18 " + + 1571-1582 Grootboek ". I did not discover any discrepancies between these accounts, and can therefore find no explanation for the substantially different totals of money and books supplied by Rooses, p. 169.

[3] Raymond de ROOVER " The business organisation of the Plantin press in the setting of sixteenth century Antwerp ", *Gedenkboek*, p. 235 and ff.

7 February 1572 were priced at 19 ½ stivers per copy, just short of a florin. On the same day 16mo breviaries were sold for 13 ½ stivers per copy. In 1573, octavo breviaries were sold for 20 ½ stivers, 16mo breviaries for 14 stivers for the one-volume edition, 32 stivers for a two-volume edition. In the same year, however, folio breviaries sold for 4 florins 10 stivers with one kind of paper, and for 5 florins 10 stivers with another. The 1574 quarto breviaries sold for 46 stivers, or 2 florins 6 stivers. A 1574 edition of two-volume octavo breviaries sold for 32 stivers a set, or 1 florin 12 stivers. It can be seen that the prices approached a ratio of two-thirds, one, two, four, for the four formats in ascending size. There were also occasional surplus charges, for copper-plate engravings in place of the usual woodcuts, for parchment copies, and for other kinds of special work.

The total value of the liturgical books shipped to Spain in these years was fixed at 110,136 florins 14 ½ stivers. Roughly a third of this handsome sum was for breviaries. The accounts reveal that all of the debits that went to make up this total were met by prompt cash payments by officers of the Spanish crown. These men also arranged for shipment of the books, sometimes by ship from Antwerp harbor, in other cases overland to some French port. The end of these accounts trails off, and it is not clear that Plantin received payment of the final 5717 florins 10 stivers, or that he delivered the last lot of books.

An exceedingly odd fact about the royal account is that it does not include any discounts, even though Philip II was buying in greater quantities than any other customer Plantin ever had. Perhaps the special prices negotiated for this order were supposed to include discounts. The actual prices make this supposition dubious, however. The unit price of 13 ½ or 14 stivers for the one-volume 16mo breviaries is well below the usual retail price of 16 stivers, though not quite enough to equal the price with discount which Plantin gave his best bookseller customers. The unit price of 19 ½ or 20 ½ stivers for the one-volume octavo breviaries, however, is about the normal retail price, with no provision for discount at all. Perhaps the notoriously poor credit of Philip II's treasury justified what seems to be an overcharge.

It is hard to estimate Plantin's profits on these breviary sales. Perhaps they can be guessed by extension from earlier editions for which we have fuller information on costs. Professor and Mrs. de Roover have studied a number of the earlier Plantin accounts, and conclude that he normally set his prices to obtain a profit of a little better than 100%, providing the entire edition sold out [1]. This is

---

[1] E.g., Florence EDLER (de ROOVER) " Cost Accounting in the Sixteenth Century : the books of account of Christopher Plantin, Antwerp, Printer and Publisher ", *The Accounting Review*, XII, No. 3 (September, 1937), p. 232.

XIX

an estimate of gross profit. Many of Plantin's workers, like many
workers of any sort in that day, obtained free lodgings in their
master's house. Plantin's estimates of wage costs, therefore, were
probably misleadingly low. An estimate of net profits would have
to take into account Plantin's household expenses, but of these
there are no records.

In any case, it is clear that Plantin prospered during the years
in which his biggest business was with the King of Spain. He bought
several new presses, increased his stock of types, matrices, and
foundry equipment, and in 1576 bought the building which the firm
used for the next three centuries and which is now the site of the
Plantin-Moretus Museum. Most of his fixed capital which has survived
seems to have been bought with Spanish profits.

These facts must cast suspicion on Plantin's later bitter complaints
against his treatment by the Spanish crown, which were aired in a
public letter issued from Protestant Leiden in 1583[1]. Some of the
figures in this letter can be demonstrated to be exaggerated[2]. And one
suspects Plantin of ulterior motives in defending his new business
with Dutch Protestants by claiming that he had been forced to it,
by the bad financial treatment he suffered from Philip II.

Other men also placed large orders with Plantin, though none
ever even approached the King of Spain's in size. An example of
one of the more prominent is Gilbert d'Oignies, Bishop of Tournai.
He paid Plantin one hundred ecus to subsidize the printing of an
antiphonary and a psalter, and ordered from him a number of breviaries and other liturgical books, presumably for the use of priests
in his diocese[3]. The numbers of copies in these orders are not specified
in the correspondence.

* * *

These, then, were the ways in which one of the largest sets of
sixteenth-century editions were produced and distributed. If there
were space, it would be instructive to compare them with arrangements in the Protestant camp for the production and distribution
of the similar set of editions of the Huguenot Psalter, details of which
have recently been uncovered[4]. Perhaps it would be more useful,

[1] Text in ROOSES, p. 410-417.

[2] Raymond de ROOVER in *Gedenkboek*, p. 240 and ff.

[3] PLANTIN, *Corr.*, II, 150-151, 16 July 1570, Plantin to d'Oignies; II, 168-169,
22 October 1570; II, 303-304, 15 March 1572; and *passim*.

[4] E. DROZ " Antoine Vincent : la propagande protestante par le psautier ", *Aspects
de la propagande religieuse* (Geneva : Droz, 1957), p. 276-293, hereafter cited as *Aspects*.
Cf. Paul CHAIX, *Recherches sur l'imprimerie à Genève de 1550 à 1564: étude bibliogra-
phique, économique et littéraire* (Geneva : Droz, 1954), *passim*, and Robert M. KINGDON,
Geneva and the Coming of the Wars of Religion in France, 1555-1563 (Geneva : Droz,
1956), p. 99 and ff.

however, to conclude by venturing some generalizations which might serve as hypotheses for future research.

Large-scale publication in the sixteenth century seems to have depended in part on political patronage. Every one of the printers most famous to bibliographers for the quality of his products had behind him the interest and the financial support of powerful political leaders. The Aldines were patronized by the Popes. The Estiennes were patronized by the Kings of France. The Plantin-Moretus were patronized by the Kings of Spain. A printer who aspired to European-wide reputation and substantial financial success, was almost required to become a diplomat, to establish contacts at a powerful court, and to win the financial interest of a ruler. He won from his patron not only financial backing, but also prestige and a variety of legal advantages, the most common of which were privileges. The only areas in which this is not strikingly apparent are Germany and Switzerland, where the printing and publishing industry was indeed strong. Here, if Geneva can provide a pattern, local governments met some of the need by providing legal regulation, and private investors, such as Ulrich Fugger and Laurent de Normandie, helped supply the capital [1].

Large-scale publication in the sixteenth century also seems to have required a list which included at least one book that could appeal to the largest market of the day—the religious market. This does not mean, of course, that printers had to be personally orthodox or even especially pious. Plantin at one point early in his career joined a heterodox religious group called the " House of Love "; he later accepted the financial help of Calvinist partners and helped found a clandestine Calvinist press; toward the end of his career he was printing books for both the Spanish crown and its arch enemy, the States-General of the Netherlands. And all during this bewildering career, his letters to Spain kept insisting on his devotion to the Roman Catholic faith [2]. But the fact remains that Plantin made probably the most important part of his fortune from the publication of breviaries and missals, the Estiennes made probably the most important part of their fortune from the publication of a Reformed Bible, and so it went. Perhaps this might even lead us to an explanation of the entire rise of the printing industry. Western civilization has long been distinguished by a religion which places peculiar importance on a written Scripture as an ultimate source of truth. Hence the persistent demand for many copies of the Bible and of devotional books such as the breviary and the psalter which

[1] Heidi-Lucie SCHLAEPFER " Laurent de Normandie ", *Aspects*, p. 176-230; Robert M. KINGDON " The business activities of printers Henri and François Estienne ", *Aspects*, p. 258-275.

[2] See L. VOET " The Personality of Plantin ", *Gedenkboek*, p. 199-213, for a skillful recent study of the problem of Plantin's religious connections.

are partly or wholly derived from the Bible. This demand may well have led to Gutenberg's initial invention of the printing press. And it certainly must have been enormously strengthened by the Reformation, with its renewed emphasis on the importance of Scripture, and its continuing demand that Scripture be made available in the vernacular. Hence the enormous growth of the printing and publishing industry in the course of the sixteenth century [1].

In any case, we are dealing here with economic phenomena which cannot be explained internally, by reference to other economic phenomena. They demand reference to the general culture of the period.

---

[1] For further evidence for this view, see H. J. MARTIN " Ce qu'on lisait à Paris au XVIᵉ siècle ", *Bibliothèque d'Humanisme et Renaissance*, t. XXI (1959), p. 230, an interpretation of material in R. DOUCET, *Les bibliothèques parisiennes au XVIᵉ siècle* (Paris : Picard, 1956).

XX

Christopher Plantin and His Backers, 1575-1590

A Study in the Problems of Financing Business during War *

The problems of conducting business during a war, in an area where fighting is actually taking place, can be exceedingly serious, even insurmountable. This logically ought to be particularly true for a firm as dependent on sales and as deeply involved in the ideological concomitants of warfare as a large publishing house. One such firm which managed to survive and surmount a series of military crises with astonishing success, was the firm established by Christopher Plantin in Antwerp, shortly before the beginning of the eighty-years war between the Spanish and Dutch which devastated and finally split irrevocably the provinces of the Netherlands.

Christopher Plantin had to face the problems posed by war particularly from 1576 on. In 1576 the sack of Antwerp by mutinous Spanish troops, known to us as the Spanish Fury, not only threatened his business with physical damage, but also led to suspension of the subsidies and huge purchase orders awarded to him by King Philip II of Spain, for the printing of quantities of Roman Catholic devotional and liturgical books. These subsidies and orders had made it possible for Plantin to buy the presses, types, and real property which made him probably the largest publisher in all of Europe during that period. Their withdrawal left him with this property intact, but with a constant need for substantial sums of money to purchase the supplies (above all paper) and to cover the other expenses of operating a business of some size.

The times were not propitious for the solution of this problem. Antwerp had barely recovered from the Spanish Fury and the subsequent occupation of the city by Dutch Calvinist troops and, for a time, their French allies, when the advancing Spanish armies of the Duke of Parma invested the city, in 1584. And the capitulation of the city, in 1585, after

* I am indebted to Professor and Mrs. RAYMOND DE ROOVER for helpful criticism of a draft of this article.

a long and bitter siege, left its important trade artery to the sea, the river Scheldt, blockaded by Dutch fleets for decades to come.

In spite of all this turmoil, the Plantin firm did find the financing it needed, it did survive, and, when Plantin died in 1589, he left to his heirs a business so well established that it flourished for more than two hundred years, down into the nineteenth century. It is toward an explanation of this economic " miracle " that this paper is addressed.

Many of the elements in such an explanation have already been suggested by experts on Plantin studies, above all by Max Rooses, the dean of them all. A full explanation of this phenomenon must wait upon an exhaustive study of the Plantin business papers preserved in the Plantin-Moretus Museum, particularly of the firm's account books. Some elements of an explanation can be gleaned, however, from a rather mixed set of manuscript instruments of credit which can be found among these business papers and which have recently been called to my attention by Dr. L. Voet, curator of the museum.[1] It is from these unpublished documents that the substance of this paper is derived.

Most of these instruments of credit are simple promissory notes. They are all signed by Plantin. A few are also countersigned by his son-in-law Jan Moerentorf (or Moretus), who was then his principal assistant and book-keeper, and who was to become his principal heir. They promise repayment of a specified sum of money, to a specified payee or his representative, generally on a specified date, sometimes in a specified place. A few also describe property which is to serve as collateral. A few also reveal that interest is to be paid on the loan and specify the rate. A few seem to involve re-financing of earlier loans. One provides for repayment in installments, over a five-year period.

An analysis of this latter note, which is particularly elaborate, provides useful illustrations of many of these facts. It is payable to Charles van Bomberghen and his brothers Daniel and François, and is dated October 8, 1582.[2] It is for the rather large sum of 1600 pounds groat (" livres de gros monnoye de Flandres "), equivalent to 9600 florins, the currency unit more commonly used in these records. As collateral this note, after generally pledging the drawer's person and his property ("biens tant meubles qu'immeubles présents et à venir"), lists several named houses at specified addresses in Antwerp, houses known to be

---

[1] Museum Plantin-Moretus, Archives, No. 98, contains these papers. Hereafter cited as MPM, Arch., 98. A somewhat cursory and imprecise inventory of this dossier can be found in J. DENUCÉ, *Inventaris op het Plantijnsch Archief*, Antwerp 1926, pp. 27-29. Hereafter cited as DENUCÉ, *Inventaris*.

[2] MPM, Arch., 98, pp. 463-466.

sites of Plantin's business operations. The most unusual feature of this note, of course, is the provision for repayment in installments. These installments are to be paid semi-annually, and each must total at least 150 pounds. They are to be paid, not at the home addresses of either Plantin or the van Bomberghen, but rather at the semi-annual Frankfurt book fairs. These fairs were no doubt often used for transactions of this sort. They constituted centers of great importance for the European book trade of the sixteenth century. Plantin always had representatives at them ; no doubt the van Bomberghen did too.

A series of twelve receipts attached to this note, all signed by Charles van Bomberghen, reveal precisely how the installments were paid. The first receipt, dated only a few days after the note itself, assigns over to a third party some 950 florins of the total due, to be paid in ten installments at the fairs of Frankfurt, the first eight installments to be of 100 florins, the last two of 75, the payments to begin at the spring fair of 1583. This whole arrangement was apparently spelled out in another promissory note, no doubt between Plantin and the third party, and there is no further mention of it here. The next ten receipts were all for 800 florins, generally paid at the fair itself to Charles van Bomberghen by one of Plantin's agents, normally either Moerentorf or Jan Dresselaer. A few of the payments were not paid on time, however, and not all of them were actually paid at the fairs—at least one receipt was signed in Antwerp. Several of these ten receipts also reveal that Plantin's agents paid parts of the installments to third parties, at van Bomberghen's instructions. The final receipt assigns the balance of the debt, some 650 florins, over to Charles van Bomberghen's brother Daniel. At the Frankfurt fair of September 1588, Daniel signed for this final payment. A postscript notes that Plantin now had all the receipts in his possession. The total semi-annual installment Plantin usually paid, therefore, came to 900 florins, or exactly the specified minimum of 150 pounds. The total sum Plantin paid, of course, came to 9600 florins, or exactly 1600 pounds.

It seems possible that the entire operation revealed by these documents is a re-financing of an earlier loan. This is suggested partly by a clause which concludes Plantin's original note of 1582 and is echoed in the van Bomberghen ratification of the note, a clause which reads in Plantin's version: " It is understood also that by this obligation all other contracts, obligations and accounts between me [Plantin] and the said Seigneurs van Bomberghen are broken and of no efficacy or value " (" Bien entendu aussi que par ceste obligation tous aultres contracts, obligations, et comptes d'entre moy et lesdits Segnieurs de Bomberghe sont casses et de nulle efficace ou valeur "). Furthermore, other records

XX

reveal that on April 6, 1577, shortly after the Spanish Fury, Plantin
had borrowed exactly 1600 pounds from the three van Bomberghen
brothers, to finance his continuing operations in Frankfurt[1]. The scholars
who note this fact say nothing of an immediate repayment of this sum.
Pending closer studies of the accounts, perhaps we can suppose that
arrangements for repayment of this loan were delayed until 1582.

The other notes in this collection have many features in common with
those dealing with the van Bomberghen loan, although none is for such
a large sum of money and none provides for repayment in installments.
Only one other mentions collateral. It is a note payable to Louis Perez,
drawn in Antwerp on October 24, 1582, only a short time after the note
drawn to the van Bomberghen brothers. It acknowledges receipt of
200 pounds groat delivered by Martin de Barron (Perez' son-in-law and
business associate), and it promises either repayment with interest one
year later to Perez or the bearer of the note, or assignation to Perez of
the " first rent " from a specified house which Plantin had just purchased
in Leiden[2]. This building had been purchased by Plantin to house a new
branch of his publishing business in the city to which the rebellious
Dutch had just awarded a new university. Other scholars who have
studied this transaction believe that the sum advanced by Perez served
as a down payment for purchase of this house[3]. Plantin's note thus gave
Perez what amounted to a first mortgage on the property.

Another interesting feature of the Perez note is that it specifies
that Plantin will pay interest on the sum advanced, and indicates the
rate—6 $\frac{1}{4}$ % per annum. A similar rate is specified in a note drawn to
Plantin's son-in-law, Jan Moerentorf, on January 2, 1589[4]. A somewhat
higher rate, 8 % per annum, is specified in a note drawn to a certain
Jean Laurent, apparently in 1579[5]. Neither of the latter two notes
specifies a date for repayment ; both require three months notice before
payment. All three notes were payable to either the designated person
or the bearer.

Even more about Plantin's interest payments is revealed by study
of a note which does not even mention interest on its face, but about
which other relevant material has been published. This note was payable

[1] MAX ROOSES, *Christophe Plantin, imprimeur anversois*, Antwerp 1883,
p. 316; COLIN CLAIR, *Christopher Plantin*, London 1960, p. 218. Hereafter
cited as ROOSES and CLAIR. Clair gives as his source: MPM, Arch., Grand
Livre signé C, p. 110.
[2] MPM, Arch., 98, p. 383.
[3] ROOSES, p. 352; CLAIR, p. 151.
[4] MPM, Arch., 98, p. 471. Cf. below, page 311, footnote 3.
[5] *Ibid.*, p. 479. The date is not clear on my photocopy.

to a certain "Monsigneur Ferdinando Ximenez", and was drafted in
Antwerp on January 24, 1586 [1]. It acknowledges a debt to Ximenez of
212 pounds groat, for a sum which Plantin had received from a certain
Jehan Cassiopin at Ximenez' instruction. It promises full repayment to
Ximenez or the bearer, on January 4 of the next year. Before 1586 was
over, however, this loan was extended for a second year, by correspondence between Plantin and Ximenez. And both Plantin's letter and a
published entry from one of his account books reveal that the actual
sum which Plantin had received was only 200 pounds [2]. The extra
twelve pounds, therefore, constituted an interest charge. Actually the
account calculates this charge to be twenty-five pounds for two years,
slightly more than the twelve pounds per year suggested by the note.
The rate, of course, is Plantin's normal one of $6\frac{1}{4}\%$.

Most of the other notes do not make any mention of interest charges,
including, notably, the large van Bomberghen note. Since they were,
however, clearly business notes, it seems highly improbable that Plantin
did not pay anything for use of these sums. Perhaps interest on these
loans was also added to the amount actually lent in calculating the total
amount due, just as in the Ximenez note.

Records of the Ximenez transaction also reveal certain other aspects
of Plantin's business methods. The Ximenez loan was renewed for several
years, and had not yet been repaid when Plantin died in 1589. Shortly
after his death, Moerentorf acknowledged the debt in a letter to Ximenez,
told him that the interest had been paid up to January 1589, and asked
that the loan be extended for yet another year [3]. Even though no attempt
to repay any part of the 200 pounds principal was made during these
years, apparently the accrued interest was paid every year. The interest,
in other words, was not compounded. This should not surprise us, since
some thinkers of the day rejected the very principle of compound
interest as immoral. The identity of the person who collected the greater
part of these annual interest payments, however, does seem to add an
unusual ingredient to these transactions. It was a young woman named

---

[1] *Ibid.*, p. 419.

[2] *Correspondance de Christophe Plantin*, ed. by MAX ROOSES and
J. DENUCÉ, 9 vol., Antwerp *et al.* 1883-1918, VIII-IX, pp. 99-100. Hereafter
cited as Plantin, *Corr.* The extract from the account book notes a debit of
25 pounds for two years interest. This actually makes $12\frac{1}{2}$ pounds per year,
slightly more than the sum specified in the note.

[3] *Ibid.*, pp. 561-562. The fact that this debt was still outstanding, incidentally, destroys the contention of ROOSES, p. 316, and CLAIR, p. 218,
that *all* of Plantin's debts, save those to Perez, were repaid by the time of
his death.

Marguerite van Breen, who lived with her parents in the secluded little town of Lierre, not far from Antwerp. Every year she appeared at the Plantin establishment to collect the sum of 50 florins, which was debited to the Ximenez interest account, and would use up two-thirds of the annual interest. Why Ximenez assigned this sum over to the young woman is not explained. Perhaps it was an act of charity.

Even this brief analysis of a random collection of credit instruments suggests one surprising conclusion : they all indicate a great degree of normality in Plantin's business operations. Rather than explaining his success in the face of adversity, they make it seem all the more miraculous. Obviously Plantin had little difficulty, during this period of chaos, in raising really substantial sums of money. Furthermore the rates of interest which he paid on these loans were modest indeed for the period, less than commercial rates paid in some other localities, much less than rates which rulers had to pay on war loans. In addition, the rates which he paid fluctuated remarkably little [1]. Plantin also had no difficulty in persuading his creditors to accept as security real property, located in dangerous areas, on *both* sides of the battle line dividing the Low Countries—in Leiden and in Antwerp. Neither Plantin's agents nor his creditors seem to have had any real difficulty in leaving the country for the semi-annual Frankfurt book fairs. Installments of his debts to the van Bomberghen were paid at nearly every one of these fairs during the critical 1583-1587 period. Other records reveal, furthermore, that Plantin's agents carried on many other kinds of business at these same fairs [2]. One would hardly believe, on the basis of these business documents, that they were drafted by a man whose headquarters in these very same years was in a city which was the focal point of a bitter religious war [3].

This paradox could well lead us to some rather interesting reflections on how bitter actually were the religious wars which supposedly devas-

---

[1] ROOSES, p. 316, says that Plantin paid interest at $6\frac{1}{4}$ % per annum on all his debts ; CLAIR, p. 218, more prudently indicates that this was the rate he paid on most of them.

[2] *Inter alia*, MPM, Arch., pp. 849-1052, inventoried in DENUCÉ, *Inventaris*, pp. 117-118. On Plantin's trade in Frankfurt, cf. FRIEDRICH KAPP, *Geschichte des Deutschen Buchhandels*, Bd. I, *Geschichte des Deutschen Buchhandels bis zum siebzehnte Jahrhundert*, Leipzig 1886, pp. 505-507.

[3] Plantin did, however, have to reduce substantially the quantities he published, if not the length of his list, during these years. On fluctuations of his actual production in Antwerp, see RAYMOND DE ROOVER, " The business organisation of the Plantin press in the setting of sixteenth century Antwerp ", in *Gedenkboek der Plantin-Dagen, 1555-1955*, Antwerp 1956, pp. 230-246.

tated Europe during the early modern period. To explore such heresies, however, would be to wander some distance from the subject at hand. In any case, further light on how Plantin met his particular problems can be gained by studying these promissory notes from yet another angle—by studying the people to whom they were drawn.

None of the payees named in these notes was really a banker or financier of the modern sort, whose relationship to his creditors is strictly financial, and who remains quite objective and impersonal in his dealings with them. Many of Plantin's creditors were business associates of his, often of long standing, often directly involved in the publishing business, although sometimes in a rather peripheral way. Many of them were also close personal friends of Plantin, and had been his friends for a long time.

Charles van Bomberghen, to begin with him, had actually been a partner of Plantin, along with his cousin Cornelius, in the 1563-1567 period which saw the first step in the growth of the Plantin firm from a humble one-man operation of the type most common in the period, to a business of some size and importance. In this partnership, the two van Bomberghen and three other partners had provided the capital. Plantin had provided most of the equipment and had been the principal working partner. The van Bomberghen had also made certain other contributions. Charles had provided a set of matrices for the making of Hebrew types. Cornelius had served as book-keeper for the firm, and had kept the books in a form which is exceedingly interesting to students of accounting history [1]. They were in double entry and were used for an unusually advanced system of cost accounting which had been developed in Venice. They were even kept in Italian. This should not strike us as curious, however. The van Bomberghen correspondence was occasionally also in Italian.

The van Bomberghen family knew Italy well. Daniel van Bomberghen, the father of Charles, had emigrated from Antwerp to Venice, and had there become one of Europe's most prominent early printers, particularly well known as a pioneer in the printing of Hebrew texts [2]. When his descendants returned to Antwerp, they brought with them some unusual printing materiel, a knowledge of the most advanced business methods in Europe, considerable funds, and commercial contacts in Italy which

---

[1] See FLORENCE EDLER [DE ROOVER], " Cost accounting in the sixteenth century : the books of account of Christopher Plantin, Antwerp, printer and publisher ", in *The Accounting Review*, 12 (1937), pp. 226-237.

[2] HENRI VAN BOMBERGHEN published a *Généalogie de la famille van Bomberghen*, Brussels 1914, which I have not been able to secure. See review in *De Gulden Passer*, n. s. 1 (1923), p. 88.

could be used for what was apparently their chief business interest—trade with Italy in tapestries and other luxury products.

Their return to Antwerp was short-lived, however. In the very years of this partnership, the van Bomberghen became deeply interested in the Calvinist faith which was then spreading like wildfire through the Low Countries. They became active members in an active Calvinist church in Antwerp itself. This fact came to the attention of the authorities. And when the Duke of Alva came to the Low Countries with plenary powers to stamp out heresy, and to do so created the notorious Council of Troubles with instructions to prepare a list of known heretics as a basis for outright persecution, four of the van Bomberghen were on the list, including both Charles and Cornelius [1]. They prudently left the country, and seem to have used Cologne as headquarters most of the time from then on.

These developments naturally embarrassed Plantin. They led to dissolution of the partnership, and forced Plantin to some fairly fancy maneuvering to escape the obvious guilt by association which such business connections would inevitably entail. He escaped this embarrassment triumphantly, however, by securing the direct patronage of his Most Catholic Majesty Philip II of Spain, and entered into the period of his greatest prosperity. It is nevertheless interesting that he did not abandon his relations with the van Bomberghen entirely. As soon as the royal subsidies stopped, he returned to Charles van Bomberghen for financial support, this time as a borrower rather than as a partner.

Louis Perez was even closer to Plantin during this whole period. He was the younger son of a wealthy Spanish Jewish couple who had been converted to Christianity, probably during the period of general repression late in the fifteenth century, and had emigrated to the North, first to Zeeland, then to Antwerp. Louis' brother Marcus had become an ardent Calvinist, had arranged for the translation into Spanish of Protestant books and had supervised their smuggling into Spain. He had also become a leader of the Calvinist church in Antwerp. Like the van Bomberghen, Marcus Perez had been formally proscribed by the Council of Troubles [2], and had prudently left the country. He settled in Basel, with a large group of Spanish and Italian Protestants, and used his fortune to find them work and his influence to establish for them a

---

[1] A. L. E. VERHEYDEN, ed., *Le Conseil des Troubles : liste des condamnés (1567-1573)*, Brussels 1961, p. 398, Nos. 10156-10158.

[2] *Ibid.*, p. 323, No. 8120. For more on the family, see article on Marcus Perez in the Belgian *Biographie nationale*.

refugee church. Louis, however, managed to avoid the religious troubles which plagued his family. He carried on from Antwerp as headquarters a flourishing trade in a variety of products, largely with Spain, but also with Italy and even occasionally with the new Spanish colonies in Mexico. Both he and Plantin became warm personal friends of the erudite Benito Arias Montano, sometime chaplain to Philip II, who was sent by the king to Antwerp to negotiate for the publication projects which the king subsidized and to supervise actual work on them. Perez is often mentioned in the many letters exchanged between Arias and Plantin subsequent to Arias' return to Spain, and on occasion arranged for transfers of cash and books and other materials between the two.

Several of the promissory notes which we have been considering were drawn to Perez. The sums thus raised were apparently used to finance enterprises as various as the establishment in Leiden of a branch publishing house, and the export to Salamanca of books for sale in Spain and the Spanish colonies [1]. Furthermore, studies of Plantin's accounts reveal that Perez also advanced to the printer sums for a good many other purposes. During the critical 1576-1582 period, for example, he loaned Plantin more than 20,000 florins [2]. Much of this debt was never paid off by Plantin himself. Some of it was still on the books at his death, and was assumed as a charge against his estate by Moerentorf.

Plantin also borrowed money from his employees. Moerentorf, his son-in-law, for one. We have already referred to a note drawn to him [3]. It seems to have been testamentary in character, designed to give Moerentorf a larger share of Plantin's estate than other heirs who had contributed less to the family business. It was drafted on January 2, 1589, only a few months before Plantin's death, and was for the rather large sum of 790 pounds. The text of this note makes it clear that only part of the sum represents a cash loan from Moerentorf to Plantin, and that the rest represents a remnant of dowry, annual wages, and house rent. There is no break-down of how much money belonged in each of these categories.

Another employee who loaned Plantin money was Jan Dresselaer, who served as Plantin's agent at the Frankfurt fairs several times during this period. He was so valuable to Plantin that shortly after he was

---

[1] MPM, Arch., 98, p. 428 (?), note of August 2, 1586, countersigned by Moerentorf, drawn for the purpose of buying up a contract between Martin de Barron (or Varon) and Jan Poelman. Poelman was a bookseller in Salamanca who frequently handled Plantin's publications. For more on the relations among these three, see Plantin, *Corr.*, *passim*, and CLAIR, p. 208.

[2] CLAIR, p. 218.

[3] MPM, Arch., 98, p. 471. See above, page 306, footnote 4.

released by a group of bandits who captured him on the way back from Frankfurt in 1586, Plantin signed an agreement to pay half the ransom if Dresselaer was ever again held up while working for Plantin [1]. The note made out to Dresselaer, dated July 24, 1584, is a fairly straightforward acknowledgement of a debt of 100 pounds groat (" pondt vlaams ") [2].

Occasionally Plantin's creditors were other publishers with whom he did business. One of the earliest notes which survive, dated April 5, 1561, during a period when Plantin's business was still small and obscure, acknowledges a debt of 88 pounds and 8 sous to Antoine Vincent, in return for a stock of books purchased and received [3]. Antoine Vincent was one of the most prominent of the great Calvinist printers of Geneva. He also had a substantial business in Lyons, and in this very period was organizing a large syndicate of printers for the printing and distribution of huge editions of the Calvinist psalter [4]. Other evidence indicates that Plantin not only entered this syndicate, but somehow persuaded the censors of the Spanish government in the Low Countries to certify his edition of this psalter to be orthodox [5]. That was a kind of game which he could not continue to play when he became prominent.

From the period in which we are primarily concerned, dates the note to Jean Laurent whose interest rate we have already mentioned. Laurent was a bookseller in Tournai, an important episcopal center, and seems to have been close to the bishop, who also subsidized some of Plantin's religious printing. Jean Laurent, and later Nicholas Laurent, his apparent successor and perhaps his son, both served as intermediaries in deals between Plantin and church authorities in Tournai [6].

Another bookdealer from whom Plantin borrowed money was Ferdinando Ximenez of Cologne. At least this seems almost certainly to have been the identity of the man to whom Plantin drew the note for 212 pounds. Plantin also had dealings with a prominent ecclesiastic in Rome of the same name, who helped him in arranging certain of his publication projects [7]. It seems at least possible that Ximenez of Cologne, like the Perez, was of Jewish descent. A good many of the merchants with

---

[1] Plantin, *Corr.*, VIII-IX, pp. 147-151, text of contract of February 5, 1587. Cf. CLAIR, p. 205.

[2] MPM, Arch., 98, p. 497.

[3] *Ibid.*, p. 88.

[4] E. DROZ, " Antoine Vincent : la propagande protestante par le psautier ", in *Aspects de la propagande religieuse*, Genève 1957, pp. 276-293.

[5] *Ibid.*, p. 287, n. 4.

[6] Plantin, *Corr.*, III, pp. 311-313 ; VIII-IX, p. 415.

[7] Plantin, *Corr.*, *passim.*

Spanish names operating in northern Europe during these years certainly were.

There is one general characteristic of Plantin's creditors which bears emphasis. Not only were they all his friends and business associates. Almost all of them also had religious views which were decidedly peculiar. We have already noted that several of them had Jewish friends and relatives, in a day when this opened men to suspicion. We have also noted that several of them became practicing Calvinists, in a day and place where this invited violent persecution. But an even closer look at their religious interests reveals that most of them had additional connections of an even more exotic sort—to a curious group which called itself the " House of Love ". These connections are not easy to discover. Record of them was left deliberately obscure. For the " House of Love " was one of a good number of radical religious sects in the Low Countries in those days which aroused the violent hostility of all established groups in society. Basically it was mystic and spiritualist in character. Its founder, Hendrik Niclaes, had had revelations direct from God of the ecstatic sort which typify the mystic [1]. Its members all hoped to achieve similar experiences. Their beliefs were not highly structured or dogmatic. They remained basically Christian and Biblical. But they did not believe in religious persecution, and had little use for the violent controversies in which the established churches were engaged. In the period and in the milieu which we are now studying, Niclaes' place as head of the group had been taken over by Hendrik Jansen van Barrefeldt, who used the pseudonym " Hiel " in his publications [2].

Two characteristics set this sect apart from most of the other radical religious groups of the period. One was the fact that it remained secret, and did not proselytize actively or openly. The other was the fact that it was " Nicodemite ", and did not prevent its members from professing adherence to Catholicism or Calvinism if that seemed to be a necessity or a convenience. It is in some ways inaccurate even to call the group a sect, since it was fundamentally nothing more than a group of like-

[1] See RUFUS M. JONES, *Studies in Mystical Religion*, London 1909, ch. XVIII, for analysis of Niclaes' ideas. Guillaume Postel is another sixteenth-century character who also became interested in the House of Love, perhaps through Plantin: see WILLIAM J. BOUWSMA, *Concordia Mundi : the career and thought of Guillaume Postel (1510-1581)*, Cambridge, Massachusetts 1957, pp. 27-28.

[2] See H. DE LA FONTAINE-VERWEY, " Trois hérésiarques dans les Pays-Bas du XVIe siècle ", in *Bibliothèque d'Humanisme et Renaissance*, 16 (1954), pp. 312-330, particularly for a biographical sketch of Barrefeldt, also for useful information on Niclaes and David Joris.

minded men bound together in brotherly love but without much theology or formal ritual, and, under Barrefeldt's leadership, relatively little ecclesiastical organization. Perhaps it might better be called a fraternity. Or one might use as labels the terms the members themselves used, and call it a " house " or " family ".

Scholars have long known that Plantin was an active member of the " House of Love ", and that he published many of their most important devotional books. There is even evidence that in an early stage of his career, he was supported financially by the group. Perhaps it has not been fully realized, however, that Plantin's business associates were also deeply involved in the group, and that, at least in an indirect way, the " House of Love " continued to underwrite his business throughout his career. This hypothesis is supported most strongly by a series of letters written by Barrefeldt to Plantin in his final illness and to Moerentorf just following the death of his father-in-law. Their real purpose is to provide religious consolation to the dying printer and to his bereaved son-in-law. And in doing that, they confirm the importance of Plantin to the group, and suggest that Moerentorf was also a member. But they also refer with frequency to Louis Perez, usually identified only by his initials, especially in passages urging Moerentorf to seek the advice and support of Perez in the difficult problems of assuming management of the family business [1].

Other records reveal other connections. The chronicle of the " House of Love ", which reveals in detail the importance of Plantin to the group, also speaks of the role of the van Bomberghen in his business [2]. Were they perhaps members too ? If Plantin could combine familism with Roman Catholicism, perhaps the van Bomberghen could combine it with Calvinism. There is also evidence which links Jan Dresselaer to the sect [3].

But there are connections of an even more sensational sort. Maurits Sabbe revealed several years ago that even Benito Arias Montano, the chaplain and agent of Philip II, knew of the group. As Sabbe pointed out, there is some evidence to suggest that Arias may have actually supplied money to finance publication of some of Barrefeldt's writings [4].

[1] Plantin, *Corr.*, VIII-IX, pp. 528-530, 536, 537, 583, 593-597, 607-610.

[2] See excerpts published by M. VAN DURME, ed., *Supplément à la correspondance de Christophe Plantin*, Antwerp 1955, especially p. 287, and n⁰ 6, p. 290.

[3] Plantin, *Corr.*, VIII-IX, p. 595, reference in letter from Barrefeldt to Moerentorf, and n⁰ 3, p. 597.

[4] MAURITS SABBE, " Hoe stond Benedictus Arias Montanus tegenover de Leeringen van Hendrik Jansen Barrefelt (Hiël) ? ", in *De Moretussen en hun kring*, Antwerp 1928, pp. 27-51.

Among other things, that is a possible partial explanation of several peculiar cash remittances which Arias made to Plantin through Perez shortly before Plantin died [1].

From this point of view, the correspondence between Plantin and Ferdinando Ximenez is also of great interest. Some of these letters do not deal entirely, or even primarily, with business matters. They also contain long passages in which Plantin talks very guardedly about religious matters and congratulates Ximenez on his spiritual progress [2]. It seems very likely that Ximenez also became a member of the " House of Love " during these years, and it is intriguing to suppose that Plantin used business dealings with Ximenez partly to convert him to the faith and initiate him in its tenets.

This line of inquiry has brought us to a problem of the precise relations between religion and business of a sort which has been intriguing and plaguing historians of early modern European history for several generations. In Plantin and his creditors we have uncovered a group which resembles in miniature the larger, more important, and longer-lasting group of financiers of the seventeenth and eighteenth centuries, known as " la banque protestante " to generations of Frenchmen, and recently studied with brilliance and precision by Herbert Lüthy [3]. And perhaps we should conclude, as did Lüthy, that the primary forces binding people of this sort together in important and profitable financial combines are ties of blood and friendship. However, it seems to me that one can go farther, and find connections more analogous to those which the late Max Weber sought in his studies of the relationships between puritanism and capitalism. I would suggest that the beliefs of the members of the " House of Love " were a positive economic advantage to businessmen operating in situations as uncertain and as ridden with ideological tensions as those which prevailed in sixteenth-century Antwerp and its economic hinterland. A set of beliefs which were secret, " nicodemite ", and emphasized brotherly love, permitted its members to avoid the disasters which could overtake any businessman, particularly any printer, who had become so thoroughly committed to a dogmatic position, either Catholic or Calvinist, that he could not accommodate himself to a new political regime enforcing an opposite point of view.

---

[1] Plantin, *Corr.*, VIII-IX, pp. 192-194, 231-236, 294-295, 335-336, 359-361, 389-391, 421, 429-430—mostly simple acknowledgements of the receipt of small sums of cash.

[2] Plantin, *Corr.*, VIII-IX, pp. 257-261, 265-268.

[3] HERBERT LÜTHY, *La banque protestante en France de la révocation de l'édit de Nantes à la révolution*, 2 vols., Paris 1959 and 1961.

316

These beliefs made it possible for a businessman to deal with any other businessman, committed to any one of the possible contemporary religious opinions, on both sides of the ideological battle lines which divided Europe. They help explain why Plantin could, as he did, deal with Rome and Geneva, Salamanca and London, Antwerp and Leiden.

To suggest all this is not to deny that the members of the " House of Love " were sincere, or any more hypocritical than anyone who adopts a " nicodemite " position must of necessity be. It merely provides yet another example of the ways in which religious conviction and economic self-interest can reinforce each other powerfully.

State University of Iowa, U.S.A.

XXI

Pamphlet Literature
of the French Reformation

France witnessed a significant outpouring of pamphlet literature
during the period of the Reformation. That part of this literature
which has attracted the most interest to date was published in the
second half of the sixteenth century and was explicitly political in
content. It thus accompanies in both time and topic the ferocious
wars of religion which ravaged France, beginning with the massacre
of Vassy in 1562, reaching one climax after the St. Bartholomew's
massacres in 1572, a second during the siege of Catholic Paris from
1591 to 1594, and ending only with the promulgation of the Edict of
Nantes in 1598. Of these political pamphlets the most widely studied
were written by Protestants during the beginning of the wars of religion in the 1560's and after the St. Bartholomew's massacres in the
mid-1570's. The Protestant pamphlets provoked by these massacres
developed particularly sophisticated arguments for armed resistance
to tyrannical government that were designed to attract support for
Protestant-led revolts against the French royal government. There
was an even greater number of Catholic political pamphlets, however, and they are attracting increasing interest. Catholic pamphlets
written during the siege of Paris also developed arguments for armed
resistance to a tyrannical government, but were designed to justify
the Catholic League's revolts against the French royal government.
Their arguments often parallel those advanced by Protestants. Together these two series of pamphlets have long been recognized as
having articulated a body of political ideas of continuing importance in justifying resistance to tyranny, and as having considerable
historical significance in explaining the great revolutions which led
to modern forms of government in England, America, and France.

The concentration of scholars upon pamphlets that are political in
content can thus be explained in part by the interest and significance

of the political ideas which many of them contain. But it can also be explained in part by the fact that a great many French pamphlets of the period concentrated on specific political issues as well. This poses a problem of interest to historians. The most obvious explanation can be found in the political history of France during the Reformation period. A royal government which had arguably been the richest and most powerful in Europe early in the sixteenth century was torn by the most vicious forms of political rivalry and warfare late in the century. These tensions grew in part from a pronounced weakness in the monarchy itself, stemming from a series of royal minorities following the accidental death of Henry II in 1559 as three of his weak sons succeeded him in turn. These periods of rule by boys or young men provoked crises inherent in the royal form of government as powerful aristocrats competed for effective control of governmental machinery either as regents or in less obvious positions at court. These tensions also grew in part from the increasingly bitter controversy among religious factions. The rapid spread of militant Calvinism in France after 1550 and of militant forms of Catholicism after 1560 boiled over into political rivalry. The political explosions provoked by these two sets of reinforcing tensions created a natural appetite among the literate public for political news. They also created an understandable appetite among the more reflective for fresh ideas about the nature of the state, the functions of the state, and the legitimacy of resistance to the state. Political pamphlets fed both appetites.

A second explanation for a concentration by the French upon pamphlets political in content, however, may well be found in the dynamics of the printing industry. In periods of peace and prosperity most printers tended to concentrate their resources on selected widely selling staples: editions of the classics for the scholarly market; Bibles and service books and summaries of theology for the religious market; collections of laws and commentaries on these collections for the lawyers' market; other standard references for a number of other, and usually smaller, markets. In times of war and economic uncertainty, however, a number of printers tended to divert resources to the publication of topical pamphlets. Hans Joachim Bremme has demonstrated that this was true of Geneva in the decades after Calvin died when Protestantism was fighting for its life in France. Such religious staples as Calvin's books tended to remain in publishers' inventories, and printers switched to publishing contemporary histories and political pamphlets.[1] Denis Pallier has demonstrated that this was also true of Paris in the decade when the Catholic League dominated its politics. The religious and legal staples that sustained most Parisian printers sold poorly and printers switched to publishing political pamphlets.[2] These switches may be explained in part by a shift in the tastes of the market for printed matter. They should also be explained, Pallier argues, by the economics of the publishing industry. Warfare tended to disrupt seriously the trade in printed matter. Fairs, networks of peddlers, and other channels of distribution were unable to do their normal work of relaying standard books to their usual purchasers. In desperation, printers on the edge of bankruptcy turned to grinding out small and inflammatory topical works that required little investment of capital and that could be sold quickly and easily in local markets.

It would be misleading to conclude that French printers produced only political pamphlets, or that their political pamphlets contain nothing of religious, economic, or social interest. Salvo Mastellone (1972) demonstrated that many suggestive conclusions about the social relationships and economic positions of French aristocrats can be gleaned from political pamphlets of the late sixteenth century.[3] And Donald R. Kelley provides significant new insights into the family, the congregation, the university, and the legal profession, in addition to fresh observations on confessional and political parties, in his book (1981) based on these pamphlets.[4] It is nevertheless fair to conclude that most of the French pamphlets of the Reformation period are obviously political in content and that most of the attention paid to this literature by scholars has focused upon its political content. This essay, consequently, is primarily about French political pamphlet literature of the Reformation period.

Where We Are

A useful introductory guide to the political pamphlets produced in France during the Reformation period can be found in Hauser (1906–1915). Although this overview is old, compiled well before the triumph of the school of the *Annales* within France and its de-

[1]Bremme (1969), 89–93.
[2]Pallier (1976), 119–130.
[3]Mastellone (1972). In some respects this is a sequel to Caprariis, (1959) which is also based on French political pamphlets. Mastellone, however, adopts a significantly broader perspective.
[4]Kelley (1981).

mands for "total history," its very age makes it useful. For Hauser's generation history was still primarily political history: dates, kings, and diplomacy were important. Thus he is careful to direct his readers to sources of political significance. Within the scope of his reference work, it was possible to hit only the high spots, but he was conscientious and shrewd, and his comments are thus usually useful and reliable. They include remarks about a number of the more interesting single pamphlets and guidance to a number of widely circulated composite works which were in reality collections of contemporary pamphlets.

More specific, if somewhat technical, information on specific pamphlets can be gained from the works of descriptive bibliographers. Some of this information is scattered through works of more general reference. Some of it has been focused more specifically upon pamphlets. These bibliographical studies are normally devoted to specific printers or publishers, sometimes gathered within a specific publishing center. Of the publishing centers then producing books in French, Paris, of course, was by far the largest and most important, for it was several times larger than any other French city, housing both the capital of the French royal government and the largest and most important French university. Paris thus supplied the largest single market for reading matter in French. The French royal government deliberately tried to increase the centralization of publishing in Paris with subsidies and laws in order to bring the industry more closely under government control. Many technical studies of individual Parisian printers and publishers have been written, though there is still more to be done on many of them. Masses of fresh information on their business activities is hidden in the manuscript notarial records of legal transactions deposited in the *Minutier Central* of the National Archives in Paris, and is in the process of being extracted and examined by dozens of scholars. The most important of the reports on this research are being published under the name of Philippe Renouard, based on notes he gathered before his death some time ago, which are now being checked, completed, and published by teams of modern scholars. These include a general *Répertoire des imprimeurs Parisiens, libraires, fondeurs . . . jusqu'à la fin du XVIe siècle* (Geneva, 1965), complemented by an ongoing series of volumes supplying more specific information on individual printers and publishers, arranged alphabetically (Geneva 1965–). This series is only beginning.

Lyon was the second largest French center of publication. While the city may not have been larger than Rouen, there were no other French cities of the second rank after Paris that were much larger. Lyon also possessed massive commercial and financial ties with Italy, complemented by significant if probably less important ties with Germany through Switzerland. The city was also sufficiently far from Paris to be free to carve out a somewhat independent market. The standard work of reference on early printing and publishing in Lyon is Baudrier (1895–1921), with a supplementary volume of index tables (1965).

Geneva was the third largest center of publication in French, but only in the later part of the sixteenth century. It became important because of the establishment of the Calvinist Reformation there. Calvin succeeded in luring to Geneva many of the most eminent printers of Paris and Lyon to join him in organizing an ambitious and strenuous attempt to win all of France to the Reformed religion. Of these emigrating printers, the most prominent were Robert Estienne, the royal printer in Paris, and Antoine Vincent, a particularly successful printer of Lyon, but they were accompanied by many others. The Genevan printing industry has been studied by Chaix (1954) and Bremme (1969), complemented by a useful general bibliography compiled by Chaix, A. Dufour, and G. Moeckli (1966).

These three centers were all large and flourishing, devoted to the publication of many kinds of books. While they published the majority of pamphlets printed in French, they published even more books of a larger and more continuing utility. Studies of these centers and their printers necessarily cannot focus solely upon pamphlets. There were other minor centers of French publication, however, that published little other than pamphlets. Bibliographical studies of their production, therefore, necessarily make more direct contributions to our knowledge of literature in pamphlet form.

The great pioneer in the technical study of French pamphlets of the Reformation period was Eugénie Droz, perhaps better known for her work in launching and directing the most important modern publishing house devoted to the scholarly study of French culture during the periods of the Renaissance and Reformation. Until her death at an age near ninety Mlle. Droz found time from her business and editorial career to pursue her own bibliographical studies, many of which she published in her own house. Her highly technical analyses of specific pamphlets or specific printers are scattered about in articles published in the *Bibliothèque d'Humanisme et Renaissance*, gathered in a series of four post-retirement collections (1970–1976), and elsewhere. Probably the most important of these studies is a three-volume set Mlle. Droz prepared jointly with Louis Desgraves (1960). This work is simply an extended list of pamphlets published in La Rochelle by the printers Berton, Haultin, and Portau, but it is several times longer than any previous list of La Rochelle printings. During the wars of religion the port of La Rochelle became a key military center for the Protestant effort to conquer France. Its few printers supported this effort energetically by publishing inflammatory pamphlets, most of them political in content, designed to advance the Protestant cause and undermine Catholic political reaction to that cause. Because of their inflammatory content, most of these pamphlets were clandestine, with either no indication of printer and place of publication or with false addresses. Sometimes the false addresses were in Protestant centers beyond the reach of French royal power, like Basel; sometimes they were in good Catholic centers, like Paris. The printers of La Rochelle clearly felt that only clandestine pamphlets had much chance of circulating widely in a country that remained largely Catholic in government and that tried to impose strict censorship to prevent circulation of works regarded as subversive. For modern scholars to connect these pamphlets to the printers of La Rochelle requires great technical expertise, including the ability to examine closely decorative matter and individual letters to establish the printer who actually used that material in the sixteenth century. Precisely these skills were developed by Droz and Desgraves to establish the origins in La Rochelle of these many pamphlets. Their skills are fully displayed in this joint study, which is accompanied by copious photographic reproduction of the materials upon which their attributions are based. Both scholars used the same skills elsewhere to identify the origins of other French Protestant political pamphlets, Desgraves most notably in his book on Eloi Gibier (1966) of Orléans, which reconstitutes the production of another provincial printer of pamphlets, Droz most notably in a series of articles on individual French pamphlets published outside of France in such places as Geneva, Basel, and Heidelberg.

Few of these technical studies, however, can be completely satisfactory to most general historians. They are extremely useful works of reference, indispensable for identifying specific pamphlets and for establishing the context in which they were produced, but they tell us relatively little of the content of these pamphlets or of the markets for which they were intended.

Greater guidance on matters of this sort is provided by a group of scholars stimulated by the *Annales* school which dominates contemporary French historiography. The most seminal of these scholars was a man who helped found the school, Lucien Febvre. Among the many desiderata he presented to the scholarly community of types of historical study which could broaden our knowledge of the past beyond traditional political chronologies to an understanding of past cultures in the totality, was a suggestion for a new history of the book. Febvre wanted this subject to be studied not just by establishing lists of individual works and printers but by reconstructing the entire book industry, placing it in its social, economic, and political context and examining the markets that it created and served. Febvre prepared a sketch of this study late in his own life, then turned his notes and outline over to a younger scholar, Henri-Jean Martin. The result was an essay published as their joint work (1958) and translated into English without any change or updating (1976). It remains the most thoughtful and sensible single general survey of the development of the printing industry and its impact on society throughout Europe between 1450 and 1800. Martin then proceeded to develop a distinguished career as the world's greatest authority on early modern French publishing. He laid a particularly persuasive claim to this status with his monumental dissertation on the seventeenth-century Parisian publishing industry (1969), based on decades of massive archival research in Paris. Martin also stimulated, encouraged, and patronized a number of additional monographic studies on aspects of early modern French printing. A number of these studies have appeared in a series of publications sponsored by the fourth section of the École Pratique des Hautes Études in Paris, under the general title *Histoire et civilisation du livre*, published by the Librairie Droz in Geneva.

Many of these studies, to be sure, do not deal with the Reformation period, and even those that do are not limited to use of pamphlets. But some do, the most notable of which is probably Pallier (1976). This meticulous study is in part an exhaustive list with descriptions of more than 870 pamphlets published in Paris during the years of great political tension from 1585 to 1594 including many written while the city was under siege. Most of them are by more or less fanatical Catholics, railing against Protestantism and against any government inclined either to include Protestants within its ranks or even to tolerate Protestants within the country. But Pallier goes well beyond his simple list to provide a great deal of fresh information on the printers who produced these pamphlets, on how they were organized and related to the political and ecclesiastical leaders of the city, and on the publics to which they sold their wares.

Even a study as fresh and as detailed as Pallier's, however, cannot exhaust its subject. Many of these pamphlets contain highly individual, even idiosyncratic arguments developed in an intricate, ingenious, or erudite manner. The more interesting or influential of them deserve intensive separate study.[5] Baumgartner (1976), has undertaken this task in his unpretentious analysis of several of these pamphlets. He pays particular attention to just two of them, Jean Boucher's *De justa abdicatione*, and the anonymous *De justa reipublicae christianae authoritate*. A number of studies have been devoted to the particularly radical and interesting *Dialogue d'entre le maheustre et le manant*, another anonymous product of the Paris Catholic League, attributed to François Cromé. This pamphlet has been skillfully edited by Peter M. Ascoli (Geneva, 1977), and is the subject of thoughtful though sharply differing analyses in articles by Ascoli and J. H. M. Salmon.[6] Salmon finds in this treatise, and particularly in its very first edition, a whiff of authentic democratic radicalism. Ascoli finds in it a more traditional set of popular Catholic objections to compromise with Protestantism.

Some of the earlier French Protestant political pamphlets, particularly those labelled "monarchomach" because of their calls for armed resistance to royal government, have been subjected to even more intensive examination. Thus François Hotman's *Franco-Gallia*, with its stirring appeal to a peculiar view of French constitutional history in order to justify resistance, has been published in a splendid variorum Latin edition by Ralph E. Giesey with an English translation by J. H. M. Salmon, encased in a magnificent critical apparatus (Cambridge, 1972). By including texts of the changes made in this pamphlet through several editions, Giesey and Salmon demonstrate how Hotman adjusted his arguments to fit changing political circumstances between 1573 and 1586. Similarly Theodore Beza's *Du droit des magistrats*, which combines legal, historical, and Biblical arguments to justify resistance to the French crown and which was written by Calvin's successor as leader of the internation-

---

[5]For a good general and recent introduction to the content of those French pamphlets of special interest to historians of political thought, see Skinner (1978) *passim*, especially chs. 7–9.

[6]Ascoli (1974), 3–22; Salmon (1972), 540–576.

al Reformed movement but published anonymously to win non-Protestant support to the cause of resistance, has been presented in modern critical editions: of the Latin version by Klaus Sturm (Neukirchen—Vluyn, 1965) and of the French version by Madeleine Marabuto (Saint-Julien-l'Ars, 1968) and Robert M. Kingdon (Geneva, 1971). The anonymous *Vindiciae contra tyrannos* has similarly been subjected to intensive study, perhaps most notably by Ralph E. Giesey, who has demonstrated its striking and innovative use of arguments drawn from Roman private law.[7].

Where We Seem to be Going

As in so many fields, the positions in which we find ourselves help indicate where we are going. There is clearly room for further useful development of all the approaches to French pamphlet literature of the Reformation period already sketched. The highly technical study of pamphlets issued by individual printers, demanding a sure control of descriptive bibliography, has much to teach us still. It can give us a surer knowledge of the geography of the publication of these often incendiary and clandestine pamphlets. My own recent studies have convinced me, for example, that there were more French political pamphlets published in London than has previously been realized. Some were printed in French, some in Latin, some in English translation. Some were surreptitiously sponsored by the English crown and even distributed in France through diplomatic channels.[8] Others may not have been inspired directly by officials of the Elizabethan government, but were still the products of a printing industry very closely supervised by the crown including many printers with personal ties of friendship and patronage to government leaders. Their publishers often worked in close collaboration with printers in La Rochelle and elsewhere on the continent.

A similar story of the publication of pamphlets outside of France to support precise political goals within the kingdom can be put together for the city of Geneva and probably also for such German cities as Basel, Strasbourg, and Heidelberg. A first step toward doing so, however, must be the discovery of just which pamphlets were published where. This often requires the technical skills of the bibliographer.

More study is needed of the production of pamphlets within the

---

[7]Giesey (1970), 41–56.
[8]Woodfield (1973), 24–33.

economic, social, and political context of the French publishing industry. The primary materials to make possible studies of this kind exist in the unpublished sets of notarized legal documents preserved in most French departmental and municipal archives. Most of these sets are not yet fully catalogued, and their use has necessarily been somewhat haphazard and random. Documents detailing the business careers of printers and publishers, to be sure, have probably been collected more extensively than those of practitioners of other trades, but there is more to be gathered on them and even more to be gathered on their business associates—the merchants who supplied publishers and printers with supplies, or the professional men who supplied publishers with their most lucrative markets. A few inventories of the private libraries of professional men prepared after their deaths, for example, have already provided rich suggestions about the markets for various kinds of books, including pamphlets.[9]

Finally, analysis of individual pamphlets of interest or influence is needed. The most popular of the "monarchomach" pamphlets provoked by the St. Bartholomew's massacres, for example, was probably the anonymous *Reveille-matin*. It is less interesting as a work of political theory than the pamphlets that have already been edited. But it went through many more editions at the time, and there is evidence that it had an inflammatory effect on groups of French noblemen considering resumption of war against the crown. It poses great problems of interpretation. Its lines of argument are somewhat inconsistent and suggest the possibility that it is actually a combination of pieces written by at least two polemicists,[10] and parts of it are needlessly offensive to certain segments of the natural audience for pamphlets of this type. It contains some nasty remarks about the religious policy of the English government, for example. These no doubt explain why it was never translated into English or published in London. The evidence of its contemporary influence, however, suggests that it deserves more intensive attention than it has as yet received.

In addition to the continued exploitation of existing ways of studying French political pamphlets, we can also expect the development of new approaches. As the works of Mastellone (1972) and Kelley (1981) suggest, there may well be further attempts to extract new types of information from these sources. Politics in the sixteenth

---

[9]E.g. Doucet (1956).
[10]Suggested by Salmon (1959), 19, n.7. Cf. Kelley (1981), 301 and ff.

century involved rivalry of tightly-knit extended aristocratic families supported by sizable groups of organized clients. Political pamphlets thus can tell us something about the structures and loyalties of aristocratic families. Politics also involved the dispersal of considerable sums of money, often under the ultimate control of royal treasuries. Political pamphlets can thus tell us something about the finances of royal governments and the economies upon which they draw.

Yet more speculative possibilities are suggested by the provocative and stimulating study by Elizabeth L. Eisenstein (1979). This fascinating exploration into the impact upon European culture of the revolution in communications accomplished by the development and institutionalization of printing deliberately omits consideration of the impact of printing upon politics. Yet surely this impact must have been considerable, in France as elsewhere. The kings of France were quick to see political advantage in the invention of printing. They poured substantial subsidies into the publication of works of humanist scholarship, no doubt in part to gain the respect and support of the scholarly community. They used the press to disseminate the texts of laws, and thus to gain greater knowledge of and respect for royal law. And they were particularly sensitive to the use of pamphlets to manipulate public opinion in the court, in aristocratic circles, and in wider parts of the community. The theologians of the Sorbonne and the governments of Paris and Lyon were encouraged to keep a close watch on pamphlet literature and to move quickly to suppress those who published or disseminated pamphlets with subversive or heretical ideas. The royal court itself was aware of the circulation of political pamphlets offensive to its interests and occasionally instructed ambassadors to file protests with foreign governments for permitting the publication of individual pamphlets. I have found record of the filing of such protests by French ambassadors to both the court of England and the federated Swiss cantons.[11] The invention of print and its use by alert governments no doubt should be an important ingredient in explaining the general increase in the power of many governmental units in the Reformation period. Further studies of how governments supported and used printers

[11]For an example of a complaint to the English court, in 1571, see Hector de la Ferrière, ed., *Lettres de Catherine de Médicis*, IV (Paris, 1891), 92–93, complemented by *Correspondance diplomatique de Bertrand de Salignac de la Mothe Fénélon*, IV (Paris and London, 1840), 301, 305. For examples of complaints to the Swiss, see the sources cited by Bremme (1969), 83–86.

or sought to control and muzzle them could be very revealing. Among these governments, the French royal government and the municipal governments of Paris and Lyon should certainly be included, as should the de facto governments created by great aristocrats who dominated the extreme Protestant and Catholic factions within France in defiance of royal authority. These aristocrats also hired printers, issued manifestoes designed for publication, and sought to manipulate and control the press in other ways as did various local governments. The publishing industry was also exploited by governments outside of France that had vital interests in the kingdom, such as in the Rhenish Palatinate, and England.

How We Get There

Obviously the most important raw materials for the study of French pamphlets during the Reformation are the pamphlets themselves. There are thousands of them scattered widely throughout the world. The most important of these collections are in Paris, above all in the *Bibliothèque Nationale*, but also in the *Arsenal, Mazarine*, and *Sainte-Geneviève* libraries, and in the library of the *Société de l'histoire du protestantisme français*. There are also important collections elsewhere in France and in cities ringing France. The *British Library* in London and the *Bibliothèque publique et universitaire* in Geneva possess important collections as do libraries in such cities as Basel. There are even important sets of French pamphlets in research libraries scattered through the United States. Effective bibliographical control of this mass of material, however, is far from satisfactory. Many of the libraries possessing these pamphlets, particularly the older ones in Europe, have over the centuries bound together in large volumes groups of vaguely connected pamphlets. Indexes or catalogues to these libraries often provide very incomplete and misleading guides to these volumes, and thus to the library's total holdings of pamphlets. There can, therefore, be no substitute for spending hours in rare-book libraries, calling up volume after collective volume, and carefully inspecting each to discover its full content of pamphlets.

There are, nevertheless, certain bibliographical guides of some value. The printed catalogues of the *British Library* and *Bibliothèque Nationale* note the presence of a number of pamphlets, as do the often unpublished catalogues of other libraries. For scholars working in America there is a useful introductory guide compiled by Lindsay and Neu (1969). It supplies a short-title list of the pamphlets contained in some fifteen American research libraries, arranged

chronologically with an index of authors and titles. It is far from
perfect. Several additional American research libraries possess significant numbers of these pamphlets, and even the libraries inventoried for this catalogue contain pamphlets which are not listed,
sometimes because they were purchased more recently, sometimes
because they had not been fully catalogued locally—perhaps
because they had been purchased in bound collective volumes of the
sort one finds commonly in Europe—at the time Lindsay and Neu
visited these libraries. Still, this catalogue supplies a very useful
preliminary guide to pamphlet collections in the United States.
Monographs using this catalogue as a starting point have already
been published.

For the English speaking world a useful supplementary guide to
the location of some pamphlets is supplied by the superb *Short-Title
Catalogue of Books Printed in England, Scotland & Ireland, and of
English Books Printed Abroad, 1475-1640* (London, 1926), now being revised by Katharine F. Pantzer, in part with materials gathered
by W. A. Jackson and F. S. Ferguson (London, 1976). It is, of
course, only of peripheral use to the student of French pamphlet literature, including only the few French pamphlets published in Britain and a few translations into English or Latin of pamphlets originally printed in French.

More useful are a number of catalogues and lists for specific printers, authors, and places. They range from old classics compiled in
the nineteenth century to such modern bibliographies as the lists of
Chaix, Droz, Desgraves, and Pallier mentioned above. The old classics, incidentally, should not be neglected. There is still no better
guide to the printings of the house of Estienne, which worked in
Paris for several kings of France and in Geneva for John Calvin and
his successors, than Renouard (1843). Few of the Estienne printings
were pamphlets, to be sure, but some of them certainly were.

Those who would like to explore some of the more technical ways
of studying pamphlets of the sixteenth century, should learn some
descriptive or analytical bibliography. There are a number of good
guides to this discipline. A reliable classic is McKerrow (1927). It
can be supplemented by Gaskell (1972). Gaskell's main contribution, however, is to the study of books printed after 1800 and the introduction of machine presses. Although Gaskell slightly updates
and corrects McKerrow here and there, McKerrow remains adequate for most students of the sixteenth century. Both these surveys
are intended primarily for the students of books produced in England, but the printing technology they describe and the types of

book they analyze were virtually the same in France and, for that matter, elsewhere on the continent. It is possible to develop even greater technical expertise in this field by following the paths indicated by great technicians such as Fredson Bowers. Most historians will not want to go that far. They tend not to be much concerned with such problems as those posed by the minor variations among various states within a single edition.

Those who would like to examine the economic context in which printers of sixteenth-century pamphlets operated should use studies of the Plantin press in Antwerp, particularly as summarized by Voet (1969, 1972). The Plantin press, thanks to encouragement and subsidy from King Philip II of Spain, became the largest and most prosperous publishing house in all of Europe in the late sixteenth century. Plantin was originally French, continued to trade with France after his establishment in Antwerp, and produced a few French pamphlets himself. He made his greatest profits, however, from printing the Catholic service books whose use was mandated by the Council of Trent. He used these profits and Spanish subsidies to erect a large building in downtown Antwerp which still stands. It continued to be used as the headquarters of a publishing empire for nearly three centuries after Plantin's death by his heirs of the Moretus family. Then it was turned into a museum with all its equipment and records intact. The equipment includes ancient hand presses, foundries, and fonts of type. The records include accounts detailing Plantin's running expenses for labor and supplies as well as his sales to wholesale houses, to patrons, and to retail customers. With them one can reconstruct the precise cost and market of an individual book, including an individual pamphlet. And since the technology and organization of the sixteenth-century publishing industry seems to have been fairly uniform, one can extrapolate informed guesses on the probable costs and sales of pamphlets elsewhere. One can also find precise information on the few French pamphlets Plantin printed himself, usually in support of the royal Catholic cause. He printed, for example, a pamphlet containing the royal excuses for the Saint Bartholomew's massacres, in which King Charles IX takes full responsibility for the butchery, but claims it was necessary to avert a plot against his life.[12]

[12]"*Discours sur les causes de l'execution faicte es personnes de ceux qui avoyent conjuré contre le roy et son estat*. En Anvers, de l'imprimerie de Christophe Plantin, 1572." From the bibliography of Plantin works compiled by C. Ruelens and A. de Backer, *Annales Plantiniennes, 1555–1589* (Paris, 1866), 126–127.

Those who wish to speculate must depend on their own general knowledge of the period, their own imaginations, and the daring example of such scholars as Elizabeth Eisenstein. Whatever the approach, however, there remains much to be done with French pamphlets of the Reformation period. They provide evidence available nowhere else of the rather volatile states of public opinion in sixteenth-century France. They provide even stronger evidence of the ways in which leaders of French society sought to manipulate that opinion.

Bibliography

Ascoli, Peter M., "A Radical Pamphlet of Late Sixteenth Century France: le Dialogue d'entre le maheustre et le manant," *Sixteenth Century Journal*, V/2 (1974): 3–22.

Baudrier, Henri, *Bibliographie lyonnaise*, vols. 1–12 (Lyon, 1895–1921); Index (Paris, 1965).

Baumgartner, Frederic J., *Radical Reactionaries: The Political Thought of the French Catholic League* (Geneva, 1976).

Bremme, Hans Joachim, *Buchdrucker und Buchhändler zur Zeit der Glaubenskämpfe: Studien zur Genfer Druckgeschichte, 1565–1580* (Geneva, 1969).

Caprariis, Vittorio de, *Propaganda e pensiero politico in Francia durante le guerre di religione, 1559–1572* (Naples, 1959).

Chaix, Paul, *Recherches sur l'imprimerie à Genèva de 1550 à 1564* (Geneva, 1954).

———, Dufour, Alain, and Moeckli, Gustave, *Les livres imprimés à Genèv de 1550 à 1600* (Geneva, 1966).

Desgraves, Louis, *Éloi Gibier, imprimeur à Orléans* (Geneva, 1966).

Doucet, R., *Les bibliothèques parisiennes au XVIe siècle* (Paris, 1956).

Droz, Eugénie, *Chemins de l'hérésie* (Geneva, 1970–76).

———, and Desgraves, Louis, *L'Imprimerie à La Rochelle* (Geneva, 1960).

Eisenstein, Elizabeth L., *The Printing Press as an Agent of Change* (Cambridge, 1979).

Febvre, Lucien, and Martin, Henri-Jean, *L'apparition du livre* (Paris, 1958); English translation, *The Coming of the Book* (London, 1976).

Gaskell, Philip, *A New Introduction to Bibliography* (Oxford, 1972).

Giesey, Ralph E., "The Monarchomach Triumvirs: Hotman, Beza, and Mornay," *Bibliothèque d'Humanisme et Renaissance*, XXXII (1970): 41–56.

Hauser, Henri, *Les sources de l'histoire de France, XVIe siècle*, vols. 1–4 (Paris, 1906–1915).

Kelley, D.R., *The Beginning of Ideology: Consciousness and Society in the French Reformation* (Cambridge, 1981).

Lindsay, Robert O., and Neu, John, *French Political Pamphlets, 1547–1648: A Catalog of Major Collections in American Libraries* (Madison, 1969).

Martin, Henri-Jean, *Livre, pouvoirs, et société à Paris au XVIIe siècle* (Geneva, 1969).

Mastellone, Salvo, *Venalità e Machiavellismo in Francia, 1572–1610* (Florence, 1972).

McKerrow, Ronald B., *An Introduction to Bibliography, for Litarary Students* (Oxford, 1927).

Pallier, Denis, *Recherches sur l'imprimerie à Paris pendant la ligue, 1585–1594* (Geneva, 1976).

Renouard, Ant. Aug., *Annales de l'imprimerie des Estienne* (Paris, 1843).

Salmon, J. H. M., *The French Religious Wars in English Political Thought* (Oxford, 1959).

——, "The Paris Sixteen, 1584–1594: the Social Analysis of a Revolutionary Movement," *Journal of Modern History*, XLIV (1972): 540–576.

Skinner, Quentin, *The Foundations of Modern Political Thought*, vol. 2, *The Age of Reformation* (Cambridge, 1978).

Voet, Leon, *The Golden Compasses, A History and Evaluation of the Printing and Publishing Activities of the Officina Plantiniana*, vols. 1–2 (Amsterdam, 1969, 1972).

Woodfield, Denis B., *Surreptitious Printing in England, 1550–1640* (New York, 1973).

INDEX